AN INTRODUCTION TO NONPROCEDURAL LANGUAGES

USING NPL™

AN INTRODUCTION TO NONPROCEDURAL LANGUAGES

USING NPL™

Thomas D. Truitt
Stuart B. Mindlin

DeskTop Software Corporation

With contributions by

Tarralyn A. Truitt

McGRAW-HILL BOOK COMPANY

New York   St. Louis   San Francisco   Auckland   Bogotá
Hamburg   Johannesburg   London   Madrid   Mexico   Montreal   New Delhi
Panama   Paris   São Paulo   Singapore   Sydney   Tokyo   Toronto

This book was produced using WordStar on an Altos computer.
It was typeset by computer in Times Roman by AZTECH Document Systems Inc.
The editors were Charles E. Stewart and Joseph F. Murphy;
the production supervisor was Joe Campanella.
The cover was designed by Rafael Hernandez.
Halliday Lithograph Corporation was printer and binder.

Cover photograph courtesy of Melvin L. Prueitt, Los Alamos National Laboratory.

AN INTRODUCTION TO NONPROCEDURAL LANGUAGES
Using NPL™

The information in this document is subject to change without notice and should not be construed as a commitment by DeskTop Software Corporation. The software described is furnished under a license and may be used or copied only in accordance with the terms of such license.

Apple II, Apple III, and Apple Pascal are trademarks of Apple Computer Inc. UCSD PASCAL and UCSD p-System are trademarks of Regents of the University of California. IBM Personal Computer is a trademark of International Business Machines Corporation. PDP-11 and RT11 are trademarks of Digital Equipment Corporation. CP/M is a registered trademark of Digital Research.

1 2 3 4 5 6 7 8 9 0 HALHAL 8 9 8 7 6 5 4 3

ISBN 0-07-065301-1

Library of Congress Cataloging in Publication Data

Truitt, Thomas D.
      An introduction to nonprocedural languages.

      Bibliography: p.
      Includes index.
      1. Nonprocedural languages (Programming languages)
2. NPL (Computer program languages) I. Mindlin, Stuart B. II.
Truitt, Tarralyn A. III. Title.
QA76.7.T78 1983   001.64′24   82-17315
ISBN 0-07-065301-1

TO ANNE

CONTENTS

FOREWORD ix

PREFACE xi

SECTION ONE   **BASIC LANGUAGE FEATURES**   **1**

1   Introduction   3

2   Listing, Sorting, and Numbering   13

3   Counting, Summing, and Averaging   33

4   Screening Records for Particular Values   51

5   Calculating New Variables   63

6   Better Looking Reports   81

7   Creating New Files from Old   109

8   Datafile Descriptions with the Master File   121

9   Indexing and Selecting a Subfile   141

10   Exec Program Files   151

11   Displaying, Revising, and Creating Records in Data-Form Mode   161

12   Preparing Data-Form Programs   173

13   Techniques for Better Results   185

SECTION TWO   **ADVANCED FEATURES FOR DATABASE MANAGEMENT AND APPLICATION DEVELOPMENT**   **217**

14   Database Names and Relational Functions   219

15   Procedural Commands   243

16   Database Functions   257

17   Multisegment Records   265

18   Array Variables   275

19   Multiple Verb and Nested Sets   287

SECTION THREE   **LANGUAGE REFERENCE SECTION**   **313**

SECTION FOUR	AN NPL TUTORIAL FOR THE APPLE II COMPUTER	369
SECTION FIVE	APPENDIXES	439
A	Nonprocedural Language Systems for IBM 370 Computers	441
	1 FOCUS Information Management System	444
	2 RAMIS Management System	447
	3 The NOMAD2 System	450
	4 Structured Query Language (SQL)	454
	5 The INQUIRE System	460
B	Master Files Used in This Book	465
C	NPL System Guide Card	471
D	NPL Microcomputer Characteristics	475
	1 Apple II Pascal and the UCSD p-System	476
	2 Apple III Pascal System	477
	3 CP/M Operating System	477
	4 IBM/PC DOS Operating System	477
	5 RT11 Operating System for the PDP-11	478
	BIBLIOGRAPHY	481
	INDEX	483

FOREWORD

As Tom Truitt has noted in his Preface, I have been an advocate of the nonprocedural approach to computer application development for some years. Fortran and Cobol and Pascal will be around through our lifetimes, for a combination of good and bad reasons, but the excitement as we move through the eighties is in the nonprocedural arena.

Accordingly I was delighted to be asked by McGraw-Hill to review the manuscript of this book. I found the subject to be a familiar one, based on my own experience with a system that runs on the big mainframes, NO-MAD, and I was astounded that something with a significant portion of the NOMAD capability could run on an Apple II Plus. The Apple is an impressive machine in its own right, but far from the capabilities—and price—of the machines in the IBM 370 line.

I expressed my enthusiasm to McGraw-Hill and gave Tom a call, asking if I could try out the system. No sooner said than done. I used NPL for a variety of record-keeping chores in connection with my college teaching, plus various other applications. A demonstration to a graduate database course resulted in a deeply impressed group of students and faculty.

You're going to be hearing a lot about NPL, especially as it becomes available on some of the newer and more powerful small computers. And the book is highly readable. A modest investment of reading and practice will have you doing things with a computer that would have been completely out of the reach of even the professional programmers a mere decade ago, and which even today are otherwise available only on very much larger computers.

Daniel D. McCracken
Author and Consultant
Professor of Computer Sciences
City College of New York

PREFACE

LANGUAGES FOR COMPUTERS AND PEOPLE

This is a book to teach you a whole new approach to coping with the lists of names and addresses, quantitative data, and other miscellaneous information that seem to clutter your life. There are five major sections. Three are tutorial in style, and two are reference material.

First-time users of computers may begin with Chapter 1, or with the Section Four tutorial. Choose the latter if you are already familiar with the Apple computer. This preface and Chapters 16 to 18 are written for more experienced computer users. The sections are organized as follows:

- Section One *Basic Language Features:* Chapters 1 through 13 present the nonprocedural language features required for data entry, for the query of datafiles, and for report writing.
- Section Two *Advanced Features for Database Management and Application Development:* Chapters 14 to 19 introduce the language features required for describing and using relational and hierarchical database structures, for file maintenance, and for executive level control of complex processes.
- Section Three *Language Reference Section:* A complete specification, in alphabetic order, of all features and keywords of the NPL language.
- Section Four *An NPL Tutorial for the Apple II Computer:* Three lessons offer step-by-step instructions for self-teaching the many features of the NPL language on a specific computer.
- Section Five *Appendixes:* Includes detailed language comparisons of five nonprocedural systems for IBM 370 computers, i.e., RAMIS II, FOCUS, NOMAD2, INQUIRE, and SQL.

PURPOSES

The book has three purposes:

- To introduce the first-time user of a microcomputer to an easier way of transforming raw data into useful information—i.e., easier than attempting to program with BASIC, COBOL, or other popular programming languages
- To provide a tutorial, a user's guide, and a reference manual for the NPL language, without the specific dimensions of the NPL software product intruding too much on the first purpose
- To suggest that microcomputers with nonprocedural software systems can become a natural training ground for people who must have access to data on very large computers, by showing the strong resemblances of

several large-computer, nonprocedural database systems and the methods taught throughout the book.

LANGUAGES

For better or worse there are hundreds of programming languages in use today. Some observers worry that a tower of Babel has been created by computer specialists and that as the number of languages grows the level of useful communications actually may be diminishing. Others are active in pursuing national and international standards for programming languages.

While the computer industry ponders these weighty matters, the practical people who have requirements for convenient access to their data and for methods of producing lists, tabulations, charts, and statistics have moved toward a different kind of standard, i.e., the English language. Computers are now beginning to listen in the language of their masters. This is an exciting trend, for it opens the doors for almost everyone to be a computer master, *without becoming a computer programmer.*

James Martin, in the preface to his *Application Development without Programmers,* writes, "Applications development did not change much for twenty years, but now a new wave is crashing in. A rich diversity of nonprocedural techniques and languages are emerging."

Daniel McCracken [1978] writes, "Most nonprocedural methods are used by people without data processing experience—which is another way of saying that the methods are used directly by the people with problems to solve, without going through the intermediary of a programmer at all. Taking all the factors together, I will venture to say that by the mid-'80s more than half of all computer time will be spent running applications programs constructed with nonprocedural oriented languages."

Software Terms and Tools

We think of *data* as numbers and words, which with appropriate sifting and sorting can be transformed into useful *information*—for accounting, financial planning, scheduling, and general support of decision making. Such data are stored in a *database,* which is generally a disk device with suitable software to provide convenient access. The most convenient of these software products employ a *query language* or an *application language* that is intended for people with a need for information but with no time or inclination to write conventional programs to get it. The table below lists selected database software products in four functional groups. Martin shows a larger list of software tools with additional classifications, and he discusses and compares the merit of many of the best products.

DATABASE SOFTWARE TOOLS FOR NONPROGRAMMERS

Software	Computer	Source
Text retrieval systems		
INQUIRE	IBM 370	Infodata Systems, Inc.
STAIRS	IBM 370	IBM
Database query languages		
ASI/INQUIRY	IBM 370	Applications Software Inc.
DATATRIEVE	DEC 11	DEC
EASYTRIEVE	IBM 370	Pansophic
MARK IV	IBM 370	Informatics General, Inc.
ON-LINE ENGLISH	IBM 370	Cullinane, Inc.
QUERY-BY-EXAMPLE	IBM 370	IBM
QWIK QUERY	several	CACI
SQL	IBM 370	IBM
SYSTEM-2000	several	MRI Systems Inc.
High-level application tools and database systems		
ADMINS/11	DEC 11	Admins Corporation
APL*PLUS	several	STSC, Inc.
EXPRESS	IBM 370	PRIME Management Decision Systems
INFO	PRIME	HENCO Inc.
INQUIRE	IBM 370	Infodata Systems, Inc.
MANTIS	several	Cincom
NPL	micros & minis	DeskTop Software Corporation
RAMIS II	IBM 370	Mathematica, Inc.
SPSS	several	SPSS, Inc.
TROLL	IBM 370	National Bureau of Economic Research Inc.
Application development systems **(Fourth-generation languages)**		
FOCUS	IBM 370	Information Builders Inc.
NOMAD2	IBM 370	National CSS, Inc.
MAPPER	UNIVAC 1100	Sperry Univac

Nonprocedural Systems

Many of the software tools listed in the table may be characterized, at least partly, as using a *nonprocedural* language, in which the "nonprogrammer" user makes requests. This term simply means the user states *what* he wants but not *how* the computer is to process the request.

Users of certain of the nonprocedural systems have been reporting enormous increases in productivity, that is, they have shortened the time to develop new database applications by factors of 4:1 to 12:1. So successful are they in quickly bringing satisfaction to end users that the name "Fourth Generation Languages" is used by some writers to distinguish nonprocedural database systems from others. Martin offers the criteria that the "Fourth-Generation" label be restricted to systems that provide development times of less than one-tenth those required by programming new applications in COBOL.

While the idea of nonprocedural programming is emphasized throughout this book, nonprocedurality is not an end in itself but rather a means of simplifying for *people* certain kinds of requests to *computers*. All complex applications use procedural steps, but these are higher-level processes required by the end user, not detailed computer instructions.

For example, when you give instructions for your car to be lubricated, have its oil changed, and its wheels balanced, it is sufficient to state what you want without telling the mechanic how to proceed. However, if you also wish the car to have an official state inspection, have the brake lights repaired, be waxed and polished, have scratches retouched with spray paint, and be washed, you probably would state these instructions in a preferred sequence.

Our nonprocedural request to the reader is that you lay aside apprehensions you may have about computers, or preconceived ideas about programming, as well as the notion that you "are not mathematically inclined." Just follow all the examples in the text, and you will soon know a new language, after only ten chapters.

Acknowledgments

We extend our sincere thanks for the seemingly perpetual assistance of David Oakley, Robert Mills, Richard Meyer, Diane Robertson, Carol Manela, and Dennis Papara; for editorial assistance by Lorraine Sichel; and for critical review and advice by Larry Manire.

Thomas D. Truitt
Stuart B. Mindlin

AN INTRODUCTION TO NONPROCEDURAL LANGUAGES

USING NPL™

BASIC LANGUAGE FEATURES

CHAPTER 1

INTRODUCTION

The wonders of electronic technology developed during the 1970s have placed powerful computers in the hands, in the briefcases, and on the desktops of persons in all fields of endeavor — people who have practical uses for a machine that can bring order to some of their records or reduce the drudgery of some of their functions. In the same period a software industry has flourished, searching in all directions for methods, sometimes called *languages*, for improving communications between people and computing machines.

At the beginning of the 1980s neither the industry nor the larger community of users of computer languages have agreed just which are better than others, much less which languages are best for average persons wishing to analyze data critical to their jobs. This book is an introduction to a language called NPL, which resembles a class of computer languages widely used in industry for analysis of management information with some of the largest computers. It illustrates how these same methods may be employed by persons with a microcomputer.

Anyone with a small computer can make effective use of the NPL language, if only to keep track of personal finances and a mailing list of friends and relations. While these two applications alone may not justify the costs, the point is that the ability to instruct a machine to perform useful tasks is readily available. The price for getting started is a personal effort somewhere between that required to learn to use a calculator and that needed to read this book.

To instruct your personal computer, you first learn a few commands. Then you practice, and your vocabulary will grow quite naturally. Most people have found the experience both fascinating and rewarding.

NONPROCEDURAL PROGRAMMING

In contrast to most computer languages, there is a special group of programming systems called *nonprocedural languages*, which have evolved over a period of fourteen years to have an important distinguishing quality: they require very few instructions on just *how* to achieve a particular result. Rather, they expect the user to give instructions on *what* data are to be used and *what* the output formats are to look like. It is assumed that the software will know the exact step-by-step process to be followed. Thus the user is relieved of the procedural steps. For example, Nonprocedural languages make it possible to give a set of instructions which might resemble the following hypothetical verbal request given to an assistant:

> Get that file over there, select only the records that look like this one and that are over one year old; display all of the critical data, together with the results of these calculations and comparisons, sorted by month and by these two variables, in these tabular and graphic formats, with appropriate statistical summaries.

Procedural languages usually require a host of detailed sequential steps to fulfill such requests. Procedural languages offer many more options, but at a greater cost in time and effort by the programmer, in the majority of cases. Nonprocedural systems offer convenience and savings for a larger community of users at the price of modest limitations in the variety of display formats which might otherwise be available.

FROM "DATA" TO "INFORMATION"

NPL is a tool to help you convert your collections of miscellaneous *data* into meaningful *information*. No matter how comprehensive your data collecting may be, you will gain very little if you lack the means to sort, screen, collate, merge, classify, calculate, organize, and display data. What we need from these data lies in the interrelations, the averages, the trends, and the ratios among data items. It is this kind of information that allows us to plan, to forecast, to budget, and to make decisions. To achieve this goal, you need a rational *process* for data analysis.

Here is a process you could follow:

Step 1: *Organize* the mounds of data records which clutter your life into piles that seem to have something in common.

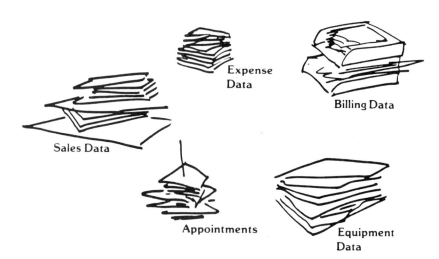

Expense Data

Billing Data

Sales Data

Appointments

Equipment Data

Step 2: *Describe* the data items (that is, the smallest units of information) which are common to each pile of records. For example, data item names associated with equipment data might be equipment name, quantity on-hand, and part number. Fieldnames associated with client data could include name, address, phone number, and social security number. The description of the common data items for a pile of records is stored in a special file called a master file.

Step 3: Once you have determined all of the fields associated with a collection of records, *capture* all the data items (e.g., names, addresses, part numbers) on a diskette. Do not copy, rewrite, or retype any item for the sake of neatness, or any other reason. Rewriting data items introduces errors. Capture the data now — make changes later. To capture data you use a special electronic form called a DATA-FORM.

Step 4: Sift, sort, screen, summarize, collate, classify, calculate, display, distribute, reorder, retype, and recap the data to your heart's content. A request that you make to NPL for information is called a *query*. NPL's response to your query is called a *report*.

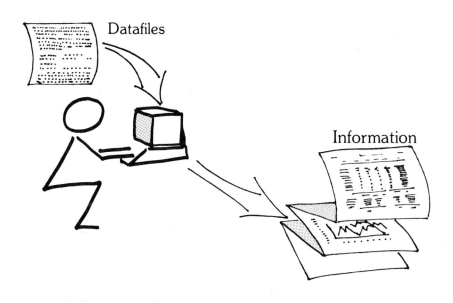

A BROAD VIEW OF NPL

Before focusing on specifics, take a look at the NPL System Guide which appears in Appendix C and in the figures on the next few pages in a simpler form. The guide is intended as a ready reference card to help you remember the NPL keywords and their relation to the various modes. You should refer to the guide often while trying the sample problems in this book.

LEVELS AND MODES

The NPL SYSTEM GUIDE is a graphic way of showing you the relationships of the several operating states of NPL. It groups these states into modes and levels. At the lowest level is the Operating System, which is the software

7

that controls the computer itself, the disks, the printer, and the display monitor.

In addition, there are two modes at the Operating System level:

- the EDIT mode is used to create program files.

- the File Directory mode, sometimes called the FILER mode, is used to transfer, to copy, and to remove files of all kinds.

The characteristics of these two modes vary from one computer to another. They are described in detail in the Operating System Reference Manual for the particular computer you are using.

To begin using NPL, you *execute*, or *run*, the NPL software from the Operating System Level. This step brings you to the NPL Command level. The NPL Command level is thought of as being at a higher level than the Operating System, because it is closer to you, the user, and your needs. Thus, when you are at the Command level you may type only one or two words, such as, CREATE, or PRINTER:, or GETFILE, to achieve a result that requires many steps at the lower Operating System level.

Two modes at the Command level are

- the DEFINE mode for storing the definitions of new variables.

- the SELECT mode for storing a definition of a subfile.

Above the Command level is the NPL Request level with REPORT mode and DATA-FORM mode. At this level all instructions to the computer are called nonprocedural requests or database queries.

Most of your use for NPL will be in these two modes, for reporting, data entry, and editing are the principal functions of NPL.

- DATA-FORM mode allows you to examine, change, and add single records on a fully formatted screen.

- REPORT mode lets you display data items which may be drawn from thousands of records and dozens of files.

The highest level is the NPL EXEC level in which you can combine all the functions of the other modes into an EXEC program file. Such programs form a library of procedures, stored on diskettes, which you may call upon at any time.

NPL MODES AND WORDS

Let's take a tour through the small house of NPL. The figure below depicts a group of rooms. In each of these rooms you must use a different vocabulary, and in each you perform different functions.

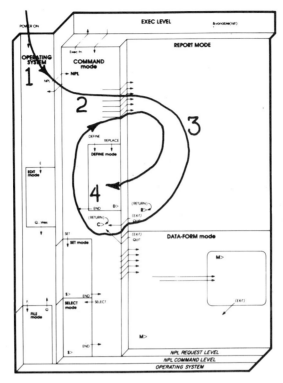

A typical path through the system to write some reports would take you first through the Operating System mode (1), to the NPL Command mode (2), and then in and out of the Report mode (3) for each NPL report you may need. Each time you are in the Command room you might give a command to change some NPL function, like ECHO or PRINTER:. Examine the list of options on the NPL System Guide.

A side trip between reports could take you to the DEFINE mode (4) for setting up one or more temporary variables for use in additional reports. When the reports are complete, the FINISH command returns you to the Operating System level.

Another path (refer to the step numbers in the figure below) might be used to perform the following tasks:

1. Create and store a new set of NPL instructions (or revise an existing one) for capturing data at the terminal. Enter the NPL statements in the Edit mode and store them in an Exec file called NEWDATA.E. (The .E in the name of a file identifies an executable NPL program.)

2. Now execute the program called NEWDATA.E, thereby setting up a new format on your monitor.

3. When the new format is displayed, NPL actually enters the DATA-FORM mode from Exec level. (Notice the broken line in the figure below), under the control of the NEWDATA.E program.

4. After you have entered all the new data, control is returned to the Command mode.

5. At that point you may enter the Report mode to examine your new datafile.

6. You may next return to the Edit mode in order to write another exec file, for preparing special reports from the new datafile.

7. On the other hand, if there are errors or omissions in the datafile you might move from Command mode back to the DATA-FORM room to make changes in individual data items.

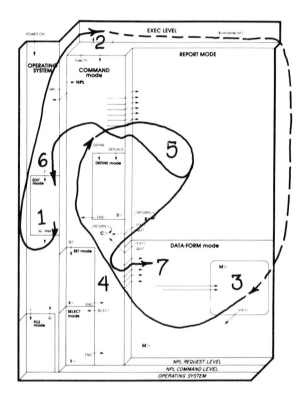

COMMANDS

There are two kinds of NPL commands. One kind, which we could call mode-changing commands, directs NPL to move from Command mode to another mode. Notice that in the NPL System Guide there are arrows into each adjoining room, and that there are several choices of commands for moving to the Report mode. The second kind of command, called direct action command, causes some action to take place within the Command mode.

MODE-CHANGING COMMANDS

Each of the following commands is associated with an arrow in the NPL System Guide, which shows transition from one room to another.

FINISH	• Terminate the NPL session and return to the Operating System level.
EXEC	• Fetch an Exec file; enter the Exec level and read NPL instructions from the file.
SELECT	• Enter the Select mode to specify a subfile of the currently active file.
DEFINE	• Enter the Define mode to define new variables.
REPLACE	• Enter the Define mode to redefine a new variable.
MODIFY	• Enter the DATA-FORM mode to build new datafiles or to edit existing files.
CREATE	• Enter the DATA-FORM mode to describe the format of a new data record.
PRINT SUM COUNT WRITE FETCH HOLD	• Enter the Report mode, and beginning with a verb phrase, write NPL requests for reports and extract files. Each request ends with a period (.), which returns NPL to the Command mode.
IF	• Enter Report mode, beginning with an IF phrase.
BY	• Enter Report mode, beginning with a BY phrase.

DIRECT ACTION COMMANDS

The direct action commands are:

DIRECTORY	• Displays the list of file names for all active diskettes.
GETFILE	• Causes a new file name to be stored as the currently active file.
FILE?	• Displays the fieldnames and other information about the currently active files.
TYPEFILE	• Displays a file on the Apple monitor or on your printer.
COPYFILE	• Copies one or more files to a new file.
DELETEFILE	• Deletes a file from a disk directory.
PRINTER:	• Directs reports and other displays to your printer.
REMOUT:	• Directs reports and other displays to a remote output port.
DISK:	• Directs reports and other displays to be stored on a disk, in a file of your choice.

CONSOLE:	• Directs reports and other displays to appear on the console screen.
INDEX	• Causes an index file to be created, to provide rapid access to records in a large file.
MEMORY?	• Shows how much memory space is available for sorting.
ECHO ON	• Activates a state in which the NPL instructions in an EXEC file are displayed while being executed. ECHO OFF reverses the action.
CLEAR	• Deactivities the current definitions of new variables or the active index file.

Once you enter the Report mode using any one of the keywords that initiate a major phrase (verb, IF, or BY), you can type as many lines as your NPL request requires without changing mode. The prompt characters, R>, appear on each line. Pressing the ESCAPE key cancels the request and returns you to the Command mode. Pressing the period (.) key submits the request for execution, after which control returns to the Command level, where the prompt characters are C>. The prompt characters for each mode are shown on the NPL System Guide. These characters tell you what mode you are in and when it is your turn to type.

While reading this book you should refer often to the NPL System Guide. Throughout the book the NPL *keywords*, which appear in the Guide, are printed in bold letters as a memory aid. If you see a word in bold letters with which you are not familiar, look for it in the Reference Section, where all keywords are defined.

CHAPTER 2

LISTING, SORTING, AND NUMBERING

Fetching and sorting records and printing reports are the fundamental processes required of a database query language. Nonprocedural languages let you, the computer user, describe only the rows, the columns, and the headings you wish, after which the computer interprets those wishes. If the requests cannot be interpreted, the computer will question you about your intent.

The rules and style of the query language are central to the nonprocedural system. Both rules and style resemble those of the English language, although the full flexibility and variability of English is not possible with a machine having a limited memory. Since your personal computer has limited tolerance of fuzzy instructions, it is most important that you, the speaker, follow all NPL rules closely.

The query language is introduced in this chapter with the keywords and phrases for sorting records and printing data items in rows and columns. NPL keywords appear on the NPL System Guide and they are printed in bold typeface throughout the book. The first keywords you should meet are:

a) the **PRINT** verb

b) verb object lists with **AND, OVER,** and **ROW#**

c) **BY** phrases for sorting records, with **RESET#** and **HIGHEST** modifiers

d) **NOSORT, END, QUIT** and **.** options

e) printing reports with **PRINTER:** and **CONSOLE:**

To use the Report mode you begin by identifying the file you wish to query, with the command,

---

GETFILE filename

NPL searches for the datafile and a master file which describes the names and formats of the data items (master files and file formats are discussed in Chapter 8). NPL reads the specified master file from your disk, allowing you to refer to any of the fields described in it in the body of your request. In this chapter STUDENTS.M, a master file, and STUDENTS.D, a datafile, are used as examples. See Appendix B for copies of those files.

The principal components of a Report mode request are illustrated here.

```
GETFILE STUDENTS                   - specifies a file
  HEADING "STUDENT REPORT"         - a page title
    PRINT LNAM AND FNAM AND PROG   - a verb phrase
        AND GRDT
            BY DGR PAGE            - sort phrase with an
                                     option
            BY SSN                 - a second sort phrase
    IF DGR IS BS OR BA             - an IF phrase
  END                              - request terminator
```

Names of data items like LNAM, PROG, GRDT, and DGR are the brief form of names, called aliases, for which the corresponding fieldnames are LASTNAME, PROGRAM, GRAD-DATE, and DEGREE. Fieldnames and aliases for the STUDENTS file are listed in Appendix B.

A report request may be entered on as many lines as you choose. Whenever you end a line with the **RETURN** key, the computer prompts with the characters **R>** to indicate that it is ready to accept the rest of your request. The **R** indicates Report mode. A short request may be typed on a single line. Commas may be used to separate phrases.

```
GETFILE STUDENTS, PRINT LNAM AND FNAM AND ADDR2.
```

Once a filename has been specified, that file remains active until the next **GETFILE** command names another. Thus, a second Report mode request, after the request above, could be written as,

```
PRINT LNAM, PROG, DGR AND GRDT.
```

PRINT VERB

PRINT is one of several verbs used in the Report mode requests. A verb phrase consists of a verb followed by one or more verb objects, which are separated by **AND**, or **OVER**, or a space, or a comma.

PRINT SSN, FNAM **AND** MI [**AND** fieldname...]

In the examples of this book square brackets are used, as above, to indicate words which are optional. The three dots indicate that the words may be repeated. The request above is interpreted as, "print the ssn, first name, middle initial, and *any other data fields.*"

The verb **PRINT** generates a simple report, listing the data values for a named field in the order they appear in the data records.

PRINT LNAM.

LASTNAME

PONG
SMITH
TAYLOR
SUMMER
WINTER
SPRING
FALL
WHITE
PLUM
GREEN
BLACK
CARD
JONES
.
.
.

The word LNAM is short for last name, which appears in the report as the word LASTNAME, since it is the FIELDNAME that is associated with LNAM in the master file. Refer to Chapter 8 for information about master files.

Sometimes you may wish to number each line, or row, in a report. A special verb object, **ROW#**, produces such a column.

```
GETFILE STUDENTS
PRINT ROW# LNAM FNAM.


ROW       LASTNAME           FIRST

  1       PONG               ERIN
  2       SMITH              MARK
  3       TAYLOR             OLGA
  4       SUMMER             JOHN
  5       WINTER             MEGAN
  6       SPRING             DAVE
  7       FALL               LINDA
  8       WHITE              PAUL
  9       PLUM               MARY
 10       GREEN              THOMAS
 11       BLACK              LYNN
 12       CARD               RICHARD
 13       JONES              KATHY
 14       VIOLET             SUE
 15       GOLD               WILLIAM
 16       SILVER             BRUCE
 17       ROSE               CAROL
 18       BROWN              LOIS
 19       TAN                CECIL
 20       LEMON              JOHN
 21       NICKEL             JEAN
 22       APPLE              ARTHUR
 23       GATES              JANE
 24       LIGHT              RAY
 25       CRAB               JOE
```

Note that the columns of the report appear across the page in the order requested and that the name of each field in the master file (see Appendix B) is displayed as the column heading.

Practice Problems

Write Report requests to produce the following reports from the STUDENTS file.

LASTNAME	TOWN	COURSE
PONG	PRINCETON	PSYCHOLOGY
SMITH	PRINCETON	CHEMISTRY
TAYLOR	PRINCETON	PASCAL
SUMMER	PRINCETON	ENGLISH LITERATURE
WINTER	PRINCETON	SOCIOLOGY
SPRING	SPRINGFIELD	PASCAL
FALL	TREE HOLLOW	PSYCHOLOGY
WHITE	CAMDEN	THEATRE
PLUM	PITTSVILLE	CHEMISTRY
.		
.		
.		

LASTNAME	ROW	DEGREE	ADVISOR
PONG	1	BA	WOLF
SMITH	2	BS	FOX
TAYLOR	3	BS	FISH
SUMMER	4	BA	EAGLE
WINTER	5	BA	WOLF
SPRING	6	BS	FISH
FALL	7	BA	WOLF
WHITE	8	BA	EAGLE
PLUM	9	BA	FOX
.			
.			
.			

Solutions

```
GETFILE  STUDENTS
PRINT  LNAM,  TOWN  AND  COURSE.
```

```
PRINT  LNAM  ROW#  AND  DGR  AND  ADV.
```

INTERACTIVE ERROR CORRECTION

If NPL does not recognize a word in your request, a correction is requested. For example, try misspelling the alias for DEGREE. NPL responds with

```
UNKNOWN  OR  NON-UNIQUE  NAME:  DGGR
PLEASE  REPLACE:
```

At this point you may do the following:
   a) Press **RETURN** to replace the unknown word with a blank (i.e., to erase the word, which perhaps was caused by a mistaken key stroke), or
   b) type the intended word correctly and press **RETURN**
   c) type several words which will be substituted for the unknown word, or
   d) type **QUIT**, or press the **ESC** key, to return to the Command Level.
If the spelling error is in the first word following the Command mode prompt, the response is different; for example, if you type:

```
C>PRNIT  LAST  NAME  BY  AGE.
```

NPL responds with this statement:

```
INVALID  COMMAND:  PRNIT
```

You should retype the whole request again, spelling **PRINT** correctly.

SORTING RECORDS

Often it is more useful to see your data sorted in either alphabetic or numerical order. NPL allows you to select one or more fields, known as **BY** fields and as sort keys, to be used as the basis for this sorting. The sorting is specified in a **BY** phrase which has the form:

```
BY fieldname              (or alias)
```

The **BY** phrase generates a column of data, which appears in the leftmost position of the report. When the sorting causes several records to be grouped together, the **BY** field value is printed only on the first line of the group.

Using several **BY** phrases in one Report mode request causes sorting and subsorting of the records. In the resulting reports the **BY** fields appear on the left side of the page in the order given in the request.

GETFILE STUDENTS

PRINT LNAM **BY** TOWN.

TOWN	LASTNAME
CAMDEN	WHITE
CANTON	VIOLET
FRANKLIN	BROWN
HAMILTON	SILVER
HAMINGTON	BLACK
LEESVILLE	GATES
MIDDLETOWN	JONES
MOON CITY	CARD
N.Y.C.	NICKEL
NEWARK	GREEN
PHILADELPHIA	GOLD
PITTSVILLE	PLUM
PLEASANTVILLE	APPLE
PRINCETON	PONG
	SMITH
	TAYLOR
	SUMMER
	WINTER
ROPER	LIGHT
SEABROOK	LEMON
SPRINGFIELD	SPRING
	ROSE
SURF CITY	CRAB
TREE HOLLOW	FALL
WILLINGBORO	TAN

BY PHRASES WITH ROW#

When sorting and counting with the special verb object **ROW#**, you can reset the row counter with each change of the **BY** field. The result is numbering of rows by groups. The keyword **RESET#** must follow the **BY** phrase.

PRINT ROW# LNAM **BY** DEGREE **RESET#**.

DEGREE	ROW	LASTNAME
BA	1	PONG
	2	SUMMER
	3	WINTER
	4	FALL
	5	WHITE
	6	PLUM
	7	BLACK
	8	CARD
	9	JONES
	10	SILVER
	11	ROSE
	12	BROWN
	13	NICKEL
	14	GATES
	15	LIGHT
BS	1	SMITH
	2	TAYLOR
	3	SPRING
	4	GREEN
	5	VIOLET
	6	GOLD
	7	TAN
	8	LEMON
	9	APPLE
	10	CRAB

With more than one **BY** phrase, the row counter is reset by the phrase containing **RESET#**.

PRINT ROW# LNAM, **BY** DEGREE **RESET#**, **BY** CREDITS.

Notice the sort fields appear on the left in the order stated, followed by the two verb objects, i.e., row number and LNAM.

DEGREE	CREDITS	ROW	LASTNAME
BA	3	1	PONG
		2	SUMMER
		3	WINTER
		4	BLACK
		5	CARD
		6	JONES
		7	SILVER
		8	ROSE
		9	NICKEL
		10	GATES
		11	LIGHT
	4	12	FALL
		13	WHITE
		14	PLUM
		15	BROWN
BS	3	1	TAYLOR
	4	2	SPRING
		3	GREEN
		4	VIOLET
		5	GOLD
		6	TAN
		7	LEMON
		8	APPLE
		9	CRAB
	5	10	SMITH

In general, the special modifier **RESET#** may be placed in any **BY** phrase, thereby causing the row numbering to be reset to 1 with the changing of that **BY** field. In any case, however, the position of the row numbers in the table is determined by the position of **ROW#** in the list of verb objects. **RESET#** is only used with **ROW#**.

Practice Problems

Write Report requests to produce the following reports from the STUDENTS file.

GRAD-DATE	ROW	SSN	LASTNAME
80/06	1	455566674	LIGHT
81/06	1	098789541	FALL
	2	456129975	BROWN
82/06	1	111222333	GREEN
	2	198987834	BLACK
	3	778902388	JONES
83/06	1	155403322	WINTER
	2	345876345	SPRING
	3	666777534	PLUM
	4	109203473	GOLD
	5	123960876	TAN
	6	567009831	NICKEL
	7	345888999	GATES
	8	231990789	CRAB
83/09	1	456987123	SILVER
	2	567809237	LEMON
84/06	1	209362084	PONG
	2	209372084	SMITH
	3	209382084	TAYLOR
	4	209392084	SUMMER
	5	345098711	WHITE
	6	557788423	CARD
	7	555888973	VIOLET
	8	444333888	ROSE
	9	234008891	APPLE

DEGREE	GRAD-DATE	SSN	LASTNAME	ROW
BA	80/06	455566674	LIGHT	1
	81/06	098789541	FALL	2
		456129975	BROWN	3
	82/06	198987834	BLACK	4
		778902388	JONES	5
	83/06	155403322	WINTER	6
		666777534	PLUM	7
		567009831	NICKEL	8
		345888999	GATES	9
	83/09	456987123	SILVER	10
	84/06	209362084	PONG	11
		209392084	SUMMER	12
		345098711	WHITE	13
		557788423	CARD	14
		444333888	ROSE	15
BS	82/06	111222333	GREEN	1
	83/06	345876345	SPRING	2
		109203473	GOLD	3
		123960876	TAN	4
		231990789	CRAB	5
	83/09	567809237	LEMON	6
	84/06	209372084	SMITH	7
		209382084	TAYLOR	8
		555888973	VIOLET	9
		234008891	APPLE	10

Solutions

```
GETFILE STUDENTS
PRINT ROW# SSN AND LNAM BY GRDT RESET#.
```

```
PRINT SSN LNAM ROW# BY DEGREE RESET# BY GRDT.
```

NOSORT

Sometimes records of a file are already stored in a sort sequence that is the same as you require for a report. To save time you can avoid sorting a presorted file by including the NPL keyword **NOSORT** either before or after the **BY** phrases. For example:

```
GETFILE POPULATION
PRINT MALE FEMALE TOTAL BY COUNTY BY TOWN NOSORT.
```

This request will print a proper table only if the file is already sorted by county, by town. Otherwise the result is disastrous, because the records will not be grouped properly by county.

Notwithstanding the last comment, **NOSORT** is used sometimes as a convenience when testing a complex NPL report request to avoid taking the time to sort while adjusting the report format. The **NOSORT** keyword is removed before the final report is prepared.

OVER, AND, AS

The word **AND** is used as a separator between verb objects. Its use, like the use of commas, is optional, and it has no meaning except when it appears in the same phrase with the word **OVER**. The **AND** separates two fields which are to appear side by side on the report page, while **OVER** causes the first to be printed above the other.

The use of **OVER** results in reports with quite a different format. Instead of a vertical column for each verb object, there is a row for each when **OVER**s separate all verb objects. Column headings are not printed. However, in order to provide labels for the rows of data items, you may use an **AS** phrase after each verb object — or after only a selected few. These labels appear to the left of the data items in the report.

The **AS** phrase consists of the keyword **AS** followed by a label of as many as twelve characters. If the label contains a space character then it must be surrounded by quotes.

For example,

PRINT A **AS** A1=, **OVER** B **AS** B1=, **OVER** C **AS** C1=.

                              yields   A1=   5
                                                      B1= 37
                                                     C1= 64

PRINT A **AS** A2=, **AND** B **AS** B2=, **OVER** C **AS** C2=,
AND D **AS** D2=.

                              yields   A2=   5   B2= 37
                                                    C2= 64   D2= 14

PRINT A **AS** A3=, **OVER** B **AS** B3=, **AND** C **AS** C3=,
OVER D **AS** D3=, **OVER** E **AS** E3=, **AND** F.

                              yields   A3=   5
                                                     B3= 37   C3= 64
                                                     D3= 14
                                                       E3= 22   16

In the list of verb objects each **AND** causes the next variable to be placed to the right, while each **OVER** causes a return to the leftmost position on the next line. Each **AS** phrase creates a label, but notice the last item above: there is no label for the value of F.

The **OVER** option is particularly useful in printing mailing labels, to place name over street over city. When **OVER** is used NPL does *not* automatically print headings or labels for the data. Thus a request

---

PRINT FNAM LNAM OVER STREET OVER CITY ST ZIP.

---

produces a mailing label format for each record:

JOHN   JONES
27 MAPLE ST
CENTERVILLE   PA   19333

On the other hand, the **AS** phrase provides labels, as follows:

```
PRINT FNAM AS NAME:   LNAM AND AGE AS AGE:   OVER
STREET AS ADDRESS:    PHONE AS 'TEL NBR:'    OVER
CITY ST ZIP.
```

with the result, for each record:

```
NAME:       JOHN       SMITH            AGE: 28
ADDRESS:    12 MAPLE AVE       TEL NBR: 218-394-5041
HARPERVILLE MN 74442
```

Notice that the label 'TEL NBR:' requires quotes because of the embedded space character. The word **AND** is optional, as in other Report mode requests.

END & QUIT

Use a **period**, or the word **END**, to complete a Report mode request and then return to NPL Command level. Use **QUIT** to return to Command level without preparing the report.

When you press **RETURN** in the middle of a request NPL displays **R>** to prompt for additional request phrases. The **period** followed by a **RETURN** causes NPL to process the request and then prompt with **C>** to indicate that you are in the Command mode.

Enter **QUIT** on any line to abort the request and return to Command mode. Pressing the **ESC** key has the same effect.

```
C>PRINT  LNAM
R>BY  SEX                        (Report  mode)
R>END
C>


SEX     LASTNAME

F       VIOLET
        BROWN
        BLACK
        GATES
        JONES
        NICKEL
        PLUM
        PONG
        TAYLOR
        WINTER
        ROSE
        FALL
        TAN
M       WHITE
        SILVER
        CARD
        GREEN
        GOLD
        APPLE
        SMITH
        SUMMER
        LIGHT
        LEMON
        SPRING
        CRAB
```

```
C> PRINT INC BY SEX END


SEX     INCOME

F     17000.00
       6258.00
      12000.00
       1267.50
      50000.00
       5000.00
       1200.00
       1372.00
       3568.00
       6339.00
       5275.00
       1200.00
       1300.00
M      7000.00
       1379.00
      13000.00
       4000.00
       7473.00
        100.00
        400.00
      13000.00
       1079.00
       1200.00
       1438.00
       4000.00
C>                (Command mode)
```

SORT SEQUENCES

NPL returns to the Command mode after every Report mode request. The initial phrase, **GETFILE** STUDENTS, is required only once to identify the file. NPL remembers the filename until a new one is specified. Thus once STUDENTS is selected a Report request may be initiated by any of the key phrase words, like **PRINT, BY, IF**. The key phrase words appear on the NPL System Guide in the Command mode room with arrows pointing into the Report mode.

Sorting is one of the most important features of a query language. Two variations on the basic forms illustrated above are:

- Many sort keys may be used (up to ten)

> **PRINT** LNAM **BY** AGE **BY** SEX **BY** CLASS **BY** COURSE **BY** SSN.

- Any sort key may be reversed

> **PRINT** LNAM **BY HIGHEST** AGE **BY HIGHEST** COURSE.

The keyword **HIGHEST** precedes the fieldname. It causes sorting by numeric fields from high to low values, and it reverses the sorting by alphanumeric fields (i.e., from z to a).

EXTERNAL SORTING

Small files can be sorted using only the high-speed RAM memory of the computer. Large files, however, require much more memory space, in the form of disk memory space (called external storage) for sorting and indexing. A feature of NPL is that it detects when a file is too large for internal sorting and it switches automatically to the use of disk storage. There are no user options in this matter. External sorting requires more time, but much larger files may be sorted — limited only by the availability of free disk space. Be sure there is ample disk space before starting to sort a large file. See the Chapter 7 section on Managing Disk Space. See Chapter 13 for further discussion of sorting.

PRINTER: AND CONSOLE:

Normally the results of an NPL request are displayed on the console monitor. You may choose, however, to send them to a printer, to another computer or to store them in a file. The word **CONSOLE:** refers to the computer monitor. To direct the display of a report to your printer, simply type the command **PRINTER:** before you type the Report request. The **PRINTER:** command remains active until you type **CONSOLE:**, after which all displays are on the monitor.

To send a report (or the results of a **TYPEFILE** command) to another computer you must have a communications device and an active output channel, which is called REMOUT: by the operating system. Then you can type the command **REMOUT:** to send reports to the output communications channel.

A report may be stored in a new disk file. First type the command:

```
C>DISK: filename
```

where *filename* is a name of your choice. Then you type your report request, and the result is stored on a diskette. The **DISK:** command does not remain active; rather, subsequent displays go to the monitor (as if you had typed **CONSOLE:**). Now, having stored a report in a file, you may type **PRINTER:** and use the **TYPEFILE:** command to print two or more copies of the report, without rerunning the NPL request.

This chapter introduced these keywords:

GETFILE
PRINT
AND
ROW#
BY
RESET#
HIGHEST
NOSORT
OVER
AS
END
QUIT
. (period)
PRINTER:
CONSOLE:
DISK:

CHAPTER 3

COUNTING, SUMMING, AND AVERAGING

In Chapter 2 you used the Report request to retrieve data and to print tables. However, retrieval of raw data items is rarely sufficient. Most applications require counting, summing, averaging, and other calculations. Here we present the verbs **WRITE**, **SUM**, and **COUNT**, and several other tools for data manipulation.

In this chapter you will become familiar with:

a) the **WRITE** verb

b) performing computations using the prefixes **SUM.**, **AVE.**, **MAX.**, **MIN.**, **LST.**, **FST.**, **CNT.**

c) **COUNT** and **SUM**

d) the use of **SUBTOTAL**, **COLUMNTOTAL**, and **NOTOTAL**

With the **PRINT** verb, each line in a NPL report is based on information contained in a single record in the datafile. Using **BY** phrases in a report request puts the rows in a different order. Using **IF** phrases means only those records that satisfy each condition are included in the report (see Chapter 4). Nevertheless, once the records are screened and ordered, when the verb is **PRINT**, each line in the report always comes from a single record. This is a fundamental property of the verb **PRINT**.

NPL can also produce reports whose lines are based on *groups* of records. Let us first define a group. In the simplest case, i.e., when no **BY** phrases are used, the entire file is one group. If a single **BY** field is used, the reports in the file are divided into several groups, one group for each unique value of the **BY** field. When a second **BY** field is used, the groups which resulted from the first **BY** field are further subdivided into groups, and so on.

For example, if a file is to be sorted **BY** age and **BY** sex, all the records for the 18-year-olds are retrieved. Within that group the records for the women (F) are placed before the records for the men (M); then all the records for 19-year-olds are retrieved; and so on. **BY** phrases specify the sort keys. As more **BY** phrases are added to a Report mode request, the resulting groups of records become smaller and more numerous.

PREFIXES

The verb **WRITE** tells NPL to choose, for each verb object, a single value to describe each group and to write those values as a line on the report — *one line for each group*. A prefix is placed before each verb object to specify how this value is to be chosen. The possible prefixes are:

SUM	• The sum of the values for a numeric field.
CNT	• The number of records in the group.
AVG	• The average of the values for a numeric field.
MIN	• The lowest of the values for a numeric field; for an alpha field, "lowest" in the sort sequence.
MAX	• The highest of the values for a numeric field; for an alpha field, "highest" in the sort sequence.
FST	• The first value in the group.
LST	• The last value in the group.
ASQ	• The average sum of the squares; i.e., each value is squared, the resulting squares are added together, and the resulting sum is divided by the number of records in the group.

In a report request, the prefix is separated from the verb object by a period. Let us consider some examples using a file of invoice data called INVOICE. Here is the master file description of the data fields in the file. See Chapter 8 for a full discussion of master files and the data format codes.

```
FIELD=PRODUCT   ,PART     ,A8    ,A8   ,$
FIELD=AREA      ,REGION   ,A5    ,A5   ,$
FIELD=CUSTOMER  ,NAME     ,A16   ,A16  ,$
FIELD=MONTH     ,MTH      ,I2    ,A2   ,$
FIELD=UNITS     ,NUMBER   ,I3    ,A3   ,$
FIELD=AMOUNT    ,PRICE    ,F6.0  ,A6   ,$
FIELD=          ,...      ,      ,A1   ,$   END-OF-RECORD
```

and here are the twenty records in the datafile:

```
AXLES     NORTHAjax Co.           1  2   113
AXLES     SOUTHHarris Motor Co.  1 83   362
BUSHINGSNORTHEdison Tools Co.  4 65   397
AXLES     SOUTHDavis Motors     10 42   121
FLANGES EAST Isaac's Sons     10 33   388
BUSHINGSEAST Davis Motors      9 52   318
FLANGES WEST Franklin Corp.   11 32   218
COUPLES EAST Coleman Brothers 8 85   303
COUPLES SOUTHFranklin Corp.    4 87   289
AXLES     SOUTHIsaac's Sons    10  8   261
COUPLES EAST Coleman Brothers10 83   372
AXLES     WEST Coleman Brothers10 84   344
BEARINGSWEST Ajax Co.          1 28   111
FLANGES NORTHIsaac's Sons     12 71   368
BUSHINGSWEST Garrison & Sons  8 55   297
AXLES     NORTHHarris Motor Co. 7 82   331
BEARINGSSOUTHIsaac's Sons     10 50   383
BEARINGSWEST Ajax Co.         12 62   231
AXLES     EAST Isaac's Sons     1 48   281
BEARINGSWEST Garrison & Sons   6 53   325
```

The request **PRINT** AMOUNT produces the following report:

```
PRINT AMOUNT.

                        AMOUNT

                           113
                           362
                           397
                           121
                           388
                           318
                           218
                           303
                           289
                           261
                           372
                           344
                           111
                           368
                           297
                           331
                           383
                           231
                           281
                           325
```

While the request **WRITE SUM**.AMOUNT produces this single-line report:

```
WRITE SUM.AMOUNT.

                         SUM
                         AMOUNT

                         5813
```

Because there are no **BY** fields in the report request, NPL considers the entire file to be a single group. Therefore, the resulting report consists of a single line.

Here are some other examples:

```
WRITE CNT.AMOUNT.


                              COUNT
                              AMOUNT

                                20
```

```
WRITE AVG.AMOUNT.


                              AVG
                              AMOUNT

                               291
```

```
WRITE MIN.AMOUNT.


                              MIN
                              AMOUNT

                               111
```

```
WRITE MAX.AMOUNT.


                              MAX
                              AMOUNT

                               397
```

```
WRITE FST.AMOUNT.


                              FST
                              AMOUNT

                               113
```

```
WRITE LST.AMOUNT.

                                    LST
                                    AMOUNT

                                        325
```

```
WRITE ASQ.AMOUNT.

                                    ASQ
                                    AMOUNT

                                       92279
```

A **WRITE** request can contain multiple verb objects, and each may have a different prefix. Here is an example request and report:

```
WRITE MIN.AMOUNT, MAX.AMOUNT, LST.CUST.
AND MAX.CUST.
```

MIN AMOUNT	MAX AMOUNT	LST CUSTOMER	MAX CUSTOMER
111	397	Garrison & Sons	Isaac's Sons

Now consider a report request in which the phrase **BY PART** is used. If the records are ordered by part names, the records appear like this:

PRODUCT	AREA	CUSTOMER	MONTH	UNITS	AMOUNT
AXLES	NORTH	Ajax Co.	1	2	113
	SOUTH	Harris Motor Co.	1	83	362
	SOUTH	Davis Motors	10	42	121
	SOUTH	Isaac's Sons	10	8	261
	WEST	Coleman Brothers	10	84	344
	NORTH	Harris Motor Co.	7	82	331
	EAST	Isaac's Sons	1	48	281
BEARINGS	WEST	Ajax Co.	1	28	111
	SOUTH	Isaac's Sons	10	50	383
	WEST	Ajax Co.	12	62	231
	WEST	Garrison & Co.	6	53	325
BUSHINGS	NORTH	Edison Tools Co.	4	65	397
	EAST	Davis Motors	9	52	318
	WEST	Garrison & Sons	8	55	297
COUPLES	EAST	Coleman Brothers	8	85	303
	SOUTH	Franklin Corp.	4	87	289
	EAST	Coleman Brothers	10	83	372
FLANGES	EAST	Isaac's Sons	10	33	388
	WEST	Franklin Corp.	11	32	218
	NORTH	Isaac's Sons	12	71	368

The records are now in five groups, one for each value of the PART field; the groups are in order.

Here are some example reports:

WRITE SUM.AMOUNT BY PART.

PRODUCT	SUM AMOUNT
AXLES	1813
BEARINGS	1050
BUSHINGS	1012
COUPLES	964
FLANGES	974

```
WRITE CNT.AMOUNT BY PART.
```

| | COUNT |
PRODUCT	AMOUNT
AXLES	7
BEARINGS	4
BUSHINGS	3
COUPLES	3
FLANGES	3

```
WRITE AVG.AMOUNT BY PART.
```

| | AVG |
PRODUCT	AMOUNT
AXLES	259
BEARINGS	262
BUSHINGS	337
COUPLES	321
FLANGES	325

WRITE MIN.AMOUNT **BY** PART.

	MIN PRODUCT	AMOUNT
AXLES		113
BEARINGS		111
BUSHINGS		297
COUPLES		289
FLANGES		218

WRITE MAX.AMOUNT **BY** PART.

	MAX PRODUCT	AMOUNT
AXLES		362
BEARINGS		383
BUSHINGS		397
COUPLES		372
FLANGES		388

WRITE FST.AMOUNT **BY** PART.

	FST PRODUCT	AMOUNT
AXLES		113
BEARINGS		111
BUSHINGS		397
COUPLES		303
FLANGES		388

```
WRITE LST.AMOUNT BY PART.

                                        LST
                          PRODUCT     AMOUNT

                          AXLES          281
                          BEARINGS       325
                          BUSHINGS       297
                          COUPLES        372
                          FLANGES        368
```

```
WRITE ASQ.AMOUNT BY PART.

                                        ASQ
                          PRODUCT     AMOUNT

                          AXLES        76205
                          BEARINGS     79499
                          BUSHINGS    115647
                          COUPLES     104571
                          FLANGES     111164
```

As before, a **WRITE** request can contain multiple verb objects, and each report may have a different prefix. Here is an example request and report:

```
WRITE MIN.AMOUNT, MAX.AMOUNT, LST.CUST, AND MAX.CUST
BY PART.
```

PART	MIN AMOUNT	MAX AMOUNT	LST CUSTOMER	MAX CUSTOMER
AXLES	113	362	Isaac's Sons	Isaac's Sons
BEARINGS	111	383	Garrison & Sons	Isaac's Sons
BUSHINGS	297	397	Garrison & Sons	Garrison & Sons
COUPLES	289	372	Coleman Brothers	Franklin Corp.
FLANGES	218	388	Isaac's Sons	Isaac's Sons

The following report provides a list of the kinds of parts in the file:

```
WRITE FST.PART BY PART NOPRINT.

                              FST
                              PRODUCT

                              AXLES
                              BEARINGS
                              BUSHINGS
                              COUPLES
                              FLANGES
```

In a **WRITE** request there is one verb object value in the report for each group. If a prefix is not specified for a verb object, then the value is picked according to the following rules:

- The assumed prefix for a numeric field is **SUM**.

- The assumed prefix for an alpha field is **LST**.

Thus, the requests:

```
WRITE SUM.AMOUNT SUM.UNITS AND LST.REGION.

WRITE SUM.AMOUNT UNITS AND REGION.

WRITE AMOUNT, UNITS, AND REGION.
```

produce virtually the same report. Try such requests, and you will see the report vary only in whether the prefix appears in the column headings.

```
AMOUNT   UNITS   AREA

 5813    1105    WEST
```

The most common prefixes are **SUM** and **CNT**. Therefore, to simplify certain report requests, NPL provides two alternatives to the verb **WRITE**:

- The word **SUM** is a synonym for the word **WRITE**.

- The word **COUNT** may be used as a verb, in which case the assumed prefix is **CNT**. for verb objects with no prefix specified.

Here are some examples:

```
SUM AMOUNT.

                         AMOUNT

                          5813
```

```
COUNT AMOUNT.

                         COUNT

                          20
```

```
SUM AMOUNT AND AVG.AMOUNT.

                                    AVG
                         AMOUNT     AMOUNT

                          5813       291
```

```
SUM AMOUNT BY PART.

                                    PRODUCT        AMOUNT

                                    AXLES            1813
                                    BEARINGS         1050
                                    BUSHINGS         1012
                                    COUPLES           964
                                    FLANGES           974
```

```
COUNT AMOUNT BY PART.

                                    PRODUCT        COUNT

                                    AXLES              7
                                    BEARINGS           4
                                    BUSHINGS           3
                                    COUPLES            3
                                    FLANGES            3
```

The **CNT.** prefix produces the same number of records for the group regardless of which fieldname is prefixed. Thus, the fieldname does not appear in the column heading. The count is an integer, with a format of I5.

Practice Problem

Write a Report request to print the following report.

PROGRAM	SEX	COUNT	MAX SALARY	MIN SALARY
CS	F	2	30000	21000
	M	3	35250	22000
HU	F	3	40750	22000
	M	2	25750	25000
NS	F	2	45000	30750
	M	4	40550	21250
SS	F	4	28000	20000

45

Solution

```
GETFILE  FACULTY
COUNT  SSN  AND  MAX.PAY  AND  MIN.PAY
BY  PCODE  BY  SEX
END
```

Practice Problems

Using the data in the table, prepare three Report requests to produce the reports below.

MONTH	DEPT	ORDERS	AMT
Jan	A	39	1950
Feb	A	31	1550
Mar	A	18	900
Jan	B	7	350
Feb	B	12	600
Mar	B	10	500

DEPT	ORDERS	AMOUNT
A	39	1950
	31	1550
	18	900
B	7	350
	12	600
	10	500

DEPT	ORDERS	AMOUNT
A	88	4400
B	29	950

DEPT	MAX ORDERS	AVE AMOUNT
A	39	1466
B	12	336

Solutions

```
BY DEPT, PRINT ORDERS AND AMT.
```

```
BY DEPT, SUM ORDERS AND AMT.
```

```
BY DEPT, WRITE MAX.ORDERS AND AVE.AMT.
```

47

COLUMN TOTALS

To produce a grand total for each numeric field in a report, include the word
COLUMNTOTAL.

```
GETFILE FACULTY
PRINT PAY AND COLUMNTOTAL BY PCODE BY SSN.


PROGRAM     SSN              SALARY

CS          200151551        30650
            200251771        35250
            200501231        21000
            200551241        22000
            200801291        30000
HU          200101441        22950
            200301881        40750
            200351991        25750
            200701271        22000
            200751281        25000
NS          162051331        21875
            200401761        30750
            200451775        40550
            200601251        45000
            200651261        25000
            200851221        21250
SS          151011221        20000
            200211661        23450
            200901331        28000
            200951441        25000

                            556225
```

Totals may require a wider column than the individual line items. If the column total appears to be misaligned, you should increase the width of the PRINTING format in the master file.

SUBTOTALS

   SUBTOTALS of all numeric variables may be printed in any report for
each unique set of values of the **BY** fields. These lines will write a summary of
census figures for all New England towns, with subtotals for each county:

```
C>GETFILE CENSUS80
C>WRITE POPULATION BY STATE,
R>BY COUNTY SUBTOTAL, BY TOWN,
R>IF STATE IS RI OR CT OR MA OR NH OR ME.
```

The report will have a grand total but no subtotals at the state level. Inserting
SUBTOTAL after **BY STATE** yields both sets of subtotals.
Consider this Report mode request for average population per town for each
county with state subtotals

```
C>WRITE CNT. TOWN SUM.POPULATION AVE.POPULATION
R>MIN.POPULATION MAX.POPULATION
R>BY STATE SUBTOTAL, BY COUNTY,
R>IF STATE IS NJ.
```

STATE	COUNTY	COUNT MUNICIPALITY	SUM POPULATION	AVE POPULATION	MIN POPULATION	MAX POPULATION
NJ	ATLANTIC	23	194119	8440	254	40199
	BERGEN	70	845385	12077	19	39007
	BURLINGTON	40	362542	9064	597	39912
	CAMDEN	37	471650	12747	9	84910
	CAPE MAY	16	82266	5142	255	17105
	CUMBERLAND	14	132866	9490	604	53753
	ESSEX	22	850451	38657	2363	329248
	GLOUCESTER	24	199917	8330	1129	27873
	HUDSON	12	556972	46414	1923	223532
	HUNTERDON	26	87361	3360	643	10855
	MERCER	13	307863	23682	2001	92124
	MIDDLESEX	25	595893	23836	955	90074
	MONMOUTH	53	503173	9494	369	62574
	MORRIS	39	407630	10452	1043	49868
	OCEAN	33	346038	10486	363	64455
	PASSAIC	16	447585	27974	5142	137970
	SALEM	15	64676	4312	1290	13848
	SOMERSET	21	203129	9673	530	31358
	SUSSEX	24	116119	4838	150	16302
	UNION	21	504094	24004	1785	106201
	WARREN	23	84429	3671	26	16647
		567	7364158	306142	21450	1547820

Look at the subtotal figures. From the left, the first is the count of towns in the state, the second is the state population, and the other three subtotals have little or no meaning. The sum of the average town populations for the twenty-one New Jersey counties has no relationship to the average county population or to the statewide average town population. The min and max subtotals are simply the population of twenty-one small towns and twenty-one large towns.

This report can be improved by suppressing the printing of all totals for the last three columns, subtotals and columntotals. This you can do with keyword **NOTOTAL**, as follows:

```
WRITE CNT.TOWN SUM.POPULATION AVE.POPULATION NOTOTAL
MIN.POPULATION NOTOTAL MAX.POPULATION NOTOTAL,
BY STATE SUBTOTAL BY COUNTY.
```

This chapter introduced these keywords:

```
WRITE
SUM
AVE.
CNT.
FST.
LST.
MAX.
MIN.
SUM.
SUBTOTAL
COLUMNTOTAL
NOTOTAL
COUNT
```

CHAPTER 4

SCREENING RECORDS FOR PARTICULAR VALUES

Often you must pick only some of the records in a datafile and report on them alone. You may need to retrieve information for particular years, or for a range of account numbers, for example, without printing the entire contents of a large file.

The **IF** phrase is used to screen out records not meeting certain criteria. The **IF** phrase sets a condition against which all records are tested. Only the records passing the test are included in the report. For example, to produce a report only on the students in the humanities, include the following statement in the Report request.

```
IF PROGRAM IS HUMANITIES
```

An **IF** phrase consists of a fieldname (or alias), the test condition, and the values that are of interest.

Test conditions may require
  a) numeric equality or inequality
  b) equivalence of words, or strings of characters
  c) inclusion within high and low limits (numeric or alphabetic)
  d) the presence or absence of certain characters

The **IF** phrase takes the general form:

```
IF fieldname relational operator value [OR value...]
```

The fieldname used may be any of those in the master file list, or an alias, or a defined field. It need not appear in the verb object list. The **relational operator** must be one of the following: **IS, IS-NOT, EQ, NE, LT, GT, LE, GE, IS. . .TO, IS-NOT. . .TO, EXCEEDS, IS-LESS-THAN, IS-MORE-THAN, CONTAINS,** or **OMITS.**

IF phrases may appear at the beginning, the end, or in the middle of a Report request. Any number of **IF** phrases may be used. Too many **IF**s may completely eliminate the report, since every test must be satisfied simultaneously for a record to be included in the report.

VALUE COMPARISON

Value tests use one of these relational operators.

Relational Operators	Meaning	
IS	is	) These operators
EQ	equal	) are interchangeable.
IS-NOT	is not	) These operators
NE	not equal	) are interchangeable.

For example,

IF SEX **IS** FEMALE	) These requests	
IF SEX **EQ** FEMALE	) are the same.	
IF SEX **IS-NOT** MALE	) These requests	
IF SEX **NE** MALE	) are the same.	

All of the above may be used with either numeric or alphanumeric fields. To retrieve records pertaining to clients who live in Pennsylvania, you might write the following request:

```
GETFILE CLIENTS

PRINT LASTNAME ACCOUNT AND AMOUNT
BY EMPLOYER
BY CITY
IF STATE IS PA
END
```

Quotation marks must surround any value with an embedded space or a leading or ending period (as in 'C.O.D.').

```
PRINT LASTNAME SSN
IF EMPLOYER IS 'ACME STORES'.
```

To compare dates, be sure to use consistent data formats for every record. See Chapter 8 for a full discussion of format codes. For example, the field EN-DATE may have the PRINTING format I4, which means the field is an integer, four digits wide. Two digits may be used for the year, followed by two for the month. September 1980, then, is printed 8009.

To retrieve and report on records pertaining to students enrolled during September 1979, you could write the following Report request:

```
GETFILE STUDENTS

PRINT DEGREE AND ENDATE
BY PROGRAM
BY SSN
IF ENDATE IS 7909
END
```

In this case the date is displayed with the year first, that is, a YYMM format. Other formats may represent the same month as 0979. The date September 15, 1979 can be recorded as 790915 or 091579 or 150979. All of these are used. The choice is yours, but you must be consistent. The first one (YMD or year-month-day) has the advantage that sorting by date is easier than with the others.

MULTIPLE VALUES

One test condition can be applied to a list of values. Each value is separated by the keywords **OR** or **NOR** for inequalities. **NOR** is used only with **NE** and **IS-NOT**. For example:

```
IF ENDATE IS 7903 OR 7906 OR 7909 OR 7912 OR 8003

IF STATE NE CA NOR NY NOR MA
```

When the list of test values is long, it may be convenient to store the test values in a datafile and then to select against those values, by referring to the filename as follows:

```
IF fieldname IN filename OR filename OR ...
```

Several files may be specified in the same statement. The test values must start in the first column of each record of the file, and have the same format as the field format. If the total list in the file is very long, the process may fail due to a shortage of computer memory space.

To check whether a value lies within a given range, use the following logical operators.

Logical Operator	Meaning
LT	less than
LE	less than or equal to
GE	greater than or equal to
GT	greater than
IS m TO n	specifies a range
IS-NOT m TO n	omits a range
IS m TO n OR p TO q	specifies two ranges
IS-NOT m TO n NOR p TO q	omits two ranges

The letters, m, n, p, and q represent literal values, which may be either numeric or alphanumeric. Consider these examples:

To report on students who enrolled *during or before* September 1979:

```
GETFILE STUDENTS

PRINT LNAM AND ENDATE IF ENDATE LE 7909.
```

To report on students whose last names begin with Q through Z:

```
PRINT FNAM, MI, BY LNAM, IF LNAM GE Q.
```

If you know the minimum and maximum values, use **IS. . .TO** to retrieve records with values in a desired range. The syntax is as follows:

```
IF fieldname IS value TO value OR value TO value...
```

For example,

```
SUM INC BY DEGREE
IF INC IS 300 TO 800.
```

The valid range includes the end values of 300 and 800. More than one range can be checked by using the **IS. . .TO** form with **OR**. For example, to report on students whose grade point average is between 2.0 and 2.5 or between 3.0 and 3.5, write the following:

```
IF GPA IS 2 TO 2.5 OR 3 TO 3.5
```

You may also use the **IS. . .TO** form with fields containing alphanumeric values or dates. For example, to report on students whose last names start with D or K or any letter in between, write the following:

```
IF LNAM IS D TO KZZ
```

The Zs are needed to make the range embrace all names beginning with K. To report on students who enrolled in 1980, you could say

```
IF ENDATE IS 8001 TO 8012
```

A variation on these is given by the examples:

```
IF AGE IS 6 TO 15 OR 20 TO 30 OR 35 OR 50 TO 60

IF AGE IS-NOT 6 TO 15 NOR 20 TO 30 NOR 35
NOR 50 TO 60
```

MULTIPLE SELECTION CRITERIA

There are two ways of combining several selection criteria into a single request.
   a) Listing a series of test values or ranges, separated by the word **OR**, in a single **IF** phrase. Records will be selected if the field passes any of the tests.
   b) Using several **IF** phrases, which results in retrieval of only those records that satisfy all criteria simultaneously. Care should be taken when using two or more **IF** phrases that the selection criteria are not mutually exclusive, thereby rejecting all records.

Some applications require the use of combinations of test conditions and two or more field values. When the two forms above are inadequate, a special new variable may be defined for use in the **IF** phrase. Defining new variables is presented in Chapter 5.

Practice Problems

For practice write a Report request to produce a report showing last names in alphabetical order, first names, middle initial, and the grade point average of students who enrolled in 1978 or in 1980.

LASTNAME	FIRST	MIDDLE	GRADE - PT - AVE
APPLE	ARTHUR	D	2.90
BLACK	LYNN	L	3.00
CARD	RICHARD	K	2.75
GREEN	THOMAS	R	3.25
LIGHT	RAY	L	3.00
PONG	ERIN	A	3.50
ROSE	CAROL	S	3.00
SMITH	MARK	B	3.00
SUMMER	JOHN	D	3.50
TAYLOR	OLGA	C	3.00
VIOLET	SUE	F	3.50
WHITE	PAUL	F	3.12

Write a Report request to produce last names in alphabetical order, first names, middle initials, and the grade point average of students who enrolled in 1978 or in 1980 and whose grade point average is greater than 3.1.

LASTNAME	FIRST	MIDDLE	GRADE - PT - AVE
GREEN	THOMAS	R	3.25
PONG	ERIN	A	3.50
SUMMER	JOHN	D	3.50
VIOLET	SUE	F	3.50
WHITE	PAUL	F	3.12

Solutions

```
GETFILE  STUDENTS
BY  LNAM
PRINT  LNAM  AND  MI  AND  GPA
IF  ENDATE  IS  7801  TO  7812  OR  8001  TO  8012
END
```

```
BY  LNAM,
PRINT  FNAM  AND  MI  AND  GPA,
IF  ENDATE  IS  7801  TO  7812  OR  8001  TO  8012
IF  GPA  GT  3.1
END
```

SUBSTRING COMPARISONS

Use the **CONTAINS** or **OMITS** operator in the **IF** phrase to check whether a value contains specific characters. This kind of test can be performed only with alphanumeric fields.

To display all students who live in a state which has NEW in its name, use the following **IF** phrase. Notice that the STATE field in the STUDENTS.M file (Appendix B) has an A30 format to allow for the full spelling of state names.

```
IF  STATE  CONTAINS  NEW
```

Use two **IF** phrases to display all students whose degree includes the letter S and who live in a state with NEW in its name:

```
IF  STATE  CONTAINS  NEW
IF  DEGREE  CONTAINS  S
```

To retrieve records pertaining to science programs other than natural science, you might say:

```
IF  PROGRAM  CONTAINS  SCIE
IF  PROGRAM  OMITS  NAT
```

To select records with programs which contain NAT or SOC in their names, the following statement could be made:

```
IF PROGRAM CONTAINS NAT OR SOC
```

The following statements ask for records in which programs include SCIE in their names and degrees which do not include an A.

```
IF DEGREE OMITS A
IF PROGRAM IS SCIE
```

Practice Problems

For practice write a Report request to display the number of students in each program who have BS degrees.

PROGRAM	COUNT
CS	3
NS	7

Write a Report request to display the total incomes for women students according to their degrees, plus the number of women in each group.

DEGREE	INCOME	COUNT
BA	94182.50	10
BS	17597.00	3

Solutions

```
GETFILE STUDENTS
COUNT SSN BY PROGRAM
IF DEGREE CONTAINS S
END
```

```
SUM INC AND CNT.SSN, BY DEGREE
IF SEX IS F
END
```

SUBSTRING COMPARISONS WITH MASKS

Screening for certain account codes may require the testing of only certain characters in a long account number. For example, suppose that in a ten character ACCNT field, the third through sixth positions contained department codes, and the ninth is a number code for a class of products:

```
ACCNT

02MRKT374B
08MRKT101B
52ENGR771R
57ENGR4973
33ADMN0040
08ADMN0010
    .
    .
    .
```

The following screening statements could be used to find certain departments and product classes, while ignoring the other characters in ACCNT:

```
IF ACCNT CONTAINS $$ENGR$$$$ OR $$MFTG$$$$

IF ACCNT CONTAINS $$MRKT$$4$

IF ACCNT OMITS $$$$$$$7$
```

The dollar signs "mask out" the character positions that are of no interest. In this example the mask, or test string is the same length as the field ACCNT, and as a consequence each non-$ character is tested against the corresponding character in ACCNT.

The test string may be shorter than ACCNT, and then a pattern search moves the masked string across the ACCNT code, looking for a match. For example, an address field might contain both city name and state code or state name in a free format. To find records for a state, screen with:

```
IF ADDRS CONTAINS '$$ WA ' OR '$$ WASH' OR '$$ Wash'
                     b  b        b             b
```

where the bs on the second line mark the spaces that should be in the test strings. It is assumed that all the city names have at least two characters. The **IF** phrase accepts addresses with the name Washington or containing the letters WA or Wash, provided they are preceded by a space and at least two other characters.

The quotes are required when the string contains space or period characters. If the test string is longer than the comparison field, all records fail to pass the screen.

Practice Problems

- Write a screening statement to find all Boston addresses, using the ZIPCODE field.

- Find records with Kansas telephone numbers.

- In a FULLNAME field find records with a first name of JOHN.

Solutions

```
IF  ZIPCODE  CONTAINS  02$$$
```

```
IF  TELNO  CONTAINS  316$$$$$$$$$  OR  913$$$$$$$$$
```

```
IF  FULLNAME  CONTAINS  JOHN
IF  FULLNAME  OMITS  $JOHN
```

Write a Report request to display, by program, the maximum and minimum income of female students and the number in each program. Also show the total income of women by program, the number of women, and the maximum and minimum income values for each program.

PROGRAM	SUM INCOME	COUNT	MAX INCOME	MIN INCOME
COMPUTER SCIENCE	5000.00	1	5000.00	5000.00
HUMANITIES	11410.50	4	5275.00	1267.50
NATURAL SCIENCES	13797.00	3	6339.00	1200.00
SOCIAL SCIENCES	81572.00	5	50000.00	1200.00

Solution

```
GETFILE  STUDENTS
WRITE  SUM.INC  CNT.SSN  MAX.INC  AND  MIN.INC
BY  PROGRAM
IF  SEX  IS  F
END
```

This chapter has presented the screening **IF** phrase. There is another use of the keyword **IF**, and that is in the **IF. . .THEN. . .ELSE** expression, which is introduced in Chapter 5. Both forms use the relational operators, but take care not to confuse the rules and purposes of the two. Further, there is a **SELECT** command which bears a resemblance to the **IF** phrase. Chapter 9 discusses the important difference between **SELECT**ing a subfile of records and screening out individual records.

The chapter introduced these keywords:

IF	
IS	**EXCEEDS**
IS-NOT	**IS-MORE-THAN**
EQ	**IS-LESS-THAN**
NE	**CONTAINS**
LT	**OMITS**
GT	**IN**
LE	**$$$**
GE	**IS...TO...OR...TO**
IS...TO	**IS-NOT...TO...NOR...TO**
IS-NOT...TO	

CHAPTER 5

CALCULATING NEW VARIABLES

Reviewing briefly, the principal operations in NPL are:

- screening of retrieved records, according to **IF** phrases,

- sorting the order of the records as rows in a report, according to one or more **BY** phrases,

- choosing particular data fields from each record for display in columns, as specified in a VERB phrase.

All of the Report mode functions discussed so far refer only to data items that have been specified in advance, as fields in the datafile. Now we look at several ways to *create and use new* data variables.

DEFINING NEW VARIABLES

You may invent new variable names, as long as they do not conflict with the master file names. See Chapter 8 for a full discussion of master file names. Unlike master file variables, the new variables have only one name, i.e., no aliases. Such a variable is defined in this form:

```
fieldname = expression
```

where an expression typically is a simple arithmetic expression. For example:

```
BIRTHYEAR = CURRYEAR - AGE

HOURS     = SECONDS / 3600

NETPRICE  = PRICE * (100 - DISCOUNT) / 100
```

Also, you may select the format of the new variable, as in this example:

```
CHANGE/F4.1 = (AMT - OLDAMT) / OLDAMT
```

The format codes are defined in Chapter 8. If you do not specify one, then F10.2 is used. Be sure to assign a format code to every alphanumeric variable. For example:

```
HEIGHT/A5 = IF HGT GT 72 THEN 'TALL'
            ELSE IF HGT GT 65 THEN 'AVE'
            ELSE 'SHORT'
```

The expressions which may appear to the right of the equal sign are many. Several kinds of expressions are introduced in this chapter:

a) the **IF...THEN...ELSE** expression

b) arithmetic functions

c) the **CLIP** function and the "adding" of character strings

d) the **LAST** function.

Before discussing each kind, you should understand where and when new variables may be defined. Consider the NPL System Guide (Appendix C) while reading what follows.

After specifying a file with a **GETFILE** command, typing the word **DEFINE** takes you into the **DEFINE** mode. Next, you type one or more definitions. For a single definition a complete entry might be:

```
DEFINE BIRTHYR = 1982 - AGE.
```

The **period**, or the word **END**, returns you to the Command mode. Any number of definitions may be entered before the period. All of the expressions are remembered by NPL until the end of the NPL session, or until you replace the definitions with a new group of definitions or request a new file.

```
C>GETFILE ACCOUNTS
C>DEFINE
D>BALFWD   = CURRBAL + CREDITS - DEBITS
D>AMOUNT   = QTY * UNITPRICE
D>END
C>
```

Remember—in **DEFINE** Mode you are simply telling NPL to hold onto a group of definitions (or expressions), which are used later by report requests. For example:

```
C>PRINT QTY AMOUNT CREDITS DEBITS BALFWD
R>BY CUSTOMER.
```

is a request which uses the new defined names interchangeably with the master file fieldnames. It is important to understand that the actual calculation, that is, the evaluation of the expressions for *AMOUNT* and *BALFWD* takes place each time NPL fetches a record from the disk file. Thus the values of the new variables become available to NPL at essentially the same time the regular master file data fields are read into the computer for each record. Hence, the new variables may be treated as if they were regular data fields.

The newly **DEFINE**d variables are always associated with a particular file (i.e., a master file and a datafile). The definitions remain active throughout as many Report mode requests as you need from that file. You may add another definition to an existing group simply by typing another **DEFINE** statement.

```
C>DEFINE NEWPRICE = UNITPRICE * 1.15
D>END
C>
```

NEWPRICE is appended to the current set of definitions associated with the ACCOUNTS file. All definitions are cleared when a **GETFILE** command selects a new file, and by the command

```
C>CLEAR DEFINE
```

After storing several definitions you may decide to change, or correct, one of them. To do so without reentering all the definitions, use the **REPLACE** command.

```
C>REPLACE NEWPRICE = UNITPRICE * 1.21
D>END
```

The rules for the **REPLACE** and **DEFINE** commands are the same. However, if a **DEFINE** statement assigns a name that is already defined, NPL rejects it and keeps the old definition. With **REPLACE** NPL cancels the old and uses the new definition. With **REPLACE** you must spell out the full name of an existing defined variable. You may change the expression and the format width, but not the **A**, **I**, or **F** format-type code.

SCREENING WITH DEFINED VARIABLES

DEFINEd variables obey all the rules of master file variables and are used in the same ways. That is, they may appear in verb, **IF**, and **BY** phrases and in **COMPUTE** and other **DEFINE** statements. There is one exception to this rule, which has to do with timing.

Most of the time when using a nonprocedural language you need have no interest in how the software processes your request; yet, in a few situations, it helps to know the following:

- Screening **IF** phrases are evaluated before other phrases, regardless of their order in a request.

- *Exception*: When the field in an **IF** phrase is a **DEFINE**d variable, all definitions are evaluated before the screening phrases.

The first rule is for the general case, for it would be wasteful to evaluate a group of definitions for a record just retrieved before knowing if the record will be accepted by the screening conditions. The exception is necessary, for otherwise NPL would not be able to evaluate the **IF** phrase test.

THE COMPUTE PHRASE

In contrast with the **DEFINE** mode, there is another place where new variables are specified. The form is the same, that is:

```
newfieldname/format = expression
```

As with **DEFINE**, a format of F10.2 is assumed, if none is specified.

The **COMPUTE** phrase contains only one definition and is used for a rather special purpose. **COMPUTE**d variables should not be confused with **DEFINE** mode variables. The processing is different, and the rules for use are different.

- The **COMPUTE**d variable is always a verb object.

- The **COMPUTE** phrase is only used to compute new columns in a report.

For example:

```
BY D, SUM A B C AND COMPUTE ABC = A*B*C.
```

produces a report with these column headings:

D	A	B	C	ABC
10	22	5	2	220.00
11	20	3	7	420.00

where ABC is the new fieldname and A*B*C means its value is calculated as the product of A times B times C.

• The expressions in a **COMPUTE** phrase are *not* remembered by NPL but are only used in the current Report request.

• **DEFINE** statements are evaluated at *retrieval* time, while **COMPUTE** statements are evaluated at *printing* time.

• Variables used in **COMPUTE** statements *first must appear as verb objects in the same verb phrase.*

• **COMPUTE**d fields may not be used in **BY** phrases or in **IF** phrases.

COMPUTE phrases are *not* evaluated on a record by record basis, but rather they operate on the *sums* of data values from groups of records (according to the **BY** fields) at the point when each line on the report is being written. Compare the following cases.
Case 1:

```
DEFINE RATIO = A/(B+C).
SUM A B C RATIO, BY D.
```

Case 2:

```
SUM A B C AND COMPUTE RATIO = A/(B+C), BY D.
```

These two cases yield different results, because the sum of many ratio values (Case 1) does not equal the ratio of the sum of those values. That is (2/3 + 3/7 + 4/5) is not equal to (2 + 3 + 4)/ (3 + 7 + 5).

EXAMPLES OF COMPUTE PHRASES

The verbs **PRINT, COUNT**, and **WRITE** (and its synonym **SUM**) are primary verbs, which determine the overall character of an NPL request. **COMPUTE** is a secondary verb, which may be used after the primary verb to compute new columns in a report from the values in the columns already formed (reading left to right). For example:

GETFILE FINANCE
SUM FUNDS **AND** TUITION **AND** GRANTS **AND** **COMPUTE**
REVENUE = TUITION + GRANTS
BY YEAR.

REVENUE is a new field with a full set of new data values created by adding together values from the fields TUITION and GRANTS (which are specified in the FINANCE master file). In order to create the new column, we specify a name (REVENUE) and an expression (TUITION + GRANTS).

In the example above, the expression for REVENUE is an arithmetic formula. Arithmetic expressions may contain any of the standard algebraic operators:

Symbol	Operation
+	addition
-	subtraction
*	multiplication
/	division
( )	grouping symbols

A standard order of execution applies; multiplication and division take precedence over addition and subtraction. For example:

$4 + 3*5 = 19$ The multiplication takes place first, then the addition.

$4 + 6*3/2 = 13$ The multiplication takes place first, followed by the division, and then the addition.

Division and multiplication may be performed in either order without affecting the result. The standard order may be overridden by placing parentheses around the part of an expression to be calculated first.

$(4 + 3) * 5 = 35$

MULTIPLE COMPUTE PHRASES

Several **COMPUTE** phrases can appear in the same request. The computed fields may be placed anywhere in the verb object list, not necessarily at the end. In all cases, however, the only fields that may be used in a **COMPUTE** calculation are those which have already appeared in the verb object list, whether master file fields, **DEFINE**d variables, or newly computed fields.

```
GETFILE FINANCE
SUM   FEES, FUNDS, GRANTS, WRKSTUDY AND
COMPUTE MONIES/I7 = FUNDS + GRANTS
COMPUTE STUMONIES/I9 = MONIES + WRKSTUDY
BY YEAR.
```

When computed variables are intermixed with datafile variables in the list of verb objects, the word **COMPUTE** must precede each computed variable, as in this example:

```
SUM A, B AND COMPUTE XX = A * B, AND C, D
AND COMPUTE YY = XX * ( A - B ),
E, F, G COMPUTE ZZ = ( 3 * YY - XX )
        COMPUTE RR = ( 5 * YY + XX )
        COMPUTE SS = XX / RR
BY H.
```

NOPRINT

To print the results of a computation without printing the values used to arrive at the results, place the word **NOPRINT** after the fieldnames to be suppressed. The desired calculation is not affected, and the fields used to obtain it will not appear in the report.

```
SUM FEES, FUNDS NOPRINT GRANTS NOPRINT
AND COMPUTE MONIES/I7 = FUNDS + GRANTS
BY YEAR.
```

Practice Problem

Write a request for a table to show student incomes and fees paid and to compute a field named CASH, which is equivalent to students' incomes less fees paid. List the sums by graduation dates.

69

Solution

```
GETFILE STUDENTS
SUM INC AND FEE AND COMPUTE
CASH/F9.2 = INC - FEE
BY GRADATE
END
```

PREFIXED FIELDS AND COMPUTE

When prefix operators like **AVE** appear in the verb object list, the prefixed fields may also appear in a **COMPUTE** phrase.

```
WRITE AVE.PAY AND MAX.PAY AND COMPUTE
RATIO/F9.2=AVE.PAY/MAX.PAY
BY PCODE.
```

NOTOTAL is a verb object modifier, similar to **NOPRINT**. Any numeric verb object, including **DEFINE**d and **COMPUTE**d variables, may be followed by **NOTOTAL** to inhibit the accumulation of the row value to form sub and columntotals.

Now, consider a **COMPUTE**d variable:

```
GET CENSUS80

SUM POPULATION BLACK HISPANIC AND
COMPUTE %BLACK = 100*BLACK/POPULATION NOTOTAL
COMPUTE %HISPANIC = 100*HISPANIC/POPULATION NOTOTAL
BY STATE SUBTOTAL BY COUNTY.
```

NOTOTAL is used because the sum of many percentages is not equal to 100 times the ratio of the individual sums. Therefore, for each state the calculations must be performed using the values of BLACK, HISPANIC, and POPULATION that appear in the subtotal line. One rule to remember is:

- Use **NOTOTAL** after a **COMPUTE** which includes division by one of the variables (rather than just a constant) or includes a nonlinear function like **ABS** or **IF...THEN...ELSE**.

When you follow a **COMPUTE** with **NOTOTAL**, something special happens. The accumulation of values is suppressed, but the values for the subtotal line are actually computed using the accumulated values of the other verb objects.

A	B	A/B		
3	4	.75		
5	10	.50		
24	6	4.00		
32	20	1.60	=	32/20

In this example notice that a value for the lower-right corner value could be obtained two ways: by totaling the figures vertically in the column, or by computing the ratio (horizontally, so to speak). Only one of them yields the correct value.

NOTOTAL means to suppress totaling vertically but, in the case of **COMPUTE**s, to compute the subtotal and columntotal values horizontally. The printing of a value for a computed column on a subtotal line is not suppressed; **NOTOTAL** simply determines which way the total is calculated.

Practice Problems

Write a Report request for the following report using the FACULTY file.

PROGRAM	MAX SALARY	MIN SALARY	RANGE
CS	35250	21000	14250.00
HU	40750	22000	18750.00
NS	45000	21250	23750.00
SS	28000	20000	8000.00

Write a Report request to show the range of salaries by program.

PROGRAM	MAX SALARY	MIN SALARY	DIF
CS	35250	21000	14250.00
HU	40750	22000	18750.00
NS	45000	21250	23750.00
SS	28000	20000	8000.00

Solutions

```
GETFILE FACULTY
WRITE MAX.PAY AND MIN.PAY AND COMPUTE
RANGE/F9.2 = MAX.PAY - MIN.PAY
BY PCODE
END
```

```
WRITE MAX.PAY AND MIN.PAY
AND COMPUTE
DIF/F9.2 = MAX.PAY - MIN.PAY
BY PCODE
END
```

IF...THEN...ELSE

This kind of expression has the form:

```
NEWFIELD/format = IF condition THEN expression#1
                               ELSE expression#2
```

The effect of the statement is to assign either the value of expression#1 or the value of expression#2 to the new field, depending on whether the **IF** condition is true or false. If it is true, then NEWFIELD takes the value of expression#1, otherwise, the value of expression#2.

You should take care to distinguish between the form above and the **IF** phrase which is presented in Chapter 4 as the means for screening records based upon some condition.

a) The general form of the *screening* **IF** phrase is:

```
IF condition   (if true, accept the record)
```

Where the condition is illustrated by these examples:

```
IF  AGE  EQ  0
IF  SEX  IS  F
IF  YEAR  IS  1976  OR  1980  OR  1984
IF  NAME  CONTAINS  ACME
```

b) In the *screening* **IF** phrase the form of the condition is restricted to a single fieldname and a single relational operator.

However, in the **IF. . .THEN. . .ELSE** form, which is used for defining new variables, the condition may take many additional forms. These are shown in the examples below. One word of caution is in order. Unlike the rules for the screening **IF** phrase, whenever literal values of alphanumeric variables, like 'ACME' and 'F' above, appear, they must be enclosed in quotation marks.

All of the relational operators presented in Chapter 4 (except those defining a range) may be used in the **IF. . .THEN. . .ELSE** conditional phrases. In addition, masks with dollar signs may be used with **CONTAINS** and **OMITS**. They are only listed here; refer to Chapter 4 for discussion and examples.

EQ	**IS**
NE	**IS-NOT**
GT	**LT**
GE	**LE**
CONTAINS	**OMITS**
IS-MORE-THAN	**IS-LESS-THAN**
EXCEEDS	**. . .$\$xx\$. . .**

IF...THEN...ELSE EXAMPLES

```
IF  CR  EQ  0  OR  5  THEN. . .ELSE. . .

IF  FUNDS  GT  1000  THEN. . .ELSE. . .
```

Unlike the case with record screening, alphanumeric values must be enclosed in quotation marks.

IF DGR **IS** 'BS' **THEN**...**ELSE**...

IF LNAM **CONTAINS** 'SCHMI' **THEN**...**ELSE**...

Extended capabilities of **IF**...**THEN**...**ELSE** are illustrated by the following examples. Two fieldnames, or many, may appear in the relational expressions.

IF GRANTS **EXCEEDS** FUNDS **THEN**...**ELSE**...

IF (WRKSTUDY + STIPEND) **LT** (FEES + ROOM + TUITION)/2
THEN...**ELSE**...

Compound conditions are created by nesting one **IF**...**THEN**...**ELSE** phrase within another. Indenting is recommended to avoid confusion. There are several possibilities: the second phrase follows either the word **THEN**, or the word **ELSE**, or both of them. In these examples, the letters W, X, Y, Z stand for three different expressions, and C1, C2, C3 stand for conditional expressions.

---

1) IF C1 **THEN**   IF C2 **THEN** W **ELSE** X
            ELSE Z

2) IF C1 **THEN** X
            ELSE   IF C3 **THEN** Y **ELSE** Z

3) IF C1 **THEN**   IF C2 **THEN** W **ELSE** X
            ELSE   IF C3 **THEN** Y **ELSE** Z

When it is necessary to employ more levels of nesting of such phrases, only the second form is recommended. The others are more difficult to write without making errors—not to mention being certain to confuse the reader. Most applications can be written in the second form. Also it helps to write in this format:

```
        IF  AGE  LT   2   THEN   'BABY'
ELSE  IF  AGE  LT  13   THEN   'CHILD'
ELSE  IF  AGE  LT  20   THEN   'TEENAGER'
ELSE  IF  AGE  LT  66   THEN   'ADULT'
                            ELSE   'GRAY  PANTHER'
```

The next example is taken directly from the I.R.S. Circular E Employer's Tax Guide (Publication 15, Rev. July 1982), to compute the Federal withholding tax deductions for a biweekly payroll.

```
PRINT EMPNBR STATUS OTFACTOR W4 RATE FICA HOURS OVRTIME
COMPUTE GROSS = HOURS*RATE + OVRTIME*OTFACTOR*RATE
COMPUTE TAXABLE = GROSS - 38.46*W4
COMPUTE TAX = IF STATUS IS 'SINGLE'
THEN
IF TAXABLE LE    54   THEN      0                                    ELSE
IF TAXABLE LE   123   THEN            0.12 * ( TAXABLE -    54 )     ELSE
IF TAXABLE LE   342   THEN    8.28 + 0.16 * ( TAXABLE -   123 )     ELSE
IF TAXABLE LE   481   THEN   43.32 + 0.20 * ( TAXABLE -   342 )     ELSE
IF TAXABLE LE   650   THEN   71.12 + 0.24 * ( TAXABLE -   481 )     ELSE
IF TAXABLE LE   865   THEN  111.68 + 0.30 * ( TAXABLE -   650 )     ELSE
IF TAXABLE LE  1069   THEN  176.18 + 0.34 * ( TAXABLE -   865 )     ELSE
                            245.54 + 0.37 * ( TAXABLE - 1069 )
        ELSE
IF TAXABLE LE    92   THEN      0                                    ELSE
IF TAXABLE LE   234   THEN            0.12 * ( TAXABLE -    92.)     ELSE
IF TAXABLE LE   461   THEN   17.04 + 0.16 * ( TAXABLE -   234 )     ELSE
IF TAXABLE LE   713   THEN   53.36 + 0.19 * ( TAXABLE -   461 )     ELSE
IF TAXABLE LE   908   THEN  101.24 + 0.24 * ( TAXABLE -   713 )     ELSE
IF TAXABLE LE  1112   THEN  148.04 + 0.27 * ( TAXABLE -   908 )     ELSE
IF TAXABLE LE  1315   THEN  203.12 + 0.32 * ( TAXABLE - 1112 )     ELSE
                            268.08 + 0.37 * ( TAXABLE - 1315 )
END
```

To summarize, return to the general form:

```
NEWFIELD/format   =   IF condition THEN expression#1
                                   ELSE expression#2
```

Expressions#1 and #2 may each take one of several forms, independent of each other.

a) They may be simple literal values, enclosed in quotation marks if alphanumeric.

```
MOOD/A5 = IF GPA GT 3.0 THEN 'HAPPY' ELSE 'SAD'

GI-BEN/F6.2 = IF VETERAN IS 'Y' THEN 500 ELSE 0
```

b) They may be fieldnames or arithmetic expressions.

```
NEWPAY/I6  = IF PAY LT 15000 THEN 1.2*PAY ELSE PAY
```

c) The expressions may be **IF. . .THEN. . .ELSE** phrases themselves, nested within the larger **IF. . .THEN. . .ELSE** phrase. Any number of levels of nesting is permissible.

```
FUTURE/A20 = IF GPA LT 2.0 THEN "FATHER'S BUSINESS"
       ELSE    IF GPA LT 3.5 THEN 'BIG CORP' ELSE 'DOCTOR'
```

When an alphanumeric string contains a quote character (single or double), the surrounding quotes must be of the other kind. Such a string may not contain both kinds of quote characters.

d) The functions described in the remainder of this chapter may be used in **IF. . .THEN. . .ELSE** expressions as well as in **COMPUTE** and **DEFINE** expressions.

ARITHMETIC FUNCTION

The absolute value function may appear in any arithmetic expression. This function simply evaluates the expression within the parentheses and reverses the sign if it is negative.

```
DIFF/I4 = ABS(FIRST - SECOND)
```

The arguments of the function, that is, data items on which the functions operate, may be literal values, or arithmetic expressions involving fields and literals. For example,

$$X = \mathbf{ABS}(153 - Y*Y/2)$$

"ADDING" ALPHANUMERIC VARIABLES

A field of three characters can be attached to another of five characters to form a new eight character variable (format A8). A group of characters between quotes may be treated as a field with a constant value. Fields are attached with the + operator. For example, these definitions of a new alphanumeric variables may be used in **DEFINE** and **COMPUTE** statements:

```
                                              Results

        THREE/A3   = 'ABC'
        FIVE/A5    = 'DEFGH'
        CODE/A8    = THREE + FIVE               'ABCDEFGH'

          YR/A2    = '81'
        YEAR/A4    = '19' + YR                  '1981'

        DEPT/A5    = 'ADMIN'
  ACCOUNTYPE/A5    = 'EQUIP'
  DEPT-ACCNT/A11   = DEPT + '-' + ACCOUNTYPE    'ADMIN-EQUIP'

       FIRST/A10   = 'JOHN       '
    LASTNAME/A10   = 'JONES      '
          MI/A3    = 'J. '
        FULL/A27   = 'MR. ' + FIRST + MI + LASTNAME
                                  'MR. JOHN       J. JONES        '
```

Two observations should be made. First, in each example the length of the new variable in characters just equals the sum of the lengths of its parts. A longer field would be filled with blanks (the space character) on the right-hand end. A shorter field would chop off the last characters of the right-most field.

Second, in the last example there are too many spaces after the name JOHN. This problem of "trailing blanks" occurs because all fields have a fixed length as defined in the master file, or elsewhere, and the actual length of the data words varies.

The solution to the problem is the **CLIP** function. The form is

```
CLIP(field)
```

The function clips trailing blanks (space characters) from the right-hand end of the field—allowing two fields to be squeezed together without any intervening spaces. Thus, to obtain normal spacing for MR. JOHN J. JONES, make these changes

```
   MI/A4 = ' J. '
FULL/A25 = 'MR. ' + CLIP(FIRST) + MI + LASTNAME
```

If the middle intial is not used, then the form would be:

```
FULL/A20 = CLIP(FIRST) + ' ' + LAST
```

The formats A25 and A20 are chosen to be long enough to handle the longest likely case for the grouped fields.

THE LAST OPERATOR

The **LAST** operator gives access to data items retrieved from the file in the *previous* record. It is quite different from the **LST.** prefix operator, which selects the last record in a group of sorted records.

```
FORMER = LAST CURRENT

DIFF/F4.2 = RATE - LAST RATE

RECORDCOUNT/I4 = IF SSN EQ LAST SSN
                 THEN LAST RECORDCOUNT + 1
                 ELSE 1
```

LAST is separated from the fieldname by a space. The variable RECORDCOUNT takes on successive integer values for each record retrieved until SSN changes; then it is reset to 1.

All other functions perform calculations on data items retrieved from the same record or on sums of these calculations. Only the **LAST** operator provides access to data items or calculations from a prior record or from a prior row on a report. The form *LAST* fld is evaluated

- in a **DEFINE** statement as the value of *fld* in the preceding record *retrieved* and *accepted*;

- in a **COMPUTE** statement as the value of *fld* in the preceding report row *printed*.

The **LAST** operator has several uses, and each depends upon the nature and the sort sequence of the datafile.

- For a file which is in sort order by zip code, the **DEFINE**d variable in the example below has the value XX to mark a change of zip code:

```
MARKXX/A2  =  IF  ZIP  NE  LAST  ZIP  THEN  'XX'  ELSE  '  '
```

- If a file of daily records of temperature, humidity, and density of SO_2 air pollutant is stored in sort sequence by date, then the **LAST** operator may be used to perform a smoothing or averaging of the daily measurements.

```
DEFINE
TEMP:MAVG  =  (TEMPERATURE  +  LAST  TEMPERATURE)/2
SO2:MAVG   =  (SO2  +  LAST  SO2:MAVG)/2
END
```

These statements illustrate two methods of smoothing time sequences of data. TEMP:MAVG is the name of the moving average of the current and previous values of the measured temperature. SO_2:MAVG, however, is a moving average of the currently measured value of SO_2 and the previous value of the moving average. This is called exponential smoothing and is equivalent to computing the average as 1/2 of the current value + 1/4 of the previous + 1/8 of the second previous + 1/16 of. . .etc.

Suppose you have a file of daily production figures and wish to print a report of just those days that fall below the average production level by more than 30 percent. You might define PRODMAVG as above for SO_2 and define PRODLOW as a code which is blank or the word LOW.

```
DEFINE
PRODMAVG    =  (PROD  +  LAST  PRODMAVG)/2
PRODLOW/A3  =  IF  PROD  LT  0.7*(PRODMAVG)
               THEN  'LOW'  ELSE  '  '.
```

Next, you would screen all records with the **IF** phrase:

```
IF PRODLOW IS LOW
PRINT DATE PROD PRODMAVG SUPERVISOR DEPT.
```

This example illustrates the importance of the exception to the rule about screening with **DEFINE** variables given earlier in the chapter. The exception is:

- When a **DEFINE**d variable appears in a screening **IF** phrase, all **DEFINE** statements are evaluated before the **IF** phrase is evaluated. Hence, **LAST** fld in such a **DEFINE** statement has the value of the *preceding record in the file.*

As stated above for the usual case, **LAST** fld has the value of the preceding record retrieved and **accepted** by the **IF** phrase screen. The usual case has the advantage that time is not wasted evaluating all of the **DEFINE** statements for records which are to be excluded by the **IF** phrase.

In the production example above, however, the moving average must be calculated for *every* record in order to be able to determine which records have low production figures and hence are to be included in the report.

This chapter introduced these keywords:

```
DEFINE
CLEAR
REPLACE
COMPUTE
NOPRINT
NOTOTAL
IF...THEN...ELSE
ABS
CLIP
LAST
```

CHAPTER 6

BETTER LOOKING REPORTS

Good reports require more than data. Titles, spacing, and column headings all help to convey more information. This Chapter introduces these report writing options:

a) **HEADING,** $<$n, $<$+n, $<$/n, and $<$field
b) **BY** phrase modifiers: **NOPRINT, SKIP, FOLD, PAGE**
c) **SET** phrases: **SET LENGTH = SET WIDTH =**
d) The **AS** phrase for special labels
e) The special variables, **REC#** and **PAGE#**

HEADINGS

Text is placed at the top of every page of a report with the **HEADING** option. The rules for the use of the option are simple.

```
HEADING
"first line of heading   "
"          .             "
"          .             "
"last line of heading    "

(Report  request)

END
```

The **HEADING** phrase may appear before or after any other request phrase, though typically it is placed first following the **GETFILE** line. The text itself follows the **HEADING** keyword on the same line or the next. Double or single quotation marks are used (in pairs) to delimit each line of heading. The number of lines is limited only by the size of the page. A single line of **HEADING** text may be entered as two or more input lines by pressing **RETURN** in lieu of one of the space characters.

```
GETFILE STUDENTS
HEADING
'  SEMIANNUAL  SUMMARY  REPORT'
'       STUDENT  STATISTICS        '
' '
' '
PRINT SSN AND LNAM
BY PROGRAM.
```

Blank lines are inserted by a pair of quotes with no intervening characters. Single or double quote characters themselves may appear in the text of a heading provided that only one kind of quote is included and that the other kind is used for the surrounding quotes.

```
SEMIANNUAL  SUMMARY  REPORT

    STUDENT  STATISTICS


PROGRAM                   SSN            LASTNAME

COMPUTER  SCIENCE         109203473      GOLD
                          209382084      TAYLOR
                          345876345      SPRING
HUMANITIES                198987834      BLACK
                          209392084      SUMMER
                          345098711      WHITE
                          456129975      BROWN
                          557788423      CARD
                          567009831      NICKEL
                          778902388      JONES
NATURAL  SCIENCES         111222333      GREEN
                          123960876      TAN
                          209372084      SMITH
                          231990789      CRAB
                          234008891      APPLE
                          555888973      VIOLET
                          567809237      LEMON
                          666777534      PLUM
SOCIAL  SCIENCES          098789541      FALL
                          155403322      WINTER
                          209362084      PONG
                          345888999      GATES
                          444333888      ROSE
                          455566674      LIGHT
                          456987123      SILVER
```

VERTICAL AND HORIZONTAL TABS

As a space saving convenience, you may insert codes in text lines to "tab" to specific columns, or skip a certain number of positions, or even cause over-printing of characters in the **HEADING**. The following codes are available:

<n — Tab to an absolute position, the nth column

The character immediately to the right of the integer n is placed in column n of the current line.

HEADING "ABCDEFG<25HIJKLMNOPQRSTUVWXYZ"

produces

ABCDEFG   HIJKLMNOPQRSTUVWXYZ

If n is past the current column position, the appropriate number of blank spaces are written. If n is prior to the current column position, then the printhead is returned to the left-most position and then n spaces are written. Note that this allows overprinting on a printer, but erases prior data on a monitor screen.

<+n — Tab n columns to the right

---

n blank spaces are written.

HEADING "ABCDE<+2FGHIJKLMNOPQRSTUVWXYZ"

produces

ABCDE   FGHIJKLMNOPQRSTUVWXYZ

</n — Move down n lines

84

The character immediately to the right of the integer is positioned n lines down.

HEADING   "ABCDE</2FGHIJKLMNOPQRSTUVWXYZ"

produces

ABCDE

FGHIJKLMNOPQRSTUVWXYZ

BY PHRASE MODIFIERS

Reports which sort the records into groups, according to various **BY** field values, are often enhanced by spacing or paging between groups. For this purpose, these **BY** phrase modifiers are used.

```
BY fieldname SKIP n
BY fieldname FOLD
BY fieldname PAGE
BY fieldname NOPRINT
BY fieldname SUBTOTAL
```

Several modifiers may appear in a list and in any order. For example:

```
BY fieldname FOLD SKIP 3 SUBTOTAL
```

Commas, may separate the items in the list, but not the word **AND**. **NOPRINT, NOTOTAL**, and the **AS** precede the other modifiers. A modifier only takes effect when the value of the sort field changes and just before the data pertaining to the new value is printed.

SKIP

This option skips one or more lines on the report page for each **BY**-field value. **SKIP 1** and **SKIP** are equivalent.

```
PRINT FNAM AND CREDITS
BY PROGRAM SKIP, BY LNAM.
```

PROGRAM	LASTNAME	FIRST	CREDITS
COMPUTER SCIENCE	GOLD	WILLIAM	3
	SPRING	DAVE	3
	TAYLOR	OLGA	3
HUMANITIES	BLACK	LYNN	3
	BROWN	LOIS	3
	CARD	RICHARD	3
	JONES	KATHY	3
	NICKEL	JEAN	3
	SUMMER	JOHN	3
	WHITE	PAUL	3
NATURAL SCIENCES	APPLE	ARTHUR	3
	CRAB	JOE	5
	GREEN	THOMAS	3
	LEMON	JOHN	5

.
.
.

In the following case **SKIP** follows the verb phrase, and a blank line is inserted between every line of the report. This is possible only with the **SKIP** option. Other modifiers may be used only in **BY** phrases.

```
    PRINT LNAM SKIP BY TOWN.


TOWN                          LASTNAME

CAMDEN                        WHITE

CANTON                        VIOLET

FRANKLIN                      BROWN

HAMILTON                      SILVER

                              BLACK

LEESVILLE                     GATES
  .
  .
  .
```

The two uses of the **SKIP** option may appear in the same request, for example:

```
PRINT FNAM AND CREDIT BY PROGRAM SKIP 3
BY DEGREE SKIP 2, AND SKIP.
```

The last **SKIP** results in two report lines per record.

FOLD

FOLD causes a report line to be folded into two lines at the change of a sort field. The values of the preceding sort fields are printed on one line, and the columns of data begin on the next line but *under* the sort field headings. The option is useful for reducing the width of a report.

```
        PRINT LNAM AND GPA, BY PROGRAM FOLD, BY SSN.


PROGRAM
   SSN              LASTNAME              GRADE-PT-AVE

COMPUTER SCIENCE
   109203473        GOLD                      3.90
   209382084        TAYLOR                    3.00
   345876345        SPRING                    3.75
HUMANITIES
   198987834        BLACK                     3.00
   209392084        SUMMER                    3.50
   345098711        WHITE                     3.12
   456129975        BROWN                     3.25
   557788423        CARD                      2.75
   567009831        NICKEL                    3.25
   778902388        JONES                     3.20
NATURAL SCIENCES
   111222333        GREEN                     3.25
   123960876        TAN                       3.70
   209372084        SMITH                     3.00
   231990789        CRAB                      4.00
   234008891        APPLE                     2.90
   555888973        VIOLET                    3.50
   567809237        LEMON                     3.45
   666777534        PLUM                      2.50
SOCIAL SCIENCES
   098789541        FALL                      4.00
   155403322        WINTER                    3.25
   209362084        PONG                      3.50
   345888999        GATES                     3.45
   444333888        ROSE                      3.00
   455566674        LIGHT                     3.00
   456987123        SILVER                    2.90
```

FOLD, SKIP, and **OVER** are often used together to good effect. **FOLD** may be used with more than one **BY** field. The next example illustrates some of the possibilities. Notice the two **DEFINE**d fields, BLANK and LINE. They are used as aids in laying out the report.

The keywords **OVER** and **AS** are used to insert labels that lie to the left of the data item (see the discussion of the **AS** phrase later in this chapter). The data items of a single record are printed on eight lines in a carefully designed format.

```
GETFILE PERSNL

DEFINE
BOARD/A15    = IF CERT EQ '1' THEN 'BOARD Eligible'
                             ELSE 'BOARD Certified'
NAME/A30     = CLIP(FNAME)+' '+MI+'. '+LNAME
EMPSTATUS/A9 = IF FT EQ '1' THEN 'Full Time' ELSE
                IF FT EQ '2' THEN 'Part Time' ELSE 'Consulting'
BLANK/A10    = '          '
LINE/A34     = '................................'
END

HEADING
"<36Group Health Association "
"</1 <36PHYSICIAN STATUS REPORT"
BY ACNO AS ' ' FOLD
PRINT NAME PHONE BLANK EMPSTATUS
 OVER STREET
 OVER CTY ST ZP
 OVER LINE LINE
 OVER HDATE AS 'Date of Hire' BLANK SPEC  AS 'Specialty:'
 OVER CDATE AS 'Contract    ' BLANK BOARD AS 'Status    :'
 OVER TDATE AS 'Date of Term' BLANK HOSP1 AS 'Hosp Priv:' HOSP2
END
```

                    Group Health Association

                    PHYSICIAN STATUS REPORT

001
  Mary G. Akins   401-351-2333   Full Time
  1615 Charles St.
  Providence   RI   02906
....\..................
Date of Hire 070176   Specialty: Medicine
Contract   010181   Status   : BOARD. Certified
Date of Term   Hosp Priv: RI General   St Mary's

003
  Stephen R. McDowell   401-331-7011   Full Time
   .   .   .
   .   .   .
   .   .   .

NOPRINT

NOPRINT suppresses the printing of a field named in a Report request, verb object or **BY** field. This option is used when the value appears elsewhere in the report, in order to avoid duplication. If used, **NOPRINT** must precede BY-field modifiers.

GETFILE CLIENTS
PRINT ROW# LASTNAME ACNO INC **NOTOTAL** AMOUNT
BY EMP **RESET# SUBTOTAL BY** AMOUNT **NOPRINT.**

Within the numbered groups the rows are ranked by increasing amounts, which appears on the right hand side of the page.

EMPLOYER	ROW	LAST	ACCOUNT	INCOME	AMOUNT
ALLIED CHEMICAL	1	STILWELL	Q18327	26	17
	2	MCNAMARA	Q08703	33	26
					43
AMERICAN CAN	1	TAYLOR	R45590	28	7
	2	LODGE	G73839	26	18
	3	JOHNSON	G49488	26	21
	4	HARKINS	F94871	31	22
					68
AT&T	1	STILWELL	Q62953	33	2
	2	TAYLOR	F44236	33	5
	3	THOMSON	F23430	43	11
	4	HUMPHREY	F18222	25	11
	5	JOHNSON	Q67952	24	16
					45
BOEING	1	MCNAUGHTON	R54168	36	2
					2
CHASE MANHATTAN	1	TAYLOR	Q79560	22	8
	2	RUSK	J19004	24	18
	3	KENNEDY	G42462	28	19
	4	THOMSON	K31975	44	24
	5	JONES	R49093	41	28

.
.

PAGE, PAUSE, PAGE#

You may break a report into a number of independent pages, each page dealing with a single value of a sort field, by using the **PAGE** option following a **BY** field. When a new page starts, under the control of **PAGE**, the column and page headings are repeated. The request:

```
WRITE BUDGET AND EXPENSES BY PROJECT
BY DEPT SUBTOTAL PAGE.
```

produces a departmental summary of project expenses on separate pages.

Of course, if there are too many project (report lines) for a single page, paging also takes place. The page length depends upon the number of report lines

91

that you wish to print on a page, and the paper size in your printer. Thus, you may set the report page size with the commands:

```
C>SET LENGTH = n      (n= report lines per page)
C>SET WIDTH  = w      (w= character positions up to
                          the right margin)
```

When NPL is started, the initial settings are:

```
LENGTH = 58
WIDTH  = 80
```

Current settings may be displayed with the command:

```
C>SET?
```

LENGTH limits the number of lines appearing on a page, including report data, headings, and intervening blank lines. If a report exceeds the length setting, a new page is started and all headings are repeated.

If the keyword **PAUSE** appears in this request, printing stops before each new page, whether caused by the **LENGTH** or a **BY** field **PAGE** option.

When **PRINTER:** is active and no heading phrase is used, the page number is automatically printed at the top of each page at the right-hand margin, as determined by the **WIDTH** setting. The page count is stored in a special system variable named **PAGE#**. As with **ROW#**, **PAGE#** is always available for use as a verb object. In the **HEADING** phrase, you can position the number in the text lines with a "field marker," as in:

```
HEADING
" Feb 1, 1982          Budget Report          </2 Page <PAGE# "
```

which places the **PAGE#** two lines below the report title.

FIELD MARKERS

The field marker is a general feature of the **HEADING** phrase by which data values can be inserted into the text lines of a **HEADING**. The fieldname of any verb object (prefix operators are allowed), or **BY** field, is preceded by the < character to mark the position for inserting the data value. The value printed in the **HEADING** is that which would appear on the first line of the page. For example:

```
HEADING
" Expense Item Report                    Pg.<PAGE#   "
" For the <DEPT    Department   "
" Project Nbr. <PROJ            "
" For the month of <MONTH   1982   "
PRINT
ACTIVITY AND EXPENSE
BY Dept NOPRINT
BY PROJ NOPRINT
BY MONTH NOPRINT PAGE
BY DATE.
```

The variables DEPT, PROJ, and MONTH are printed in the **HEADING** rather than in the body of the report. A typical page begins like this:

```
     Expense Item Report              Pg.    3
     For the SALES Department
     Project Nbr. 1345
     For the month of March   1982


DATE    ACTIVITY                 EXPENSE

03-82   TRAVEL                   $120.00
03-82   LITERATURE               $151.65
03-82   DEMONSTRATIONS           $106.50
   .
   .
   .
```

Practice Problem

Write a Report request to produce a report listing students alphabetically by college degree, each degree appearing on a separate page.

```
PAGE NBR    1

DEGREE   LASTNAME          FIRST          SSN

BA       BLACK             LYNN           198987834
         BROWN             LOIS           456129975
         CARD              RICHARD        557788423
         FALL              LINDA          098789541
         GATES             JANE           345888999
         JONES             KATHY          778902388
         LIGHT             RAY            455566674
         NICKEL            JEAN           567009831
         PLUM              MARY           666777534
         PONG              ERIN           209362084
         ROSE              CAROL          444333888
         SILVER            BRUCE          456987123
         SUMMER            JOHN           209392084
         WHITE             PAUL           345098711
         WINTER            MEGAN          155403322


PAGE NBR    2

DEGREE   LASTNAME          FIRST          SSN

BS       APPLE             ARTHUR         234008891
         CRAB              JOE            231990789
         GOLD              WILLIAM        109203473
         GREEN             THOMAS         111222333
           .                 .              .
           .                 .              .
                             .              .
         VIOLET            SUE            555888973
```

Solution

```
GETFILE STUDENTS
HEADING "PAGE NBR<PAGE# </1"
PRINT FNAM AND SSN BY DGR PAGE BY LNAM.
```

Practice Problem

Write a Report request to produce the following report:

```
                                                       PAGE    1

PROGRAM   NAME                          GRANT     SALARY

CS        COOK                 1        25000     30000
          EAGLE                2        50000     30650

                                        75000     60650


                                                       PAGE    2

PROGRAM   NAME                          GRANT     SALARY

HU        CROCKER              1        15000     40750

                                        15000     40750


                                                       PAGE    3

PROGRAM   NAME                          GRANT     SALARY

NS        JAMES                1       100000     45000
          TREE                 2        60000     30750
          WOLF                 3        75000     21875

                                       235000     97625


                                                       PAGE    4

PROGRAM   NAME                          GRANT     SALARY

SS        FLEMMING             1        15000     23450
          LYON                 2        40000     28000

                                        55000     51450
```

Solution

```
GETFILE FACULTY
SET WIDTH = 57
PRINT ROW# AS ' ' GRANT AND PAY
BY PROGRAM RESET# SUBTOTAL PAGE
BY NAME
IF GRANT GT 1000
END
```

REC#, ROW#, PAGE#

There are three system variables, which may always be used in reports, in addition to master file variables, **DEFINE**s, and **COMPUTE**s.

   a. **REC#**—The record number
   REC# is the physical sequence number of the records. It is like a **DEFINE**d field and may be used as any other **DEFINE**d field.

   b. **ROW#**—The row number
   ROW# is the line number in the report. It is like a **COMPUTE**d field and can be used where any other **COMPUTE**d field is permitted. (i.e., verb phrases, but not **IF** or **BY** phrases).

   c. **PAGE#**—The page number
   PAGE# contains the page number of the report. It starts with the value 1 and is incremented each time the report advances to a new page. It is like a **COMPUTE**d field.

To see the difference between **REC#** and **ROW#**, consider the following report requests made on a file containing 5 records:

```
PRINT PAGE# ROW# REC# CUST AND AMOUNT.


PAGE    ROW    REC    CUST                    AMOUNT

  1      1      1     Benson Brothers           325
  1      2      2     Ajax Corporation          193
  1      3      3     Issac's Sons              225
  1      4      4     Ajax Corporation          203
  1      5      5     Garrison Corpoation       285
```

```
PRINT PAGE# ROW# REC# CUST AND AMOUNT
BY AMOUNT NOPRINT.


PAGE   ROW   REC   CUST                  AMOUNT

  1     1     2    Ajax Corporation        193
  1     2     4    Ajax Corporation        203
  1     3     3    Isaac's Sons            225
  1     4     5    Garrison Corpoation     285
  1     5     1    Benson Brothers         325
```

System variable names may not be truncated in report requests.

THE AS PHRASE AND NEW COLUMN HEADINGS

Column headings for reports are defined in the master file. Each fieldname is a report column heading. These may be replaced, however, in a report request by other more suitable headings. The **AS** phrase defines a new column heading. The syntax is:

```
...fieldname AS 'new heading'...
```

Quotation marks must enclose the new title if there are spaces in the title, or if it contains quote characters or begins or ends with a period or comma (as in 'C.O.D.'). The **AS** phrase may follow the fieldname of any field that generates a report column, whether a verb object, a **BY** field, or a **COMPUTE** phrase.

```
GETFILE STUDENTS
SUM FEE AS 'TOTAL FEES'
BY PROGRAM.


PROGRAM                  TOTAL FEES

COMPUTER SCIENCE          3280.00
HUMANITIES                4150.00
NATURAL SCIENCES          4800.00
SOCIAL SCIENCES           5300.00
```

The width of any column in a report is determined by the size of the printing format of the field or by the length of its column heading whichever is larger. Thus the **AS** phrase may be used to control the spacing of columns by specifying longer or shorter column headings, up to a maximum of twelve characters. **AS** phrase titles longer than 12 are truncated to 12 characters. A column heading may be made blank with **AS** ", that is, a title string of *no* characters surrounded (so to speak) by a pair of quote marks.

```
GETFILE FACULTY
SUM SALARY AS 'TOTAL INCOME'
BY PROGRAM
BY SEX AS ' '   END



PROGRAM        TOTAL INCOME

CS        F          51000
          M          87900
HU        F          85700
          M          50750
NS        F          75750
          M         108675
SS        F          96450
```

Column headings are suppressed when using **OVER** in a Report mode request. When labels for data items are needed, the **AS** phrase is used. In this case, the **AS** phrase label is printed to the left of the data, rather than as a column heading. For example:

```
GETFILE COLLEGE
PRINT FNAM AND LNAM OVER ADDR1 OVER
ADDR2 OVER ADDR3 AND PROGRAM AS 'ACADEMIC DIVISION:'
SKIP 2
END



LINDA              FALL
321 OAK DR
TREE HOLLOW
DELAWARE           ACADEMIC DIVISION: SOCIAL SCIENCES


WILLIAM            GOLD
3100 CHESTNUT ST
PHILADELPHIA
PENNSYLVANIA       ACADEMIC DIVISION: COMPUTER SCIENCE


THOMAS             GREEN
89 B TOWER LANE
NEWARK
NEW JERSEY         ACADEMIC DIVISION: NATURAL SCIENCE
```

Practice Problem

Write a Report mode request with an **AS** phrase to display the information in the following report from the students file.

PROGRAM		SOC-SEC-NO
BA	BLACK	198987834
	BROWN	456129975
	CARD	557788423
	FALL	098789541
	GATES	345888999
	JONES	778902388
	LIGHT	455566674
	NICKEL	567009831
	PLUM	666777534

Solution

```
GETFILE  STUDENTS
PRINT  SSN  AS  SOC-SEC-NO
BY  LNAM  AS  ' '
BY  DGR  AS  'PROGRAM'
IF  DGR  IS  BA
END
```

The next example uses the **FOLD**, **AS**, and **OVER** options, together with two dummy **DEFINE**d fields (BLANK5 and BALHDG) to achieve a special report layout. In addition, the **LAST** operation is used in the NETHOURS definition to provide a running balance of vacation hours, which is reset for each new ACNO to the value of a data item named JAN1HRS. Each record for an individual account has hours which are deducted from the balance. The phrases, **BY** BALHDG, **BY** JAN1HRS are included as a formatting trick to place JAN1HRS above the NETHRS variable.

REQUEST

```
GETFILE LEAVE
DEFINE NETHOURS/I6 = IF ACNO NE LAST ACNO THEN JAN1HRS
                                    ELSE LAST NETHOURS - HRS
       BLANK5/A5   = '      '
       CITYST/A25  = CLIP(CTY)+', '+ST+' '+ZP.
       BALHDG/A36  =' ........ Jan 1 Balance ........'  END

HEADING
"Page<PAGE# "
"<27GROUP HEALTH ASSOCIATION   "
" "
"<24EDUCATIONAL LEAVE STATUS REPORT   "
" "
"<56Hours   Balance "
BY ACNO FOLD SKIP 3,
  BY NAME, BY BALHDG BY JAN1HRS FOLD,
   PRINT CONFERENCE CME AS CREDITS: BLANK5 HRS NETHOURS
     OVER BLANK5 FRDATE AS FROM: TODATE AS TO:
     OVER SPONSOR CONAME AS CONTACT:
     OVER STREET PHONE AS 'PHONE   :'
     OVER CITYST,
   AND SKIP.
```

```
REPORT

Page    1
                         GROUP HEALTH ASSOCIATION

                      EDUCATIONAL LEAVE STATUS REPORT

                                              Hours    Balance

   ACCT #
   NAME

   003
      CARTER,H                     ........ Jan 1 Balance ........    80
         PEDI CARDIOLOGY              CREDITS: 25            24        56
             FROM: 040581    TO: 040681
         HARVARD                      CONTACT: MARY JAMES
         19 ROCK ST
         BOSTON, MA 01764

         PEDIATRIC BOARDS             CREDITS: 0             24        32
             FROM: 082781    TO: 082981
         AMERICAN PEDI BOARD          CONTACT: JEAN PEARS
         91 8TH ST.
         NEW YORK, NY 91110


   007
      HARRIS, R                    ........ Jan 1 Balance ........    96
         INT MEDICINE                 CREDITS: 34           30        74
         .                            .       .            .         .
         .                            .       .            .         .
```

The various formatting options discussed here may be employed in myriad combinations to meet your most demanding report formatting requirements.

LETTER REPORTS

The **HEADING** phrase field marker feature provides some useful possibilities in the preparation of letters and memo reports to people whose names and addresses are in a datafile. Not only can you apply names, addresses, and "Dear John's" to a standard letter, but you can have the selected data items and phrases in the letter vary, dependent upon the data values in the file.

Letter reports may either have columns of report data or not. In the latter case, data values appear only in the field markers in the **HEADING** text, and this is accomplished by *omitting the verb phrase.* Thus a Report mode request may consist of only a **HEADING** phrase containing one or more verb objects as field markers, in which case the **WRITE** verb is *implicitly* the active verb.

DEFINEd variables, **BY** phrases, and **IF** phrases may be used with such letter reports; however, when there is no explicit verb the **BY** phrase variables are not printed, unless they appear in field markers. If **COMPUTE** phrases are needed, then use a normal verb phrase, followed by **COMPUTE**. and use

NOPRINT after each verb object and **BY** field to suppress the usual columnar report.

An example of a letter report with an implicit **WRITE** verb follows. Letters printed by this NPL program have different text in the second paragraph, depending upon each salesperson's ratio of sales to quota.

```
REQUEST

GETFILE SALES
DEFINE
   FULL NAME/A30 = CLIP(FIRSTNAME) + ' ' + MI + ' ' + LASTNAME
   MRMS/A3 =      IF SEX IS 'F' THEN 'Ms.' ELSE 'Mr.'
   COMMENT/A70 =  IF SALES GE 1.2*QUOTA THEN
      'Congratulations, '+ CLIP(FIRSTNAME)
                          + ', you made the "Golden Circle" this year.'
   ELSE IF SALES GE QUOTA THEN
      CLIP(FIRSTNAME)+ ', you had a good year. Keep up the good work.'
   ELSE
      "Let's all work for a better year, next year."
   SCORE/F5.1 = 100*SALES/QUOTA.

HEADING
"<21 JARVER MANUFACTURING COMPANY, INC."
"<21     Interoffice Memorandum "
"  "
"<52 January 20, 1983. "
"</4 <9 To:      <MRMS <FULLNAME   "
"</2 <9 FROM:    Mr. Sidney Q. Poppinhurst, President "
"</3 <9 Subject: Sales Team Competition Results for 1982 "
"</2 <9 Our Vice President for Sales, Mr. Owen Swazeys, has shown"
"<9 the results of the Ninth Annual Jarver Sales Sweepstakes, fifty "
"<9 teams, from every state in the country, were in competition this "
"<9 year. The first score for your team for 1982 is <SCORE % of quota."
""""
"<9 <COMMENT "
"<9 I certainly am proud of the hard work that all the team "
"<9 members put into this fine program. "
"</4  <40 Sincerely,"
"</4  <40 Sidney Q. Poppinhurst "
"<9 SQP/npl "
BY LASTNAME PAGE NOSORT.
```

REPORT

JARVER MANUFACTURING COMPANY, INC.
Interoffice Memorandum

January 20, 1983.

To: MR. PHILIP A. WALTERS

FROM: Mr. Sidney Q. Poppinhurst, President

Subject: Sales Team Competition Results for 1982

Our Vice President for Sales, Mr. Owen Swazeys, has shown
the results of the Ninth Annual Jarver Sales Sweepstakes. Fifty
teams, from every state in the country, were in competition this
year. The first score for your team for 1982 is 146.7 % of quota.

CONGRATULATIONS, PHILIP, you made the "Golden Circle" this year.
I certainly am proud of the hard work that all the team
members put into this fine program.

Sincerely,

Sidney Q. Poppinhurst
SQP/npl

The next example shows a letter report that includes a table of data items from the datafile, and hence the request has an explicit verb phrase.

REQUEST

```
GETFILE PAYABLES

DEFINE    MRMS/A4 = IF SEX IS 'F' THEN 'Ms. '  ELSE 'Mr. '
    FULLNAME/A30 = CLIP (FIRSTNAME) + MI + '. ' + LASTNAME
    CITYST/A20 = CLIP(CITY) + ', ' + ST + ' ' + ZIP
    SALUTATION/A20 = 'DEAR ' + MRMS + CLIP(LASTNAME) + ':'
              DATE/A20= &DATE
              PAYMNT/A4= IF PURCHASE LE &LATEDATE THEN 'LATE' ELSE ' '.
HEADING
"  <55<DATE  "
"  </4<FULLNAME   "
"  <COMPANY    "
"  <STREET     "
"  <CITYST     "
"  "
"  <SALUTATION"
"  "
" Our records indicate that your account is in arrears. "
" Kindly review the items listed below and forward full"
" payment immediately. </1"
"                      Thank you, "
" </4              Willa Collect "
"                  Accounts Receivable Dept. "
BY ACCOUNTNBR PAGE
BY PURCHDATE BY ITEM, PRINT DESCRIPTION QTY PRICE AMOUNT
IF PAYMNT IS LATE.
```

REPORT

October 13, 1982

PATRICIA A . BARNES
SIMI RESEARCH
1622 LAWSON ST
DURHAM , NC 27703

Dear Ms. BARNES:

Our records indicate that your account is in arrears.
Kindly review the items listed below and forward full
payment immediately.

Thank you,

Willa Collect
Accounts Receivable Dept.

ACCOUNTNBR	ITEM	QTY	AMOUNT	AMOUNT	AMOUNT
146.90	AXLES	2	113	113	226.00
157.30	AXLES	42	121	121	5082.00
470.60	AXLES	83	362	362	30046.00
516.10	BUSHINGS	65	397	397	25805.00
		192	993	993	61159.00

This chapter introduced these keywords:

```
HEADING
BY phrase modifiers
 NOPRINT
 SKIP n
 FOLD
 PAGE
PAUSE
AS phrases
REC#
PAGE#
SET LENGTH
SET WIDTH
```

CHAPTER 7

CREATING NEW FILES FROM OLD

An important feature of all nonprocedural systems is the ability to create new database files as readily as to print reports.

In manipulations of data by hand we are accustomed to taking data items from one or more sources and listing and summarizing them on a worksheet. Perhaps two or three successive worksheets are required for some tasks. It should not seem unnatural, then, when tackling a complex problem with a computer, to ask it to extract and summarize some data in one step and hold the results in a work file, or a **HOLD** file, in preparation for a second step.

In NPL the word **HOLD** appears in several forms, but it always has the same meaning, which is to

• suppress printing of any reports

• create a new datafile to hold all data items that would have been printed

• create a new master file defining the format of the records in the new datafile.

The two files are named **HOLD.D** and **HOLD.M**.

Since both a master file and a datafile are created, the next step in a sequence of tasks may proceed with standard NPL requests. The process of creating extract files may be repeated, of course, until you have the desired information. Reports may be printed from the intermediate extract files as needed.

These new files are created in the Report mode even though no tables are printed. The general form of the request is the same, whether you **PRINT** something or **HOLD** it as a work file. This is fairly natural, since you may want both to print *and* to save your worksheet data.

The keyword **HOLD** is a secondary verb, like **COMPUTE**. It must be accompanied by a primary verb (**WRITE, PRINT, SUM,** or **COUNT**). An extract file is created in a Report mode request when the secondary verb **HOLD** appears in the request. It may appear before, after, and between other phrases. For example:

```
C>PRINT FNAM LNAM SSN AND HOLD.

C>SUM PAY HOLD BY PROGRAM.

C>HOLD, COUNT SSN, SUM.FEE-PAID, AVE.GPA,
R>BY COURSE BY SEX.
```

Records are screened, certain fields are specified, and the resulting records are sorted and held as a temporary file. A master file describing the temporary records is created. If you wish it to be a permanent file you may assign a filename.

Some allowable forms for **HOLD** requests are illustrated here:

```
PRINT A B C AND HOLD BY D.

HOLD PRINT A B C D ROW#.

SUM M N BY D HOLD.

HOLD AND SUM M N BY D.

HOLD AND WRITE AVE.M CNT.A BY D.

WRITE MAX.M BY D HOLD.
```

where A, B, C, D, M, and N are fieldnames; M and N are numeric data items. **BY, IF,** and **COMPUTE** phrases are allowed in any of these forms. **PRINT** implies one record in the extract file for each input record. When **SUM** or **WRITE** is present, input records are clustered to produce an output record for each value of the sort keys.

HOLD.D files are datafiles created for use as input to other NPL programs. Columntotals, subtotals, headings, and other report display options are never part of a datafile, hence it is not appropriate to use such options in a **HOLD** request. Each record does contain, however, all the data values that would be printed if **HOLD** were not used.

The **HOLD** files remain on the disk. Only one pair of files with the name HOLD may be active at a time. Creation of a second pair of HOLD files replaces the first. A *named* **HOLD** file, created by the command,

```
HOLD AS  filename
```

remains on the disk until you remove it. "Filename" may contain a volume name to cause the **HOLD** files to be written on a particular diskette. If a file with the same name already exists, it is replaced by the new file. Any number of named **HOLD** files may be created.

As an alternative to the foregoing you may cause the new datafile to be *appended* to an existing datafile with the **INTO** phrase:

```
HOLD INTO  filename
```

In this case, a new master file is not created. You must be quite sure that the old and the new datafiles have the same record length.

BINARY

In addition to ASCII characters, binary integer and real values may also be written to hold files. This will effect a performance improvement since NPL will process binary data faster than ASCII.

To cause all fields in a hold file to be binary, the keyword BINARY is used after the word HOLD. For example,

```
PRINT A, B, AND C, AND HOLD BINARY.
```

If **AS** (or **INTO**) is used, the word **BINARY** and the **AS** phrase may be in either order. For example,

```
PRINT A, B, AND C, AND HOLD BINARY AS MYDATA.   or
PRINT A, B, AND C, AND HOLD AS MYDATA BINARY.
```

111

Fields in hold files may individually be made binary by using the field option **BINARY** on the selected fields instead of as an option on the HOLD phrase. For example,

---

PRINT A, B BINARY, AND C AND HOLD AS MYDATA.

C>**GETFILE** FACULTY
C>**PRINT ROW#** NAME FAC-CODE **AND** SALARY
R>**BY** PROGRAM **RESET#** BY SSN **HOLD AS** FAC2.

C>**TYPEFILE** FAC2.M

```
FIELD=PROGRAM        ,PCODE    ,A2      ,A2 ,$
FIELD=SSN            ,SSN      ,A9      ,A9 ,$
FIELD=ROW            ,         ,I5      ,A5 ,$
FIELD=NAME           ,FLAST    ,A17     ,A17,$
FIELD=FAC-CODE       ,FCODE    ,A2      ,A2 ,$
FIELD=SALARY         ,PAY      ,I8      ,A8 ,$
FIELD=               ,...      ,        ,A1 ,$ END-OF-RECORD
```

Each field is stored in the **HOLD** file in the form of characters, numbers, and letters with a field width equal to the **PRINTING** format width in the original file. Thus the **FILE** format for SALARY is A8 (eight alphanumeric characters) because the **PRINTING** format width is eight in the FACULTY master file (see Appendix B).

Numeric **PRINTING** formats must be wide enough to accommodate summary values for groups of records and must provide space for a minus sign, *even though* all values are known to be positive. For possible large values, F8.1 or F9.2 or wider are recommended as the safest choice. If a **PRINTING** format is too narrow, irregularities may occur in the HOLD datafile.

The special variable **ROW#** produces a fieldname of ROW in the HOLD.M file. Verb objects that are prefixed by **MIN, MAX, AVG**, etc., produce fieldnames which begin with **MIN:, MAX:**, and **AVG:**, etc., in the master file. If the original fieldname exceeds eight characters in length, characters on the right end are lost.

Next we prepare a report from the FAC2 **HOLD** file.

```
C>GETFILE FAC2
C>PRINT PROGRAM ROW AS COUNT NAME FCODE SALARY.
```

PROGRAM	COUNT	NAME	FAC-CODE	SALARY
CS	1	ALDEN	11	21000
CS	2	ROWE	12	22000
CS	3	COOK	17	30000
CS	4	EAGLE	04	30600
CS	5	BEERS	06	35200
HU	1	BRITT	15	22000
HU	2	FOX	03	22900
HU	3	MAYER	16	25000
HU	4	DUNCAN	08	25700
HU	5	CROCKER	07	40700
NS	1	BROOKS	18	21200
NS	2	WOLF	02	21800
NS	3	BOND	14	25000
NS	4	TREE	09	30700
NS	5	RULE	10	40500
NS	6	JAMES	13	45000
SS	1	FISH	01	20000
SS	2	FLEMMING	05	23400
SS	3	TRENT	20	25000
SS	4	LYON	19	28000

The contents of each record (except SSN) in the **HOLD** file are displayed here, yet it is not a good report, because the first column repeats the common values for each program. A better request would be:

```
C>BY PROGRAM SKIP NOSORT
R>PRINT ROW AS COUNT, NAME FCODE SALARY.
```

In this request, the use of a **BY** phrase results in suppression of the repeated PROGRAM codes. The **NOSORT** option then is added to prevent resorting of a file which is already in the desired sort sequence.

The **COMPUTE** command creates data fields in the **HOLD** datafile exactly as they would appear in a report without **HOLD**.

```
C>GETFILE FACULTY
C>PRINT NAME SALARY NDP AND COMPUTE
R>ADJ-PAY = PAY/(NDP + 1)
R>BY PROGRAM
R>HOLD.


C>TYPEFILE HOLD.M
```

```
FIELD=PROGRAM        ,FCODE    ,A2      ,A2 ,$
FIELD=NAME           ,FLAST    ,A17     ,A17,$
FIELD=SALARY         ,PAY      ,I8      ,A8 ,$
FIELD=NDP            ,NDP      ,I2      ,A2 ,$
FIELD=ADJ-PAY        ,         ,F10.2   ,A10,$
FIELD=               ,...      ,        ,A1 ,$ END-OF-RECORD
```

You may also examine the active file fieldnames and formats with this command:

```
           C>FILE?


FILE:    FACULTY

RECORD LENGTH:   46

    FIELDNAME    ALIAS    PRINT

    NAME         FLAST    A17
    FAC CODE     FCODE    A 2
    SSN          SSN      A 9
    PROGRAM      PCODE    A 2
    SEX          SEX      A 1
    SALARY       PAY      I 8
    GRANT        GRANT    I 6
    NDP          NDP      I 2
```

Using a **HOLD** file permits screening on the values of the computed fields, as in the next example.

```
GETFILE HOLD
PRINT SSN AND NAME AND ADJ-PAY
BY PROGRAM   SKIP BY SALARY
IF ADJ-PAY GT 20000
END
```

PROGRAM	SALARY	SSN	NAME	ADJ-PAY
CS	21000	200501231	ALDEN	21000
	22000	200551241	ROWE	22000
	30000	200801291	COOK	30000
	30600	200151551	EAGLE	30650
	35200	200251771	BEERS	35250
HU	22000	200701271	BRITT	22000
	22900	200101441	FOX	22950
	25000	200751281	MAYER	25000
	25700	200351991	DUNCAN	25750
	40700	200301881	CROCKER	40750
NS	21200	200851221	BROOKS	21250
	21800	162051331	WOLF	21875
	25000	200651261	BOND	25000
	30700	200401761	TREE	30750
	40500	200451775	RULE	40550
	45000	200601251	JAMES	45000
SS	20000	151011221	FISH	20000
	23400	200211661	FLEMMING	23450
	25000	200951441	TRENT	25000
	28000	200901331	LYON	28000

Any Report mode request may be applied to the contents of a **HOLD** file. Recall that **COMPUTE** commands only contain fieldnames of verb objects or of previously computed fields. For computation involving sort control fields, sort the file and **HOLD** in the first pass over the data, then do the computation in a report request on the **HOLD** file.

```
GETFILE FACULTY
PRINT SSN AND NDP BY PROGRAM BY SALARY,
HOLD AS TEST.


GETFILE TEST
PRINT SALARY AND SSN AND NDP AND COMPUTE
ADJ-PAY = SALARY/(NDP+1) AS 'ADJUSTED WAGE'
BY PROGRAM SKIP NOSORT.
```

PROGRAM	SALARY	SSN	NDP	ADJUSTED WAGE
CS	21000	200501231	0	21000.00
	22000	200551241	2	7333.33
	30000	200801291	0	30000.00
	30650	200151551	3	7662.50
	35250	200251771	2	11750.00
HU	22000	200701271	0	22000.00
	22950	200101441	1	11475.00
	25000	200751281	1	12500.00
	25750	200351991	1	12875.00
	40750	200301881	1	20375.00
NS	21250	200851221	2	7083.33
	21875	162051331	0	21875.00
	25000	200651261	2	8333.33
	30750	200401761	2	10250.00
	40550	200451775	3	10137.50
	45000	200601251	0	45000.00
SS	20000	151011221	0	20000.00
	23450	200211661	0	23450.00
	25000	200951441	0	25000.00
	28000	200901331	3	7000.00

Practice Problem

Write a request to generate a **HOLD** file containing the total amount of salaries paid to all faculty members in each program.

Then write a Report mode request to print the following:

SALARIES	FACULTY	PROGRAM
96450	4	SS
136450	5	HU
138900	5	CS
184425	6	NS

Solutions

```
GETFILE FACULTY
HOLD AND SUM SALARY AS SALARIES
AND CNT.SSN AS FACULTY
BY PROGRAM.


GETFILE HOLD
PRINT FACULTY AND PROGRAM BY SALARIES.
```

The **HOLD** master file is described by the table below. The third data item is actually the *count* of the records for each program, even though the original fieldname was SSN. SALARIES is the sum of all salaries for each program. The second and third fieldnames come from the **AS** phrases.

FIELDNAME	ALIAS	PRINTING FORMAT	FILE FORMAT
PROGRAM	PCODE	A2	A2
SALARIES	PAY	I8	A8
FACULTY	SSN	I5	A5

To select records from a file based upon a computed field or on a summation of values, create a hold file first. For example:

```
GETFILE FACULTY
HOLD AND WRITE AVE.SALARY CNT.SSN BY PROGRAM.


GETFILE HOLD
PRINT PROGRAM AVG:SALARY BY CNT:SSN AS FACULTY
IF AVG:SALARY GT 28000 END
```

AVG:SALARY is the fieldname assigned when the verb object AVE.SALARY is saved in a **HOLD** file (Note: **AVE** and **AVG** are synonyms).

Be careful not to confuse the following two groups of names. Those with periods are prefixed verb objects, and the others are all just fieldnames created by the **HOLD**ing process.

Prefixed verb objects	HOLD.M Fieldnames
MIN.AMOUNT	**MIN:**AMOUNT
MAX.EXPENSES	**MAX:**EXPENSES
AVE.SHIPMENTS	**AVG:**SHIPMENT
CNT.SSN	**CNT:**SSN

MANAGING DISK SPACE

Care should be taken to ensure there is sufficient disk storage space before creating a new file, particularly if you have recently created one or more **HOLD** files and if the files are large. To understand how disk space might be used up before you expect it, think of a long bookshelf with thirty books (analogous to files) stacked against each other and against the left end of the shelf, with free shelf space at the right end. As new books are shelved they are placed in the first position (l-to-r) that is wide enough—or at the right end.

Now, as **HOLD** files are created their width is not known until fully created, hence these new books are always placed in the largest available open-shelf position (usually the right end).

After a new pair of **HOLD** files is created, the previous **HOLD** files (master and data) are removed, to avoid there being two files with the same name. This leaves empty spaces on the shelf. The result of a sequence of holding operations can be that there is no space at the right end of the shelf, while several small spaces occur across the shelf.

In order to place a large, new book on the shelf you would have to take hold of the right-most book and slide all books to the left. On a diskette this action is called "crunching" the files together—to make space at the end of the file directory for a new file.

Use the **DIRECTORY** command to find out how much free space you have on a particular diskette. With some UCSD and Apple Operating Systems the free space may be distributed among the files in several small pieces. This space can consolidated by "crunching" your files with a special command in the Filer mode. Other operating systems may not require you to consolidate the free disk space.

This chapter introduced these keywords:

HOLD
HOLD AS
HOLD BINARY

CHAPTER 8

DATAFILE DESCRIPTIONS WITH THE MASTER FILE

NPL retrieves, analyzes, and displays information from your datafiles. There are *only two* constraints placed upon the type or format of your datafiles:

• All records in a file must contain the same number of characters.

• Data items, or fields, in each record must be in the same relative position.

NPL does not have a unique or preferred database file format of its own. You are the one to specify record size and content, and there are NPL procedures to simplify even that process.

SOURCES OF DATAFILES

Datafiles may come from several sources, and each can require different steps to make them accessible by NPL. For example, let's assume that you have an Apple III computer and then consider these possibilities:

a) *Situation number one*: A friend with an Apple III has a datafile prepared using the Apple Pascal System. You have seen the datafile displayed on the monitor, or printed, using the Transfer command in the Filer mode, and it consists of readable characters in a regular format in records of fixed length.

To use this file with NPL, have your friend transfer the file to an empty (and newly formatted) diskette or to one of your Apple Pascal diskettes.

Next, ask for a detailed description of all the data items in a typical record. That is, what is the item called? How many characters in the data field (maximum)? Is it a numeric quantity, a code, a name, a date? Then run NPL and use the **CREATE** command to provide NPL with a complete description of the file.

b) *Situation number two*: Your friend lives two thousand miles away, OR your friend's computer is of some other brand and uses a "funny" diskette format, OR your friend's Apple III datafile is in some "funny" file format (that is, different from Apple Pascal file format). Also, the file is very long and to retype it into your Apple III would run a large risk of introducing errors into the data.

If both computers have the right peripheral cards, connectors, cables, and perhaps modems, the file can be transferred from one Apple computer to another — if you know what you are doing. It is not hard to do, but ask for advice the first time you try it. The significant point to be made here is that because the transfer is made in a universal serial I/O format the disparity between the diskette formats in the two computers is of no consequence.

c) *Situation number three*: Your friend is a mogul of the programming department of a firm with a time-sharing computer, and has offered to give you dial-up access to his or her file.

You need a special program to run on your Apple Pascal System which makes your computer function as a time-sharing terminal. Your microcomputer becomes an "intelligent terminal" with which you call up and log on to the time-sharing system. Your friend will tell you how to instruct his or her computer to transfer the file to your computer memory. Again, the differences in storage formats are resolved by transmission in a standard communications format.

d) *Situation number four* (and perhaps the most likely): your friend has never been near a computer and his or her data is only in a printed form. Hence you will enter the data directly into your computer.

CREATE A MASTER FILE

In every case, you must provide NPL with a full description of the datafile. To do so you run NPL and type **CREATE**. NPL then asks you for the information needed to create a *master file* for your datafile. Every NPL datafile must have an associated master file. Several datafiles with exactly the same description (e.g., sales figures for three successive years, stored in three separate files) may be associated with a single master file.

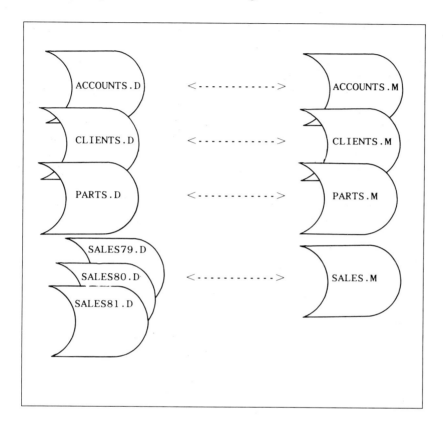

In Section Four, An NPL Tutorial for the Apple II Computer, there is a step-by-step presentation of the use of the **CREATE** command. This chapter provides a complete definition of the elements of a master file.

ELEMENTS OF A DATAFILE

There are these elements of a datafile, which are stored as descriptors in the master file:

```
1)   FILENAME


2)   Data Field descriptors

        FIELDNAME
        ALIAS
        PRINTING Format codes
        FILE Format codes


3)   End-of-Record character(s)
```

Items 1 and 3 are specified once for the file; they do not change. Item 2 is specified once for each data item in a record.

Now, you may say there are other critical descriptors of a datafile, such as record length and file size. That is so, of course, but as for length, you will see that NPL can compute record length from the **FILE** Format codes.

File size is measured either in total characters stored or in the number of records. Though it may seem strange, NPL does not require an a priori knowledge of the number of records. You can find that number by using the **COUNT** command in a Report mode request.

RULES FOR DESCRIPTORS

FILENAME

In general, a *full* filename has three parts, i.e.:

```
/volume-id/name.suffix
```

The exact form of these parts varies from one operating system to to another. See Appendix D for specific information. These examples illustrate the essential options:

```
/NPL/CLIENTS.D.DATA

.D2/CLIENTS.M.TEXT

/MARY/CENSUS80.E.TEXT
```

A *volume-id* identifies either a disk drive, a diskette, or a portion of a disk. Its use is optional and it is omitted in most of the examples in this book.

At the NPL level only the name need be mentioned, for NPL knows from the context whether you need a Datafile (**.D**), a Master file (**.M**), an Exec file (**.E**), or an Index file (**.I**). The *name* is assigned by you; it must consist of letters, digits, colon, hyphen, or # and must begin with a letter. Depending upon the operating system, names may have up to six or eight characters.

FIELDNAME

A field is a storage place for a data item to be held on a diskette. A **FIELDNAME** (abbreviated **FIELD**) is a name for a particular storage place in a particular position in a record. The position is the same in every record.

The word **FIELD** is widely used throughout this book to refer to data items in various ways, such as these:

- **FIELD** and **FIELDNAME** refer to a label of up to twelve characters (any printable characters) which is used as a column heading in reports.

- Field is used interchangably with variable to refer to the values of a data item throughout a file.

- **BY field** is a data item or defined variable used as a sort key.

- **IF field** is a data item or defined variable used in an **IF** phrase.

- Key field is a master file **FIELD** for which an index file exists.

- fld often appears in this book in definitions as an abbreviation of the word field.

While a **FIELDNAME** used only as a *column heading* may include any printable characters (including the space character), if you intend to refer to the item in any NPL statement (that is, use **FIELDNAME** as an *identifier*) the character set is restricted as for other identifiers. See Alias.

FIELDNAMEs may be changed at any time in the Edit mode.

ALIAS

This descriptor is a field *identifier*, and as such has these properties:

- It may have up to twelve characters beginning with a letter.

- The characters are limited to letters, 0 to 9, colon, hyphen, and #.

- Embedded spaces are not allowed.

- It should not be spelled exactly like an NPL keyword (ignoring upper- and lowercase differences).

- It must be unique among all other identifiers associated with this partic- ular datafile.

The **ALIAS** is an alternative to **FIELD** as an identifier. If **FIELD** satisfies the criteria above, then **ALIAS** may be blank. It is good practice, however, to use the **ALIAS** as a unique and brief field identifier. Brevity is for convenience in typing, but it should not compromise clarity. That is, for example, FNAM or FNAME may be better for "first name" than FN.

In a report request, any identifier may be truncated (on the right) to the min- imum number of characters with which it retains its uniqueness. This may be as few as only one character, say, *F* for FNAM, provided no other **ALIAS** or **FIELDNAME** begins with the letter F.

ALIASes may be changed at any time in the Edit mode, but take care to observe the rules for an identifier.

Format codes are the means by which you tell the computer three things about each data item:

- the **width** of the data field on the diskette—which is the same as saying the largest number of characters that may occur in a particular item,

- in the case of quantitative data, the **kind** of numeric quantities, that is, integer or real numbers (see discussion below), and

- the display format of quantitative data, that is, how names, numbers, and fractional values appear on the printed page.

The first of these is specified by the **FILE** format code.

The second and third pieces of information make up the **PRINTING** for- mat code.

TYPES OF DATA ITEMS

NPL processes four types of data items. These types are identified by the first character of the **PRINTING** format code, as follows:

Code	Type of Data Item	Alternative Name
A	Alphanumeric	Alpha
I	Integer (16-bit)	
F	Floating point (32-bit)	Real
D	Double-precision integer (40-bit)	Dollar

The alternative names are often used in this book to refer to the format codes or to data items.

FORMAT CODES

Alphanumeric Characters

For some data items the **PRINTING** and **FILE** format codes are the same, as for these familar items:

FIELDNAME	PRINTING FORMAT	FILE FORMAT	EXAMPLE
LAST NAME	A20	A20	HOSSENPHEFFER
MIDDLE INIT	A1	A1	A
FIRST NAME	A20	A20	JOHN
TELEPHONE	A12	A12	401-594-3764
SSN	A9	A9	015204336
ZIP CODE	A5	A5	02912

The "**A**" prefix stands for alphanumeric, which means any letter, number, or punctuation character, including the space character; that is, all printable keyboard characters. There is no limit on the size of A format codes other than the width of the printed page and the desired length of the file data record. There is no limit to the length of records.

127

Integer Numbers

Numbers which represent counts and quantities as whole numbers are called integers, and the **PRINTING** format code for such data items begins with the letter **I**. For example:

FIELDNAME	PRINTING FORMAT	FILE FORMAT	EXAMPLE
AGE	I2	A2	27
EDUC-YRS	I2	A2	14
NBR DEPENDNT	I3	A2	3
NBR OF CARS	I2	A1	3
UNITS SOLD	I4	A3	523
DISTANCE(MI)	I5	A5	8450

These **FILE** format codes range from A1 to A5, depending upon the maximum size of integers to be expected in the data. A2 means a maximum value of 99, which is adequate for the first three items above. A3 allows for 999 UNITS SOLD. WARNING: A5 would appear to permit values up to *99,999,* but there is a limit of about 32,000 on integer values. The limit results form the internal representation of numbers as sixteen binary bits. If negative values are expected, an extra character position is included for the minus sign.

The number in the **PRINTING** format code may vary from 1 to 9 or larger. Its only effect is to determine the space provided on the printed page (or screen), that is, the width of the column for the data item in a report. This width should be equal to or larger than the width of the **FILE** format. Why larger ? ...to allow for group or grand totals which exceed the width of the individual items. Actually, NPL allows the field width to be any integer value up to 999. Such a large number is not useful, but you may vary printing format widths to produce wide spaces between columns.

While I2 would suffice for the data field on the number of dependents, the **COLUMNTOTAL** for this field over a large group of records could exceed 99, hence I3 is a better choice for the **PRINTING** format code.

When the verb **HOLD** is used in a request, integer variables are stored as numeric characters, i.e., **FILE** format An, where n is the width of the **PRINTING** format, except when the **BINARY** option is used, in which case the **FILE** format in the **HOLD** file for **I** variables is **I2**.

Real Numbers

Now, clearly the computer must also handle larger numbers and fractional values as well. Most computers employ a different kind of number representation internally for this purpose—called *Real* numbers, or, alternatively, *Floating point* numbers. The letter **F**, from the latter name, appears in the **PRINTING** format code. For example:

FIELDNAME	PRINTING FORMAT	FILE FORMAT	EXAMPLE
MILES/GAL	F5.2	A5	32.18
TOTAL MILES	F12.3	A8	83622.700
ERROR RATE	F7.6	A7	.001488

Take a close look at the three example values and count the characters— particularly those to the right of the decimal point.

```
   32.18                                              F5.2
 |<--->|                    the total width is       5
   |<>|                     the fractional part is    2


   83622.7                                           F12.3
|<---------->|              the total width is        12
      |<->|                 the fractional part is     3


   .001488                                           F8.6
 |<------>|                 the total width is        8
 |<---->|                   the fractional part is    6
```

Floating point variables may have values that are infinitesimally small up to astronomical values. Yet in all cases the precision is limited to about six significant decimal digits. This is a result of the internal numerical representation by 32 binary bits.

PRINTING format codes for real numbers (rather than small integers) consist of the letter **F** followed by two numbers. The first number, as you can see from the examples above, specifies the field width of the field on the printed page—including the decimal point. The number to the right of the decimal point is the number of fractional digits, and so determines the location of the point itself. The latter number may vary from 0 to 9.

The **PRINTING** format code may vary from F1.0 to F999.9. In the last example notice there is just enough width for a negative sign on the left. In general, the number of fractional digits should be two less than the width, to allow for sign and decimal point. As noted above, large field widths are used only to create large spaces between columns. The width should be large enough to accommodate subtotals and columntotals.

After data values have been stored in a datafile you must not change the **FILE** format codes which reside in the master file description of the datafile. You may, however, change the **PRINTING** format codes at any time, being careful only to avoid making the field width less than the data requires.

When the verb **HOLD** is used in a request, real number variables are stored as numeric characters, i.e., **FILE** format An, where n is the width of the **PRINTING** format, except when the **BINARY** option is used, in which case the **FILE** format for **F** variables in the **HOLD** file is F4.

Occasionally the computer will be required to print, or store in a **HOLD** file, a very large number which does not fit the field width provided by the format code. For example, the number 936,552 cannot be printed with a format of F5.0. Some computers flag this error by filling the field with asterisk characters. Others, like the UCSD and Apple Pascal Systems print the number in a special format (the so-called engineering format), 9.365E07— which means 9.365 times 10 raised to the 7th power or 9.365 x ten million. To avoid this result you can change the **PRINTING** format to F8.1 or F9.2.

Double-Precision 40-bit Integers

Special requirements arise for accounting applications, where very large values *and* fine precision may be needed at the same time. To process variables which measure billions of dollars while keeping track of the pennies, NPL uses special software and a special type of data, called **D** format variables. The values may represent counts from zero to over a trillion. If the data item is in dollars and cents, values of about 11 billion dollars may be processed with precision to the penny. The internal representation of these values is an integer number of pennies, by integers of forty binary bits.

Because the most frequent use of **D** format is for precise representation of money variables, the data type is called a Dollar format variable, even though the use of the dollar sign is optional. **D** format also has an option for two fractional decimal postitions, in order to display dollars and cents.

Dollar format variables are stored on the disk as alphanumeric characters, hence the **FILE** format is an **A** code. In response to the **HOLD** verb **D** format variables are stored on disk in **A** format, unless the **BINARY** option is used, in which case the **FILE** format is **D6** and the variables are stored as forty-bit binary integers.

The **PRINTING** format offers a choice of widths and options. The two basic formats are illustrated here as *whole numbers* and *dollars & cents* (decimal values with two fractional digits).

Whole Numbers			Dollars & cents		
PRINT Format	FILE Format	Example Item	PRINT Format	FILE Format	Example Item
D13	A13	3210987654321	D13.2C	A13	32,098,654.21
D7	A7	9999999	D7.2	A7	9999.99
D9C	A9	9,999,999	D9.2C	A9	-9,999.99
D10CL	A10	$ 10,000	D12.2CL	A12	$ -500.00
D10CR	A10	$10,000	D12.2CR	A12	-$500.00
D10CB	A10	(999,999)	D12.2CB	A12	(999,999.99)

The two general forms of the **D** format are:

```
Dn     and     Dn.2
```

where n is an integer, from 0 to 999. In addition these four option codes may follow the above:

```
C     Commas at every third position

B     Brackets around negative values

L     Left-most postion contains a $ sign

R     Right-most position, before the value,
      contains a $ sign
```

You must be careful to make n large enough to accommodate the largest possible value, plus commas and decimal point and cents, plus a minus sign (or parentheses), plus the dollar sign.

Addition, subtraction, and column summation are performed by software which processes one digit at a time. Calculation between **D** format variables and **F** or **I** variables yields **D** results. Division by a **D** variable is achieved by an internal conversion of all values to **F** format.

Format Conversions

Conversions of a variable from one Printing format to another are done either in the master file, or, for a temporary change, with a **DEFINE** statement, as

```
DEFINE NEWVAR/D12.2 = OLDVAR
```

This process is completely flexible. Any type data item (**A, I, F,** or **D**) may appear on the left side of the equal sign or on the right side. That is, for example, you can convert a **D**, or **F**, or **I** variable into an **A** variable—and *vice versa*. This seems like a contradiction of terms, but, then of course, it only makes sense for numeric values; yet consider these cases (let OLDVAR be an alphanumeric string of digits).

	OLDVAR value	*NEWVAR value*
NEWVAR/D12.2	$5,943.25	5943.25
NEWVAR/D12L	$5,943.25	$ 5943
NEWVAR/F12.4	$5,943.25	5943.2500
NEWVAR/I12	$5,943.25	5943

I and **F** format conversions ignore commas and $ signs (and letters as well). **D** format may selectively ignore commas, $ signs, and cents, depending on the C, B, L, and R option codes. Conversion to **A** format accepts all such symbols and the result is right justified (as if it were being printed).

UCSD Pascal Long Integer Format

With UCSD and Apple Pascal operating systems you may write a datafile with a Pascal program other than NPL, as *Long Integers*, and then these values may be read by NPL by assigning an **L** format code as the **FILE** format. The **L** format code may not be used as a **PRINTING** format. The form for FILE format is:

```
Ln
```

where n is the maximum length of the *Long Integer* as declared in the Apple Pascal Program.

Unlike other FILE format codes, Ln does not indicate the number of character positions in the data field on the disk. The actual field width is two greater than n divided by two and rounded up to an even integer.

The **PRINTING** format associated with long integers must be **D**. When a request contains the phrase, **HOLD BINARY**, any **D** format variables are stored in the Long Integer, Ln, format on the disk.

UCSD Pascal String Format

With the UCSD and Apple Pascal operating systems, alphanumeric values stored as strings by a Pascal program other than NPL are made accessible to NPL by assigning an **S** format code as the **FILE** format. The **S** format codes may not be used as a **PRINTING** format. The form for the FILE format is:

```
Sn
```

where n is the maximum number of characters in the Pascal string as declared in the Apple Pascal programs. The number of character positions used to store the string is the next even number greater than the number of characters declared for the string. Like the **L** format, the **S** format code does not indicate the actual field width on the disk.

The **PRINTING** format associated with strings must be **A**. When a request contains the phrase, **HOLD BINARY**, any **A** format variables for which the **FILE** format is Sn are stored on the disk in string format, Sm, where m is an even number equal to n or n + 1.

Binary File Formats

Numeric data may be recorded in datafiles either as a group for numeric characters or as binary numbers. You cannot read the binary formatted numbers by displaying the datafile on your monitor; however, the disk space required for binary numbers is much less than for the numeric characters. Also NPL can read the binary data faster.

NPL recognizes three binary **FILE** format codes, **I2**, **F4**, and **D6**. The first means that the data for a particular field is stored on the diskette not as a series of digits (which you could read on the monitor) but as 16-bit binary integers. Such numbers take the same space in memory as two characters. The **FILE** format code I2 is used.

When the datafile contains 32-bit floating-point binary numbers, the storage space required is four characters wide, and the **FILE** format is F4.

D format binary variables are stored as forty-bit integers, representing pennies, and the **FILE** format is **D6**.

Automatic Assignment of Format Codes

When defining new numeric variables, in the **DEFINE** mode or in **COMPUTE** statements, a **PRINTING** format code is assigned to each new name. As a convenience NPL assigns a format code of **F10.2** whenever you omit the code.

```
This statement:           X = A * B


is treated like this one:  X/F10.2 = A * B
```

However, you must assign a **PRINTING** format code, between **A1** and **A999**, when the new variable is alphanumeric.

Notice that no **FILE** format code is needed for **DEFINE**d and **COMPUT**Ed variables, since by their very nature they only exist at run time and do not appear in the file itself.

END-OF-RECORD CHARACTER(s)

Some datafiles have a character or two separating one record from the next, and some do not. Typical characters for this purpose are the **RETURN**, vertical tab, space, null characters. The first two of these correspond to the carriage return and line-feed controls on a typewriter. The use of one or both of these characters makes it easier to display a datafile on the monitor or printer. Otherwise the computer may attempt to display the whole file on one line of the screen — spilling thousands of characters on top of each other!

NPL doesn't care what character is used, as long as you count it. The standard End-of-Record for NPL on some computers is the **RETURN** character. On others it is two characters: **RETURN** and **LINE-FEED**. When you use the **CREATE** command to build a new master file, NPL inserts the standard End-of-Record character. You may change from this standard to one or more special characters or to none.

When there is no End-of-Record character, the last field in the master file is for the last data item you described using **CREATE**.

The **CREATE** command always assumes you want the *standard* NPL character (which varies from one operating system to another), and it adds this field description:

```
FIELD =           ,...   ,      ,A1   ,$ END-OF-RECORD
```

The **FIELDNAME** and **PRINTING** format are blank. The **ALIAS** is three periods and the **FILE** format is A1 for the **RETURN** character.

For other kinds of datafiles you may change the format to be A2 or A3, or you may delete the whole line. To make changes to the master file use the Apple Pascal Edit mode.

When the option **BINARY** follows the verb **HOLD**, the resulting master file *omits* the End-of-Record field.

Sometimes there are parts of a data record which are of no interest, such as blank fields. There could be one or more blanks between all data items, which you may prefer to skip. Sections of a data record are ignored simply by recording blank values for **FIELDNAME, ALIAS,** and the **PRINTING** Format in the master file, with a **FILE** format equal to the width of the skip zone. For example:

```
FIELD =First Name ,FNAM   ,A15  ,A15 ,$
FIELD =           ,       ,     ,A2  ,$
FIELD =Last Name  ,LNAM   ,     ,A15 ,$
FIELD =           ,       ,     ,A2  ,$
FIELD =Account Nbr,ACNO   ,A6   ,A6  ,$
FIELD =           ,       ,     ,A30 ,$
FIELD =Balance    ,BAL    ,F9.2 ,A9  ,$
FIELD =           ,...    ,     ,A1  ,$ END-OF-RECORD
```

When the number of data items in a single datafile is quite large, say, two hundred (which is greater than the maximum allowable number of active fieldnames), it is possible to use several master files, each with different skip fields, and thereby to "activate" several groups of 50 names for different purposes.

HOLD MASTER FILE

Format codes in a **HOLD** master file are determined as follows:

- **HOLD PRINTING** formats are copied from the original **PRINTING** format.

- **HOLD FILE** formats are **An**, where n equals **PRINTING** format width

• **HOLD BINARY FILE** formats are determined by the **PRINTING** format as follows:

PRINTING	FILE
An	An
Im	I2
Fm	F4
Dm	D6

where n and m are field widths. For UCSD and Apple Pascal operating systems there are two additional cases:

- when **PRINTING** format is **An** and the original **FILE** format is Sm, then the **HOLD FILE** format is Sn (n is an odd integer equal to m or m + 1).

- when **PRINTING** format is **Dm** and the original **FILE** format is Lm, then the **HOLD FILE** format is Ln (n is 4, 8, 12, or 16, whichever is equal to or just greater than m).

CHANGES TO THE MASTER FILE

Use the Edit mode for any changes to a master file. Do not use the **CREATE** command to append new fields to an existing master file.

If the datafile has not been formed yet, you may change any element of a master file. You may delete or add data items (records in the master file). You may change names and formats.

Once you have a datafile and an associated master file, you must not change any **FILE** formats without knowing precisely what you are doing. **FIELDNAME**s, **ALIAS**es, and **PRINTING** formats may be changed at any time, within the normal rules for those file descriptors.

To make changes in any **FILE** format code, observe these rules:

- The sum of all the **FILE** format widths must equal the actual length of a data record, including the End-of-Record characters.

- Any alphanumeric field may be subdivided in two or more fields, as long as the sum of the **FILE** format widths is the same.

- Similarly, alphanumeric fields may be combined, provided all the character positions are counted in the new field.

- Changing numeric fields for an existing datafile is hazardous. However, a field representing a date, with both formats equal to A6 (ddmmyy), can be divided into DAY, MO, YR fields, each with **PRINTING** format of I2 and **FILE** format of A2.

FILE?

A special command is used to show you just what file is active currently and which index file has been selected. Type:

```
C>FILE?
```

The following is an example using the CLIENTS file after two new variables have been **DEFINE**d:

```
C>GETFILE CLIENTS
C>DEFINE
D>FULLNAME/A30 = CLIP(FN) + ' ' + MI + '.' + LN
D>CITYST/A26 = CLIP(CITY) + ',' + STATE + ' ' + ZIP.
C>FILE?


FILE:    CLIENTS

RECORD LENGTH:    150

        FIELDNAME       ALIAS           PRINT

        TITLE           PREFX           A 6
        FIRST           FN              A15
        MIDDLE          MI              A 1
        LAST            LN              A15
        SUFFIX          SUFX            A 6
        SSN             SSN             A11
        STREET          STR             A15
        CITY            CTY             A12
        STATE           ST              A 2
        ZIPCODE         ZP              A 5
        TELEPHONE       PHONE           A12
        AGE             AGE             I 3
        SEX             SEX             A 1
        DEPENDENTS      DEPS            I 2
        YR EDUC         EDYRS           I 3
        YR EMPL         WRKYRS          I 3
        EMPLOYER        EMP             A15
        INCOME          INC             I 6
        ACCOUNT         ACNO            A 6
        ACCOUNTYPE      TYP             A 4
        AMOUNT          SIZE            I 6
DEF     FULLNAME                        A30
DEF     CITYST                          A26
```

This chapter introduced the keyword:

FILE?

and the master file structure.

CHAPTER 9

INDEXING AND SELECTING A SUBFILE

Finding a particular book, or a group of books on a single subject, in a large library would be a formidable task if the library kept only an alphabetic list of titles. Yet with a device as simple as a card catalog, any student can make one stop at the catalog and then walk directly to the correct shelves to find the desired books.

You might have a file of 2000 records which are sorted alphabetically by customer name. To find the records of all customers with particular ZIP Codes would require you to read and test each record, a process which could take many minutes. On the other hand, if you have an *index file* for ZIP Codes, you can find the desired records *in seconds*.

An index file, like a card catalog, tells NPL the exact location of the desired records. That is, NPL obtains the location of the records on your diskette, from the index file, after searching the ordered index table for particular ZIP Codes.

This chapter presents several related topics:

- Selecting one datafile from among several with the **GETFILE** command

- Selecting a subfile with the **SELECT** command using an **INDEX** file

- Creating an **INDEX** file

- Automatic sorting using an **INDEX** file

SELECTING A FILE

An NPL datafile is a collection of records with an associated name (containing .**D**). In the broadest sense we may consider "the sales file" to be a collection of records of sales data for several years, stored in several NPL files with names like SALES79.D, SALES80.D, SALES81.D, and so on. Now, to print reports from these files we need a master file, but by our present rules the master and datafiles have the same name. Do we need *three* master files, even though the datafiles have identical formats?

The answer, of course, is no; because the **GETFILE** command has an option for selecting a particular datafile. The general form is:

```
C>GETFILE (dfile) mfile
```

To prepare reports with the SALESREP.E Exec file for three years, follow these steps:

```
C>GETFILE (SALES79) SALES
C>EX SALESREP
C>GETFILE (SALES80) SALES
C>EX SALESREP
C>GETFILE (SALES81) SALES
C>EX SALESREP
```

where the SALESREP.E Exec file contains this report request:

```
SUM ITEM QTY PRICE
AND COMPUTE AMOUNT = QTY*PRICE
BY MONTH SUBTOTAL, SKIP
END
```

Exec files are discussed in detail in Chapter 10. The master file has the name SALES.M. Notice that the Exec file does not include the **GETFILE** statement; rather, you must type it first before running the Exec program.

A more convenient way to prepare the same report from several datafiles uses a feature described in Chapter 10, the *amper-variable*:
The *SALESRPT.E* exec file contains:

```
GETFILE (&DATAFILE) SALES
SUM ITEM QTY PRICE AND COMPUTE AMOUNT = QTY*PRICE
BY MONTH SUBTOTAL BY RECORD.
```

The ampersand character, **&**, in an exec file causes NPL to display to the operator the request:

```
ENTER DATAFILE
```

As the operator, you would reply by typing SALES79, SALES80, or SALES81. Your reply replaces the amper-variable (that is, replaces &DATAFILE) during the execution of SALESRPT.E, so that you may choose a different sales file each time you run the Exec program.

The datafilename option of the **GETFILE** command is not limited to use with Exec files. It is quite general. In fact you may find it useful for specifying a datafile which is on a disk drive other than where the master file resides. For example (using volume notation for the Apple II), **GETFILE** (#11:AC-COUNTS) ACCOUNTS first locates ACCOUNTS.M master file on the primary disk and then selects the datafile #11:ACCOUNTS.D from disk #11. Each of the following is a valid statement for selecting a pair of files:

```
GETFILE (#4:SALES79) #11:SALES

GETFILE (MYDISK:NEWORDER) ORD:ORDERS

GETFILE (JAN.HRS) #11:HOURS
```

Disk drives are identified as #5:, #11:, etc., in the UCSD and Apple II Pascal operating systems, and diskettes have volume names which end with a colon, like MYDISK: and ORD:

You may think of the datafilename option as a *pointer* to any datafile of your choice. The name must appear within parentheses and must precede the master file name.

SELECTING A SUBFILE

Just as you may select from several NPL datafiles, you may also select a portion of the chosen file for use in subsequent processing. The **GETFILE** command assigns a particular file to be the currently active file. The **SELECT** command chooses (via an Index file) a particular set of records within that file to be the active subfile. Both commands establish a single selection which remains active until changed by similar commands.

```
C>GETFILE NJ
C>SELECT COUNTY = WARREN.
```

These commands select the Warren County records in the New Jersey datafile, provided that an index file exists for the COUNTY field.

From one perspective the effect of the **SELECT** command is the same as screening with an **IF** phrase. That is, from a file of many records only records that satisfy a particular condition are to be used in a report. Why then are there two keywords for this function? The answer pertains first to speed and efficiency and second to flexibility and convenience. More fundamentally, however, there is an important difference in approach between "selection" and "screening," as the words are used here.

To *select* a subfile in advance means that you do not even examine the other records in the file. To *screen* the records retrieved and "accept" those that pass a test means you read and test every record in the file.

The general form of the **SELECT** command is:

```
SELECT keyfld = list of values END
```

where keyfld means a field for which an Index file exists. A period may be used in place of the word **END**.

Like **DEFINE**, **SELECT** takes you into a special mode. The **period** or **END** returns you to Command mode. Unlike **DEFINE** mode, only one condition may be stored in the **SELECT** mode. Each **SELECT** command replaces the old selection condition with a new one. The command:

```
C>CLEAR SELECT
```

cancels the selection. A **GETFILE** command also cancels the selection.

The list of values referred to above may be typed on one or more lines. The prompt message is **S>** until the list is terminated. These examples show the allowed formats for the list of values:

```
C>SELECT COUNTY = SALEM, SUSSEX, WARREN, HUNTERDON,
S>SOMERSET, MERCER, MIDDLESEX, MONMOUTH.

C>SELECT COUNTY = ATLANTIC THRU WARREN

C>SELECT AGE = 18 THRU 65

C>SELECT AGE = LO THRU 17, 66 THRU HI
```

The keyword **THRU** specifies an inclusive range, and **LO** and **HI** mean the lowest and highest values in the file. Values with embedded blanks must be within quotes:

```
C>SELECT STATE = MAINE 'RHODE ISLAND' VERMONT...
```

Individual values and ranges may be mixed:

```
C>SELECT STATE = LO THRU AZZ, OHIO, OREGON,
S>RHO THRU HI.
```

This statement selects state names beginning with A and those beginning with RHO through Z, plus Ohio and Oregon.

Words used in **IF** phrases like **OR, EQ, IS, TO, GT, LT**, etc., may not be used in the **SELECT** command.

A second form of the **SELECT** command lets you read the list of values from a datafile:

```
C>SELECT keyfld IN filename.
```

For example:

```
C>SELECT STATE IN MIDWEST.
```

where MIDWEST.D is a datafile which contains records with state names in the first field of each record.

KEYFIELDS AND INDEXING

A keyfield (*keyfld* in the definition above) is a master file fieldname or alias for which an index file exists. The **SELECT** command can only be used when an index file exists. An index file contains a table of field values and numbers which indicate the location of records on the disk. An index file is associated with a particular field in a particular datafile. An index file is created by the commands:

```
C>GETFILE NJ
C>INDEX COUNTY
```

A file called NJ.I.CNTY is created on the same disk with the **NJ.D** file. The first four letters of the alias of the keyfield are used as the suffix in the filename, in the UCSD and Apple Pascal operating systems. With other systems the filename suffix is the line number in the master file (NJ.M in this example) of the indexed field. See Appendix D.

When the above commands are issued, NPL reads every record in the NJ.D file, extracts the county name *and its disk address* from each, and builds the index table, alphabetically by county. An index file is always sorted A to Z, or lowest to highest. Thus an index file is said to provide us with a "view" of a datafile in the sort sequence of the keyfield. The existence of a county index file makes it possible to read, or view, the file alphabetically by county name.

RAPID ACCESS TO RECORDS VIA AN INDEX

Have you ever looked for a particular topic in a book with an unhelpful table of contents and without an index? Perhaps you looked up a disease symptom in a medical book, or a tax question in an IRS publication—but without the benefit of an index. In a word, the process is slow.

Without an index you must resort to a sequential search through every chapter and page to find all occurrences of certain words. The same is true of finding particular values of data items in a datafile. But then, if you have an index table of data values you should be able to locate the desired items directly.

Indeed this is the case. To find one social security number in a file of 1000 employees might take only a few seconds, as compared with many minutes in the absence of an index for SSN. Or all employees with a last name of Greene and age less than 30 could be extracted from the file in several seconds, instead of many minutes, using an index on last names.

First, however, you must create the needed index tables. One table is needed for each data item you expect to use as an index. In the library, typically there are three index tables, called card catalogs, one for access by author, one for book titles, and one by subject.

Consider a book which might have 1000 pages, each page containing a summary description of a manufacturing company, including these data items:

Name, headquarters address, telephone, sales volume in millions, number of employees in thousands, standard industry code (SIC), first year of operation, plus textual material describing products, plant, distribution, etc.

The pages of the book are ordered alphabetically by company name. Index tables at the end of the book could be organized to provide quick access to companies by state or ZIP Code, by size in sales or employees, or by SIC code. Such index tables might appear as follows:

```
STATES                                         PAGE  NUMBER

      ALABAMA      . . . . .37,572,589,640,739,821,833
      ARKANSAS     . . . . . . 161,220,484,631,876,910
        .
        .
        .
      WEST VIRGINIA   . . . . .57,313,560,842,901,943


  SALES (IN $ MILLIONS)

      100   . . . . . . . . . . . . 41,89,302,671,842
      200   . . . . . . . . . . .7,49,162,549,708,936
      300   . . . . . . . . . . 84,87,109,187,250,251
        .
        .
        .
```

While the above is not an ordinary index for a book, you would have no trouble finding the pages for all the companies with sales between 200 and 399 million dollars.

In the NPL system you create an index file for each subject or data field to be indexed, with a command of this form:

```
C>INDEX    fieldname
```

The fieldname may be an alias or a **DEFINE**d variable.

The datafile is not changed. A separate file is created to hold the index table. Any field and any number of fields may be indexed. For example, these commands:

```
GETFILE CLIENTS
INDEX SSN
INDEX LN
INDEX ACNO
```

147

create three new files, with the names

```
CLIENTS.I.SSN
CLIENTS.I.LN
CLIENTS.I.ACNO
```

where the suffixes are the first four letters of the alias names in the master file. The three fields SSN, LASTNAME, and ACCOUNT are called the keys or keyfields of the datafile.

If the CLIENTS file records are actually ordered by ZIP Code as they are stored on a diskette, then an ordinary view of the file is sequentially by ZIP. Moreover, the presence of an index file for the LASTNAME field provides another view of the file, alphabetically by last name. Thus, if you use that view to list the names and other items, the computer does not have to take the time to resort the file; it simply reads the file via the LASTNAME index table.

SELECTING WITH KEYFIELDS

It should be clear that indexes provide direct access to stored items. A subject index, as discussed above, makes it possible to open the pages of a book directly at the desired point. A library card catalog shows the way directly to the correct shelf. In both cases you avoid a sequential search for the desired items.

Selecting a subfile with a keyfield index can be a hundred, even a thousand, times faster than sequential screening. The savings in time can be enormous for large files. However, you do pay a price for this speed. First, the index files take up disk space on the same disk as the datafile.

Second, creating index files can be a slow process if the datafile is large. Each index file must be recreated after records are added to, or deleted from, the datafile (or when a keyfield value is changed). Hence, it may be inefficient to use an index file if frequent changes are made to the file. Historical datafiles, like the 1980 census data and prior year sales and accounting datafiles, are ideal for the use of indexing, because they are complete and do not change.

The command **SELECT** STATE = OHIO, IDAHO is a directive to NPL to first find all Ohio records and then find all Idaho records. This directive is acted upon, as soon as a complete Report mode request is submitted. Each record retrieved by the **SELECT** command is processed by the report request in the order selected.

The command **SELECT** STATE = IDAHO OHIO selects the Idaho records first. This is another critical difference from the screening **IF** phrase. Moreover, **SELECT** IDAHO, OHIO, IDAHO selects *two* sets of Idaho records! Obviously this is quite different from: **IF** STATE **IS** IDAHO **OR** OHIO **OR** IDAHO, which finds only one set of records per state.

The latter feature of repeated selection of the source records may be useful in creating an expanded file, with the **HOLD** phrase, to use for test purposes. One or two records in a datafile may be copied many times into a new **HOLD** file.

Care must be taken in specifying lists of values to avoid duplicate selections. For example

```
SELECT   AGE = 25 THRU 50,   18 THRU 25.
```

yields duplicates for age 25, and

```
SELECT CODE = 7, 5, 9, 4, 2, 6 THRU HI.
```

yields duplicates for codes of 7 and 9.

SELECT specifies the subfile. Report mode requests are not changed. They still use **IF** phrases to screen records sequentially as retrieved.

The command:

```
C>SELECT keyfield.
```

establishes a file view without selecting a subfile.

SORTING WITH KEYFIELDS

The time required to sort a very large file can be quite long. If the file is never changed you may sort once and store it in the desired sequence. As long as reports are to be in the sort sequence of the file, say, by account number, the delay of sorting is avoided. But if occasionally you need a mailing list printed from the file in ZIP Code order, sorting may be needed. You should then create an index file for the ZIP Code field and **SELECT** it when needed.

- If the **SELECT** keyfld and the primary **BY** field are the same, the index file is used for both selection and sorting. The resulting sequence is that of the keyfield, unless overridden by the sequence of the list of values in the **SELECT** command.

- If the **SELECT** keyfield and the primary **BY** field are *different*, the *selection* is done via the index file and the subfile is then sorted by the standard sort procedure.

This chapter introduced these keywords:

```
INDEX
SELECT
CLEAR
THRU
LO
HI
IN
```

plus the datafile option for the **GETFILE** command.

CHAPTER 10

EXEC PROGRAM FILES

There are two methods for initiating NPL queries. Almost all of the examples in this book are presented as if you personally were typing each query request. This is sometimes referred to as the **on-line**, or **ad hoc**, method.

As you use more of the report-writing features your NPL requests will get longer and more complex. At that point it is better to use the **EXEC** file method. Instead of going to the Report mode of NPL, you first enter the EDIT mode at the operating system level and create an **EXEC** file which contains the full NPL request. In fact, several NPL queries may be typed one after the other in the file.

The statements in the **EXEC** file should be exactly the same, with punctuation, as you would have typed them on-line. When you enter NPL Command mode and type, for example, **EXEC** TESTCASE (where TESTCASE.E is your **EXEC** filename), the query statements are read from the file rather than from the keyboard. NPL responds to these statements just as if you had typed them.

If a name is misspelled or if the request is improper, NPL asks you for corrections, just as it does in the on-line mode.

RUNTIME VARIABLES

Simply storing your queries in **EXEC** files for future use is a valuable function which you should utilize whenever you can. It permits you to create a whole library of NPL queries, ready for use at any time. Moreover, if you test your **EXEC** programs well at the beginning, you can be confident they will perform correctly when you call upon them many months later.

Such **EXEC** programs become even more useful and flexible with the use of *runtime variables*. The word runtime contrasts with the time at which you created the **EXEC** file, which means you can write a program now and defer the assigning of values to certain variables until later, when you are ready to print the report.

Suppose you have written a Report mode request to print a table of expenditure and budget figures for the month of March for the engineering department. By changing MARCH to APRIL and ENGNRG to SALES you have made new programs for additional budget reports. The changes are made to these two **IF** phrases:

```
IF  DEPT  IS  SALES

IF  MONTH  IS  APRIL
```

You can simplify the situation, however, by a change to your original program which permits the selection of a department and a month at runtime—that is, when you *run* the program. Simply change the **IF** phrases to read

```
IF  DEPT  IS  &DEPARTMENT

IF  MONTH  IS  &MONTH
```

The words prefixed with an ampersand, called *amper-variables*, as well as runtime variables, are replaced by your choice of values when you execute the program. When NPL encounters the first ampersand it sends this message to the console, as a request for data:

```
ENTER  DEPARTMENT
```

You could respond with **SALES**; then NPL types:

```
ENTER  MONTH
```

to which you might reply **APRIL**

Any **EXEC** program can be made quite general purpose with the use of runtime variables. Any number of variables may be used in one program. The general form is:

```
&xxx...x
```

where the x's are letters, numbers, or any printable character *except*:

```
&  "  '  ( )  .  and the space character.
```

All of the above characters terminate an &variable string of characters. The period character has the special purpose of allowing the amper-variable to be placed adjacent to the word on the right (i.e. without space). This feature is explained later in an example. Any number of characters that fit on a line may be used in the amper-variable. Thus the variable,

&THE−NUMBER−OF−ANGELS−THAT−CAN−DANCE−ON−THE−HEAD−OF−A−PIN=

will cause NPL to prompt the user with:

ENTER THE−NUMBER−OF−ANGELS−THAT−CAN−DANCE−ON−THE−HEAD−OF−A−PIN=

Whatever you use for xxx...x becomes the string of characters appearing in the prompt line at runtime.

The next thing to happen is that whatever you type in reply to the prompt, *including spaces*, replaces the amper-variable in the original program. The result, of course, must be a valid Report mode request.

The response to runtime variable prompts can be complete phrases. The following extreme example asks the user for *all* the phrases of a report request:

EXEC PROGRAM	RUNTIME PROMPTS	POSSIBLE RESPONSES
------------	--------	---------
GETFILE &FILENAME	ENTER FILENAME	POPULATION
&VERB−PHRASE	ENTER VERB−PHRASE	PRINT MALE FEM TOTAL
&BY−PHRASE	ENTER BY−PHRASE	BY COUNTY BY TOWN
&IF−PHRASE	ENTER IF−PHRASE	IF STATE IS NY
END		

After the &variables are replaced by the responses above, the query seen by NPL is:

```
GETFILE POPULATION
PRINT MALE FEM TOTAL
BY COUNTY BY TOWN
IF STATE IS NY
END
```

Amper-variables may be embedded within a word or literal value as in the next examples. Remember that your response at runtime is a string of characters which simply replaces the &variable characters.

For this case,

```
DEFINE STARTDATE/A6 = '81&MONTH/01-12/' + '01'.
```

The runtime prompt line is:

> ENTER MONTH/01-12/

If you reply with 05, for example, the value of STARTDATE becomes 810501, or May 1, 1981.

In another example, the first statement in a program might be:

> **GETFILE** (SALES/&NAME-FOR-SALES-DATA-FILE:) SALES

and the runtime prompt line would be:

> ENTER NAME-FOR-SALES-DATA-FILE:

You reply, ACME82, and the result is:

> **GETFILE** (SALES/ACME82) SALES

Another example:

```
GETFILE &VOLUME-NAME. /BUDGET
DEFINE REPORTDATE/A4 = '&MONTH:01-12&YEAR<81-82-ETC>'.
HEADING
"       MONTHLY REPORT FOR THE &DEPT-NAME DEPARTMENT       "
"              &MONTH:JAN-DEC          &AGAIN:YEAR         "
"       ACCOUNT CODES:    4ENX&DEPT-ACNT-CODE-GROUP        "
```

The runtime prompts, with replies in bold letters would appear as follows:

```
ENTER  VOLUME-NAME  /FIN82

ENTER  MONTH:01-12    07

ENTER  YEAR<81-82-ETC>    82

ENTER  DEPT-NAME    CONSUMER  PRODUCTS

ENTER  MONTH:JAN-DEC    JUL

ENTER  AGAIN:YEAR    82

ENTER  DEPT-ACNT-CODE-GROUP    49400
```

The foregoing examples illustrate various uses of amper-variables, particularly where the reply is to be placed adjacent to other characters. The first example produces the statement

```
GETFILE  /FIN82/BUDGET
```

(i.e., Get the BUDGET file on the FIN82 disk). Notice the period character serves only to terminate the amper-variable string and does not appear in the final text. The rule is that an amper-variable begins with the ampersand, contains only letters, 0 to 9, the characters !@#$%^*_-+=\{}[]~`:;?/<>,| and ends at the first space, quote mark, period, parenthesis or nonprinting character. Amper-variables that are used to furnish literal values to **DEFINE** and **COMPUTE** statements may be placed between quote marks.

An additional feature of the amper-variable allows you to specify the values that NPL should accept when entered at runtime. For example, in the prior illustration, YEAR could be restricted to just two years as follows:

```
&YEAR<81-82>(81  82)
```

which results in a runtime prompt message of

```
ENTER  YEAR<81-82>
```

155

and the parenthetic expression lists the acceptable answers. If ten consecutive years are to be allowed, the range is stated as (75..84). The general form is:

```
&variable(list)
```

The first parenthesis must be adjacent to the amper-variable string (i.e. no space between them). The list consists of acceptable runtime responses separated by spaces. Responses that include space, quote, vertical bar, period or parenthesis characters must be surrounded by a pair of quotes. A range may appear on the list as two values separated by two periods (without spaces). Here are some examples:

```
&MONTH<QTR-II>(APR APRIL MAY JUN JUNE)
&PART-NBR(B3400 B3800 C425..C780 'C780.47'..'C780.3'
&STATE(NY 'NEW YORK' CA CAL CALIF CALIFORNIA)
```

When a response fails to match any one of the items on the list, the prompt message is presented again to the operator. This is repeated until the operator enters a valid response, presses the **Exit** key, enters **QUIT**, or presses the **Override** key. In the latter case, the previous value entered is accepted even though it is not on the list.

COMMENT STATEMENTS

As **EXEC** programs grow in complexity it is good practice to leave some notes around explaining how to use them. The best place to put the notes is in the **EXEC** file itself. You can do this by starting each line of notes with an asterisk in column one or two. Some examples:

```
*    THIS IS A COMMENT LINE IN AN NPL EXEC FILE
 *    ALL SUCH LINES ARE IGNORED BY NPL
**    COMMENT LINES MAY BE 78 CHARACTERS LONG
*******>> IMPORTANT NOTE <<*******
****  ASTERISKS PROVIDE HIGHLIGHTING   ****
 *
*    AN ASTERISK MUST APPEAR IN COLUMN ONE OR TWO
```

DISPLAYING OPERATOR MESSAGES OR A MENU

There are two uses for plain text lines in Exec files. One is to include a programmer's explanation of how the **EXEC** program should function. The second is to provide instructions to the operator. With the latter feature the person writing NPL Exec programs can build systems which will appear very simple to operate by someone who need only read instructions and answer questions. Such programs are often described as being *menu driven*, because the operator sees only a series of *menus* of options and the program proceeds only as fast as the operator responds to the menu options.

The two kinds of text or comment lines are distinguished by whether an asterisk appears in column one:

```
* in column two only: a programmer's comment line

* in column one (or both): a message to the operator
```

However, the position of the asterisk has no effect whatever unless the **ECHO** command is set to the value of *. There are four forms of the **ECHO** command:

```
C>ECHO OFF    :  The normal state

C>ECHO ON     :  Displays  on  the  monitor,  during
                 execution  of an Exec  file,  the  NPL
                 program  lines and message text  lines
                 (* in column one)

C>ECHO *      :  Displays only message text lines (* in
                 column one)

C>ECHO ALL    :  Displays  all  lines  in an  Exec  file
                 during its execution
```

The **ECHO** * form is used for displaying a menu of operator options and instructions. A simple example follows:

```
*              THE  ACME  MANUFACTURING  INVENTORY  QUERY  PROGRAM
*
*
*              >>>>QUERY  OPTIONS<<<<
*
*              A.     WIDGETS
*              B.     JARVERS
*              C.     LINKERS
*              D.     BLIVETS
*
*              CHOOSE  ONE  OF  THE  ABOVE:
*
               GETFILE  ACME
               SELECT  PART-TYPE  =  &CHOICE(A  B  C  D)     END
*
               PRINT  PARTNBR  NAME  QTY
               IF  PARTNBR  EQ  &PART-NUMBER
               END
               CLEAR  SELECT
```

When the **EXEC** program is run the operator sees only the text lines down to "CHOOSE ONE OF THE ABOVE," then NPL prompts the operator with the runtime variable **&CHOICE**:

```
ENTER  CHOICE
```

If the operator enters a choice, followed by **RETURN**, NPL next prompts with &PART-NUMBER:

```
ENTER  PART-NUMBER
```

and after the reply a report is written.

Message text lines (* in column one) are used to:

• display a whole menu of options

• provide detailed instructions before an amper- variable prompt

- send progress messages to the operator during a long, multiple-step Exec file.

- print headings and footings for reports without taking up memory space during report writing

When more than one **ECHO** command (i.e., **ON, ALL**, or *) occurs, only the first one has effect, until cleared by **ECHO OFF**. It is good practice to use these two commands at the end of an **Exec** program to reset the echo and printer status:

```
ECHO  OFF
CONSOLE:
```

The **ECHO** * command may be used in an **Exec** program, yet when you are testing the program you may type **ECHO ON** before executing the program in order to display all the program lines. In this case the **ECHO** * is redundant.

This chapter introduced these keywords:

```
EXEC
&variable(list)
ECHO  OFF
ECHO  ON
ECHO  *
ECHO  ALL
```

CHAPTER 11

DISPLAYING, REVISING, AND CREATING RECORDS IN DATA-FORM MODE

How do you examine a single record to be sure that all the field values are correct? When records contain thirty to forty or more data items, it is important to be able to verify the content of each record and to be able to revise individual items without having to reenter the whole record. The DATA-FORM mode provides access to individual records, while the Report mode, as we have seen, is used to retrieve and display information from many records at a time. The DATA-FORM mode also provides the means for changing data items and for adding and deleting records in a datafile.

The word DATA-FORM refers to the notion that almost any business data form you may find on your desk, like a receipt, a bill, a deposit slip, an application form, a personnel action form, etc., could be duplicated on the screen of your monitor. The description of the fields would appear next to blank spaces for the data items. There are physical limits, of course, on the size of such forms, and they are:

- 78-column screen width

- up to 23 lines of text

- up to 100 data items

A DATA-FORM picture on the monitor is created by an NPL program, which is usually stored as an EXEC program. Thus, you might have a series of such programs for creating different DATA-FORM images, such as:

```
CREDTAPP.E for a credit application form
 DEPOSIT.E for a deposit form
 CASHREC.E for a cash receipt form
   CHECK.E for checks written
 INVOICE.E for bills sent
   BILLS.E for bills received
 APPOINT.E for appointments
```

Eventually, you should have a DATA-FORM Exec program for every datafile for which you need to enter or examine individual records.

Before presenting how to prepare DATA-FORM Exec programs, we look at how you and others may *use* such programs; that is, how you actually write into and change data in an electronic data form appearing on the monitor. Throughout these pages and the book we refer to certain special keys by descriptive names like *Exit key, Back-Space key, Tab key,* and *Override key.* This is because the actual keys vary from keyboard to keyboard; see Appendix D for specific examples.

EXAMPLE SCREEN PICTURES

A few sample DATA-FORM screen pictures appear on the next pages. The Exec programs to produce these screens are presented in Chapter 12.

The command EXEC CHECKBK results in the screen picture:

```
                CHECKBOOK  TRANSACTIONS

          CHECK  OR  DEPOSIT:

                              ‾‾‾      ‾‾‾‾
                              C/D      NBR
      /    /

    ‾‾ ‾‾ ‾‾
    MO DA YR
                                  $

    ‾‾‾‾‾‾‾‾‾‾‾‾‾‾‾‾‾‾‾‾‾‾‾   ‾‾‾‾‾‾‾‾‾‾‾
      PAYEE / PAYOR             AMOUNT

    ‾‾‾‾‾‾‾‾‾‾‾‾‾‾‾‾‾‾‾‾‾‾‾   ‾‾‾‾‾‾‾‾‾‾‾
    DESCRIPTION               ACCOUNT
              CANC  OR  VOID

                              ‾‾‾
                              C/V
```

The checking program may be used for entering business checks and deposits into a datafile together with accounting codes. It is also used for examining the existing file of checking account transactions.

This form is used for creating a record for each client account. One client could have several accounts, each with different account numbers, and each with a record in the file. To see the Exec programs that produce the screen-picture, type **ECHO ON**, and then execute the program CLIENTS.

```
| ................ CLIENT   INFORMATION ..................... |
|                                                             |
| Name:                                                       |
|     ------    ----------------   -   ----------------  ----- |
|   Mr,Mrs,Ms                                   Jr,Esq,PHD    |
|                                                             |
| Social Security Number:        Telephone Number:           |
|                    --- -- ----              --- --- ---- |
|                                                             |
|                                                             |
|     ----------------   -------------     --     -----       |
|   Street Address    City                State   Zip Code   |
|                                                             |
|               Age:          Annual Income :    ,000        |
|               Sex:                             ---          |
|   Number of Dependents:        Account Number:             |
|   Years of Education   :                                    |
|   Years of Employment  :       Account Type   :   ------    |
|                                                ----         |
|   Employer:                    Account Amount:    ,000     |
|             ----------------                   ---          |
|                                                             |
```

In the illustration, no data appear in the form, because the Exec program has specified that the *initial* condition of the screen be set up for appending new records. We can change that condition now, in order to illustrate another condition, by pressing the **Exit** key. Two things happen: first, each field of the form is filled with data; second, the **M>** prompt characters appear in the top left corner of the screen. See the figure on the page after next.

LOCATING RECORDS

When the DATA-FORM picture first appears, the first record of the file is displayed in the form. If you press the **RETURN** key, the second record is displayed. To find particular records, you may step through the whole file by pressing **RETURN**, once for each record. After the last record, you hear a warning beep, and the computer types the message: END OF FILE. You may type **TOP** (and press **RETURN**) to return to the first record, or type **UP** (and press **RETURN**) to move back one record.

You may search for a particular record, i.e., for a particular field value, by typing (after the **M>** characters) a search condition like one of these:

```
    LN=SMYTHE
   ZIP=39400
ACCOUNT=B347
   REC#=B347
```

NPL reads forward through the file, testing each record for the desired value. If you search for the 567th record, as in the fourth example, the search is completed within seconds, regardless of the size of the file. If you begin at the top of the file, NPL can search the whole file, stopping at the first record to satisfy the search condition. If the search begins in the middle, the first part of the file is not searched. Wherever the search stops, a record is displayed, and you may continue searching by stepping through the records one at a time using the **RETURN** key, or by typing **UP**. You may type **TOP** or **BOTTOM**, at any time, to move to one end of the file or the other.

REVISING FIELD VALUES

Once you locate a particular client record, press the **Tab** key, and the cursor will move to the beginning of the first field. You should think of this as a step *into* the DATA-FORM where a particular record is displayed. In this mode, you can move the cursor about with the **Tab** and **Back-Space** keys, but you cannot select a new record. To select another record with the cursor at the beginning of any field, press the **Exit** key to escape from the record.

Before doing that, however, let's change some data items. First, select a data field by moving the cursor to it, by pressing the **Tab** key. Then begin typing a new value for that field, say, for example, a new street address. As soon as you press the first key, the field is cleared, and the new characters are entered. If you change your mind before completing the field, pressing **Exit** restores the original street address. A spelling error is corrected by using the **Back-Space** key.

The **Back-Space** key moves the cursor from field to field when you are *in the record*, but it is a backspace key when you are *in a field*. The **Exit** key aborts the field changes when you are in a field. When the cursor is at the beginning of a field, however, the **Exit** key lets you escape *from this record*.

If the new street address is short, press **RETURN** to complete the data items. If it is long, you may hear a soft tone from the speaker, depending upon what computer you have, as you approach the end of the allowed field length. This is like the bell on a typewriter; it warns you that you are within three characters of the end. If you keep typing, a tone signals that the cursor has moved to the next field. At that point, if the street address is not correct, press the **Back-Space** key to move the cursor back to the beginning of the street field and then reenter the address.

After changing all the fields requiring correction, press the **Exit** key, and a message, which, for example, on Apple computers is **RETURN or ESC >** (**ESC** is the **Exit** key), appears at the top of the screen with the cursor, as shown here:

```
|M>                    RETURN or ESC >
|
|
|   ............... CLIENT   INFORMATION ......................
|
|Name:Mr        Philip           A   Walters
|    ------      ---------------   -   -----------------   ------
|   Mr,Mrs,Ms                                        Jr,Esq,PHD
|
|Social Security Number:321-21-4321 Telephone Number:215-446-3231|
|                       --- -- ----                   --- --- ----|
|
|   37 Market St       Philadelphia        PA      19104
|   -----------------  ------------        --      -----
|   Street Address     City                State   Zip Code
|
|                   Age: 29            Annual Income : 22 ,000
|                   Sex:M                               ---
|   Number of Dependents:1            Account Number:B44200
|   Years of Education  :16                           ------
|   Years of Employment :8            Account Type   :MMKT
|                                                     ----
|   Employer:Wayne Oil Co             Account Amount:  5 ,000
|            ---------------                           ---
|
|
```

RETURN keeps -- **Exit** key cancels

If you press **RETURN** the changes just made to the record are written to the disk file. The **Exit** key cancels those changes and restores the display of the record to the original values. In either case, the cursor returns to the **M>** position to await your next record selection. While you are using the DATA-FORM mode, the datafile is stored partially in computer memory and from time to time the file changes are written to the disk file.

APPENDING NEW RECORDS

Returning now to the empty screen displayed by the Exec program CLI-ENTS at the beginning of the chapter, type **APPEND** after the **M>** characters. NPL clears the data values, positions the cursor at the first field, and waits for you to enter new data values. At first, the cursor will seem to behave inconsistently—sometimes waiting for you to press **RETURN**, sometimes refusing to move when you do press **RETURN**, and other times skipping ahead to the next field before you can press **RETURN**.

Just what happens as you enter values may vary from field to field, and it depends upon your Exec program. You can expect things like the following:

- The computer will only accept letters in name fields and only numbers in ZIP, AGE, and DATE fields.

- Names and address fields do not have to be filled, hence **RETURN** is used to end an item, except for ZIP, which must be filled. The **RETURN** key is ignored.

- When a field is filled, the cursor moves to the next field automatically.

- Integer fields, like AGE and NBR OF DEPENDENTS, reject the decimal point, but real numbers (i.e., floating point numbers) accept the point, and commas as well, which are ignored.

- Some fields are optional and may be skipped by pressing **RETURN**. Others are required, and **RETURN** causes an error beep and a message at the top of the screen.

- Fields may be restricted to specific values like Y or N; M or F; GA, SC, NC, VA, MD, DE, PA, NJ, NY, CT, RI, MA, NH; or to a range of values, alphabetic or numeric.

- When you violate these restrictions, a beep tells you to look at the top line for a message about the allowed values. To learn the values, press the **Tab** key to display each value of the list of allowed values.

Occasionally, you may wish to override one of the restrictions for a field. To do this, first enter the desired value. For example, the CLIENTS field called ACCOUNT TYPE accepts only these codes: BOND, MMKT, MARG, and FUND. When you type CASH the computer beeps, clears the data field, and tells you to " Press Tab for Values." Each time you press the **Tab** key a different ACCOUNT TYPE value appears at the top of the screen. These are the only valid codes for that field. If desired value, say, CASH in this example, is not a valid code you may press the **Override** key. Instantly, the value CASH reappears and the cursor moves on to the next field.

When you have filled all the fields on the screen, the cursor moves to the top line of the screen, and you have the option of pressing the **RETURN** or the **Exit** key. As before:

RETURN keeps—**Exit** key cancels

That is, press **RETURN** to write the new record to the file, or press the **Exit** key to erase the new record. A third option, which is almost always available, is to move the cursor to a particular field to correct a data item. When the cursor is at the top of the screen, use the **Tab** key to move it back *into* the record. After typing the corrected value, press **RETURN** to keep the item, and press the **Exit** key to send the cursor to the top. Then press **RETURN** to keep the new record, which also clears the data field to prepare for the next record.

COPYING

Now let's assume that you are working with a stack of client forms and have entered a dozen records when you come to one that appears to be a duplicate of a form that you have just entered. Closer examination reveals that the name, address, and basic personnel information is the same; the account type, account number, and amount fields are different.

Now, with the cursor at the beginning of the first field, rather than retype the personnel data, just press the **Tab** key to *copy* the data from the prior record into the new record. Keep pressing the **Tab** key until all the repeated fields are filled, then enter the new account information.

Data from the last record is always held in the computer after it is written on the disk and may be copied into the screen form with the **Tab** key. Changes that you make on the screen replace the values held by the computer.

When you have finished appending records and the cursor waits at the first field, you may:

> • Press the **Exit** key once to leave the **APPEND** option and return to **M>**, where you can examine individual records.

> • Press the **Exit** key twice to terminate the DATA-FORM program and return to Command mode (**C>**).

Let's elect the first course and introduce some other features of the DATA-FORM mode.

INSERTING AND DELETING

When the **M>** characters appear at the top of the screen, you have left the **APPEND** option and may again search for a particular record. That record may be removed from the file with the command **DELETE**. NPL accepts the command but defers the actual removal of the record until you leave the DATA-FORM mode.

Sometimes with *small* files, you may find it convenient to keep the records in a particular physical order in the file. To accomplish this you may **INSERT** records into specific positions in the file. For example, after the **TOP** command, the **INSERT** command creates a new record at the beginning of the file.

When you type **INSERT**, the data fields are cleared and the cursor is positioned at the first field. After you enter data for all fields, and press **RETURN** to keep the new record, NPL writes the record to a special file. When you leave the DATA-FORM program, the special file is merged with the main datafile—at which time the new record is placed at the top of the file.

INSERT puts the new record ahead of the one being viewed at the time of the command. That record, incidentally, is held in the computer and may be *copied* into the next new record with the **Tab** key, after a second **INSERT** command. Data field edit conditions must be satisfied during entry of an inserted record, as well as when you revise values in existing records.

A variation on the use of the *copy* feature for adding new records is that you may first find a particular record, then type **APPEND**. The record you were just viewing is carried with you into the **APPEND** mode. The **Tab** key displays each field on the screen. You may then change some of the fields and **APPEND** the revised record. This feature saves time when the number of fields is large and the revisions are few.

There is a disadvantage to the use of the **INSERT** and **DELETE** commands, particularly for larger datafiles. At the end of the DATA-FORM session the whole datafile must be copied to a new place on the disk, during which process records are added and removed. If file changes occcur frequently, it may be more efficient to avoid rewriting the file after each session, by **APPEND**ing all new records, and marking certain records for later removal. If, for example, you marked the records to be deleted by leaving the LASTNAME field blank, then these records may be removed from the file, periodically, with the phrase, **IF LN NE ''**, as you copy the file using the **HOLD** feature.

RAPID SEARCHING WITH AN INDEX

Searching for particular records in DATA-FORM mode is slow when the file is large, say, several hundred records. However, when an **INDEX** file is present, as discussed in Chapter 9, the access time to any record is only a few seconds, almost independent of the size of the file.

You may select an **INDEX** file with a **SELECT** command before executing the DATA-FORM Exec program, or if the Exec program contains the **GETFILE** command (which clears the active **INDEX**), you can type after the M> character in the top left corner of a DATA-FORM picture, for example, **SELECT ZIP**. If a ZIP **INDEX** file exists, the record with the lowest ZIP value appears on the screen—i.e., the **TOP** of the file as viewed from the ZIP **INDEX**.

Now, with an active **INDEX**, there are a few special features and restrictions to the DATA-FORM mode:

a) Using **DELETE** and **INSERT** commands will invalidate the indices. NPL warns you and provides the opportunity to abort and save the indices. If you proceeded the indices must be recreated. The **UP** command is inhibited.

b) The subfile feature of the **SELECT** command, which allows you to specify a range of values of an **INDEX**, is inoperative in the DATA-FORM mode.

c) If new records have been appended to the datafile since the **INDEX** file was created, type **NEWRECS** to locate the first appended (non-indexed) record.

d) The top line of the screen looks like this:

```
|                                                      |
|  Index =           ZIP     M> ▮                      |
```

To search for a value of ZIP, ignore the **M>** characters and type:

```
                        =39740

as if you were saying  ZIP=39740
```

e) A search using an **INDEX** always finds a record (the one with the nearest higher value) unless the search value is higher than the highest ZIP value in the file.

f) Since searching with an **INDEX** finds the record with the nearest, highest value, you may type approximate values like:

```
        =39           which might locate a record
with ZIP=39144.
```

If the **INDEX** is LASTNAME, typing

```
        =SMI           could lead you to a record
with LN=SMIDOWSKI.
```

g) The **RETURN** key steps through the file in the order of the **INDEX**. The **TOP**, **BOTTOM**, and **UP** commands refer to action that is relative to the Indexed order of the files.

h) You may switch from one **INDEX** to another by typing **SELECT** followed by the keyfield name. The last **INDEX** selected remains active at the end of the DATA-FORM program.

i) If you **SELECT REC#** as the **INDEX** you can then quickly locate records by their physical position number.

j) Type **APPEND** to enter new records, and press the **Exit** key to return from the **APPEND**ing (at the bottom of the file) to the **M>** condition, where you are viewing the record at the top of the file (as viewed via the **INDEX**).

UPDATING THE DATAFILE

Upon completion of a DATA-FORM session, pressing the **Exit** key (when the cursor is at the **M>** position) causes NPL to remove the screen picture and, if you have deleted, inserted, or appended any records, to ask this question:

```
Make file changes permanent? (Y/N)
```

The expected answer is **Y** for "yes," of course, but NPL gives you one last chance to change your mind about modifying the datafile. Such an option is possible because throughout the DATA-FORM session NPL does the following:

- If you change the value of a *data item*, the original item is simply overwritten with the revised item. Such changes may be reversed only by retyping the original data values.

- On the other hand, if you **APPEND** a new record, it is written in a separate datafile called filename.D.NEW, where *filename* is the name of the datafile. At the end of the DATA-FORM session, if you answer **Y** to the question above, the two datafiles are copied into one file called filename.D and the original two files are removed from the file directory.

- If you **INSERT** a new record, it, too, is written into the file called filename.D.NEW, and a note is recorded in computer memory to merge it into the original datafile (rather than attaching to the end) upon exit from DATA-FORM mode.

- If you **DELETE** a record, a note is recorded in computer memory to skip that record when the datafile is copied into a new datafile upon exit from DATA-FORM mode.

As you can see, no change to the structure of the datafile takes place until you answer the question about making the file changes permanent. Of course, any changes made to data fields in existing records are already permanent as you move from record to record.

SAVING CHANGES IN A NEW DATAFILE

SAVING CHANGES IN A NEW DATAFILE

Now, suppose you answer the question with **N** (i.e., "no"). NPL then asks another question (let filename be CLIENTS, for example):

```
Save new records in separate file,
NPL:CLIENTS.D.NEW ? (Y/N)
```

At this point, you have abandoned the option of inserting or deleting, but you are given the opportunity of keeping all new records (inserts and appends) in a separate file. The name of the *NEW* file varies from one operating system to another. This file may be used in two ways:

- With the **COPYFILE** command (see Chapter 13), you can join this file with any other file that uses the same master file—perhaps one on another diskette.

- The new file may be used as a datafile by itself, but you must first change its name to newname.D.

- If you answer **N** to the second question, the CLIENTS.D.NEW file is removed from the file directory.

DISK SPACE

Finally, there is one contingency which NPL allows for, i.e., there may not be enough space on the diskette to copy CLIENTS.D and CLIENTS.D.NEW into a new file. If this situation occurs, NPL asks:

```
Insufficient space
for output file on NPL: disk
Try new disk? (Y/N)
```

If you answer **N** you are allowed to keep the new records in a separate file. An answer of **Y** requires you to tell NPL the name of the new diskette and then to insert the diskette in a disk drive that does not hold the two datafiles.

This completes the discussion of how to *use* a DATA-FORM program for data entry and editing. The next chapter discusses the writing of DATA-FORM programs.

This chapter introduced these keywords:

```
TOP
UP
APPEND
INSERT
DELETE
SELECT
NEWRECS
BOTTOM
COPYFILE
```

CHAPTER 12

PREPARING DATA-FORM PROGRAMS

From reading Chapter 11, you should have an idea of what can be done in the DATA-FORM mode. Now we consider how to prepare your own DATA-FORM Exec programs. All of what follows may be performed in a direct, on-line manner just by typing the commands. However, DATA-FORM programs are almost always stored as Exec programs, because they are long and complex, and because we want to save and reuse them many times.

The shortest DATA-FORM request is just two words, **MODIFY RUN**, while the general form of a request looks like this:

```
MODIFY
    PROMPT   fld fld fld eeee...
             fld eeee fld...
             ...

    FORM "text <fld text <fld ...
         ... text       <fld      text <fld ...
         ...            text ...
         ...          <fld ...
                          .
                          .
                          .                  text    <fld ...    "

    VALIDATE
        fld eeee
        fld eeee
        ...
RUN
```

where fld means any fieldname or alias, eeee stands for edit codes, text is any group of characters, and the dots mean "et cetera." The layout of the text between the quotes is entirely up to you.

The DATA-FORM *program prompt*s you at the console to enter selected fields (*fld*) of data in a particular *form* on the screen of the monitor. What you type is *validated* against certain edit criteria (*eeee*). When values for all fields have been typed, NPL appends a record to the datafile. The format of the record is controlled by the currently active master file.

Acceptable DATA-FORM requests include

- a **MODIFY** statement alone

- **MODIFY** and **PROMPT** statements

- **MODIFY** and **FORM** statements

- **MODIFY** and **VALIDATE** statements

- **MODIFY, FORM**, and **VALIDATE** statements

- **MODIFY, PROMPT**, and **FORM** statements

The keyword **RUN** completes the request and initiates its execution.

The special case that combines all four types of statements in one request as illustrated on the previous page is cumbersome and is not used. A feature of the **PROMPT** statement, which is explained later in this chapter, lets you combine the **PROMPT** and **VALIDATE** function.

BRIEF FORMS

The simplest request is one which prompts the operator for the full list of fieldnames in the master file:

```
C>GETFILE CLIENTS
C>MODIFY RUN
```

This request accepts data items until the operator presses the Exit key *twice* in succession to cause NPL to leave the DATA-FORM mode. No edit checks are performed upon the data items entered.

You may specify fewer fields than those listed in the master file to correspond, say, with a particular paper form of the raw data— other data elements being added later. To do so requires a **PROMPT** statement. Thus, the record might be created with this request:

```
C>GETFILE CLIENTS
C>MODIFY
M>PROMPT FNAM MI LNAM PHONE
M>RUN
```

The sequence on the screen is determined by the order of the names in the **PROMPT** statement, which must be fieldnames, aliases, or unique truncations. Fields not mentioned in the **PROMPT** statement are filled with blank (space) characters in the new records created.

FIELD EDITING CONTROLS

Data testing is available at the field level. That is, NPL can perform a variety of tests on each data item, as it is entered. If these tests fail, the operator is alerted with audible and visual signals. Moreover, the operator is held at the particular field until the edit criteria are satisfied.

Since the possible number of edit tests are many, it is convenient to use a shorthand notation. The name of each field in a **VALIDATE** statement is followed by one or more three-letter codes. For example,

```
VALIDATE LNAM REQ LTR
```

means an operator's response for lastname is *required*, and it must consist of *letters*, not numbers.

```
VALIDATE SSN REQ FIL NBR
```

In the second case, SSN is not only *required*, but the operator must *fill* the nine character field, and only with *numbers*.

```
VALIDATE PARTNBR REQ VAL (E53..E84, E95, F95, G50)
```

The third case *requires* a PARTNBR *value* that is on the list within the parentheses. The list consists of a range of values E53 through E84 and three other values.

The **REQ** and **VAL** codes are used with fields of all types, while the **FIL,** **NBR,** and **LTR** code can be applied only to alphanumeric variables (fields with PRINTING format of A). The **REQ** and **FIL** tests accept blanks (i.e., space characters) and **VAL** does not reject a null response from the user, but such responses *are* rejected when **REQ** and **VAL** are combined as in the third example above.

The restrictions of **NBR** and **LTR** tests are relaxed slightly to allow you to enter the slash, period, hyphen, and comma characters. Thus a date of 10/21/81 is accepted by a **NBR** test. Hyphens may be entered with SSN and telephone numbers, and "Smith, John R." is accepted by an LTR test.

Ranges of values and single values may be mixed in the **VAL**ue list, separated by commas or spaces, and the range limits separated by two periods. Alphanumeric values containing spaces, periods, or quote marks must be surrounded by quotes.

Numeric fields (I, F, and D formats) reject the entry of characters other than 0 to 9, a minus sign, a decimal point, and commas. The commas are ignored, for they have no meaning to the computer. The minus sign (hyphen) may be entered as the first or last character.

Additional examples of range and value checks follow:

```
 TIMEOUT VAL (0000..2400)

    YEAR VAL (1952..1964)

 ZIPCODE VAL (07000..08999)

  Knames VAL (Kaaaaa..Kzzzzz)

   TITLE VAL ('Mr.' 'Mrs.' 'Ms.' 'Dr.' 'Rev.' 'Hon.')

 CLASSES VAL (1981 1976 1971 1966)

  STATES VAL (AL AK AR AZ CA CO CT DC DE FL GA
              HI IA ID IL IN KS KY LA MA MD ME
              MI MN MO MS MT NC ND NE NH NJ NV
              NY OH OK OR PA RI SC SD TN TX UT
              VA VT WA WI WV WY)

 WEEKDAY VAL (MON TUE WED THU FRI)
```

PROTECTED FIELDS

One additional edit code is available for blocking all data entry to an existing field. That is, once a record has been entered into a file you may wish to protect certain fields from change. For example, the principle identifying fields like LASTNAME and SSN should be protected—particularly, if the fields have been **INDEX**ed. The **NOC** edit code (for no change) prevents the DATA-FORM program from changing a particular field, though in the **APPEND** mode **NOC** has no effect, since the field value is being entered to create a new record.

A BRIEF FORM WITH VALIDATION

The **VALIDATION** statement lists just those fieldnames that require edit checking. The following sample program causes NPL to prompt the user for all of the fields in the Master file—in Master file order—while performing tests only on four fields.

```
GETFILE CLIENTS
MODIFY
  VALIDATE
    LASTNAME REQ LTR NOC
         SSN REQ NBR NOC
         SEX VAL (M F)
         AGE VAL (14..100)
  RUN
```

If it is intended to prompt for only, say, six items—the four above, plus TELEPHONE and EMPLOYER—a **PROMPT** statement with six fieldnames could be added to the sample program. However, having lists of fieldnames in both the **PROMPT** and **VALIDATE** statements is too wordy. You may drop the **VALIDATE** statement and add the edit codes after the four names in the **PROMPT** statement. The sample program becomes the following:

```
GETFILE CLIENTS
MODIFY
  PROMPT
    LASTNAME REQ LTR NOC
         SSN REQ NBR NOC
         SEX VAL (M F)
         AGE VAL (14..100)
    TELEPHONE
    EMPLOYER
  RUN
```

Edit checks may be added to the last two fields but they are not required. In a **VALIDATE** statement all fields listed have at least one edit option. **VALIDATE** and **PROMPT** statements are alternative sites for the edit option codes. You should use a **VALIDATE** statement when the selection and sequencing feature of the **PROMPT** statement is not needed.

FORMATTING THE MONITOR SCREEN

In the foregoing examples, the monitor screen format is automatically determined by NPL by displaying a list of fieldnames from the master file. You may, however, override this format and create your own monitor display.

The keyword **FORM** is like the keyword **HEADING** in Report mode. It is followed by lines of free text surrounded by a pair of quote marks. A simple program has this form:

```
MODIFY
    FORM
    "              text ...

        text <name      text <name

                   text <name

             text...                 "
RUN
```

The display is arranged to fill up to twenty-three lines (up to seventy-eight characters wide) of the monitor screen. You may design the screen to resemble the format of the paper forms which have the raw data. Alternatively, you may design for maximum speed in keying the data.

Use the Edit mode to lay out the **FORM** statement. Whatever text appears on the monitor in the Edit mode is what you see when entering data. The so-called fieldmarkers illustrated above as <name, specify where on the screen the cursor is to pause for the operator to type the data. The screen cursor advances from fieldmarker to fieldmarker as each field is filled. Every field in the master file may appear as a fieldmarker in one DATA-FORM layout. The upper leftmost character position and the lower-right corner of the layout must contain a quote character.

With a **FORM** statement the list of fields is specified by the fieldmarkers, hence the **PROMPT** statement may not be needed. However, the **PROMPT** and **FORM** statements *may* be used together when you wish to control the *sequence* of prompting. Without **PROMPT** the sequence is determined by scanning left-to-right, top-to-bottom across the **FORM**. The **PROMPT** statement can make the cursor move from fieldmarker to fieldmarker around the screen in any pattern.

Thus when a special sequence is needed, you should use **PROMPT** and **FORM** statements (in that order). Edit check codes may be added to the fields in the **PROMPT** statement.

The alternative is to use a **FORM** and a **VALIDATE** statement (in that order), with the edit check codes listed in the **VALIDATE** statement.

DATA-FORM PROGRAMS

Let's look now at the Master files and **DATA-FORM** programs that were used to produce the example screens presented in Chapter 11. First, the CHECKBK master file:

```
FIELD=C/D          , TRANCODE    , A1      , A1     , $
FIELD=NBR          , SERIAL      , I4      , A4     , $
FIELD=YEAR         , YR          , A2      , A2     , $
FIELD=MON          , MO          , A2      , A2     , $
FIELD=DAY          , DA          , A2      , A2     , $
FIELD=CANC/VOID    , CAN         , A1      , A1     , $
FIELD=NAME         , PAYEE       , A25     , A25    , $
FIELD=DESCRIPTION  , ITEM        , A25     , A25    , $
FIELD=ACCOUNT      , CODE        , A4      , A4     , $
FIELD=AMOUNT       , AMT         , F10.2   , A10    , $
FIELD=             , ...         ,         , A1     , $ END-OF-RECORD
```

Next we show the CHECKBK.E exec file.

```
GETFILE CHECKBK

MODIFY

  PROMPT

        TRAN REQ FIL VAL (C D)
         NBR
          MO REQ FIL VAL (01..12)
          DA REQ FIL VAL (01..31)
          YR REQ FIL VAL (82 82)
         CAN VAL (C V '')
        NAME REQ LTR
         AMT REQ
        ITEM REQ
        CODE

  FORM

      "          CHECKBOOK TRANSACTIONS

                  CHECK OR DEPOSIT:<TRAN <NBR

                                   C/D    NBR

        <MO<DA<YR
        __/__/__
        MO DA YR

      <NAME                       $<AMT

      _____     _____
        PAYEE / PAYOR              AMOUNT

      <ITEM                       <CODE

      _____     _____
      DESCRIPTION                 ACCOUNT

                                  <CAN

      C/V

  APPEND
```

In these files notice that the date field has been divided into its three parts to permit range checks of 1 to 12 and 1 to 31 for months and days. The three acceptable values for the CANCEL field are: C for cancelled, V for void check, and a space character for entry of a new check or deposit record.

```
GETFILE CLIENTS

MODIFY

    PROMPT

                    TITLE
                    FIRST  REQ LTR
                    MIDDLE LTR
                 LASTNAME REQ LTR
                   SUFFIX
                      SSN REQ FIL
                   STREET REQ
                     CITY REQ
                    STATE REQ FIL LTR
                  ZIPCODE REQ FIL NBR
                TELEPHONE REQ FIL
                      AGE REQ VAL (14..100)
                      SEX VAL (M F)
                     DEPS REQ VAL (0..12)
                    EDYRS REQ VAL (8..18)
                   WRKYRS REQ VAL (0..40)
                 EMPLOYER REQ
                      INC REQ VAL (0..500)
                     ACNO REQ FIL
                      TYP REQ VAL (MMKT MARG FUND BOND)
                     SIZE REQ VAL (0..500)
    FORM

"......................CLIENT  INFORMATION........................

Name :<TITLE    <FIRST.........  <MI   <LAST.........  <SUFFIX
      ------    ---------------   -    ---------------  ------
      Mr,Mrs,Ms                                        Jr,Esq,Phd

Social Security Number:<SSN           Telephone:<TELEPHONE
                       ___ __ ____               ___ __ ____

       <STREET          <CITY            <ST    <ZIP
       ---------------  ---------------   ---    ------
       Street Address   City             State  Zip Code

               Age:<AGE            Annual Income :<INC    ,000
               Sex:<SEX                              ---
Number of Dependents:<DEPS         Account Number:<ACNO
Years of Education  :<EDYRS                        ----
Years of Employment :<WRKYRS       Account Type  :<TYP
                                                   ---
       Employer:<EMPLOYER          Account Amount:<SIZE  ,000
       --------------------                        ---         "
RUN
```

The CLIENTS.E **DATA-FORM** program above includes both the **PROMPT** and **FORM** statements. When this is so, you must ensure that all the desired fieldnames (or aliases) appear in each statement (and only once in each). Between the quote mark on the first line of the **FORM** statement and the one on the last line, the text can say anything. Following each bracket, < , there must be a fieldname referring to the above **PROMPT** lines.

Notice the rows of dots after some of the fieldmarkers. These are not required, but are suggested as a way to remind yourself how long the fields are. The dots extend the fieldmarker out to the full field length—see the **FILE** format in the master file. The dots are not visible at run time because they are covered by the data entry field.

RUN vs. APPEND

Either one of the Keywords **RUN** or **APPEND** may be used to initiate the running of the **DATA-FORM** program. When the purpose of the **DATA-FORM** exec is to enter new records, use the Keyword **APPEND** to bring up a blank screen. When data editing is the purpose, use **RUN**, which brings up the screen filled with the first record in the datafile, and waits for you to search for other records. **RUN** performs like **APPEND** when no datafile exists.

RUN and **APPEND** are alternative commands. With **APPEND** the DATA-FORM session begins at the *end* of the file, with an empty screen; however, pressing the **Exit** key takes you to the top of the file. With **RUN** the session starts at the top of the file, yet you can then type the **APPEND** command to get to the end of the file. When an Index file is **SELECT**ed, *top* of the file means at the first **INDEX**ed value.

TESTING A DATA-FORM PROGRAM

When you have completed the writing of a DATA-FORM program and are leaving the Edit mode, assign a name to the file which suggests the Exec program is for data entry rather than for report writing. For example: NEW-CASE.E, NUCLIENT.E, NEWRECRD.E.

Next, enter the NPL system, and before executing the DATA-FORM program, type the command **ECHO ON**, so you can see each step of the Exec as it is read by NPL. NPL examines your CLIENTS.E exec file in great detail. If an error is found in your Exec program, a message appears below the line being examined. After such a message, you may press **RETURN** to continue processing or press **Exit** key to return to Command mode. Continuation allows you to see other error messages that may occur; thus you may have to revise the CLIENTS.E file only once.

The possible error messages	*Some possible errors in the Exec program*
• INVALID CHECK TYPE:	The option list code is not **REQ, FIL, NBR, LTR, VAL**, or **NOC**.
• ONLY 160 CHECKS ALLOWED:	A range check counts as one, and each value check item counts as one. The limit is on the total for all fields.
• NAME NOT IN MASTER FILE:	A misspelled fieldname or alias in the **PROMPT**, **FORM**, or **VALIDATE** statement.
• FIELD ALREADY PROMPTED:	A duplicate use of a field in the **PROMPT** statement.
• FIELD ALREADY ENTERED IN FORM:	A duplicate use of a field in the **FORM** statement.
• FIELD MISSING FROM FORM:	A field in the **PROMPT** statement does not appear in the **FORM**.
• VARIABLE HAS NO PROMPT:	A field in the **FORM** statement does not appear in the **PROMPT** statement.
• FORM TOO WIDE:	**FORM** width exceeds seventy-eight columns.
• TOO MANY LINES IN FORM:	**FORM** length exceeds twenty-three lines.

In the event of an error, if you allow the processing to run to completion, NPL attempts to bring up a DATA-FORM screen display, notwithstanding the errors. Sometimes this helps you to discover what is wrong in the Exec file. In any case, NPL does not allow you to proceed in filling the screen, for the resultant **DATA-FORM** might damage the datafile. You must correct the Exec file first, and then try to execute it.

To leave NPL to correct any mistakes, type **FIN**, and then enter the EDITOR mode. Bring the **NPL:CLIENTS.E** file into the Editor. You may have to repeat these steps more than once before the DATA-FORM program works correctly.

This chapter introduced these keywords:

```
MODIFY
PROMPT
FORM
VALIDATE
RUN
REQ
FIL
NBR
LTR
VAL
NOC
```

CHAPTER 13

TECHNIQUES FOR BETTER RESULTS

This chapter discusses a variety of programming issues. It assumes you have studied the rest of the preceding chapters and may have practiced using NPL on your computer. The examples used here only begin to suggest the many additional ways that NPL may be employed to turn your data into useful information.

COPYING FILES

The **COPYFILE** command is used to copy one or more files of alphanumeric data into a single file, as in this example:

```
C>COPYFILE SALES81 + SALES82 TO SALES
```

Another way to copy a datafile is first to set up the output channel with the **DISK:** command and then to use the **TYPEFILE** command.

```
C>DISK:NEWDISK/CLIENT.D

C>TYPEFILE CLIENT.D
```

The copy may be placed on a different diskette, or, if a different name is used, the copy may be placed on the same diskette.

Also you can copy a file by use of the **HOLD** keyword. Simply mention all the fieldnames in a print statement followed by the phrase "**AND HOLD AS** newname." A new master file is also created. This process is most useful when you wish the new file to contain only a portion of the records in the original file. You can use the **SELECT** command and the **IF** phrase to determine which records are copied.

Two warnings are needed:

- If the length of, the number of, or the order of the records is changed in the process discussed above, any Index files that may exist for the original datafile will not work with the new datafile and therefore the Index files should not also be copied. (Index files can be copied only with the **DISK:** and **TYPEFILE** commands, as shown above.)

- The new datafile will have a different record length than the original file if any of the PRINTING format codes have a different width than the corresponding FILE format codes.

Remember that the PRINTING format width may be arbitrarily large, to suit the needs of report formats, but when **HOLD** is used the PRINTING format *determines* the FILE format widths of the new file. Therefore, when using **HOLD** to copy files, the FILE format and PRINTING format should have the same width. You may change the PRINTING format widths in the Edit mode at any time. Do not change the FILE formats.

EXPANDING THE RECORD DEFINITION

When the need arises you may add new fields to a file. First define the new field and assign blank or zero values. Then follow the copying procedure mentioned above, adding the new fieldnames to the verb object list. For example, to add the client's birthday and the spouse's name to the CLIENTS file:

```
DEFINE
   BIRTHDAY/A6  = ' '
   SPOUSE/A15   = ' '.

PRINT  PREFIX FN MI LN SUFX SSN
       STR CTY ST ZP PHONE
       AGE SEX DEPS BIRTHDAY SPOUSE
       EDYRS WRKYRS EMP INC
       ACNO TYP SIZE
AND HOLD AS TEMP.
```

Next, delete the old CLIENTS.D file, and rename TEMP master and datafiles to CLIENTS. Then delete any CLIENTS.I files and rebuild the Index files.

You could also add a dummy field of, say, twelve characters filled with blanks. Then at a later date you could divide this one new field into several smaller fields. By planning for such a change you can avoid copying a large file a second time. To add the new fieldnames, you would use the Edit mode to revise the master file. The A12 dummy field could be replaced by two dates each with A6 format, or by three numeric quantities with formats of (I4, A4);

or even by twelve new fields of a single character each. It is important only that the sum of the FILE format widths equal the width of the original dummy field.

EXTENDING A FILE

The number of records in a file may be increased by using a property of the **SELECT** command. Suppose you have a small test file and wish to expand it. Perhaps the content of the records is of no importance to you; you simply want more records for use in testing a new exec program. If the file is CLIENTS, create an Index file for ACNO, then **SELECT** repeated records, and **HOLD** them as a new file, e.g.:

```
C>GETFILE CLIENTS
C>INDEX ACNO
C>SELECT ACNO = LO THRU HI, LO THRU HI.
C>PRINT PREFX FN MI LN SUFX SSN
        STR CTY ST ZP PHONE
        AGE SEX DEPS
        EDYRS WRKYRS EMP INC
        ACNO TYP SIZE
        AND HOLD.
```

CHOOSING DATA FORMATS

Before creating a new master file, you should consider carefully the data formats to be used. The choice between alphanumeric (**A** format), integer (**I** format), real or floating point numbers (**F** format), and high-precision decimal values (**D** format) may be evident, but there are considerations about field width and FILE formats which are worth reviewing here.

The following should be taken as guidelines, to be followed if there is no good reason to do otherwise.

- Fields upon which sums and computations will never be performed should be alphanumeric, even if they contain all numeric characters, like zip, telephone, and SSN.

- On the other hand, for numeric codes with many leading zeros that you wish to *avoid* entering in DATA-FORM mode, use Integer format to

187

right-justify the digits in the field. For example, these codes become integers:

0034	34
0702	702
0021500	21500

- Any field which is a measure of something, like AGE, WEIGHT, or DISTANCE, should be integer or floating point. See Numbers and Numeric Codes, below.

- Alphanumeric fields should have identical PRINTING and FILE formats, except when the PRINTING width is varied for special display effects.

- Keep the width of FILE formats small to save disk storage space; in particular, fields which you expect to be sort keys, in order to minimize sorting time.

- For numeric fields, decide first on the FILE format width. Then choose the PRINTING format width to handle the largest column total you would expect on a report. Include a position for a negative sign in both formats even though the values may always be positive.

- As an exception to the above, remember that if you use the **HOLD** option to create new data and master files, the PRINTING format width in the original master file becomes the FILE format width in the new master. Thus if you intend to create a new file from an old one using the **HOLD** option, and then use the same master file for both datafiles, be sure that the PRINTING and FILE format widths are the same.

- When using a screening **IF** phrase to test the value of *fld* against the first field **IN** *filename*, only the first **n** characters of each record are used, where **n** is the PRINTING format width of *fld*. Be sure that the desired first field has the same FILE format as **fld**.

- Occasionally you may want to shorten a long alphanumeric PRINTING format for a particular report, using, for example (A15, A30) as the two formats for COMPANY NAME. This causes the first fifteen characters to be printed and anything beyond that to be ignored.

• A similar thing can be done to skip over unwanted characters, or blank fields, which follow an alphanumeric field. Suppose you have a record with three blank characters after the ZIP code. Choose the two formats as (A5, A8). The FILE format of A8 accounts for the characters that actually exist, while the PRINTING format of A5 causes only the ZIP code to be printed in reports. This means you avoid an extra field in the master file, for skipping the three blanks, with a consequent saving of space in the computer memory. Do not do this with numeric PRINTING formats I and F unless the characters to be skipped are certain to be blank, i.e., space characters.

• Integer formats are for small quantities (from −32768 to +32767). When values do not require precision, as for budgets, estimates, and forecasts, you may scale the values and still use integer formats. For example, financial forecasts are often presented in thousands (or millions) of dollars. Use fieldnames like: SALES(000) and INCOME(000) to indicate that the data value is to be followed by three zeros. Thus the data item with an I5 format can represent up to 32 millions of dollars.

• F format provides numeric precision to six decimals, while D format will handle 11 billion dollars, precise to the penny.

• If you think there is an error in your datafile, use the **TYPEFILE** command to transfer it to the monitor or to the printer so you can compare the records with the record format specified in the master file. Double-check the FILE formats, and verify the total number of characters per record (including the end-of-record character).

Real Numbers, Large and Small

Real numbers may be printed with as many as six decimal places. Although a PRINTING format of F12.4 would allow four fractional positions, these positions are not precisely correct for large numbers. Consider this listing of two numbers, where N equals successive powers of ten, and X = −1.23456 x N. The computer prints values of X as follows:

N	X
1	−1.2346
10	−12.3456
100	−123.4560
1,000	−1234.5599
10,000	−12345.5986
100,000	−123455.9922
1,000,000	−1234559.8750

The inaccuracy in X is a consequence of the computer's internal binary representation of floating point numbers, which limits the precision of all values to about one part in eight million. Thus, in decimal format only the first six significant digits are certain to be without error.

In the case of the Apple Pascal operating system and other UCSD operating systems a convention is used that causes floating point numbers to be printed in the so-called *engineering format* (or scientific format) whenever you specify a PRINTING format with no fractional positions (e.g., F6.0, F12, F20.0, F4). In engineering format, the last line in the example above would appear as:

1.0E6	−1.23456E6

where the characters **E6** mean the first part is to be multiplied by ten raised to the sixth power, that is, one million.

This format may look strange to those who are not engineers, and it has the disadvantage of causing wider columns in your report when your formats are narrow. A way of avoiding the engineering format display, if your values are in the millions or above, is to scale the field by a factor sufficient to reduce the values to under one million. You can still obtain six-decimal precision in the numbers, using the F format codes. Typical values will appear as 11.678, 1.593, or 0.0354; representing, in order, $11,678,000, $1,593,000, and $35,400.

A different problem arises with very small numbers. Consider another table of two numbers, where N equals successive powers of ten, and $Y = -1.23456/N$.

N	Y
1	-1.234560
10	-.123456
100	-.012346
1,000	-.001235
10,000	-.000123
100,000	-.000012
1,000,000	-.000001
10,000,000	-.000000

In this case any error in the displayed value is due to the display width of nine characters (F9.6). The internal representation is precise to about six decimals.

Finally, take note that with APPLE and UCSD Pascal operating systems not only does the engineering format appear in your reports when data values become very large or very small, but also this format is written into **HOLD** files. This is not a problem if the PRINTING format has sufficient width. Otherwise, the field boundaries of HOLD.D will be violated and reports written from it will appear skewed or full of mysterious characters. If you suspect that this has happened, **TYPE** out a portion of the HOLD.D file and check the alignment of fields from record to record. Then recreate the **HOLD** file using wider PRINTING formats. The safest choice is to allow at least seven positions to the left of the decimal point to provide space for sign and six digits in the HOLD.D file. A character position is reserved for the sign even though the data values are always positive.

Numbers and Numeric Codes

The following data items may appear to have the same numeric value:

```
1
 1
  1
 01
```

yet if they appear in a field with an alphanumeric PRINTING format, each is different, because the blank spaces themselves have a value. Let "**b**" be used here to represent a blank or space character.

Thus, the data items are:

```
1bb
b1b
bb1
b01
```

Now, it is certain that these items have different values. Naturally if you are searching for a *numeric* value of one, you will not find it among these items. On the other hand, if you change the PRINTING format to I3, with the above items stored on the disk (FILE format = A3), the computer transforms all four items into the numeric value of one. When the items are printed they appear right-justified in the three-character field and the leading zero is suppressed.

When data items are entered into a file in DATA-FORM by persons who should not have to be concerned with the above distinctions, it is important for you to anticipate potential sources of error. For example, proper entries for an AGE field with format of I2 are:

Proper Entries	Data Stored	Derived Value(I2)
7	7b	7
32	32	32
4	4b	4
2	2b	2
10	10	10

If AGE is to be a sort field, an **INDEX** key, or a screening **IF** phrase field, then the PRINTING format must be I2 to avoid the wrong interpretation of the blank characters.

CHANGING A MASTER FILE

After a datafile has been built, you may change the names and format codes in its master file, provided only that the sum of the FILE format widths remains equal to the number of characters in a record.

Changing PRINTING formats and fieldnames is an aid to designing reports. Changing aliases may be needed to avoid duplicate names. FILE formats do not normally change, except in cases where you want to reassign the characters represented by them to other fields. For example, you could replace a group of fields by one skip field (i.e., a dummy field). You could also assign a group name, which would then be used to retrieve groups of data items (packed side by side). There are several uses for this:

- If the codes for Age, Race, and Sex are side by side in the record, renaming them as a group called ARS would permit you to build a single Index file using the combined codes.

- City, State, and ZIP can be treated as a single field, if state codes are stored in an A3 field to provide a space between ST and ZIP.

- Skipping a large number of fields which are infrequently used leaves more room for defined fields by reducing the number of active Master file names.

- Long account numbers, with names for sub-elements, like FUND, DIV, DEPT, OBJECT, may usually be printed as one string of characters.

Most important is the situation when the data record has more than the maximum number of data items allowed by the system, say, 150 or 200, as with large survey questionnaires. Skip fields are used to deactivate large portions of the record at a time. Alternatively, clusters of characters representing several survey responses (often single-character codes) can be printed in groups, with a fieldname for each group.

The latter idea, of clusters of one-character items, also may be used with DATA-FORM mode for entering data records of many items. A special master file of up to, say, 100 clusters of data items could be used when the maximum number of fields allowed is 100. Instructions on the screen (in the **FORM** statement) would identify the individual items.

For reporting, survey forms of, say, 180 items divided into three sections of sixty questions each could be handled with three master files called SURVEY1.M, SURVEY2.M, SURVEY3.M. Each would skip the fields that are active in the others. To activate a particular master file for use with the single datafile SURVEY.D, use the command:

```
GETFILE (SURVEY) SURVEY2.
```

TIME AND SPACE

As your use of NPL grows you will employ more and more of its features. Most likely, you will add more fieldnames, define more new variables, and try more elaborate sorts and displays. Each new step should come easily to you, but the cumulative effect of many new requirements may push the capacity of the computer to its limits. Therefore, it is well for you to understand these limits and how you might get around them.

The essence of a nonprocedural language is that you need only state what output information and formats you want, without specifying how the computer should proceed in order to meet your requests. Nevertheless, a little knowledge about just how the software does process requests can help you improve its overall performance. For example, you may be able to avoid making requests that would be very inefficient and time consuming.

In some cases, NPL places no limits, or the limit is so high as to have no practical effect on your choices. Most limits are a function of the size of the memory for a particular computer. There are no limits on the number of characters in a record nor on the number of records which may be in a file. Field widths may be as wide as 999 characters. There are, of course, practical limits, like the number of records, or characters, that fit on particular disks.

For computers with up to 128,000 characters of computer memory, typical limits are:

- No more than 100 active names, i.e., master file fieldnames plus **DE-FINE**d names plus **COMPUTE** names

- No more than ten **BY** fields in a Report request

- No more than thirty verb objects

- No more than 160 check values in DATA-FORM mode

Of greater importance than these individual limits, however, is the overall limit of computer storage and memory space, and how it affects what you can accomplish with NPL. There are two space dimensions: disk storage space and the random access, or RAM, memory of 64K to 256K characters or more. You can overcome disk space limits by adding more disk drives. RAM memory, also called the main memory, or core memory by old-timers, cannot be expanded as readily.

If a complex NPL request runs into a space limit due to the memory capacity of the computer, you can usually achieve the desired result by breaking the request into two or more simpler ones. You are trading time for memory space. Each of the simpler steps, by using the **HOLD** feature described in Chapter 7, creates an intermediate, and perhaps smaller, file to be used in the next step. The last step prints your report. For example, screening and sorting the records may be done in one step, while summing, computing complex functions, and formatting the ultimate report may have separate steps.

SORTING LARGE FILES

Sorting of records into the order requested, through your choice of **BY** phrases, is the single most demanding operation with respect to memory space. It should be helpful for you to understand how NPL sorts records.

As an analogy, suppose you are given an encyclopedia and a list of fifty historical events, such as the publication of the following:
- the Declaration of Independence
- the Magna Carta
- the Monroe Doctrine
- the Emancipation Proclamation
- the United Nations Charter
- the Treaty of Versailles
- the Treaty of Kent
- the Gutenberg Bible
- the Yalta Agreements

etc....

Now you are asked for a brief description of each document, to be copied from the encyclopedia onto a sheet of paper *in chronological order.* You may write the information only once.

Unless you can perform the difficult feat of retrieving from your own memory the fifty dates, you would most likely proceed as follows. First, look up each event and record its date, together with the page number for its description. Only after you have a complete list of dates and page references would you be able to pick the earliest event, find the text, and write the brief description. You would then repeat this sequence for each successive event.

When NPL reads a request like

```
GETFILE EVENTS, BY DATE PRINT NAME AND ...
```

it follows such a procedure. NPL reads the EVENTS.D datafile, and it writes into computer memory each date and the physical location on the diskette of each record. Thus NPL reads the whole file once to create in RAM memory a **sort key table.** DATE is the sort key, and the table holds the location of each record of a particular date. Moreover, the dates are stored in numerical order.

Next NPL uses the sort key table in main memory to retrieve, in chronological order, of course, each record for printing a report. At no time during the sorting process is the datafile read into the RAM memory; only the sort key table is stored in computer memory.

Sorting is a two-step process: (1) find and store the keys and the record location, (2) fetch and print the records in sorted order. If the file is large, the process can take a lot of time. There are choices you can make, however, to mimimize the time required to complete the first step.

It should be evident that for large files and a small computer, the sort key tables will not fit into the available space in main memory. The main memory must hold the software for the operating system and for the active parts of NPL. The space available for the sort keys may, for example, be only 5000

195

characters. The next section, however, explains that the size of a file that may be sorted is not limited to this RAM memory limit.

EXTERNAL SORTING

When the memory limit is reached during a sort, NPL shifts into a different mode, called *external sorting*, because the external memory, that is, disk storage, is used. Consider this analogy.

You are asked to hold some playing cards in your hand, always keeping them sorted by suit and by rank, as you are dealt one card at a time. If the process continues through several decks of cards, at sixty cards or so you will have to put the stack of sorted cards down. You would then continue to hold and sort the new cards into a second stack.

Later you can merge the two stacks into a completely sorted stack. If you could place the two stacks on a table, you should be able to continue indefinitely; that is, sorting a stack of sixty cards in your hand, then merging that stack into the larger sorted stack on the table.

In the example, the limited capacity of your hand corresponds to the finite memory of the computer, and the table performs the function of the external memory, i.e., the disk storage. It holds the table of keys already sorted while sorting continues. To do this, NPL creates a temporary file called NPSORT.DATA on one of your disks (the one with the most unused space). If you see such a file listed in your disk directory, you may remove it, for it has served its purpose.

There is no question that external sorting is a slow process, yet it does allow you to sort almost any number of records. The only limit is the amount of disk space available for the NPSORT.DATA file. (A rule for estimating the required space is discussed under Disk Space Management in this chapter).

Just how slow is external sorting and what can you do about it? The number of "sort/merge" cycles, that is, sorting the keys from a portion of the file and then merging them with the existing, partially sorted key table, depends on three factors:

- the size of the work space available in computer memory

- the length of the sort keys

- the number of records and the number with unique keys

You may be able to influence these factors and thus speed up the sorting process.

196

Available Memory Space

First, consider the memory work space. There are many elements in a complex Report mode request that compete for the available space; for example (in approximate order of importance):

- the number of definitions stored in **DEFINE** mode

- the number of **COMPUTE** phrase definitions

- the number of fieldnames stored in the master file

- the number of characters stored for the report heading

- **SELECT** and **IF** phrase criteria

- **EXEC** mode requires extra space

- **PRINTER:** and **DISK:** commands also use space

After these memory requirements have been met by NPL, sorting must work with whatever space remains.

To begin, you should use the commands **CLEAR DEFINE** and **CLEAR SELECT** to recover space used by the **DEFINE** and **SELECT** modes. Further, you can increase the space available for sorting by employing a separate request just for sorting or even using screening with sorting to reduce the number of records. An initial request would reduce the number of records to be sorted by using **SELECT** and **IF** criteria to find the desired records. Only then would it sort and **HOLD** them. A second request would **DEFINE** new variables, summarize the records, and **PRINT** the report.

Sort Keylength

The effect of the choice of sort keys upon the sorting capacity of a computer is illustrated here with some examples.

The sort keylength is computed by adding the lengths of each **BY** field in the NPL request. The length of each alpha field is the length of its FILE format. The length of a **D** format field is eight. The length of each integer field is two and the length of each real field is four. In addition the sort keylength must be rounded up to an even number, if any **BY** field is an integer, and, if any **BY** field is a real number, rounded up to the next number divisible by four.

For example, consider some requests which use **BY** fields selected from the following list:

Fieldname	Type	Internal Keylength
CUSTOMER	alpha	20
AGE	integer	2
RACE	alpha	2
SEX	alpha	1
REGION	alpha	5
SALES	real	4
AMOUNT	dollar	8

request: **BY CUSTOMER BY REGION**

keys: JONES, B R   NORTH
             GREENSPAHN, JOS.   EAST
characters |<--------20-------->|<-5->| keylength = 25

request: **BY AGE, BY RACE, BY SEX**

keys: 34 WH F
           22 BL M
characters: | 2| 2|1| (5 + 1 = 6)   keylength = 6

request: **BY REGION BY SALES**

keys: NORTH 23462
           SOUTH 41105
characters |<-5->|<-4->| (9 + 3 = 12)   keylength = 12

Short keylengths are desirable. The shorter the keylength the more records can be sorted within main memory, and thus, for large files, fewer cycles of sorting and merging are needed.

You may shorten the keylength in four ways:

• You may drop nonessential **BY** fields.

• If extra **BY** fields are used to achieve certain report formats, use only the essential fields for sorting, **HOLD** the results, and then print the report with the extra **BY** fields and the **NOSORT** option.

• In some cases it may be sufficient to sort on only the first five or ten characters of a name field. You can:

```
DEFINE SHORTNAM/A10 = NAME.
```

And then sort **BY** SHORTNAM.

• If there is a choice between sorting on a name and a unique code, choose the code. Examples are: State names and two-letter codes (MISSOURI, MO); department names and abbreviations (Pediatrics, PEDS); inventory parts names and abbreviations.

Unique Keys

Many of the uses of sorting are not just to rank or to alphabetize records but rather to order them into groups: **BY** SEX or **BY** AGEGROUP or **BY** REGION or **BY** DEPT, etc. After clustering records into groups, or categories, each group of records may be displayed in full detail, or, more often, you will summarize the data in the cluster of records in order to write one line on a report. You may sum or average or find the minimum and maximum values for the group.

In such applications the number of unique keys may be quite small. **BY** SEX has only two unique key values. **BY** AGEGROUP **BY** RACE **BY** SEX may have only 5 x 4 x 2, or 40, unique values. When this is so, the length of the key is not important.

The number of records that can be sorted in main memory depends upon the memory space available, the keylength, and the uniqueness of the keys in the file. The actual number lies somewhere between the following two extreme situations.

a. All keys in the file are unique

```
Number of records = memory space available
                    divided by (keylength + 14)
```

b. Only one unique key

```
Number of records = memory space available
                    divided by 6
```

199

You may ask NPL for the memory available with this command:

```
C>MEMORY?
```

Thus, if memory available is 6000 bytes, to sort the file **BY** DIVISION with a ten-character keylength:

a. All unique keys • 6000/(10+14) = 250
b. One unique key • 6000/6 = 1000

The actual value lies between 250 and 1000 records.

SELECT a Sorted View of the File

Finally, you can reduce sorting time for large files with the use of Index files. One purpose of an Index file is to define a subfile; another is to provide quick and direct access to one or a few records. An equally important function of an Index file is to provide a sorted view of a datafile by storing, more or less permanently, a sort key table. (To **INDEX** a particular field of a file, NPL uses the same process of building a sort key table and the temporary NPSORT.DATA file, as discussed above for sorting). Indexing differs in that no report is written, and the NPSORT.DATA information is saved as a special Index file.

Use the **SELECT** command to activate an Index file, and then you can write a report using the sort sequence of the Index file. That is, if you use the command **SELECT** SSN. and then request a report using the single sort field **BY** SSN, NPL bypasses the sort phase and uses the Index file to read the datafile in SSN order. The resulting report is the same. The time to write it may be very much less than if sorting were done.

It is inefficient to attempt to **SELECT** an Index for one **BY** field and then to expect sorting by the other **BY** fields. Since NPL will have to sort anyway, the accessing of the records using the superfluous Index will actually make the request run slower. Thus Index files are an aid in report writing when only one **BY** phrase is needed, or when a subfile can be defined with the **SELECT** command.

Remember, however, that Index files are not limited, in themselves, to a single field. You could combine adjacent fields in the master file, say, AGEGROUP, RACE CODE, and SEX into a single master file field called ARS, provided the three fields are adjacent, by revising the master file using the Edit mode.

Then the commands

```
C>GETFILE EMPLOYEE
C>INDEX ARS
```

produce a file called EMPLOYEE.I.ARS. With this file you can prepare a report as follows

```
C>SELECT ARS.
C>BY ARS
R>WRITE AVE.SALARY MAX.SALARY MIN.SALARY.
```

The components of ARS are written as a single field. Even more options are available to you by **INDEX**ing on a **DEFINE**d variable (see Chapter 9).

Actual Sort Order

Here is a simple rule to remember. When the records of a file are already stored in the desired order, include the word **NOSORT** in the request, but also use **BY** phrases in the regular way. **NOSORT** causes NPL simply to skip the sorting phase and to read the datafile directly. Thus the lines in the report appear in the same order as the records in the file. The **BY** phrases affect the format of the report, even though sorting is not performed.

Use Short Keys for Sorting

Short sort keys lead to shorter sorting times. (Repeat rapidly out loud). The effect is important, of course, only with large files. Here are some things you can do.

Sort by last name only, or by a field defined as **CLIP(LN)+FN**. For most printed lists, however, you can use a rough sort, on, say, the first six, or maybe ten, characters of the last name or a company name. Use: **DEFINE** SHORT/A6=COMPANY. Then sort, **BY** SHORT.

The same thing applies to creating an Index file for a large field, but since the Indexed field is in the master file you must use a trick. Before using the command

```
C> INDEX COMPANY
```

make a temporary change to the master file (in the **Edit** mode). Shorten both formats for the field COMPANY, and insert a skip field as the next field:

```
change this:    FIELD = COMPANY   ,NAME   ,A25  ,A25  ,$


to this:        FIELD = COMPANY   ,NAME   ,A6   ,A6   ,$
                FIELD =            ,        ,     ,A19  ,$
```

The two File format widths must add to the original 25.

Next, build the Index file, and then return to the original master file. You can get as fine a sorting of names as you need by adjusting the length of the key field.

Another use of this technique is to use only the first three characters of the ZIP code and then sort on ZIP3 or **INDEX** ZIP3. The Post Office requires only three digit sorting on bulk mailings. Similar results can be achieved by **INDEX**ing a **DEFINE**d variable, which is discussed in Chapter 9.

DISK SPACE MANAGEMENT

Sorting large files requires both time and disk space. If you are not careful, a sort request could run for a while and then fail because you did not provide enough disk space for the computer to do its work.

Most large files require external sorting, that is, NPL creates the temporary work file, called NPSORT (or a similar name, depending on the operating system). This file is placed on the disk with the most unused space. UCSD Pascal operating systems allocate half of the unused space to NPSORT. The most demanding case is when the sort key is a large part of the record length and every record has a unique key. The work file may be almost as large as the datafile. When many records have the same key and the keylength is short, NPSORT may be only a small fraction of the size of the datafile. It will take experience to be able to estimate the disk space requirement for your files. You should take notes for various cases until you are confident of your estimates.

The disk space problem is compounded, of course, when you sort and then **HOLD** the file. The purpose of holding the file and printing the report in a second step is to make available the maximum amount of computer memory for sorting. Yet the **HOLD** file requires additional disk space, which could limit the disk available for the NPSORT file.

You should use the **DIRECTORY** command to find out what disk space is available. You may be able to direct the **HOLD** file to a particular disk, with the **AS** phrase, thereby resolving the particular conflict with the NPSORT file.

This will be so when you are certain that the **HOLD** file will be smaller than the original datafile (due to screening and/or summing). NPL can only assume the **HOLD** file will be the same size, and hence it reserves that amount of disk space.

Rules for Sorting

In summary, when working with large files you may reduce sorting time by following some of these suggestions.

• Use **NOSORT** when the datafile is stored in the desired order.

• If the datafile is changed only infrequently, and a particular sort sequence is used regularly for reports, then either sort and hold the file in that sequence or use **INDEX** and **SELECT** to provide the desired file views.

• When using an Index file for a sorted view do not use secondary **BY** fields.

• Keep the sort keylength short.

• Screen, sort, and **HOLD** in one request, and leave **DEFINE**s, **HEAD-INGs**, and printing to a separate request.

UPDATING A FILE

The data in some files do not change, for example, the 1980 Census files and stock market quotations for particular dates; i.e., all files of historical statistics are static files. Many files, however, are constantly changing in order to retain the most current information. There are four kinds of file changes:

• changed values which create new records

• additional values which replace old data in existing records

• new data which are added to old totals to form new cumulative totals

• deletion of cancelled or inactive records

These changes may be accomplished in the DATA-FORM mode, with commands like **INSERT, APPEND, INPUT**, and **DELETE**. Also, records may be deleted while copying a file, using an **IF** phrase.

As a further alternative, let's discuss a general purpose means for creating a file of changes, which is used periodically to update another file. You might, for example, build a file of changes during each day and then run an Exec program in the evening to revise the previous datafile.

The file of changes is called a transaction file, and we'll call the file to be changed the permanent file. Let's choose the names TRANS.D and PERM.D for these two datafiles. The benefits of creating a transaction file, rather than directly editing the permanent file, are:

- special error-testing reports from the transaction file provide better control of the accuracy of the datafile

- an *audit trail* may be kept on all file changes

- if damaged, the permanent file can be recreated from the transaction file and an earlier backup copy of the permanent file

When files are large or sensitive, or when they affect financial decisions, effective controls on the entry of new data are imperative. It is not a good idea to allow casual corrections or changes to be made to such files. Many people prefer to have a printed copy of all transactions and reports showing the records changed in the permanent file, in addition to retaining a copy of the transaction file for a few months.

The process is cyclic, perhaps daily or weekly, as illustrated:

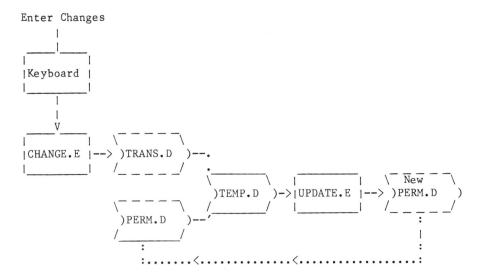

A DATA-FORM Exec program, called CHANGE.E, for example, is used to enter the new information, appending it to the transaction file, TRANS.D. UPDATE.E is a Report mode program (which you must write) to merge the old and new data. Before running the UPDATE.E program, you must create a temporary datafile, called TEMP.D, which contains both the permanent and the transaction data—in that order. To append one file to another and store the results in a file called TEMP.D. use this command:

```
C>COPYFILE PERM + TRANS TO (TEMP)PERM
```

If the files are on different disks, you should prefix each name with the volume name or number.

Next, your UPDATE.E exec is run, using the new file, which has both the permanent and the transaction records in it. For this process to work you must follow these rules:

- TRANS.D and PERM.D must have the same record length, that is, contain the same number of characters.

- The fields to be updated must be in the same character positions in both files.

- To accomplish the above, the PERM.M master file may be used as the master for both the transaction and the permanent files.

- When combining the two files into the TEMP.D file, the PERM.D records must come first.

- The TRANS.D data fields either are blank or contain values to replace or to be added to the corresponding PERM.D data items.

- Each record must contain a unique keyfield to identify the correct record to be changed.

The updating process can be explained best by using an example. Suppose that the people in your office record their working hours once a week. The form for recording staff hours might look as follows:

```
|  _____  |
| |                                                                       | |
| | WEEK ENDING:   ___   ___   ___                                        | |
| |                 MM    DD    YY                                        | |
| |                                                                       | |
| | EMPLOYEE NUMBER: ____                                                 | |
| |                                                                       | |
| |    REGULAR HOURS ____.__         OVERTIME HOURS ____.__               | |
| |                                                                       | |
| | SICK LEAVE HOURS ____.__         VACATION HOURS ____.__               | |
| |_____| |
```

Let the permanent file of year-to-date data be TOTHOURS.D, and the transaction file be WEEK.D.
Here are the two master files:

```
                        TOTHOURS . M

FIELD =EMPNBR          , END    , A3    , A3   , $
FIELD =DATE            , DATE   , A6    , A6   , $
FIELD =NAME            , NAME   , A20   , A20  , $
FIELD =YTD HOURS       , REGHRS , F5.1  , A5   , $
FIELD =YTD OVERTIME    , OVRTM  , F5.1  , A5   , $
FIELD =YTD SICKTIME    , SICHR  , F5.1  , A5   , $
FIELD =YTD VACATION    , VACHR  , F5.1  , A5   , $
FIELD =                , ...    ,       , A1   , $ END-OF-RECORD


                        WEEK . M

FIELD =EMPNBR          , ENO    , A3    , A3   , $
FIELD =MONTH           , MM     , A2    , A2   , $
FIELD =DAY             , DD     , A2    , A2   , $
FIELD =YEAR            , YY     , A2    , A2   , $
FIELD =                ,        ,       , A20  , $
FIELD =HOURS           , REGHR  , F5.1  , A5   , $
FIELD =OVERTIME        , OVRTM  , F5.1  , A5   , $
FIELD =SICKTIME        , SICHR  , F5.1  , A5   , $
FIELD =VACATION        , VACHR  , F5.1  , A5   , $
FIELD =                , ...    ,       , A1   , $ END-OF-RECORD
```

The **EXEC** program for entering the weekly data looks like this:

```
GETFILE  WEEK
MODIFY
FORM

"    WEEK  ENDING:     <MM   <DD   <YY
                       ----  ----  ----
                        MM    DD    YY

        EMPLOYEE  NUMBER:     <EMPNBR
                               - - -

        REGULAR  HOURS:       <REGHR
                               - - . -

        SICK  LEAVE  HOURS:   <SICHR
                               - - . -

        OVERTIME  HOURS:      <OVRTM
                               - - . -

        VACATION  HOURS:      <VACHR
                               - - . -              "


APPEND
```

The file TEMP.D is first formed by appending WEEK.D to TOTHOURS.D.

Now picture the two kinds of records in the combined file: ("ytd" stands for "year-to-date")

Permanent Record: TOTHOURS

empnbr	previous date	name	ytd hrs	ytd ovr	ytd sck	ytd vac

Transaction Record: WEEK

empnbr	date	blank	hrs	ovr	sck	vac

The UPDATE.E program must sort the combined file by EMPNBR, after which each transaction record follows the corresponding permanent record. Some sample records might appear as follows:

391	041682	ABERNATHY, R	520	0	0	80
391	042382		34	0	6	0
396	041682	QUEEG, K	592	24	8	0
396	042382		40	6	0	0
397	041682	LAMBERT, H	544	0	16	40
397	042382		0	0	0	40

A new permanent file is created with this request:

```
GETFILE (TEMP)TOTHOURS

WRITE LST.DATE FST.NAME
      SUM.HOURS SUM.OVERTIME SUM.SICK SUM.VACA
BY EMPNBR
AND HOLD AS TOTHOURS.
```

This single NPL request performs the sort which brings each employee's records together and creates the new permanent file. The choice of prefix operator determines what happens to each field. **LST.DATE** updates the date field, while **FST.NAME** retains the employee name from the permanent record. **SUM.HOURS**, etc., forms the year-to-date totals. The TEMP.D and WEEK.D files may now be deleted.

TWO-DIMENSIONAL TABLES

A generally useful report format is the two-dimensional table, for example:

CLASS	WOMEN	MEN
1982	360	320
1983	345	342
1984	346	350
1985	355	362
	1406	1374

To compile such a summary report for a file of student records requires that you define two new fields, WOMEN and MEN, to count the records by class and by sex.

```
DEFINE
    WOMEN/I5 = IF SEX IS 'F' THEN 1 ELSE 0
    MEN/I5   = IF SEX IS 'M' THEN 1 ELSE 0
END
```

Next the records are sorted into clusters **BY CLASS**, the two new fields are evaluated for each record, and the values are summed for each cluster. The NPL request to accomplish these steps is:

```
SUM WOMEN AND MEN BY CLASS, AND COLUMNTOTAL.
```

Compressing Long Reports

Statistical tables which are sorted by several variables often result in reports of many pages but only a few columns of data. For example, from a hospital file of patients you might request

```
COUNT PATIENTS BY COUNTY BY CITY
BY AGE BY SEX BY PHYSICIAN
```

The count field is the only true data item; the other fields are called grouping, or categorizing, variables. With several hundred towns, say, eighty-eight age values, two sex values, and twenty doctors the report could have several thousand lines. A better report might appear as follows:

PATIENT STATISTICS

COUNTY CITY PHYSICIAN	MEN			WOMEN		
	0-19	20-59	60+	0-15	16-44	45+
GREENE COUNTY						
PLATSVILLE						
SMITH, R.A.	21	6	0	10	8	0
MALTIN, M.	0	8	32	0	10	47
SOMERTON						
BALDEROL, K.	0	0	0	8	38	16

.
.
.

The report takes two of the sort fields and spreads them across the page, rather than down the page. Also, ages have been grouped into useful ranges. The result is much easier to read than a long single column of numbers.

To accomplish this, you first decide on what data columns you want printed across the page. Then define a new field for each column. In the example, we assume the original file has one record per patient with fields for COUNTY, CITY, MD, AGE, SEX. The new fields are:

```
DEFINE
   M19/I3  =  IF  SEX  IS  'F'   THEN  0
              ELSE  IF  AGE  GT  19    THEN  0
                                        ELSE  1

   M59/I3  =  IF  SEX  IS  'F'   THEN  0
              ELSE  IF  AGE  LE  19    THEN  0
              ELSE  IF  AGE  GT  59    THEN  0
                                        ELSE  1

   M60/I3  =  IF  SEX  IS  'F'   THEN  0
              ELSE  IF  AGE  LE  59    THEN  0
                                        ELSE  1


   W15/I4=...
```

Repeat the above for W15, W44, and W45, the three columns for women. Next, write this report request:

```
HEADING
"PATIENT STATISTICS "
"                          MEN                         WOMEN "
BY COUNTY FOLD PAGE
BY CITY FOLD SKIP
BY MD AS PHYSICIAN
WRITE M19 AS '0-19'  M59 AS '20-59'  M60 AS '60+'
   AND W15 AS '0-15'  W44 AS '16-44'  W45 AS '45+'.
```

To understand how the new columns are calculated, visualize the records of individual patients sorted into groups by county, by city, and by doctor. Each group corresponds to a row on the report.

One of six new fields, which act as six counters, is increased by one, through the **IF. . .THEN. . .ELSE** logic, for each record. When the group changes, the counter totals are printed and the counters are set to zero.

The names of the new fields, M19, M59, M60, W15, W44, and W45 are chosen simply to provide an association with the column headings. Any names will do, though they must begin with a letter (which rules out the use of the column headings themselves, as "0-19").

Sales Forecasts as Variances

Additional examples of multicolumn report formats are illustrated here by two examples. For each case a master file, a piece of the datafile, an Exec program, and part of the resulting report are illustrated.

The Sales.M Master File

```
FIELD=PRODUCT     , ITEM       , A8      , A8    , $
FIELD=SALESMAN    , SLSMN      , A8      , A8    , $
FIELD=DISTRICT    , DIST       , A8      , A8    , $
FIELD=REGION      , AREA       , A8      , A8    , $
FIELD=MONTH       , MNTH       , I2      , A2    , $
FIELD=SALES       , ORDERS     , F10.2   , A8    , $
FIELD=FORECAST    , ESTIMATE   , F10.2   , A8    , $
FIELD=            , ...        ,         , A1    , $ END-OF-RECORD
```

Example 1

```
GETFILE SALES

DEFINE
QUARTER/A11 =IF MONTH LE 3 THEN '1st Quarter' ELSE
             IF MONTH LE 6 THEN '2nd Quarter' ELSE
             IF MONTH LE 9 THEN '3rd Quarter' ELSE
                                      '4th Quarter'.

WRITE SALES FORECAST NOPRINT AND
COMPUTE VARIANCE    = SALES - FORECAST
COMPUTE OVER-QUOTA = IF VARIANCE GT 0
                     THEN VARIANCE ELSE 0
COMPUTE BELOW-QUOTA= IF VARIANCE LT 0
                     THEN VARIANCE ELSE 0
COMPUTE PCT-VAR     = 100*VARIANCE/FORECAST NOTOTAL
BY REGION FOLD SUBTOTAL PAGE
   BY DISTRICT SKIP 2 SUBTOTAL FOLD
      BY SALESMAN SKIP SUBTOTAL FOLD
         BY QUARTER
END
```

REGION DISTRICT SALESMAN QUARTER	SALES	VARIANCE	OVER-QUOTA	BELOW-QUOTA	PCT-VAR
EAST					
BOSTON					
ADAMS					
1st Quarter	44010.40	1187.20	1187.20	0.00	2.8
2nd Quarter	61933.90	-392.70	0.00	-392.70	-0.6
3rd Quarter	54191.90	-812.70	0.00	-812.70	-1.5
4th Quarter	58730.00	3928.41	3928.41	0.00	7.2
	218866.20	3910.21	5115.61	-1205.40	1.8
BAKER					
1st Quarter	42295.40	-191.10	0.00	-191.10	-0.4
2nd Quarter	61265.40	6957.30	6957.30	0.00	12.8
3rd Quarter	55400.80	-3234.00	0.00	-3234.00	-5.5
4th Quarter	63185.50	-3113.61	0.00	-3113.61	-4.7
	222147.10	418.59	6957.30	-6538.70	0.2
	441013.30	4328.80	12072.91	-7744.10	1.0
COLUMBUS					
DAVIDSON					
1st Quarter	40658.80	676.89	676.89	0.00	1.7
2nd Quarter	66495.10	20055.00	20055.00	0.00	43.2
3rd Quarter	48848.10	-6175.39	0.00	-6175.39	-11.2
4th Quarter	55163.50	-5516.69	0.00	-5516.69	-9.1
	211165.50	9039.81	20731.90	-11692.09	4.5
	211165.50	9039.81	20731.90	-11692.09	4.5
NEWYORK					
BAMBURG					
1st Quarter	0.00	-7236.60	0.00	-7236.60	-100.0
2nd Quarter	0.00	-7236.60	0.00	-7236.60	-100.0
3rd Quarter	57062.60	6696.89	6696.89	0.00	13.3
4th Quarter	57558.89	1026.89	1026.89	0.00	1.8
	114621.50	-6749.41	7723.79	-14473.20	-5.6
MALLORY					
1st Quarter	43534.39	-3094.00	0.00	-3094.00	-6.6
2nd Quarter	61656.70	5891.90	5891.90	0.00	10.6
3rd Quarter	54261.91	-2528.39	0.00	-2528.39	-4.5
4th Quarter	57535.10	2975.70	2975.70	0.00	5.5

Example 2

```
GETFILE SALES

DEFINE
  FCST:N/F9.2 = IF REGION IS 'NORTH' THEN FORECAST ELSE 0
  FCST:E/F9.2 = IF REGION IS 'EAST'  THEN FORECAST ELSE 0
  FCST:S/F9.2 = IF REGION IS 'SOUTH' THEN FORECAST ELSE 0
  FCST:W/F9.2 = IF REGION IS 'WEST'  THEN FORECAST ELSE 0

  SLS:N/F9.2  = IF REGION IS 'NORTH' THEN SALES ELSE 0
  SLS:E/F9.2  = IF REGION IS 'EAST'  THEN SALES ELSE 0
  SLS:S/F9.2  = IF REGION IS 'SOUTH' THEN SALES ELSE 0
  SLS:W/F9.2  = IF REGION IS 'WEST'  THEN SALES ELSE 0

  QUARTER/All = IF MONTH LE 3 THEN '1st Quarter' ELSE
                IF MONTH LE 6 THEN '2nd Quarter' ELSE
                IF MONTH LE 9 THEN '3rd Quarter' ELSE
                               '4th Quarter'
END

HEADING
"                                       REGION"
" "
"                       North      East      South      West "
WRITE       FCST:N AS FORECAST:  FCST:E     FCST:S     FCST:W
   OVER     SLS:N AS 'SALES  :'  SLS:E      SLS:S      SLS:W
   OVER
   COMPUTE VAR:N/F8.1 = 100*(SLS:N - FCST:N) / FCST:N AS VARIANCE:
   COMPUTE VAR:E/F8.1 = 100*(SLS:E - FCST:E) / FCST:E
   COMPUTE VAR:S/F8.1 = 100*(SLS:S - FCST:S) / FCST:S
   COMPUTE VAR:W/F8.1 = 100*(SLS:W - FCST:W) / FCST:W

BY PRODUCT PAGE FOLD BY QUARTER SKIP
IF FORECAST GT 0
END
```

REGION

		North	East	South	West
PRODUCT					
QUARTER					
BLENDER					
1st Quarter	FORECAST:	14307.98	27897.75	24448.50	15435.23
	SALES :	13587.75	26515.35	25948.35	14416.65
	VARIANCE:	-5.0	-5.0	6.1	-6.6
2nd Quarter	FORECAST:	21548.70	32322.37	49126.51	23170.73
	SALES :	23635.13	44348.86	48500.11	24002.32
	VARIANCE:	9.7	37.2	-1.3	3.6
3rd Quarter	FORECAST:	18696.15	38190.83	32594.40	17023.50
	SALES :	19060.65	44444.03	36668.03	20113.65
	VARIANCE:	1.9	16.4	12.5	18.2
4th Quarter	FORECAST:	13421.03	50834.25	36575.55	18236.48
	SALES :	18578.70	47922.98	42830.78	21714.75
	VARIANCE:	38.4	-5.7	17.1	19.1

REGION

		North	East	South	West
PRODUCT					
QUARTER					
COOKER					
1st Quarter	FORECAST:	8039.93	16617.82	13556.02	6564.38
	SALES :	8133.75	17062.65	16874.32	7715.25
	VARIANCE:	1.2	2.7	24.5	17.5
2nd Quarter	FORECAST:	7629.53	20545.65	23752.57	10471.95
	SALES :	10177.65	19555.43	21135.60	10746.68
	VARIANCE:	33.4	-4.8	-11.0	2.6
3rd Quarter	FORECAST:	7629.53	17588.48	16147.35	7701.75
	SALES :	7766.55	18970.88	18046.80	8538.75
	VARIANCE:	1.8	7.9	11.8	10.9
4th Quarter	FORECAST:	8040.60	15802.42	17040.37	6423.98
	SALES :	8651.48	18524.70	17064.00	7591.05
	VARIANCE:	7.6	17.2	0.1	18.2

.
.
.

This chapter illustrated how to combine various NPL features for more effective reports. In addition, programming methods were discussed for making the best use of memory and storage space. The following keywords were introduced:

```
DISK
TYPEFILE
MEMORY?
DIRECTORY
COPYFILE
```

ADVANCED FEATURES FOR DATABASE MANAGEMENT AND APPLICATION DEVELOPMENT

14

DATABASE NAMES AND
RELATIONAL FUNCTIONS

Up to this point the discussion has been about the elements of a non-procedural language and their use in retrieving data from a file for display in various forms. The remaining chapters address the broader topic of how non-procedural software packages provide complete programming solutions for important data processing applications. Beginning with the introduction of the RAMIS system in 1968, nonprocedural packages have been more than just query and report writer programs, for RAMIS had a general approach to managing complex arrays of data stored in tape files.

Today nonprocedural systems are integrally tied to some form of database management system (often called a DBMS). Moreover, they compete with the leading programming languages, COBOL, FORTRAN, PL/I, and BASIC, as the language of choice for major database applications. The principal benefits of the *nonprocedural* approach are:

- Shorter program development times

- Greater ease in making changes after the application programs are in use

- Fewer pages of program statements, more easily understood by successor programmers, or even by yourself at a later date!

These benefits translate into important cost savings, yet perhaps the greater merit derives from these two issues:

a. People in search of solutions to their information retrieval and data processing problems usually
   - are in a hurry
   - do not want to become computer experts
   - do want to be able to change their minds
   - have only a vague idea of their information needs or of how the ready access to data may affect their own operations.

b. It is evident that the demand for skilled programming talent in the business community alone will never be fully satisfied. Only by harnessing the power of the computer to help a wider class of people to prepare and operate advanced application programs will most needs be satisfied.

The relative benefits of other approaches usually are that the resultant programs, written in COBOL, BASIC, or another procedural language:

- require less computer memory

- use fewer computer cycles, i.e., cpu power or cpu seconds

These are also cost saving benefits. In the past, the balance between the two sets of cost savings resulted in greater emphasis being given to the efficient use of very large computers. As the costs of memory devices and of computer processors have dropped dramatically, and the need for scarce programming talent has risen, the balance of benefits now favors the *nonprocedural* approach.

For the nonprocedural approach to handle significant data processing applications, additional capabilities beyond those presented in earlier chapters are required. Specifically, two major functions are needed: a DBMS facility and an exec control language. The basic DBMS functions are discussed here and in the next chapter, and the second topic appears in Chapter 16.

DBMS

A minimal database management system consists of

- A means for query and retrieval of data items

- A method of describing the content and relationships of data items, record, file, and databases

- A means for inserting and deleting records and for replacing or updating data items within records

- A means for storing, moving, and combining datafiles

Most nonprocedural information systems include all of the above, plus a nonprocedural report writing system, plus a procedural Exec control language and control system. Many DBMS systems leave the latter functions to be handled by a powerful and general-purpose programming language, such as COBOL, FORTRAN, or BASIC, which is then referred to as a host language. In such cases the data processing application is prepared in the host language.

Just what is a *database*, as distinct from a datafile, you might ask. A database is a collection of related files, together with a directory for locating each file and a dictionary for describing all elements of the database system. A *database* is to a *file* as the public library is to your home library. Each contains volumes of printed pages (records), but the larger library has a complete card catalog, which provides a large amount of information about the volumes. An important function of the card catalog is to facilitate rapid access to the volumes through the use of one or more indexes. Typically, library books may be accessed by title, by author, by subject matter, and sometimes by publisher.

These are separately indexed paths to the location of the desired material. A catalog record also provides information about the size, shape, source, date, and place of publication. Similar functions may be performed by a database "catalog" (which in this book is called the master file).

In earlier chapters, a *master file* is described as defining the fields of a datafile. Such a master file is a basic element of a database. We continue to call it a master file, though it is also known as the database *schema*, for it describes the scheme by which the many elements (e.g., fields, records, files, segments, names, formats) of a database are related to each other. A *database dictionary* is a computer printout of the contents of the master file, or schema, with a listing of all codes, labels, edit values, limits, and other miscellaneous information.

While the functions performed are mostly the same for all *nonprocedural* DBMS systems, the terminology varies widely. We employ here, for tutorial purposes, a very simple set of commands, phrases, and programming rules. Variations by different software systems are presented in the appendixes.

DATABASE NAMES AND FILENAMES

Naming conventions for files vary from computer to computer. Yet it is generally true that a physically distinct file is identified by a filename and a file type, separated either by a space, a period, or a slash. The file type is treated as a suffix. In this book we use the suffixes .D, .M, .E, and .I for data, master, exec, and index files, respectively.

As we consider databases that consist of several files, we need to expand the structure of the master file to include the description of more than one datafile. A database is the assemblage of master, data, and index files that are identified in a particular database master file. Such a grouping of files is also called a *logical database*, since it includes only those files that are logically related to each other.

Two different database master files may be defined to use many of the same files, as illustrated below:

```
         The
      MARKETING DB        Miscellaneous Files
      Master  File        _____
   _____      |CUSTOMER.I.ACNO|
  | MARKETING.M |         |_____|
  |_____|                                   The
  |             |        |CUSTOMER.I.LNAM|        FINANCE DB
  |             |         |_____|       Master File
  |             |         _____
  |CUSTOMER (.M)|------>|  CUSTOMER.D  |        _____
  |             |        |_____|       | FINANCE.M |
  |             |                                 |_____|
  |PROSPECT (.M)|------>|  PROSPECT.D  |        |           |
  |             |        |_____|       |           |
  |             |         _____       |           |
  | STAFF (.M)  |------>|   STAFF.D   |<------| STAFF (.M) |
  |             |        |_____|       |           |
  |             |        |  STAFF.I.SSN |       |           |
  |             |        |_____|       |           |
  |             |         _____       |           |
  | ORDERS (.M) |------>|   ORDERS.D   |<------| ORDERS (.M) |
  |_____|        |_____|       |           |
                         |   ACCREC.D   |<------| ACCREC (.M) |
                          |_____|       |           |
                         |   ACCPAY.D   |<------| ACCPAY (.M) |
                          |_____|       |           |
                         |   VENDOR.D   |<------| VENDOR (.M) |
                          |_____|       |           |
                         |  EXPENSE.D   |<------| EXPENSE (.M)|
                          |_____|       |_____|
                          _____
                         |   CHART.D   |<--
                          |_____|  |
                          _____  |
                         |   CHART.M   |<--|
                          |_____|
```

In this illustration each box represents a physically separate file. The two database master files, MARKETING.M and FINANCE.M, are directory filenames which contain the master file information for several files. The additional files are identified in the figure with (.M) following the filename.

To access any of these files, the GETFILE command takes multiple objects, where at least the first is the name of a physical master file, that is, a *directory filename*, which is indicated by a colon.

Examples are:

```
GETFILE  MARKETING
```

which activates all the files listed in the figure under MARKETING.M.

```
GETFILES  MARKETING:  CUSTOMER,  STAFF
```

which activates only the files mentioned. The colon terminates the database name and indicates that a list of filenames follows.

```
GETFILES  FINANCE:  ACCREC, ACCPAY, VENDOR, ORDERS, CHART:
```

Notice that the suffixes do not appear. Each name specifies a master and a datafile, and possibly one or more index files. The names ending with a colon are separate directory filenames; the others are master descriptions contained in the database master file. Only the files named are made active by the command.

If the datafiles have names which differ from the master names, they must appear in parentheses before the master name. For example:

```
GETFILES  MARKETING:  (OVERSEAS) CUSTOMER,
                      (ORD81)  ORDERS, STAFF
```

Within the database master file the file designations appear as follows. Each group of field descriptors are headed by a filename. Each field that has an Index file lists the index filename suffix.

The contents of MARKETING.M could appear as:

```
FILE=CUSTOMER,
      FIELD =ACCOUNT NBR     ,ACNO   ,A9      ,A9  ,INDEX =ACNO,$
      FIELD =COMPANY         ,CORP   ,A20     ,A20,$
      FIELD =LAST NAME       ,LNAM   ,A15     ,A15,INDEX =LNAM,$
      FIELD =FIRST           ,FNAM   ,A15     ,A15,$
      FIELD =MI              ,MI     ,A1      ,A1  ,$
      FIELD =STREET          ,STR    ,A15     ,A15,$
                      .
                      .
                      .
      FIELD =SALESMAN        ,SCODE  ,A4      ,A4  ,$

FILE = PROSPECT,
      FIELD =COMPANY         ,CORP   ,A20     ,A20,$
      FIELD =LAST NAME       ,LNAM   ,A15     ,A15,$
                      .
                      .
                      .
      FIELD =TELEPHONE       ,PHONE  ,P12     ,A12,$

FILE = STAFF,
      FIELD =SOC SEC NBR     ,SSN    ,A11     ,A11, INDEX =SSN,$
      FIELD =LAST NAME       ,LNAM   ,A15     ,A15,$
                      .
                      .
                      .
FILE = ORDERS,
      FIELD =ACCOUNT NBR     ,ACNO   ,A9      ,A9  ,$
      FIELD =AMOUNT          ,AMT    ,F10.2   ,A10,$
                      .
                      .
                      .
```

NAMES FOR DATA ITEMS AND VARIABLES

Data items are given two names, FIELDNAME and ALIAS, in the master file, and at least one of the two must be unique among the names in the file. Fieldnames also serve the functions of column headings, are often longer then the alias, up to twelve characters, and often have embedded spaces. It is therefore recommended as good practice to make the aliases unique. Also they should be short, yet mnemonic, and contain only letters and numbers.

When two files are to be employed at once, the names of one must be distinguished from the names of the other. LNAM or SSN could well appear in both files. Separation of names is achieved by letting the *full* name of a data item be the FILEname followed by the FIELDNAME or ALIAS, separated by a period. For example, from the MARKETING master consider these fields:

CUSTOMER.ACNO	ORDERS.ACNO	
CUSTOMER.CORP	PROSPECT.CORP	
STAFF.ZIP	PROSPECT.ZIP	CUSTOMER.ZIP

If the double name looks like an inconvenience, we may simplify it somewhat by using an abbreviated FILEname for the first part of the full name. Moreover, when there is no ambiguity, the FILEname prefix is not required. An NPL rule is that names chosen by the user for data items may be truncated on the right as long as they remain unique identifiers. For this purpose, then, the FILEname prefix may also be used in its shortest unique form. Now, if you choose FILEnames that begin with different letters, you may use names like these:

C.ACNO	O.ACNO	
C.CORP	P.CORP	
S.ZIP	P.ZIP	C.ZIP

The shorthand notation is convenient, because the number of active files is usually not very large, so the single letters provide adequate recognition. Here we use C for customer, S for staff, O for orders, and P for prospects.

In addition to names which are specific to each file, there are names for a different kind of data element. Data items which belong to the MARKETING database master, yet are not associated with any one of the datafiles, are called "profile" variables. They have no prefix name, but to avoid confusion with similar local names they may be prefixed with a period. Thus .LNAM and .CORP may be used to identify data variables which belong to the database but are not part of a particular datafile.

The rules for assigning names to **DEFINEd** variables are similar to the above:

- **DEFINEd** variables associated with a particular file must be named with the FILEname prefix. Names appearing in the expression to the right of the equals sign must also be associated with that FILE, and the name prefix need not be stated.

225

- Other **DEFINE**d variables may be considered global to the database (rather than local to a file). Their assigned names contain only a period as a prefix; names in the expression may come from two or more files, but must be identified as such.

For example:

```
DEFINE   .FISCALYR/A4    =1982
DEFINE   .GOAL/F10.2     =1.2 * (LAST SALES.GOAL).
DEFINE C.ZIP3/A3         =ZIP.
DEFINE   .BUDGET         =HUSBAND.INCOME + WIFE.INCOME.
```

The third example provides a three digit zipcode for the CUSTOMER file, for sorting mailing labels by postal distribution districts.

RELATING RECORDS BETWEEN TWO FILES

We look now at preparing report requests which draw information from two or more files within a database in order to write a single report. To accomplish this we must know how to *relate* the records in one file to the records in another.

The words used to describe database structures (that is, relationships between files) are varied and often confusing. It is usually quite apparent that the *information content* of one datafile is somehow related to the information in other datafiles. If the objective is to pull together the related elements while screening out unrelated data, either for a report or to create a new file, the challenge to the user of the system is in understanding just how to draw upon whatever relationships exist between the files.

The central idea that helps to clarify some of the confusion in terminology is that the important relationships are those existing between a single record in one file with one or more records of a second file. Consider, for example, these two files:

Personnel File

NAME	DEPT NBR	EMP NBR	CITY	DIV
•	•	•	•	•
•	•	•	•	•
•	•	•	•	•
HENSEL	025	9287	CLEVE	SLS
HENSBERG	046	3304	NYC	ENG
HENTSCHEL	033	5561	BOSTON	SLS
HEPERKAN	007	1103	NYC	FIN
HERBERT	006	3702	DENVER	SLS
HERBERT	033	4766	HOUSTN	SLS
•	•	•	•	•
•	•	•	•	•
•	•	•	•	•

Budget File

DEPT NBR	CITY	DIV	BUDGT	ACCT
•	•	•	•	•
•	•	•	•	•
029	DENVER	SLS	4673	G034
030	NYC	ADM	5000	G034
031	ATLANTA	MAN	1570	G034
032	BOSTON	SLS	31000	G037
033	BOSTON	SLS	1750	G034
034	NYC	SLS	7320	G034
•	•	•	•	•
•	•	•	•	•
•	•	•	•	•

What are the possible relationships between the HENTSCHEL record in the first file and those in the segment of the second file illustrated above? The answer is shown here by creating composite records from the related elements:

case (a): matching **DEPT NBR** (*)

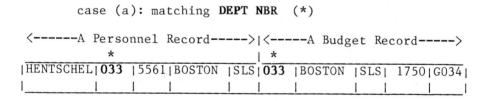

```
<------A Personnel Record----->|<-----A Budget Record----->
            *                  | *
|HENTSCHEL|033 |5561|BOSTON |SLS|033 |BOSTON |SLS| 1750|G034|
|_____|____|____|_____|___|____|_____|___|_____|____|
```

case (b): matching **CITY** (*)

```
                        |
                *       |      *
|HENTSCHEL|033 |5561|BOSTON |SLS|032 |BOSTON |SLS|31000|G037|
|---------|----|----|-------|---|----|-------|---|-----|----|
|HENTSCHEL|033 |5561|BOSTON |SLS|033 |BOSTON |SLS| 1750|G034|
```

case (c): matching **DIV**

DEPT NBR	DEPARTMENT
.	.
.	.
.	.
031	Atlanta Field Service Dept
032	Boston Improvement Sales Office
033	Boston Customer Service Dept
.	.
.	.
.	.

In the first case, the HENTSCHEL record is said to have a one-to-one (1:1, or *unique*) relationship with the records in the second file. That is so, because we can see with the second file sorted by DEPTNBR that there is only one record that matches the DEPT NBR value of 033 in the HENTSCHEL record.

In cases (b) and (c), using different fields for matching, however, the HENT-SCHEL record has a one-to-many (1:N, or *multiple*) relationship with the records of the second file. The effect of matching in such cases is to create groups of composite records, in which the HENTSCHEL information is repeated.

In most situations, there is only one common field between two files, and hence only one possible relationship. Usually, it is apparent whether the relationship is *unique* or *multiple*, for often we know whether the common field in the second file has unique values for each record. Two examples, which are typical, illustrate the point.

Let's create a relatively simple file just to hold the forty or so DEPART-MENT names and their corresponding DEPT NBRs. Then "Boston Customer Service Dept" may be printed on a report, rather than just the code number 033.

				*			*		
HENTSCHEL	033	5561	BOSTON	SLS	029	DENVER	SLS	4673	G034
HENTSCHEL	033	5561	BOSTON	SLS	032	BOSTON	SLS	31000	G037
HENTSCHEL	033	5561	BOSTON	SLS	033	BOSTON	SLS	1750	G034
HENTSCHEL	033	5561	BOSTON	SLS	034	NYC	SLS	7320	G034

A file of this special kind may be called a *lookup* table, or a **RECODE** table, for it is used simply to look up the meaning of a code field. The code must be unique. The relationships of other records to this file are one-to-one. Notice, however, that a relationship from a record in the lookup file to another datafile may be one-to-many, for many records may have the same DEPT NBR.

For the second example, let's make a file to hold the names of dependents of employees, with a record for each dependent.

EMPLOYEE NBR	DEPENDENT	RELATION	AGE
.	.	.	.
.	.	.	.
5558	MARY	W	23
5561	JOAN	W	39
5561	ROBERT	S	7
5561	JOHN	S	14
5561	JOANNE	D	17
5564	SARAH	W	51
.	.	.	.

The result of matching the HENTSCHEL employee number (5561) to the above file is this group of composite records:

```
<-------A Personnel Record------>|<--Dependents-->
              *                  |  *
|HENTSCHEL|033 |5561|BOSTON |SALES|5561|JOAN   |W|39|
|---------|----|----|-------|-----|----|------|-|--|
|HENTSCHEL|033 |5561|BOSTON |SALES|5561|ROBERT|S| 7|
|---------|----|----|-------|-----|----|------|-|--|
|HENTSCHEL|033 |5561|BOSTON |SALES|5561|JOHN   |S|14|
|---------|----|----|-------|-----|----|------|-|--|
|HENTSCHEL|033 |5561|BOSTON |SALES|5561|JOANNE|D|17|
```

While this relationship is one-to-many, observe that in reverse it is one-to-one. That is, a single record in the dependent file matches only a single record in the other file—for the obvious reason that the EMPLOYEE NBR is a unique identifier of employee records. There is an implied hierarchy here, and in such cases the employee *record* is said to be the parent (sometimes the term owner is used) of the dependent records. In more casual discussions the employee *file* is considered the parent of the dependent file. Such a concept is useful, but you must remember that it means a single record in the parent file may be matched to *one or more* records in the subordinate file.

LOOKUP TABLES

The special case of lookup tables is the simplest situation in which the records of one file are matched to those of another file. When long names appear many times in large files, it is more efficient to store short codes in the datafile and to look up the decoded value of the codes in a table of names. For example, a file of fifty records would hold a table of state names and their two letter codes. A MAILIST.M file might look like this:

```
MAILIST.M


    FILE  =NAMES,
          FIELD  =CODE        ,ST      ,A2    ,A2  ,$
          FIELD  =STATENAME   ,NAM     ,A20   ,A20 ,$
          FIELD  =            ,...     ,      ,A1  ,$
    FILE  =DONORS,
          FIELD  =FULLNAME     ,NAM     ,A25   ,A25 ,$
          FIELD  =STREET       ,STR     ,A20   ,A20 ,$
          FIELD  =CITY         ,CTY     ,A15   ,A15 ,$
          FIELD  =STATE        ,ST      ,A2    ,A2  ,$
          FIELD  =ZIP          ,ZP      ,A5    ,A5  ,$
          FIELD  =TYPE         ,TCODE   ,A6    ,A6  ,$
          FIELD  =             ,...     ,A1    ,A1  ,$
```

The **RECODE** function is used to change a code into a corresponding value. The pairs of codes and values may be stored in a datafile. To illustrate, let's print mailing labels with the full state names, using this request:

```
GETFILES MAILIST:   NAMES, DONORS

DEFINE
    D.STNAME/A20 = RECODE D.ST (N.CODE N.STATENAME)
    D.CITYST/A30 = CLIP(CITY) + ', ' + D.STNAME.

PRINT FULLNAME OVER STREET
      OVER CITYST ZIP
      BY ZIP NOPRINT AND SKIP 4.
```

In this example, a value of D.ST in a record of the first file (DONOR) is matched with a value of N.CODE. Then the corresponding value of N.STATENAME is extracted from the second file (NAMES) and is assigned the name D.STNAME, which, in turn, is used in the definition of the variable D.CITYST.

If there were only a few states to consider, the standard form of **RECODE** could be used to change the two letter codes into the names, as in:

```
DEFINE NAME/A20 = RECODE ST (CA CALIFORNIA, OR OREGON,
                            WA WASHINGTON, NV NEVADA).
```

When the table of codes and names is long, however, you may prefer to store it in a file and look up the names. In this case, the code/name pairs within the parentheses are replaced by the pair of fieldnames of the two items in this file. The full definition is:

```
DEFINE fnl.extractfld/fmt = RECODE fnl.code (fn2.code fn2.fld).
```

where

fnl is the filename, or abbreviation, of the primary datafile.

fn2 is the filename, or abbreviation, of the lookup file.

extractfld is a new name for the value extracted from the lookup file.

fn2.fld is the field in the lookup file containing possible values for extractfld.

code is a fieldname or alias in both master files for the common field (not necessarily the same name).

fmt, a format code, is taken from the fn2.M master file if not specified.

RECODE functions of this form may be used in **DEFINE** and **COMPUTE** statements. It is also convenient when several **RECODE**s are used regularly to store the **DEFINE** statements in the master file, more or less permanently. Thus, the main value of interest in the lookup table may be treated just as if they were stored in the basic datafiles.

When lookup tables are large, the time required to extract values may be noticeable. Much efficiency is gained by **INDEX**ing the code field in the lookup file.

THE GENERAL PROCESS OF MATCHING

It is evident that to coordinate the records in two files at least one field in each file must contain common data values, and that those keyfields must be compared and the values matched. When the files are large and neither, or only one, is sorted by the common field, the task can take a long time, for every record in one file must be compared with every record in the other. It is like matching a long mailing list to the names in a telephone book. Only if the list is sorted alphabetically is the task an easy one. When it is, you can lay the list on the phone book pages and scan one list of last names until it gets ahead of the other, alternating back and forth, noting matches as you go. Only one pass through the lists is required.

The task of matching is performed as part of a data retrieval request from the two files. A report mode request, for example, or as we see later in the chapter, a Modify mode request, uses a *matching* IF phrase to specify which records to retrieve from each file. Just as the screening IF phrase, described in Chapter 4, tests a field in each record against a value or list of test values, the matching IF phrase tests a field in each record of the first file against the values of a similiar field in a second file.

For example:

```
IF   A.acode  EQ  B.bcode
```

Only the EQ relational operator is used in the matching IF phrase, and when the two codes are equal the records of the two files are retained. The two kinds of IF phrases may both be used in a single request. They function similarly but their purpose is different. The matching IF phrase finds the records in one file that are *owned* by a record in a parent FILE. The screening IF phrase selects records meeting a literal value or range test.

You should think of the result of the matching, or joining, of A and B to be that a new record has been formed, consisting of all the A fields and all the B fields, but with a single copy of the common code, or keyfield, as shown here:

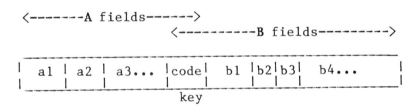

Report requests use all these fields as if only a single file exists. File A may be considered the parent of file B, and block diagrams like the following are often used to suggest a one-to-many relationship.

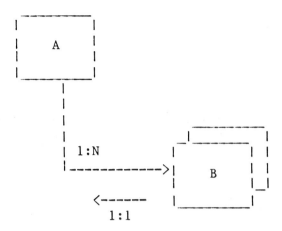

You should visualize the resulting joined records as follows:

```
<-----File A Records---->
                        <-------File B Records------>
   a1      a2      a3      code    b1      b2 b3      b4
  _____
 |SALES|1982|1250000|NYC    |180500|25|M|JONES,  R   |
 |  "  |  " |   "    |NYC    |205040|32|F|KLEIN, J   |
 |  "  |  " |   "    |NYC    | 92400|24|M|GREENE,  H |
 |SALES|1982| 900000|BOSTON| 85750|28|M|MCVEY, R    |
 |  "  |  " |   "    |BOSTON|260850|38|M|MONAHAN, P|
 |  "  |  " |   "    |BOSTON|140500|37|M|O'LEARY, J|
 |     |    |        |       |      | | |          |
 |     |    |        |       |      | | |          |
```

For each value of the code there is one record from the A file. The A fields are implicitly repeated for each record matched from the B file, as indicated by the ditto marks. The composite record consists of the A fields plus the B fields (yet each A field value really exists only once as stored data) plus a single occurrence of the common code field.

Notice that each B file record matches only one record in the A file, hence the relationship between records as viewed from below is one-to-one.

Consider a case where the quantities of parts in inventory are stored in one file, and the current price of the parts is maintained in a second file. To evaluate the potential sales values of all items you could do this (where the common keyfields are called PARTNBR):

```
GETFILES INVENTORY, PRICES

PRINT PARTNBR NAME QTY PRICE
AND COMPUTE VALUE = QTY * PRICE
AND COLUMNTOTAL
IF I.PARTNBR EQ P.PARTNBR.
```

INVENTORY FILE

PARTNBR	QTY
13	159
17	326
22	92
39	108

PRICES FILE

PARTNBR	PRICE
9	5.22
13	6.05
19	7.00
22	3.25
39	6.45

The effect of matching the tables above is shown in this combined table. Matching records are marked with an asterisk.

QTY	PARTNBR	PRICE
	9	5.22
* 159	13	6.05
326	17	
	19	7.00
* 92	22	3.25
* 108	39	6.45

Only the three lines with asterisks are retained by the matching **IF** phrase. The other lines have missing values and are dropped from the report. Part numbers 9 and 19 are not available in inventory and #17 is available, but it must be a new item for it does not appear on the current price list.

This illustrates a one-to-one relationship between records in two files. Each part in inventory must have one and only one record in the PRICE file. If it is not so, the results may be in error.

The general form of the matching **IF** phrase is:

```
IF fn1.fld1 EQ fn2.fld2
```

The filename prefixes are not required if the fieldnames are unique across all active files. Matching is performed by stepping though the first file, fn1, one record at a time, while searching the second file, fn2, at each step. The **EQ** *is* required.

In the inventory example, if prices were to be different at each regional warehouse, the price list would then be broken down by two fields, REGION and PARTNBR.

INVENTORY FILE

PARTNBR	REGION	QUANTITY
13	SOUTH	159
17	NORTH	326
17	SOUTH	60
22	NORTH	92
39	SOUTH	108
39	NORTH	58

PRICES FILE

REGN	PART	NAME	PRICE
NORTH	9	WOMUS	5.22
NORTH	13	JARVER	6.05
NORTH	19	LINKER	7.00
NORTH	22	WIDGET	3.25
NORTH	39	COLLAR	6.45
SOUTH	9	WOMUS	4.80
SOUTH	13	JARVER	5.22
SOUTH	17	PADDLE	4.05
SOUTH	22	WIDGET	3.00
SOUTH	39	COLLAR	5.90

Both the REGION and PARTNBR fields are needed to match these records, so we combine them in **DEFINE** statements, and then match using the combined keys.

```
GETFILES INVENTORY, PRICES

DEFINE VALUE = I.QTY * P.PRICE
       I.KEY/A7 = I.REGION + I.PARTNBR
       P.KEY/A7 = P.REGN + P.PART.

PRINT PARTNBR NAME NOTOTAL QTY PRICE NOTOTAL VALUE
  BY REGION
  COLUMNTOTAL
IF I.KEY EQ P.KEY.
```

The resulting report should look like this:

REGION	PARTNBR	NAME	QTY	PRICE	VALUE
NORTH	22	WIDGET	92	3.25	299.00
	39	COLLAR	58	6.45	374.00
SOUTH	13	JARVER	159	5.22	830.00
	17	PADDLE	60	4.05	243.00
	39	COLLAR	108	5.90	637.00
					2383.00

In a different example, the relationship of bosses to employees is one-to-many, yet the reverse is one-to-one, for each employee has only one immediate superior. The employee file, which holds records for both bosses and employees (since bosses are also employees, and each has a boss), could be treated as the datafile source of both kinds of persons, matching employees to boss. You might seek every employee whose salary is greater than 90 percent of their boss's salary.

```
GETFILES EMP, (EMP)BOSS

DEFINE .PERCENT = 100 * E.SALARY/B.SALARY.

PRINT EMP.NAME BOSS.NAME
IF .PERCENT GT 90
IF E.SUPVNBR EQ B.EMPNBR.
```

The master files BOSS.M and EMP.M have the same contents, but different FILEnames. They both use the same datafile. Upon execution, the supervisor number, SUPVNBR, in each record is used to search for a matching entry in the EMPNBR field to find the boss record; then the two names are printed.

JOINING FILES

The keyword **JOIN** is used when you wish to define a more or less permanent relationship between two files. With a **JOIN** statement you can avoid repeated use of the matching **IF** phrase. The processing is the same but the relationship is remembered in the master file. The command:

```
C>JOIN CUSTOMER.ACNO TO ORDERS.CUSTID
```

joins the CUSTOMER file with the ORDERS file using a field in each with common format and values, though the fieldnames may differ. No action takes place with the datafile. The **JOIN** command simply records in the master file the existence of a *joint* relationship, as shown in bold type here:

ORDERS.M

```
| FILE =CUSTOMER,                                                       |
|   FIELD =ACCOUNT    ,ACNO       ,A6  ,A6 ,JOIN = ORDERS.CUSTID,$ |
|     •                                                                 |
|     •                                                                 |
|     •                                                                 |
|                                                                       |
| FILE =ORDERS,                                                         |
|   FIELD =CUSTOMER  ,CUSTID      ,A6   ,A6 ,$                          |
|     •                                                                 |
|     •                                                                 |
|     •                                                                 |
|                                                                       |
```

The effect of the **JOIN** command on a subsequent report request is equivalent to that of a matching **IF** phrase. The **JOIN** relationship, as specified, is uni-directional; that is, a value of ACNO is first selected from the CUSTOMER file, and the ORDERS is searched for a matching value.

In another example, a file called DIVISION, containing a recording of data items for each division of a company, has a one-to-many, or *parent*, relationship to a file called PLANT with one record per plant location. Moreover, each plant has several sections, and a file called SECTION is also related to the PLANT file. We show here the parental relationships in a block diagram, where the one-to-*many* relation is indicated by the appearance of multiple boxes.

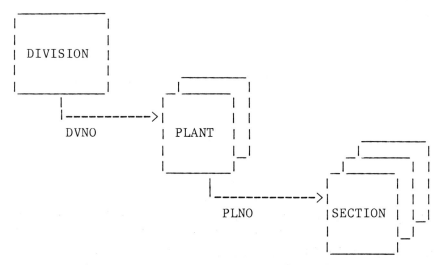

Every record in the PLANT file has a code, DVNO, to designate its parent division. Similarly, the SECTION records carry the PLNO code which ties them to a field in the PLANT file.

With matching **IF** phrases you would list the section names, according to the hierarchy of plants and divisions, with this request:

```
GETFILES DIVISION PLANT SECTION

PRINT SECTION.NAME BY DIV.NAME BY PL.NAME
IF D.DVNO EQ P.DVNO
IF P.PLNO EQ S.PLNO.
```

The last two lines are *matching* **IF** phrases, and they define the relationships between the files. The two phrases must be given with each request whenever data items are to be drawn from the three files. Now, as a convenience in situations where multifile requests are the rule rather than the exception, the **JOIN** command may be used to simplify your requests. Thus, you may request the following, in lieu of the foregoing example.

```
GETFILES DIVISION PLANT SECTION

JOIN D.DVNO TO P.DVNO
JOIN P.PLNO TO S.PLNO
```

The function of the **JOIN** command is to test for the existence of the necessary fields and to record the joint relationship in the master file. Once that has

239

been done, the matching **IF** phrases and **JOIN** commands are not required again, and the system responds as *if the files were one file of composite records.* File prefix names may be needed, as in this example:

```
PRINT SECTION.NAME BY DIV.NAME BY PL.NAME.
```

MATCHING WITH INDEX KEYFIELDS

In all of the discussion of matching records, no mention is made of sorting or of indexed fields, and yet both are of critical importance to the speed and efficiency of matching. If both files are already sorted by the matching code fields, the searching and matching process is greatly enhanced.

For discussion purposes, consider what happens when the sorted field is LASTNAME and we have stepped through the first file to the name MARTIN (the previous name was LUMBERMAN). When searching the second file, the system can save time and effort first by starting the MARTIN search at the point in the file where it finished the LUMBERMAN search. Second, when the name MEECHUM appears in the second file, the system can stop searching for MARTIN and *not* go to the end of the file looking for more cases. Then, if MARTINSON is found next in the first file the remaining records in file 2 can be skipped completely since the next record is known to be MEECHUM. Obviously, the saving in search time could be very large when the files are large and are sorted by the matching code fields.

The **INDEX** file is a device designed specifically for speeding up the search process. Its use in matching is most advantageous with the *second* file in the matching **IF** phrase, or **JOIN** statement. Given a record in the first file with LASTNAME value of MARTIN, an **INDEX** file for LASTNAME in the second file locates all the desired records in the shortest possible time — typically a few seconds, independent of the total number of records.

INDEXing of keyfields is usually done in advance, for instance, at the time of using the **JOIN** statement. Consider again the CUSTOMER and ORDERS file, and let the CUSTOMER file be stored in sorted order by NAME. ORDERS is sorted chronologically.

The latter two facts are recorded in the master file, at the time of defining the database, by assigning the special name **REC#** as the *index* of the C.NAME and O.DATE fields. **REC#** is a special system variable which is used as a counter of the records in a file. When **REC#** is given as the *index* of a field, the system knows the file is sorted physically by that field.

These commands insert the necessary information into the ORDERS.M file to **JOIN** the files with an **INDEX**ed customer number.

```
C>INDEX ORDERS.CUSTID
C>JOIN CUSTOMER.ACNO TO ORDERS.CUSTID
```

Now the master file includes the information needed to do a rapid match using the CUSTID index file.

ORDERS.M

```
 FILE =CUSTOMER,
    FIELD =ACCOUNT    ,ACNO    ,A6  ,A6 ,JOIN= ORDERS.CUSTID,$
    FIELD =NAME       ,COMPANY ,A25 ,A25,INDEX =REC#        ,$
    FIELD=
       .
       .
       .

 FILE =ORDERS,
    FIELD =CUSTOMER   ,CUSTID  ,A6  ,A6 ,INDEX= CUSTID      ,$
    FIELD =DATE       ,ORDATE  ,A6  ,A6 ,INDEX= REC#        ,$
    FIELD =
       .
       .
       .
```

In general, remember that indexing the matching field in the second, or subordinate, file can increase greatly the speed and efficiency of matching.

RELATIONS BETWEEN FILES

The three forms for specifying relations between files are summarized below. The forms are:

- A **RECODE** statement, for looking up the meaning of a code found in one file in a table of code and definitions located in a second file:

```
DEFINE fn1.name = RECODE fn1.code(fn2.code fn2.name).
```

241

- A matching **IF** phrase, which links records in two files via fields having common codes:

```
IF fn1.fld1 EQ fn2.keyfld2
```

- A **JOIN** command, for storing a relationship between files in the master file:

```
JOIN fn1.fld1 TO fn2.keyfld2
```

In addition to the above, this chapter introduced five master file attributes:

```
FILE
INDEX
REC#
JOIN
DEFINE.
```

CHAPTER 15

PROCEDURAL COMMANDS

In this chapter, we depart from the presentation of strictly nonprocedural language features to address the subject of how to use a nonprocedural system in a larger context to handle moderately complex applications. Complexity usually means that there are several, if not many, options and that there are multiple tasks to be performed—usually in a particular sequence. We assume also the intended user, or keyboard operator, has no interest in, or knowledge of, any kind of programming language. Programs of this kind are called *application programs* because they are tailored to very specific uses of particular datafiles. Also, they are *procedural*, because they are built upon a sequence of choices by the operator and upon a sequence of computer responses. Different sequences yield different results. Hence, the developer of the application, that is, you, must specify the procedural steps carefully.

The heavy emphasis on nonprocedurality in this book should not mislead you to think that there is anything wrong with sequentially oriented programming. Indeed, the latter is a necessary element in expressing *what* tasks *you* want performed as well as their **sequence**. The case for NPL and similar software systems is based upon overcoming the need to define further *how* the computer should go about fulfilling those requirements of yours.

In a rather basic way, we have already been combining procedural and nonprocedural tasks. For each exec program of two or more report requests specifies a step-by-step procedure. When the steps are many, the distinction is more evident.

For example, suppose you have two files of valuable data and several nonprocedural report requests which produce printed reports of interest to several other people. You decide to let each person have a copy of the datafiles on a floppy disk so each one may experiment with additions and changes on his or her own. However, you are reluctant to burden others with learning the details of your report requests or how to prepare their own. So you lay out the options they will need and the necessary procedural steps in a diagram like the one shown here.

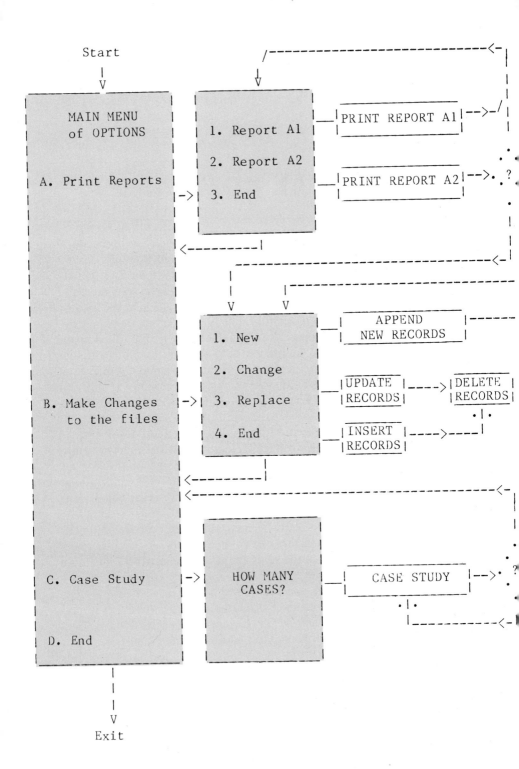

PROCEDURAL COMMANDS

The shaded boxes show the questions to be presented to the operator. The arrows show the sequence of tasks. The other boxes represent either non-procedural requests or else mixed procedural and nonprocedural statements. Following the paths in the figure, you may notice they all return in a loop to the shaded boxes. These boxes repeatedly display a *menu* of options after each choice has been executed, until the operator chooses to exit from the program.

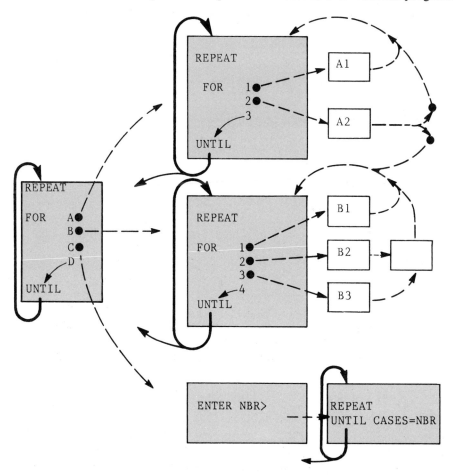

In the second figure, the illustration of the program is rearranged to emphasize two basic procedural ideas. The first is that certain steps are repeated over and over until some condition becomes true. The *repeat loops* are shown by arrows in the figure. The key words, **REPEAT:...UNTIL**, are used to tell NPL to repeat a group of statements.

The second idea is that of choosing between two or more paths in the flow diagram. The **FOR** statement is used to provide a choice of which statements to execute next. One group out of any number of groups of statements may be selected by one **FOR** statement.

The general form of these two special statements is as follows:

- The **REPEAT:. . .UNTIL** statement

```
REPEAT:
      statements...
UNTIL condition
```

where *statements...* means any number of commands, of Report requests, or of Modify mode requests may be included. At the completion of those statements the conditional expression is evaluated to determine if the group of statements should be executed again. The *condition* may be any logical expression (with a value of *true* or *false*) as defined in Chapter 5 for the **IF. . .THEN. . .ELSE** phrase.

- The **FOR** statement

```
FOR expression rel-oper 'value1': statements...
                        'value2': 'value3': statements...
                             .
                             .
                             .
                        ELSE statements...
ENDFOR
```

where *expression* may be any variable (including an amper- variable), or combination of variables, and *rel-oper* is a relational operator. The value of the *expression* is compared to one or more literal *values*, each of which is surrounded by quotes and followed by a colon. The second *value* phrase and the **ELSE** phrase are optional. More than one *value* may select the same group of statements. Each such value must have an associated colon. The keyword **ENDFOR** indicates the location of the next statement to be executed, following the selected group of statements.

As an example of the **FOR** statement consider the following:

```
FOR  COLOR  EQ  'BLUE':   blue-statements...
                'RED ':   red-statements...
                'YELLOW':yellow-statements...
ENDFOR
next-statements
```

The first *value* to satisfy the **EQ** condition selects a group of statements, after which the "next-statements" are executed.

A program to accomplish the first level of selection logic illustrated by the figures on the previous pages is as follows:

```
ECHO  *
GETFILE  ACCOUNTS
REPEAT:
*
*        MAIN  MENU  OF  OPTIONS
*            A    Print  reports
*            B    Make  changes  to  the  files
*            C    Run  a  case  study
*            D    Exit
*
    SET  CHOICE/A1=&YOUR-CHOICE(A,B,C,D).

FOR  CHOICE  EQ  'A':  EXEC  REPORTS
                'B':  EXEC  CHANGES
                'C':  EXEC  STUDY
ENDFOR

UNTIL  CHOICE  IS  'D'

ECHO  OFF
```

The two special phrases are used mostly in exec level programs, yet they are available at the command level and may be entered at the console. The following examples illustrate some simple applications.

(a)

```
C>FOR MONTH EQ 'JAN': TYPEFILE ACCOUNTS.D ENDFOR
C>
```

(b)

```
C>FOR YEAR EQ '81': GETFILE SALES81;
<>PRINT SALES BY REGION BY CUSTOMER.
<>ELSE GETFILE SALES80; SUM SALES BY REGION.
<>ENDFOR
C>
```

(c)

```
C>REPEAT: TYPEFILE SALES.M UNTIL K EQ 5
C>
```

(d)

```
C>GETFILE SALES
C>REPEAT: PRINT SALES BY PRODUCT IF BRANCHNBR EQ NBR.
<>SET NBR = NBR + 1.
<>UNTIL NBR GE 23
C>
```

In example (a), the value of MONTH is tested to determine whether the ACCOUNT.D file is to be displayed. The **ELSE** option is omitted, resulting in a simple conditional command.

In example (b), a similar test selects between two report requests. Each request is terminated by a period. The final keyword, **ENDFOR**, is required to terminate the **FOR** phrase. The system prompts the operator with <> on each new line until the **ENDFOR** is reached.

Example (c) shows an incorrect command which will type the SALES.M file again and again, forever, since no provision is made for changing the value of K between repeated excutions. An exception to this is when the initial value of K is 5, and the SALES.M file is typed only once.

Example (d) prints a sequence of reports, until the variable NBR reaches a particular value. The **SET** statement causes NBR to act as a counter. The **PRINT** and **SET** statements are repeated as a pair. The system prompts the operator with <> on each new line until the **UNTIL** phrase is executed.

DATA VALUES

If we are to use NPL to handle more complex applications, we must have access to data values other than those stored in datafiles. You have seen how the &variable feature is used to obtain data values from the operator of an Exec program. Notice in the four examples above that there are variables like DATE, K, and NBR in the conditional expressions, but no explanation of their source. How are those values established? The answer must come from the answer to a broader question; that is, what data values are available to the console operator in the command mode? The next four sections address this topic.

PROGRAM VARIABLES

So far, we have stashed all the data away in files, and a Report request is needed to fetch data for immediate use. It is as if you were standing in the center of your office with all the file cabinets in full view, poised, ready to make a rapid search of any of their bulging drawers; yet, when asked a question on any matter, however simple, you are unable to reply directly, due to the absence of data immediately in hand.

Continuing the analogy, suppose we relieve the "file drawer" problem by making these changes:

- You may hold a pencil and note pad to record important data items for quick reference.

- We replace the face of each file cabinet drawer with glass, to enable you to read the first page (i.e., record) of each file drawer (i.e., datafile) directly, without resorting to a report request.

- You may refer to any variable mentioned in the last report request executed; however, the value you receive is the *last* value taken by the variable at the completion of the nonprocedural request.

Now you are in control of the situation. Using your "notes," plus information about the first record and last report request, you can make decisions about which requests to run and in what order.

SET VARIABLES

For your "notes" the **SET** mode provides a special *scratch pad* memory for storing data values for future use. A group of sample **SET** mode statements follows:

```
SET
  CASE/I4 = 1
  DATE/A6 = '810524'
  NBR/I2  = -5
  X/I4    = 10*CASE + NBR
  Z/F8    = 0.5*SALES.QUOTA
END
```

The general form for the **SET** mode resembles that of the **DEFINE** mode (though the effect is different). Thus several definitions may appear between the **SET** command and the period (or **END**), as:

```
SET name1/format = expression
    name2/format = expression
END
```

Also, a single variable is **SET** with a one-line command in this form:

```
C>SET name/format = expression.
```

where the period is equivalent to **END**. If the format specification is missing, F10.2 is used.

The choice of name must follow the rules for defined names. The expression on the right contains constants and names of currently active variables. The last example defines Z in terms of the value of QUOTA for the first record in the SALES file.

These **SET** variable statements are executed only once (except when repeated from within a **REPEAT:...UNTIL** statement), to determine the initial values of the **SET** variables. At a later step, the value of a **SET** variable can be changed with another **SET** statement. For example:

```
SET
  CASE = CASE + 1
  DATE = '810928'
  NBR  = 2*NBR
END
```

where any expression may appear to the right, including one having the name of the **SET** variable itself.

DATAFILE VARIABLES

In addition to being available for nonprocedural report requests, datafile variables from the *first record* of the file and from the *last line* of the previous report are availale to command statements. The above example which defines the command variable Z illustrates how the first variable of a file is accessed. To refer to a variable appearing in the previous report request, use the modifier **LAST**. For example, upon completion of this report request:

```
GETFILE SALES
WRITE MIN.PRICE AVE.PRICE MAX.PRICE SUM.UNITS.
```

you may retrieve the four values computed for the whole SALES file (this is a one-line report) and assign those values to **SET** variables, as follows:

```
C>SET
S>MINP/F8.2= LAST MIN.PRICE
S>AVEP/F8.2= LAST AVE.PRICE
S>MAXP/F8.2= LAST MAX.PRICE
S>TOTUNITS/F8.2= LAST SUM.UNITS.
C>
```

Each of these statements is a *command* to define a new variable and then to compute a value for it. Were the report request to include the sort phrase **BY REGION**, the values assigned above would be those computed for only the last REGION in the report.

You may also update an existing **SET** variable, as well as a PROFILE variable, with values read from the last report request. For example:

```
C>SET NBR = LAST ROW#
C>SET .QUOTA = LAST AVE.SALES.
```

The first case saves the number of lines generated by the previous report request in the NBR exec variable. The second stores the last value reported of AVE.SALES into the field called .QUOTA, where the name QUOTA identifies a variable in the SALES/P datafile—a PROFILE datafile having a single record. The prefixed period identifies the PROFILE datafile.

PROFILE VARIABLES

For the purpose of storing control information helpful to procedural programming, any file (with name filename.D) may have associated with it a special file called a profile datafile. The profile has the name filename.P and contains a single record of one or more data items. These items are assigned fieldnames, aliases, and formats in the master file. Profile variables may be used in connection with any active datafile. Their names are distinguished from other data items by the use of period as a prefix to the name. For example, the following statement is used to assign a new value to the profile QUOTA:

```
SET .QUOTA = 85000.
```

TYPE OF VARIABLES

In summary, we see that NPL provides storage in disk files for two kinds of variables:
- Datafile variables (multiple values)
- Profile variables (single value)

where the second is a special case of the first. Then there is a temporary storage in computer memory provided for:
- **SET** variables (single value)
- **LAST** variables (single value)

where the latter type is created at the completion of a report request and disappears at the begining of the next report request. The latest values of **SET** variables are remembered until the end of the NPL session.

Elsewhere in the book two other types of *variables*, are discussed: **DEFINE**d variables and amper-variables. With the first of these there is some confusion in terminology, for what is stored in memory is the **expression** from a DE-**FINE** statement and not the current *value* of a variable. Thus whenever you use a **DEFINE**d variable the expression is re-evaluated. It is not possible to store a new value into a **DEFINE**d variable, for values are not saved.

The term amper-variable refers to the totally different concept of substituting a new string of characters into an Exec program to replace the names of a dummy variable name. See Chapter 10. We mention amper-variable here to distinguish it from the types of data variables under discussion.

The relationship of variables to Report requests, **SET** statements and DE-FINE expressions is illustrated in the figure. Notice that datafile variables may be viewed in two ways:
- by Report requests and **DEFINE**s as a sequence of data values
- by **SET** statements, as the first data value for each datafile variable

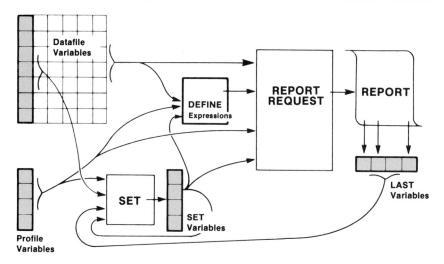

The rules for the use of these variables are:
- **SET**, profile, and datafile variables may appear in **DEFINE** expressions.
- **LAST**, **SET**, profile and initial datafile variables may be used in **SET** statements.
- **DEFINE**d, **SET**, profile and datafile variables may be used in Report requests.

THE CHECKBOOK APPLICATION

Let's put these tools to work with a simple application. The following activities are required for the keeping of records for a personal account:
- Entering new transactions (checks and deposits).

- Recording which ones have been cleared by the bank (cancelled) and returned with the bank statement.
- Reconciling your current balance with that of the bank statement.

```
ECHO  *
GETFILE CHECKREG
*
*     This Program Handles All Checkbook Entries

REPEAT:
   *
   *          CHECKBOOK BALANCING MENU OF OPTIONS
   *
   *          0   -   Exit
   *          1   -   Enter New Checks
   *          2   -   Enter Cancelled Checks
   *          3   -   Balance
   *
      SET OPTION/A1   = &YOUR_CHOICE
      FOR OPTION EQ

          '1':      MODIFY
                    FORM
                    "Paid To: <TO              Amount:   $<AMT
                     DATE    : <DAT        Check Nbr:    <NBR"
                    APPEND

          '2':      SELECT CHECKNBR.
                    MODIFY
                    FORM
                    "Cancelled Y/N?: <CAN
                     Paid To      : <TO      Amount :   $<AMT
                     Date         : <DAT Check Nbr:    <NBR "
                    RUN

          '3':      SUM AMT AS 'TOTAL OUTSTANDING'
                    IF CAN IS N OR ' '.
                    SET OUTSTANDING = LAST C.AMT
                    SET NEWDEPS = 0.
                    REPEAT:

 *   Enter Outstanding Deposit Amounts; Enter 0 to Proceed.

                    SET  DEPOSIT = &DEPOSIT_AMOUNT
                    SET  NEWDEPS = NEWDEPS + DEPOSIT.
                    UNTIL DEPOSIT EQ 0

                    SET BALANCE   = &ENDING_BALANCE
                    SET CURRENT   = BALANCE + NEWDEPS - OUTSTANDING.

 *   Current Balance= <CURRENT

      ENDFOR
UNTIL OPTION IS '0'
ECHO OFF
```

A means for displaying these options is shown in the first grey box above. The figure shows a complete exec level program. A **REPEAT:. . .UNTIL** statement reaches from the fourth line to the end of the program to allow repeated selection of options from the menu. The **SET** variable called OPTION is set with an amper-variable (&YOUR CHOICE), which prompts the operator for a value.

Next a three-level **FOR. . .ELSE. . .ENDFOR** statement tests the value of OPTION in order to select one of three groups of statements. Once the selected group of statements has been executed, NPL passes control to the line following the three-level **FOR. . .ELSE. . .ENDFOR** statement, that is, to the line that reads "UNTIL OPTION IS '0'."

For example, when OPTION has the value of 1, a DATA-FORM program is executed to append new records to the file. When the operator ends the DATA-FORM session, NPL passes control to the **UNTIL** phase and then back up to the **REPEAT:** command.

When OPTION has the value of 2, the DATA-FORM mode allows the operator to select records at random and to mark them as "cancelled."

When OPTION has the value of 3, a Report request computes the total amount for checks outstanding. Then the **LAST** value of C.AMT, just computed, is assigned to the **SET** variable OUTSTANDING, and a **SET** variable NEWDEPS is assigned the value of zero. A **REPEAT:. . .UNTIL** statement and an amper-variable cause successive prompts to the operator to obtain all the outstanding deposit amounts.

Next, the bank statement "ending balance" is requested from the operator. The current balance for your checkbook is computed, and then it is displayed by means of the form "<CURRENT", which substitutes the computed value of the variable CURRENT into a display line (a line beginning with an asterisk).

Next, the **UNTIL** phrase returns control to the top of the program, and the main menu is redisplayed. When the operator types 0, NPL exits from the program.

This chapter introduced three new statements for use in controlling the execution of NPL requests:

```
C> REPEAT: statements UNTIL condition

C> FOR condition a: statements
                  b: statements
              ELSE statements ENDFOR

C> SET name/format = expression.
```

CHAPTER 16

DATABASE FUNCTIONS

To maintain a datafile means to keep it up-to-date with changes. Many datafiles require no maintenance, because they contain historical data which does not change. Last year's financial files, the U.S. Census files, and extracts from the Dow-Jones database are dated and need never be changed (unless there are errors). For many files the data item values are changing constantly and records must be added, changed, and dropped.

There are three basic commands for making changes to datafiles:

- **INSERT** for storing a new record in a file
- **DELETE** for dropping an existing record
- **UPDATE** fld=... for changing the value of a data item

The first two of these were introduced in Chapter 11 in their simplest form.

Each command affects only a datafile activated by the **GETFILE** command, and each is further restricted to the subfile created by the active **SELECT** condition. When the **SELECT** statement is so specific as to isolate a single record, then **DELETE** and **UPDATE** affect only that record, and **INSERT** places a new record in the file immediately before the **SELECT**ed record.

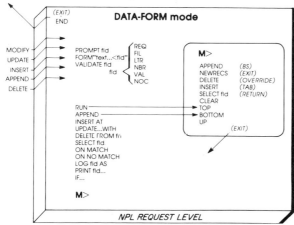

The three file maintenance commands take you into the File Maintenance mode, or Modify mode. The command **APPEND**, a special case of **INSERT**, does so also. The options in this mode are summarized in the illustration, which is taken from the NPL guide. We have used the **INSERT, APPEND,**

and **DELETE** options in DATA-FORM mode in early discussions about data entry. Their use is made more general in this chapter.

INSERTING NEW RECORDS

To insert a new record in a currently active file you must:

- Indicate which file—usually by the prefix of one or more field identifiers

- Furnish the data item values or the name of a file that contains the values

- Specify where in the file the new record is to be placed

If you are furnishing the data for each record from the console, you should use the **PROMPT**, **FORM** and **VALIDATE** phrases introduced in Chapter 12.

To specify the location for insertion at a point in the file determined by a keyfield value, you name the keyfield in an **INSERT** phrase, as in this example:

```
GETFILE SALES

INSERT AT SALES.ACNBR
  FORM "ACCOUNT NBR  <ACNBR    DATE <DATE
        <FULLNAME
        - - - - - - - - - - - - - - - - - - - - - - - - - - - -
        NAME
        STREET <STR
        CITY <CITY      STATE <ST    ZIP <ZIP "
  END
```

If SALES.ACNBR is an indexed field, the file is searched in ACNBR order to find the closest possible match between a value of SALES.ACNBR in the file and a new value of ACNBR entered by the operator.

If the physical sort order of the file is not important to you, it is better to use the **APPEND** command to store the records at the end of the file. This takes less time to execute. **INSERT**ing usually requires copying the whole file. For large files, it is sometimes better to ignore the physical order of records, to always **APPEND** new records, and to depend upon index files for locating and sorting the records.

To insert a *group* of new records, you may store the new data in a datafile with a master file of its own, called NEWACCTS, for example. Then for each record of the NEWACCTS file, the SALES file may be searched to locate the position for insertion.

```
GETFILES SALES NEWACCTS

INSERT AT S.ACNBR = N.ACNT
          S.DATE = &DATE
          S.REGION = 'EAST'
          S.SALESPERS = N.SALESMAN
          S.CUSTOMER = N.NAME
          S.* = N.* ;
IF N.ACNT EQ S.ACNBR.
```

In this example the fields of each new record intended for the SALES file are assigned values either by an &variable, or from the NEWACCTS file. When the names (or aliases) of the two master files are the same, the asterisk may be used to specify "all fields with like names," otherwise separate assignment statements are required to show the assignment of NEWACCTS values to the right fields in a SALES record. The matching **IF** phrase causes NPL to step through the values of N.ACNT searching at each step for a matching value of S.ACNBR.

DELETING RECORDS

To delete certain records you need only identify them. Both the **SELECT** command and the two kinds of **IF** phrases are used to find the records. If you know the unique identifying numbers of the records, use, for example,

```
DELETE FROM SALES IF ACNBR EQ B492X OR C137 OR F514.
```

If an index file exists for ACNO the records are located quickly by direct addressing of the disk file. Otherwise the file is searched sequentially.

One way to delete a group of records is to match a file of bad accounts numbers with the SALES datafile.

```
GETFILE SALES BADACCTS

DELETE FROM SALES IF BAD.ACNBR EQ S.ACNBR
```

NPL steps through the values of BAD.ACNBR and searches at each step for a like value of S.ACNBR.

259

More general conditions may be used for deleting records based upon data values in the sales file or in a second file. Three examples are:

```
DELETE FROM SALES IF S.AMOUNT IS 0
       AND IF BAD.ACNBR EQ S.ACNBR.

DEFINE S.VARIANCE = S.AMOUNT - BAD.AMOUNT.
DELETE FROM SALES IF S.VARIANCE IS-NOT -20 TO 20
       AND IF BAD.ACNBR EQ S.ACNBR.

SELECT S.REGION = 'NEW ENGLAND' 'MID ATLANTIC'.
DELETE FROM SALES IF S.FORECAST LT 15000.
```

When more than one file is active the **FROM** phrase specifies from which file records are to be removed. When a matching **IF** phrase is used, the specified file is usually mentioned after the **EQ** operator, resulting in a search of that file for each value of the variable in the beginning of the **IF** phrase.

UPDATING RECORDS

The **UPDATE** command specifies which records and with what values a change should be made. Hence the command options include those used with both the **DELETE** and **INSERT** commands. All of the facilities of the SELECT and DEFINE statements and of the **IF** phrase are available to assist the **UPDATE** command.

In certain respects a complete **UPDATE** command resembles a report mode request. The verb objects are the fields to be updated; expressions may determine the values used; and **IF** phrases control which records are affected. Three examples are:

```
a)   GETFILE SALES
     UPDATE S.SALESPERSON WITH 'WINKLER, H.'
         IF REGION IS NORTH
         AND IF S.SALESPERSON CONTAINS 'MARTIN$$$$'.
```

```
b)   GETFILE EMPLOYEE, SELECT DIVISION = MANUFACTURING.
     UPDATE SALARY WITH 1.15 * SALARY, IF TITLE IS BOOKKEEPER.
```

c)   **DEFINE** PAYRAISE = **IF** TITLE **IS** 'CLERK'   **THEN** 0.20*SALARY
                ELSE IF TITLE **IS** 'TECHNICIAN' **THEN** 100
                ELSE IF TITLE **IS** 'MANAGER'
                         AND SALARY **LT** 15000   **THEN** 0.15*SALARY
                ELSE IF TITLE **IS** 'MANAGER'   **THEN** 250.
       UPDATE SALARY **WITH** SALARY + PAYRAISE.

TRANSACTION FILES

Updating one file with transaction data stored in another file is most readily handled by matching, or joining, the two files. If the transaction file is smaller than the permanent file, and the latter is indexed by S.ACNBR, for example, then join the smaller to the larger with:

```
GETFILES SALES TRANSACT
JOIN T.ACNBR TO S.ACNBR
```

By using this order the **UPDATE** causes NPL to step through only the smaller file and to use the S.ACNBR index file to find the matching record. Now, if all the files in TRANSACT have names to match the corresponding fields in SALES, then all of the fields will be replaced with TRANSACT values by this command:

```
UPDATE SALES.* WITH TRANSACT.*
```

When there are fewer fields in TRANSACT than in SALES, only those fields present cause updating. The asterisk is shorthand for "all fields with like names." If the TRANSACT file has only two fields, DATE and AMOUNT, the last example would be equivalent to this request:

```
UPDATE S.DATE WITH T.DATE,
SALES.AMOUNT WITH T.AMOUNT.
```

A common requirement is to add the transaction amount to the current amount in the file and then to update the file with the new total. To do this, change the last example to read as follows:

```
UPDATE S.DATE WITH T.DATE
SALES.AMOUNT WITH SALES.AMOUNT + T.AMOUNT.
```

FILE MAINTENANCE STATEMENTS

The general forms of the four file maintenance commands are as follows:
1. The basic statements are for processing data held in a sorted transaction file (in these examples the filename is TRAN):

```
APPEND          fn.fld1 = TRAN.fld, ...
                fn.fld2 = expression, ...
                fn.*    = TRAN.* ;      END


INSERT AT fn.keyfld    fn.fld1 = TRAN.fld, ...
                       fn.fld2 = expression, ...
                       fn.*    = TRAN.* ;    END


DELETE FROM fn IF TRAN.fld EQ fn.keyfld
               IF fn.fld rel-oper value-list ... END


UPDATE          fn.fld1 WITH TRAN.fld, ...
                fn.fld2 WITH expression, ...
                fn.*    WITH TRAN.*  ;
            IF TRAN.fld EQ fn.keyfld
            IF fn.fld rel-oper value-list ... END
```

2. Similar statements are used for processing specific sets of data values (rather than a file of values):

```
APPEND    PROMPT fn.fld, fld...
          FORM "text <fld... text <fld..." END

INSERT AT fn.keyfld
          PROMPT fn.fld, fld...
          FORM "text <fld... text <fld..." END

DELETE FROM fn
          IF fn.keyfld EQ value-list
          IF fn.fld rel-oper value-list ... END

UPDATE PROMPT fn.fld, fld...
          FORM "text <fld... text <fld..."
          fn.fld1 WITH expression,  ... ;
          IF fn.keyfld EQ value-list
          IF fn.fld rel-oper value-list ... END
```

The *expressions* may contain **DEFINE**d names, and fieldnames of the file. *Expressions* may simply be specific data values. **END** may be replaced by a period.

3. There is a combination form which is used to **UPDATE** or **INSERT**, depending on whether a record exists or not for a particular keyfield value. The **UPDATE** and **INSERT** statements are selected by an **IF. . .THEN. . .ELSE** phrase in this form:

```
IF TRAN.fld EQ fn.keyfld
THEN UPDATE statement
ELSE INSERT statement.
```

All the options of the **UPDATE** and **INSERT** forms may be used.

In response to the combination statement, NPL reads a field value from the TRAN file and searches the fn.keyfld index file for a match of values. If a match is found the **UPDATE** statement is executed. If there is no match of values the **INSERT** statement is executed.

4. There are four other phrases which depend upon the outcome of the search for a match of key values. These may be included in any **UP-DATE** or **DELETE** statement before the final terminator.

```
ON MATCH PRINT fn.fld fn.fld ...
ON MATCH LOG fn.fld fn.fld ... AS filename
ON NOMATCH PRINT TRAN.fld TRAN.fld ...
ON NOMATCH LOG TRAN.fld TRAN.fld ... AS filename
```

The **PRINT** phrase writes a report, and the **LOG** phrase writes a file. In either case the verb objects are fields of the matched records, or the unmatched TRAN record, or variables **DEFINE**d with those fields.

The following keywords were introduced in this chapter:

Commands	*Others*
APPEND	**IF . . . THEN . . . ELSE**
DELETE FROM	**ON MATCH**
INSERT AT	**ON NOMATCH**
UPDATE . . . WITH	**LOG**
JOIN	

CHAPTER 17

MULTISEGMENT RECORDS

For most of the examples in this book we have been considering files with records of a fixed number of characters, that is, *fixed record length files*. Sometimes such files are referred to as **rectangular files**, or **single segment** files. Each record contains a group of data items, or fields, which describe an entity, such as an event, a person, a course, an organization, or a place.

Many files are not so simple—largely because business forms and information requirements are not simple. The most common circumstance is that a record format must accommodate multiple occurrences of a data item. For example: students take several courses; people have several dependents; and companies have many departments.

In such cases you have two choices in selecting a record format. You may use a fixed length record, by providing extra fields for the multiple occurrences of, say, course number. You must choose some maximum number of such fields, and this is called a "repeating field."

SSN	NAME	COURSE1	COURSE2	COURSE3	COURSE4	COURSE5

A more convenient choice is to define a second kind of record— a *record segment*—one which is always associated with the first kind. Any number of the second record segment type may belong to a record segment of the first type. The first type of record segment is the *owner* or *parent* of the other.

Further, the parent record segment type may own several sets of record segments of different types. Each type of record segment is a different length and contains different data items. The relationship may be illustrated by rectangles for segments, with segments clustered by types, and with clusters connected to a parent record.

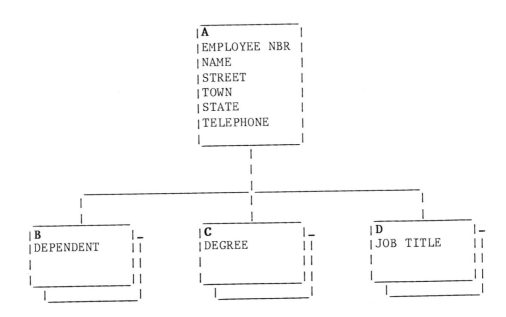

Figure 17-1

In the figure above, record segment type A is the parent of the other types, which may have these data items in them.

Record type	Entity	Possible data items
A	Employees	ID number, name, address, phone
B	Dependents	Dependent's name, relationship, date of birth, sex
C	Degrees earned	College degree, date, college
D	Jobs held	Job title, date, salary

Notice the data items of the B, C, and D segments occur together for an individual employee, but there is no association among B, C, and D items. Moreover, a particular employee record type A may own zero, or several, B-type record segments, as well as any number of C- and D-type segments.

The file in the figure above is a file of multiple segment types. It is also described as a multipath hierarchical file. The parent segment, A, owns three dependent segments with three separate paths. A path is defined as a line drawn from the most senior parent segment (or root segment) through subordinate segments to the bottom of the diagram.

To visualize how the data for the file in the figure above might be stored in a computer, first picture the data for each occurrence of segments B, C, and D as being on separate cards which are stacked below their parent, A-type, cards. The set of cards would form an ordered list like the following.

Nbr	Type	Data
1.	A	987654 JONES JOHN A 16 ELM ST SMITHBURG NJ
2.	B	SUSIE D 720116 F
3.	B	JOHN S 740107 M
4.	C	BA 65
5.	C	MA 67
6.	D	INTERN 660615 150.00
7.	D	TRAINEE 670620 180.00
8.	D	ANALYST 681101 220.00
9.	D	SR ANALYST 710305 375.00
10.	A	123456 SMITH MARY E 1087 E.40TH ST POTTSTOWN PA
11.	C	BS 74
12.	D	TRAINEE 740701 205.00
13.	A	334455 GREEN JOE S 43 PARK PL CANTON OH
14.	B	ARTHUR S 800111 M
15.	D	ANALYST 801101 230.00

The list shows fifteen record segments, but there are only three employee records (for Jones, Smith, and Green). Every B segment has the same format, and all C and D segments also look alike. The computer requires something extra to identify the segment types A, B, C and D, in order to keep its records straight.

It is sufficient to include the letter A or B or C or D as a code within each record segment. Such a code has the special name of **RECTYPE**. The **RECTYPE** code must appear in the same position in every segment. You might place it first in each segment, as in the list above.

The master file for describing the multipath file above looks like this:

PERSON.M

```
FILE=PERSONNEL ,

SEGMENT=EMPLOYEE ,
    FIELD=RECTYPE          , A     , A1     , A1    , $
    FIELD=EMPLOYEE - NBR , ENO   , A6     , A6    , $
    FIELD=LAST - NAME     , LN    , A9     , A9    , $
    FIELD=FIRST - NAME    , FN    , A6     , A6    , $
    FIELD=MIDDLE - INT    , MI    , A1     , A1    , $
    FIELD=STREET          , ADDR1 , A15    , A15   , $
    FIELD=TOWN            , ADDR2 , A12    , A12   , $
    FIELD=STATE           , ADDR3 , A2     , A2    , $

SEGMENT=DEPENDENT , PARENT=EMPLOYEE
    FIELD=RECTYPE          , B     , A1     , A1    , $
    FIELD=DEPENDENTS     , DNAM  , A9     , A9    , $
    FIELD=RELATIONSHIP , REL   , A1     , A1    , $
    FIELD=BIRTH - DATE    , DOB   , A6     , A6    , $
    FIELD=SEX             , SEX   , A1     , A1    , $

SEGMENT=DEGREE , PARENT=EMPLOYEE ,
    FIELD=RECTYPE          , C     , A1     , A1    , $
    FIELD=DEGREE         , DGR   , A6     , A6    , $
    FIELD=YEAR           , YR    , A2     , A2    , $

SEGMENT=JOB , PARENT=EMPLOYEE ,
    FIELD=RECTYPE          , D     , A1     , A1    , $
    FIELD=TITLE          , JOB   , A10    , A10   , $
    FIELD=DATE           , JDAT  , A6     , A6    , $
    FIELD=SALARY         , JWAGE , F5 . 2 , A5    , $
    FIELD=SUPERVISOR     , SCODE , A3     , A3    , $
    FIELD=PERFORMANCE    , PCODE , A4     , A4    , $
```

The first field in each segment has a very special form. That is, the fieldname is the keyword **RECTYPE** and the alias field holds the specific code value for the segment: A, B, C, or D. The alias field is *not* a name but rather the code itself. Note that any set of unique codes, with any number of characters, would work as well.

Each segment is described by a **SEGMENT** name and a **PARENT** segment name, to which you may assign names of up to eight characters beginning with a letter. You may choose words which describe the kind of data in the segment, or you could simply use the segment codes **A, B, C, D** as names. The **PARENT** names are determined by the hierarchical relationships.

Multiple segment files may have a large variety of forms. Hierarchies of data segments usually mimic the organization of institutions. For example:

```
Country              Company
  State                Division
    County               Region
      Town                 Department
                             Plant
                               Office
```

Simple structures like these have only one path from top to bottom. Others may have several paths.

A Population Datafile   A List of Record Segments

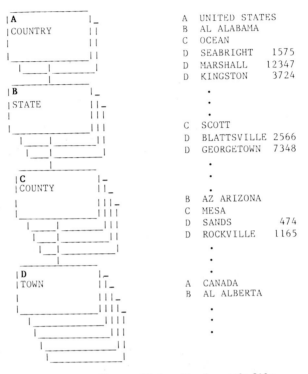

A	UNITED STATES	
B	AL ALABAMA	
C	OCEAN	
D	SEABRIGHT	1575
D	MARSHALL	12347
D	KINGSTON	3724
	•	
	•	
	•	
C	SCOTT	
D	BLATTSVILLE	2566
D	GEORGETOWN	7348
	•	
	•	
	•	
B	AZ ARIZONA	
C	MESA	
D	SANDS	474
D	ROCKVILLE	1165
	•	
	•	
	•	
A	CANADA	
B	AL ALBERTA	
	•	
	•	
	•	

Figure 17-2a. Single path file

A better way to view the records in a single path file like the one in Figure 17-2a is to place all the record segments end to end, like this:

```
|A|UNITED STATES |B|AL|ALABAMA  |C|OCEAN |D|SEABRIGHT | 1575|
|"|      "       |"|"|    "     |"|  "   |D|MARSHALL  |12347|
|"|      "       |"|"|    "     |"|  "   |D|KINGSTON  | 3724|
|"|      "       |"|"|    "     |"|  "   |•|    •     |  •  |
|"|      "       |"|"|    "     |"|  •   |•|    •     |  •  |
|"|      "       |"|"|    "     |"|  •   |•|    •     |  •  |
|"|      "       |"|"|    "     |C|SCOTT |D|BLATTSVILL| 2566|
|"|      "       |"|"|    "     |"|  "   |D|GEORGETOWN| 7348|
|"|      "       |B|AZ|ARIZONA  |C|MESA  |D|SANDS     |  474|
|"|      "       |"|"|    "     |"|  "   |D|ROCKVILLE | 1165|
```

Figure 17-2b. A rectangular file view

The ditto marks in Figure 17-2b show that while the data items in the A, B, and C segments are stored only once in the file, we may think of them as being repeated throughout a logically equivalent file, which has records of a fixed record length. Such a simplifying view is not possible with the multipath files illustrated next.

An Emergency Squad Datafile

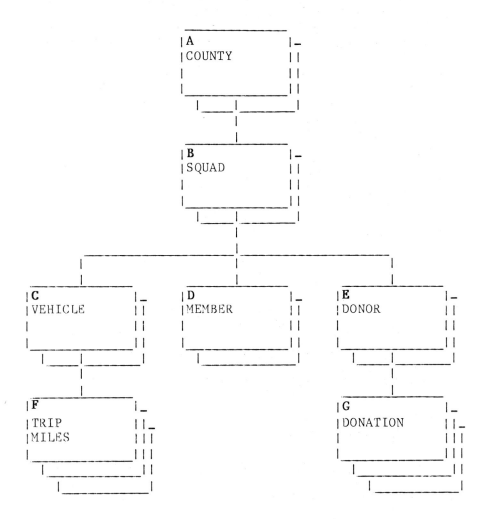

Figure 17-3. Multipath file.

A College Schedule File

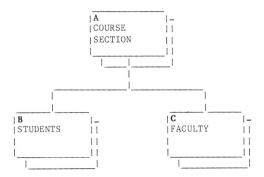

Figure 17-4. Multipath file.

A Business Accounts File

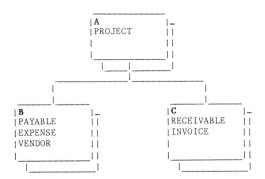

Figure 17-5. Multipath file.

REPORTING FROM MULTIPATH FILES

There are no special rules for writing NPL requests for *single path* multilevel hierarchical files. All fields are uniquely named (either by fieldnames or aliases) and are treated by NPL requests as if the file had only a single record segment of a fixed length, as in Figure 17-2b. In fact, the user may well be unaware of the actual file structure and work only with a list of fieldnames or aliases.

With *multipath* files, however, the foregoing freedom is not possible. Consider, for example, these partial requests, and refer to the figures above:

```
PRINT VEHICLE BY MEMBER.     (Figure 17-3)
PRINT FACULTY BY STUDENT.    (Figure 17-4)
 SUM  INVOICE BY EXPENSE.    (Figure 17-5)
```

In each request an item in one path is to be sorted by an item in a different path. Not only can these requests not be performed, they make no sense whatsoever, for the data in parallel paths are defined as unrelated. To avoid writing such incorrect Report requests, two rules should be observed.

Rule # 1. For verb phrases with **PRINT**, all verb objects and **BY** fields must lie along a single path from top to bottom through the **SEGMENT** diagram.

For example, looking at Figure 17-3, consider these requests:

```
PRINT TRIP AND MILES BY COUNTY BY VEHICLE    correct
PRINT DONOR BY SQUAD                         correct
PRINT TRIP AND MEMBER BY COUNTY              incorrect
PRINT DONOR BY MEMBER                        incorrect
```

Rule # 2. Verb phrases with **COUNT** or **SUM** or **WRITE** may use objects from divided paths; however, any **BY** fields must belong to **SEGMENTS** lying above the junction of the paths.

Consider these requests based on the file **SEGMENTS** in Figure 17-3:

```
COUNT TRIP AND MEMBER AND DONOR
BY COUNTY BY SQUAD.                          correct
SUM MILES DONATION BY SQUAD BY VEHICLE.  incorrect
```

The following multiverb, multipath request is correct:

```
SUM DONATION BY COUNTY;
COUNT MEMBER BY COUNTY BY SQUAD;
SUM   MILES   BY COUNTY BY SQUAD BY VEHICLE.
```

Notice that each line contains the sort fields of the preceding line. Multiple verb requests are discussed in detail in the Chapter 19.

The multi-segment files described in this chapter are distinctly different from the files discussed in all the other chapters of the book. In most cases discussed previously, datafiles have a single record type and a constant record length. The multi-segment files are a special case, and the techniques presented here are quite useful when you have such files. However, it is not always convenient or possible to mark each record segment with the **RECTYPE** code.

By describing the records of a file as a set of record segments, we gain the benefit of not having to store redundant data items for repeated occurrences of descendent **SEGMENTS** at the cost of having to mark each **SEGMENT** with a **RECTYPE** code. Another benefit is the ability to hold in a single file multiple repeating fields of data with a common **PARENT**. Such files, however, must retain the correct physical relationship of record **SEGMENTS**. They cannot be resorted conveniently; and they may not be created with the **HOLD** command.

This chapter introduced three new master file attribute names:

SEGMENT
PARENT
RECTYPE

CHAPTER 18

ARRAY VARIABLES

This chapter introduces a rather special and advanced topic; that is, the treatment of a whole table of numbers (or alphanumeric values) as if it were a single data item. The table is called an *array* of values. The advantage of grouping numbers in an array is illustrated by the following example.

A fairly common type of datafile is one that has a fixed number of records (for example, one record for each month of the year) each containing a single data item, plus one or more *descriptor* fields. Descriptor fields typically specify dates, locations, departments, age groups, account type, and other values to classify or categorize data items. The primary data items, by contrast, usually are numeric measures of an activity, a population, a value, a count, etc. For example, sales data for the divisions of a company could be stored in records with three descriptor fields, DIV, YR, MON, as follows:

```
div   yr  mon forecast

|WEST  |81|JAN|531075|
|WEST  |81|FEB|487810|
|WEST  |81|MAR|502150|
|   •  |  |   |      |
|   •  |  |   |      |
|   •  |  |   |      |
|WEST  |81|NOV|586500|
|WEST  |81|DEC|550450|
|NORTH|81|JAN|378642|
|NORTH|81|JAN|297844|
```

An alternative way of storing the same information is in a single record for each division, with two descriptors, as in this one:

```
div   yr   mon=1    2         3                           11        12
```

	WEST	81	531075	487810	502150		. . .		586500	550450	
	NORTH	81	378642	297844	361490		. . .		420192	397333	

The obvious advantage of the second form is that the descriptors, WEST and 81, are stored only once, while the month names are not recorded at all. There are only 78 characters stored, rather than 180: a 56 percent saving of disk space. This may be significant when there are many divisions and many years of data items.

The absence of the month names may seem to be a problem. Yet if there are always twelve data items, we can infer the month from the position of each item in the record. A group of data items in this form is often called a *repeating field*, and sometimes an *array variable*. In the master file we designate the group as an **ARRAY**, rather than a **FIELD**, and the group is given a name, an alias, a printing format, and a file format.

The master file for the first example file shown above looks like this:

```
FILE =SALES1,
    FIELD =DIVISION    ,DV      ,A4    ,A4    ,$
    FIELD =YEAR        ,YR      ,A2    ,12    ,$
    FIELD =MONTH       ,MTH     ,A3    ,A3    ,$
    FIELD =FORECAST    ,FRCST   ,F6    ,A6    ,$
```

The master file for the second example includes an ARRAY to describe the twelve forecast items.

```
FILE =SALES2,
    FIELD =DIVISION    ,DV      ,A4    ,A4    ,$
    FIELD =YEAR        ,YR      ,A2    ,A2    ,$
    ARRAY =FORECAST    ,FRCST   ,12F6  ,A72   ,$
```

You can see that

- The Array name is FORECAST

- The Alias is FRCST

- The Printing format calls for twelve items, each with a format of F6

- The File format reserves space for seventy-two characters (six times twelve)

A Report mode request for the sales data, in the SALES82 file, listed by month would look like this:

```
GETFILE SALES82
PRINT ROW# AS MONTH AND FORECAST BY DIVISION BY YEAR
AND COLUMNTOTAL.
```

with the result:

DIVISION	YEAR	MONTH	FORECAST
WEST	81	1	531075
		2	487810
		3	502150
		.	.
		.	.
		.	.
		11	586500
		12	550450
			- - - - - -
			6217727

Since the month number is not stored anywhere, the system variable **ROW#** is used instead.

CREATING MASTER FILES WITH ARRAYS

To create a master file description for the file in the foregoing example, execute the command:

```
C>CREATE ARRAY SALES
```

NPL then asks for the definition of each array and field item to create the SALES.M file. The dialog looks like this:

```
FILE name  >  SALES

FIELD or ARRAY Name  >  DIVISION
ALIAS                >  DV
PRINTING FORMAT      >  A4
FILE FORMAT          >  A4
SUBSCRIPT            >

FIELD or ARRAY Name  >  YEAR
ALIAS                >  YR
PRINTING FORMAT      >  A2
FILE FORMAT          >  A2
SUBSCRIPT            >

FIELD or ARRAY Name  >  FORECAST
ALIAS                >  FRCST
PRINTING FORMAT      >  12F6
FILE FORMAT          >  A72
SUBSCRIPT            >  .MONTH
```

SUBSCRIPTS

Clearly we have lost something in the foregoing sample report by not printing the month names. To regain them we need a means to store the names once (not repeatedly for each year and each division). The names must be associated implicitly with the numbers 1 to 12. The desired means is simply an **ARRAY** of names, which is specified in the master file as an array item in a **FILE** called **PROFILE**.

The array of names is employed as a *subscript* to the array of sales values. The relationship is established with this command

```
C>DEFINE SUBSCRIPT
```

which results in the asking of a series of questions. The answers are supplied here (in bold) for the example above:

```
Name of Subscript? >  MONTH
Short Name? >  MTH
Number of Subscript Values? >  12
Description of the Subscript? >  MONTH OF THE YEAR
What Printing Format? >  A9
Enter Subscript Value Names:

MONTH OF THE YEAR
    MONTH   1 >  JANUARY
    MONTH   2 >  FEBRUARY
    MONTH   3 >  MARCH
      .       .     .
      .       .     .
      .       .     .
    MONTH  11 >  NOVEMBER
    MONTH  12 >  DECEMBER
```

The system then inserts the definitions of the array under FILE =PROFILE in the SALES.M master file and stores the array values in a datafile called SALES.P. This is a special datafile which is used for storing subscripts and constants.

The next step is for you to join the SALES array and the MONTH array using a new command, **JOIN**, as follows:

```
C>JOIN SALES.FORECAST TO .MONTH
```

This command simply writes two additional pieces of information in the SALES.M master file:

- MONTH is given the attribute that is **JOIN**ed to FORECAST

- FORECAST is given the attribute that the array has a subscript called **.MONTH**

The resulting master file looks like this:

279

SALES.M

```
|                                                                    |
|FILE =PROFILE,                                                      |
| ARRAY =MONTH,MTH,12A9,A108,ARRAYTYPE =SUBS,MONTH OF THE YEAR,      |
|                JOIN =SALES.FORECAST ,$                             |
|                                                                    |
|                                                                    |
|FILE =SALES,                                                        |
| FIELD =DIVISION ,DIV   ,A4   ,A4 ,$                                |
| FIELD =YEAR     , YR   ,A2   ,A2 ,$                                |
| ARRAY =FORECAST ,FRCST ,12F6 ,A72, SUBSCRIPT =.MONTH ,$            |
|                                                                    |
```

Not only has MONTH been inserted in SALES.M, but the two arrays have been cross-referenced with the **JOIN** and **SUBSCRIPT** phrases. A record of the **PROFILE** file consists of various fields and arrays like any other file; however, only a single record is stored in the special file SALES.P. Fieldnames and array names do not need the filename prefix to assure uniqueness. These names are considered to be global to all files in the database. An initial period in the name is sufficient to identify **PROFILE** variables.

SUBSCRIPT RELATIONS

To expand on the possibilities of using array variables, let's redefine the SALES.M file now to include a second array which contains twelve values of the estimated quantity of units to be sold. Thus after the FORECAST array, insert the line:

```
ARRAY =EST-UNITS ,QTY ,12I4 ,A48    ,$
```

Then add:

```
JOIN SALES.QTY TO .MONTH
```

and let's assume that the data have been loaded into the new file. The master file now looks like this:

SALES.M

```
|                                                                          |
|FILE =PROFILE,                                                            |
|  ARRAY =MONTH    ,MTH   ,12A9 ,A108 ,ARRAYTYPE =SUBS,MONTH OF THE YEAR,  |
|          JOIN =SALES.FORECAST ,$                                         |
|                                                                          |
|  ARRAY =SEASON ,SESN  ,4A6   ,A24,ARRAYTYPE =SUBS,SEASON OF THE YEAR,    |
|                                                                          |
|                                                                          |
|FILE =SALES,                                                              |
|  FIELD =DIVISION ,DIV  ,AR    ,AR   ,$                                   |
|  FIELD =YEAR      ,YR  ,A2    ,A2   ,$                                   |
|  ARRAY =FORECAST ,FRCST,12F6 ,A72  ,SUBSCRIPT =.MONTH ,$                 |
|  ARRAY=EST-UNITS,QTY   ,12I4 ,A48  ,SUBSCRIPT =.MONTH ,$                 |
|                                                                          |
```

Next, define a new subscript array to hold the names of the seasons:

```
C>DEFINE SUBSCRIPT

Name of Subscript? > SEASON
Short Name? > SESN
Number of Subscript Values? > 4
Description of the Subscript?> SEASON OF THE YEAR
What Printing Format Code?> A6
Enter Subscript Value Names:

SEASONS OF THE YEAR
   SEASON 1 > SPRING
   SEASON 2 > SUMMER
   SEASON 3 > FALL
   SEASON 4 > WINTER
```

We know, of course, that the array of SEASON names is related to the month names, but we must tell the computer about it by defining another variable called a *subscript relation array*. The relations between the subscripts may be seen more clearly in this block diagram:

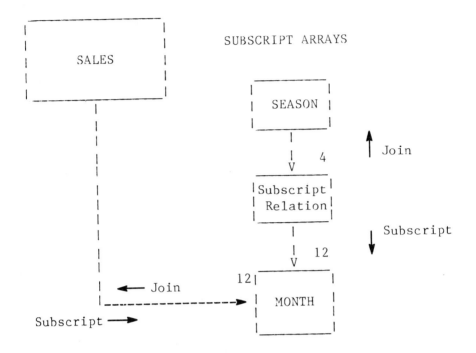

Where two boxes are connected, the lower box contains the *less aggregate sub-scripts*, e.g., twelve items versus four items. The relation, looking down the hierarchy, is described as a **SUBSCRIPT**. For example, from the perspective of the SALES file, MONTH is a subscript. Looking up from MONTH to SALES, the relation is labelled a **JOIN** in the master file. The two relations are complementary. The master file description for this example is shown on the next page.

Many subscript array variables have a direct relationship to other subscript variables, as illustrated by the SEASON and MONTH boxes in the diagram, so a special form of the **JOIN** command exists for defining subscript relations:

```
C>JOIN SUBSCRIPTS SEASON TO MONTH
```

Both subscripts have been defined as having a discrete number of values. The *less aggregate subscript* has as many as and usually more values than the other. The less aggregate subscript must follow the word **TO** in this command. The two subscript variables, SEASON and MONTH, must have been defined in the master file prior to the JOIN SUBSCRIPT command.

The system then asks for answers to these questions:

```
Name for New Variable to Hold the Relationship?  >SEAS:MTH
Short Name? >  S:M
Description of SEAS:MTH? >SEASON FOR EACH MONTH

ENTER SEASON FOR EACH MONTH
   MONTH JANUARY    >WINTER
   MONTH FEBRUARY   >WINTER
   MONTH MARCH      >SPRING
      .        .          .
      .        .          .
      .        .          .
   MONTH NOVEMBER   >FALL
   MONTH DECEMBER   >WINTER
```

After the dialog, you may write a summary report of forecasts of sales and quantities *by season*:

```
C>GETFILE SALES
C>SUM FORECAST AND QTY BY SEASON.

SEASON          FORECAST          EST-UNITS

SPRING          1632745               6472
SUMMER          1459236               5195
FALL            1556421               5870
WINTER          1569335               6103
```

The master file, with the above additions, looks like this:

SALES.M

```
|                                                                              |
|FILE =PROFILE,                                                                |
| ARRAY =MONTH    ,MTH    ,12A9 ,A108 ,ARRAYTYPE =SUBS,MONTH OF THE YEAR,|
|           JOIN =SALES.FORECAST ,$                                            |
|           JOIN =.SEAS:MTH      ,$                                            |
|                                                                              |
| ARRAY =SEASON  ,SESN  ,4A6   ,A24  ,ARRAYTYPE=SUBS,SEASON OF THE YEAR,|
|           SUBSCRIPT =.SEAS:MTH,$                                             |
|                                                                              |
| ARRAY =SEAS:MTH,S:M,12I1,A12 ,ARRAYTYPE=SUBREL,SEASON FOR EACH MONTH,|
|           SUBSCRIPT =.MONTH    ,$                                            |
|           JOIN =.SEASON        ,$                                            |
|FILE =SALES,                                                                  |
| FIELD =DIVISION ,DIV  ,A4   ,A4   ,$                                         |
| FIELD =YEAR     ,YR   ,A2   ,A2   ,$                                         |
| ARRAY =FORECAST ,FRCST,12F6 ,A72  ,SUBSCRIPT =.MONTH ,$                      |
| ARRAY=EST-UNITS,QTY   ,12I4 ,A48  ,SUBSCRIPT =.MONTH ,$                      |
|                                                                              |
```

The SALES.M master file has two kinds of array variables. The first two arrays are tables of *subscript value names*. The third array, named SEAS:MTH, is a table of twelve integers which represents the relationship of two sets of subscript values, MONTH and SEASON. The **ARRAY** name chosen for this subscript relation suggests the relation, if the colon is read as "for each." The table of integers corresponds to the answers given to the question of the **JOIN SUBSCRIPT** command. That is:

Subscript	SEASON		SEAS:MTH	
1	WINTER		4	
2	WINTER		4	
3	SPRING		1	
4	SPRING		1	
5	SPRING		1	
6	SUMMER		2	
7	SUMMER		2	
8	SUMMER		2	
9	FALL		3	
10	FALL		3	
11	FALL		3	
12	WINTER		4	

This table is created and used automatically by the system. The user need not understand this and other details of the master file to make good use of arrays and subscripts.

In summary, these are the only commands you need for working with subscripts; each command writes information in the master file.

```
C>CREATE ARRAY

C>DEFINE SUBSCRIPT

C>JOIN fn.array1 TO .subs3

C>JOIN SUBSCRIPTS .subs1 TO subs2
```

where .subs1, .subs2, and .subs3 are arrays of subscript value names.

This chapter introduced these keywords:

```
CREATE ARRAY
PROFILE
DEFINE SUBSCRIPT
JOIN
```

and these master file attributes:

```
ARRAY
ARRAYTYPE
SUBSCRIPT
SUBS
SUBREL
```

CHAPTER 19

MULTIPLE VERB AND NESTED SETS

CLUSTERING RECORDS WITH BY PHRASES—AGAIN

We have discussed how the **BY** phrases in a report request not only sort records for an ordered display, but in doing so, also bring records together into groups with common **BY** field values. Fields which are *attributes*, or *descriptors*, rather than the basic data values in a record are sometimes called classifying or categorizing variables. Examples are: AGE-GROUP, SEX, RACE, CITY, STATE, CLASS, DEPARTMENT, PROGRAM, and COLOR. These variables may assume only a fixed number of discrete values.

Other data fields do not classify records; rather, they identify specific records because of their unique values. SSN, NAME, APARTMENT-NBR, AC-COUNT-NBR, SERIAL-NO, and PART-NBR may have unique values for each record.

The basic data values usually have field names like QUANTITY, AMOUNT, CURRENT-BALANCE, AVERAGE, TOTAL AMOUNT, or RATION. These are quantitative values, which differ from record to record.

Categorizing variables, when using **BY** fields in a report request, cluster the records into cells specified by the hierarchy of the **BY** fields. That is, if sorted **BY** AGE-GROUP, **BY** RACE, and **BY** SEX, the cells are defined by this structure:

AGE-GROUP	RACE	SEX	CLUSTER #
0-20		F	#1
	NW	M	#2
	WH	F	#3
		M	#4
21-40	NW	F	#5
		M	#6
	WH	F	#7
		M	#8
40-60	NW	F	#9
		M	#10
	WH	F	#11
		M	#12
>60	NW	F	#13
		M	#14
	WH	F	#15
		M	#16

If the other fields in the records are NAME, EDYRS, and INCOME, then you may have either a long or a short report, depending on whether you use the **PRINT** or the **WRITE** verb.

• The short form results from the use of the **WRITE** verb, and one or more prefix operators, producing a report line for each of the sixteen cells in the table of categorizing variables. For example:

```
C>WRITE AVE.INCOME AVE.EDYRS,
R>BY AGEGRP BY RACE BY SEX.
```

Or, no prefix operator but only numeric variables may be used:

```
C>WRITE INCOME, BY AGEGRP BY RACE BY SEX.
```

The latter is really a brief form of **WRITE SUM.INCOME**, since the summing of numeric variables is the most frequent operation.

• The long form results when the request indicates you wish to print data from each and every record. The keyword **PRINT** has been assigned the meaning that each record is to appear in the report.

```
C>PRINT EDYRS INCOME, BY AGEGRP BY RACE BY SEX.
```

Of course, the long form also results from using a **BY** field that is not a categorizing variable but uniquely specifies each record, as in:

```
C>WRITE EDYRS INCOME BY AGEGRP BY NAME.
```

The **BY** field *NAME* has a unique value for each record, as do the two verb objects EDYRS AND INCOME; hence each record is printed.

REPORTING MISSING CLUSTERS

Now let's see what happens when the file is changed into two files, GROUP and PERSON, as follows:

289

GROUP

AGEGRP	RACE	SEX	CODE
0–20	NW	F	01
0–20	NW	M	02
0–20	WH	F	03
0–20	WH	M	04
21–40	NW	F	05
.	.	.	.
.	.	.	.
.	.	.	.
>60	WH	M	16

CODE	NAME	EDYRS	INCOME
15	CAREY	16	35500
06	HUGHES	14	27750
02	CAHILL	12	14320
12	KANE	19	28222
13	BROWN	15	19590
06	MANDEL	16	11000
12	RAGEN	16	14600

There is a one-to-many relationship between a code in a GROUP record and the PERSON.code values, through which we can join the files with the commands

```
C>GETFILES GROUP, PERSON
C>JOIN GROUP.CODE TO PERSON.CODE
```

This yields a simple hierarchy where the GROUP records are the parents of the PERSON records. Writing reports from this file structure is not changed from the previous single file case, though the resulting reports may differ. In the one file case, we can only write report lines for records that exist.

With two files the GROUP categorizing codes exist for all sixteen categories, whether or not the PERSON file has records for all the cells. You have an option, therefore, whether or not to write the data items from the parent files when there are no matching records in a second file. The rule is:

• In the normal case, the upper structure is *not* printed when matching records are not present, either in the file or after screening.

• Use the prefix **ALL** with any field from the parent file to force printing of all cases.

For example, if there are no records for females under age 41 in the PERSON file, this request,

```
C>WRITE CNT.PERSON.CODE AS NBR,
R>AND AVE.INCOME MIN.EDYRS
R>BY ALL.AGEGRP SKIP BY RACE BY SEX.
```

yields a report with four lines having dots in lieu of data values, to indicate the absence of records for those cells.

AGE GRP	RACE	SEX	NBR	AVE INCOME	EDYRS
0-20	NW	F	.	.	.
		M	18	0	6
	WH	F	.	.	.
		M	42	3240	5
21-40	NW	F	.	.	.
		M	83	11320	8
	WH	F	.	.	.
		M	124	12754	10
41-60	NW	F	9	13159	11
		M	7	13254	10
	WH	F	142	9234	12
		M	157	15375	10
>60	NW	F	43	7242	10
		M	61	6239	6
	WH	F	34	8942	12
		M	78	10139	9

The **ALL** option is used only in report requests from two or more files to ensure the printing of items from the parent file, even in the absence of data in the lower structure.

SCREENING ON CLUSTERS OF RECORDS

The screening **IF** phrases test the value of a variable for each record to determine whether or not to retain the record. If rejected the record does not participate in the sorting, summing, or printing activities that follow. Another kind of screening, which takes place *after* sorting and summing, may be used to retain or reject a whole cluster of records. We may call such screening statements the *group test* **IF** phrases.

```
WRITE  CNT.PERSON.CODE  AS  NBR,
AND  AVE.INCOME  MIN.EDYRS
BY  AGEGRP  SKIP  BY  RACE  BY  SEX
IF  AVE.INCOME  GT  10000.
```

In this example, it is evident from the **AVE** prefix in the third line that the screening must be applied to each of the sixteen clusters formed by the three **BY** field values. The report appears like this:

AGE-GRP	RACE	SEX	NBR	AVE INCOME	MIN EDYRS
21-40	NW	M	83	11320	8
	WH	M	124	12754	10
41-60	NW	F	9	13159	11
		M	67	13254	10
	WH	M	157	15375	10
>60	WH	M	78	10139	9

Thus group tests are performed using any of the prefix operators which measure some property of the cluster of records, as illustrated here:

```
...BY     DIV        IF AVE.EMP.AGE LT 50, IF EMP.SEX IS AM
...BY     COLLEGE    IF MIN.SATSCORE GT .SATMIN IF CLASS IS FRESHMAN
...BY PRODUCTTYPE    IF MAX.PRICE GT 500
...BY     DEPT       IF CNT.SSN GT 10, IF SALARY GE 15000
...BY     CLASS      IF ASQ.SCORE LE 8.7
...BY     ACTNTYPE   IF SUM.BALANCE GE 50000, IF DIV IS SALES
```

The general forms for the three kinds of **IF** phrases are:

screening: **IF** fld rel-oper value(s)
matching: **IF** fld **EQ** keyfld
group test: **IF** prefix.fld rel-oper value(s)

Notice in the examples that screening **IF** phrases may be used to qualify the records that appear in the clusters being group tested. In the second example the test value is a constant which is stored as a **PROFILE** variable called .SATMIN. Each example depends on at least one **BY** field to define the cluster of records. If no **BY** field is used the cluster becomes the whole file of records, in which case, the group test determines whether the report will be printed or not.

The prefixes **PCT** and **TOT** may also be used for group tests. They deserve special attention because the tests use the screen of a field over the whole file. Remember that **TOT** means the same thing as the **SUM** prefix but independent of the **BY** field clusters. This group test, for example, is applied to all records in the file (independent of any **BY** field clusters).

```
...BY MONTH, IF TOT.SALES GT 30000,
IF DIVISION IS AUTOPARTS
```

It tests the year-to-date total sales figure for the Autoparts Divison. Only if the total exceeds 30,000 is a report to be written; if so, however, the report is sorted by MONTH. The **BY** field does not affect the **TOT** group test.

The **PCT** prefix computes the ratios of the cluster sums over the sum for all records (after **IF** phrase screens). Consider a report from a file of election district counts of voters:

```
...BY DISTRICT, IF PCT.VOTERS GT 15
```

This test limits the report to the few districts that had the most influence, that is, those districts which represented at least 15 percent of the total vote.

Two additional prefix operators are useful in group tests for determining whether a cluster of records includes or excludes specific field values. The **ANY** and **ALL** prefix operators are restricted to group tests like these examples:

```
IF ALL.RACE EQ NW
IF ANY.AGEGRP IS '41-60' OR '>60'
IF ANY.GRADE EQ C-
IF ALL.GRADE EQ A OR A+
IF ANY.RACE EQ NW
IF ALL.GRADE NE F NOR X
IF ANY.COLOR NE BLUE NOR RED
IF ALL.COLOR NE BLUE NOR RED
```

If the other color choices are yellow and green, then the last example retains clusters of *only* yellow and green, while the previous test retains clusters with *some* yellow and green items. When the tested field is numeric, certain tests with **MIN** and **MAX** are equivalent to **ANY** and **ALL**, as in these pairs.

```
            <-----Equivalent tests----->

    IF  MIN.SATSCORE  LT  1000      IF  ANY.SATSCORE  LT  1000
    IF  MIN.SATSCORE  GT  1000      IF  ALL.SATSCORE  GT  1000
    IF  MAX.PRICE  LT  500          IF  ALL.PRICE  LT  500
    IF  MAX.PRICE  GT  500          IF  ANY.PRICE  GT  500
```

GROUP TESTS WITH COMPUTES

Finally, there is a form of group test **IF** phrase that uses a computed variable in place of the prefixed variable, e.g.:

```
GETFILE EMPLOYEE
WRITE CNT.PERSON.CODE AS NBR, AVE.INCOME, AVE.EDYRS,
AND COMPUTE RATIO = AVE.INCOME/AVE.EDYRS
IF RATIO GT 1000.
```

```
GETFILE SALES
WRITE MANAGER SUM.SALES CNT.SALESPERSON
COMPUTE PERFORMANCE=100*(SUM.SALES/(.QUOTA*CNT.SALESPERSON))
BY REGION
IF PERFORMANCE GT 80.
```

In the second example, a fixed quota per salesperson is assumed. This quota value is stored as .QUOTA in the profile datafile called SALES.P. A PERFORMANCE ratio is computed for each REGION equal to the total regional sales as a percent of the total quota.

You can see from the two examples that a group test with a **COMPUTEd** variable, like the basic group test **IF** phrase, depends upon the use of a prefixed variable. Remember that the **COMPUTE** phrase, by definition, operates upon the sum of the verb object values (or the result of a prefix operator) for a cluster of records.

COORDINATED REPORT REQUESTS

We have shown how the verb, **IF**, and **BY** phrases, with their modifiers, provide the means for organizing your data in a rather large variety of report formats. We introduce now the rules for combining two or more report requests to prepare a single report (or an extract file), providing even more ways of processing complex sets of data. To avoid confusion among all this variety, the new options are presented one at a time, each building upon the previous examples. All of the examples are based on the group of files illustrated on the next page.

The sample files may be related by four **JOIN** statements to form a hierarchy of record segments that model the sales organization of the hypothetical corporation. The highest segment, the DIVISION file, has only 3 records. The REGION file has 12 records, and below that there are 60 BRANCH office records. An average of four salespersons per office suggests there may be 240 records in the SALESPERSON file. The NEWORDER file is a journal of customer orders recorded by all branch offices. See figure on next page.

Now observe the codes used for joining the files and the following **JOIN** command. Each pair of files is linked using a slightly different technique. At the top of the hierarchy, DVNO is common to the DIVISION and REGION file; therefore, joining them, we used these commands:

```
C>INDEX  REG.DVNO
C>JOIN  DIV.DVNO  TO  REG.DVNO
```

DIV and REG are proper abbreviations for the **FILE**names. Once the **JOIN** command is executed it is not necessary to use a FILEname prefix with DVNO, for the two DVNO values are *matched* and hence are the same. At the next level the keyfield does not appear explicitly in the REGION file, so the DVNO and REGN codes are combined with a **DEFINE** statement:

```
C>DEFINE  REG.CODE/A2  =  DVNO  +  REGN.
```

Now the files may be linked with:

```
C>INDEX  BRANCH.CODE
C>JOIN  REG.CODE  TO  BRANCH.CODE
```

The BRANCH file carries a BRNBR which is a unique branch identifier. Each SALESPERSON record has a corresponding code value. An alternative code could be formed by combining the BRANCH.CODE and BRN codes and storing it in the SALESPERSON file. The resulting code would be larger, five characters rather than only two; however, the method is often used, for it provides common codes throughout the hierarchy of files.

DIVISION

DVNO	NAME	DIRECTOR	GOAL (000)	LST YR
1	PAPER PRODUCTS	A.J. Machee	5075	4800
2	FABRICS	W.M. Weaver	4700	4450
3	HOUSEWARE	R.H. Hammer	3950	3630

REGION

DVNO	REGN	NAME	MANAGER	GOAL	QUOTA
1	E	MID ATLANTIC SALES	B. Franklin	1300	1240
1	N	NORTH CENTRAL SALES	J.R. Adams	1300	1210
1	S	SOUTH & S-W SALES	R.E. Lee	1250	1212
1	W	WESTERN SALES	W.B. Hickock	1225	1185
2					
2					

BRANCH

DVNO	REGN	CODE	BRN	BR	BRANCH MGR	QUOTA	ADDRESS	CITY
2		1N	CHI	49	R. Fulton	505	600 SPRINGVALE LANE	CHICAGO ...
3		1N	MIN	51	B. West	300	324 LINCOLN STREET	MINNEAP ...
3		1N	CIN	57	N. Bly	405	10200 VERDE LANE	CINCINNA...
3		1E	NYC	63	J. Smith	261	2330 BLEEKER STREET	NEW YORK...
3		1E	BOS	64	U.S. Grant	240	43 WESTON PLAZA	BOSTON ...
		1E	PHL	65	W.			DEL...
		1E	PIT	66	A.			BUR...
		1E	WAS	67	S.			NGT...

SALESPERSON

1E	BAL	71	J.	BRNBR	SALES ID	NAME	QUOTA	MOR...
1S	RIC	72	T.					OND...
1S	MEM	74	C.	49	N1475	A. Carnegie	172	IS ...
1S	NOR	76	A.	49	N8550	Z. Grey	183	LK ...
1S	DAL	78	W.	49	N6021	C.P. Steinmetz	210	S ...
1W	POR	81	S.	51	N5999	I. Duncan	170	AND...
1W	SFR	83	P.	51				

NEWORDER

1W	LAN	84	B.	51					
1W	SDG	86	B.	51					
1W	TUS	92	M.	57	SID	PRODUCT	CUSTOMER	DATE	AMOUNT
1W	PHE	95	N.	57					
2N	IND	43	F.	57	N1475	321	AK43	0115	543
2N	DET	45	A.	63	N1475	404	B593	0222	1112
2N	CHI	49	P.	63	N1475	223	BN86	0405	400
2E	NYC	63	R.	63	N1475	540	K924	0501	125
2E	HRT	64	A.	63	N1475	404	DC30	0527	2300
2S	WAS	67	C.	64	N8550	540	BN46	0105	1515
2S	RIC	72	H.	64	N8550	238	R600	0131	600
2S	MEM	74	O.		N8550	240	R600	0314	1800
2S	DAL	78	C.		N8550	238	TY80	0519	1675
	PHE				N6021	102	E590	0201	800
					N6021	85	WS06	0402	1000

Using the smaller code, the following commands are needed:

```
C>INDEX  SALESPERSON.BRNBR
C>JOIN  BRANCH.BRNBR  TO  SALESPERSON.BRNBR
```

Next the SALESPERSON and NEWORDER records are linked by a salesperson ID code which includes a character, N, E, S, or W, for the region

```
C>INDEX  NEWORDER.SID
C>JOIN  SALESPERSON.SLSID  TO  NEWORDER.SID
```

Finally, look over the resulting master file and compare it with the picture of the files. Notice that each parent file contains a **JOIN** phrase that names an alias in the next lower file. Each field so named has an **INDEX** phrase, signifying that an index file exists.

```
SALES.M

FILE=DIVISION,
    FIELD =NBR                ,DVNO    ,A1  ,A1  ,JOIN=REGION.DVNO,$
    FIELD =NAME               ,DVNAM   ,A16 ,A16,$
    FIELD =DIV DIRECTOR,DIRECTOR,A16   ,A16,$
    FIELD =GOAL (000)  ,GOAL      ,I5  ,A5  ,$
    FIELD =SALES LASTYR,LSTYR     ,I5  ,A5  ,$
    FIELD =                ,  ...    ,   ,A1  ,$

FILE =REGION,
    FIELD =DIV NBR            ,DVNO    ,A1  ,A1  ,INDEX=DVNO,$
    FIELD =REGION NBR         ,REGN    ,A1  ,A1  ,$
    FIELD =NAME               ,RNAM    ,A24 ,A24,$
    FIELD =MANAGER            ,RMGR    ,A16 ,A16,$
    FIELD =SALES              ,RGOAL   ,I5  ,A5  ,$
    FIELD =QUOTA (000) ,RQUOTA   ,I5  ,A5  ,$
    FIELD =                ,  ...    ,,   ,A1  ,$
    DEFINE REG.CODE/A2 = DVNO + REGN.      JOIN=BRANCH.CODE,$

FILE =BRANCH,
    FIELD =REGN CODE          ,CODE    ,A2  ,A2  ,INDEX=CODE,$
    FIELD =BRANCH             ,BRN     ,A3  ,A3  ,$
    FIELD =BRN NBR            ,BRNBR   ,A2  ,A2  ,$
                                         JOIN=SALESPERSON.BRNBR,$
    FIELD =MANAGER            ,BMGR    ,A16 ,A16,$
    FIELD =QUOTA (000) ,BQUOTA   ,I5  ,A5  ,$
    FIELD =ADDRESS            ,STR     ,A20 ,A20,$
    FIELD =CITY               ,CTY     ,A16 ,A16,$
    FIELD =STATE              ,ST      ,A2  ,A2  ,$
    FIELD =ZIP                ,ZP      ,A5  ,A5  ,$
    FIELD =                ,  ...    ,   ,A1  ,$

FILE =SALESPERSON,
    FIELD =BRN NBR            ,BRNBR   ,A2  ,A2  ,INDEX=BRN,$
    FIELD =ID                 ,SLSID   ,A5  ,A5  ,JOIN=NEWORDER.SID,$
    FIELD =NAME               ,SNAM    ,A16 ,A16,$
    FIELD =QUOTA (000) ,SQUOTA   ,I5  ,A5  ,$
    FIELD =                ,  ...    ,   ,A1  ,$

FILE =NEWORDER,
    FIELD =SALESPERSON ,SID      ,A5  ,A5  ,INDEX=SID,$
    FIELD =PRODUCT            ,PCODE   ,A3  ,A2  ,$
    FIELD =UNITS              ,QTY     ,I5  ,A5  ,$
    FIELD =CUSTOMER           ,CUSTID  ,A4  ,A4  ,$
    FIELD =MONTH              ,MTH     ,I2  ,A2  ,$
    FIELD =AMOUNT             ,AMT     ,F8.2,A8  ,$
    FIELD =                ,  ...    ,   ,A1  ,$
```

PRINTING TWO SEPARATE REPORTS AT ONE TIME

To prepare a list of regional sales managers' names side by side with a list of the division managers' names, use two verb phrases in one report request:

```
C>GETFILES SALES DIVISION REGION
C>PRINT DIRECTOR; PRINT REG.MANAGER.
```

The result is:

```
DIVISION          REGION
DIRECTOR          MANAGER

A.J. Machee     |  J.R. Adams
W.M. Weaver     |  H. Clay
R.H. Hammer     |  B. Franklin
                |  A. Hamilton
                |  W.B. Hickock
                |  S. Houston
                |  T. Jefferson
                |  J.P. Jones
                |  R.E. Lee
                |  W. Penn
                |  T. Roosevelt
                |  W. Scott
```

The semicolon is optional, but the system recognizes the absence of any common element between the two requests and automatically prints a column of vertical bars. This signals that items on the same line are not necessarily related.

Now let's add sorting and screening conditions to two requests that will list the names of all the regional managers and those branch managers with quotas in excess of $100,000.

```
C>PRINT REG.MANAGER BY REG.CODE;
R>PRINT BRANCH.MANAGER AS 'BRANCH MGR'
R>BY STATE IF B.QUOTA GT 100.
```

The result is:

REGION CODE	REGION MANAGER		BRANCH STATE	BRANCH MGR
1E	B. Franklin	|	AL	R. Cody
1N	J.R. Adams	|	CA	T. Mix
1S	R.E. Lee	|	DE	C. Smith
1W	W.B. Hickock	|	FL	J. Mann
2E	W. Penn	|	IL	R. Fulton
2N	J.P. Jones	|	ME	J. Ford
2S	T. Jefferson	|	MI	B. West
2W	H. Clay	|	NY	J. Smith
3E	T. Rooselvelt	|	.	.
3N	A. Hamilton	|	.	.
3S	W. Scott	|	.	.
3W	S. Houston	|	.	.

Again the data on each line are uncorrelated, because each part of the report is sorted by a different field. Even when two files are **JOIN**ed, as these are, two verb phrases produce uncorrelated reports *unless the primary sort keys of each are the same.*

When the two requests draw data from different files they can be coordinated in one report, provided:

• The files are linked via a **JOIN** or matching **IF** statement, and

• Each request includes the common keyfield as a **BY** field.

To produce a coordinated report the prior example is modified by inserting one **BY** phrase:

```
C>PRINT REG.MANAGER BY REG.CODE;
R>PRINT BRANCH.MANAGER AS 'BRANCH MGR'
R>BY REG.CODE SKIP BY STATE IF B.QUOTA GT 100.
```

REGION CODE	REGION MANAGER	BRANCH STATE	BRANCH MGR
1E	B. Franklin	DC	R. Cody
		MD	J. Hopkins
		PA	W. Lemmon
		PA	A. Mellon
1N	J.R. Adams	IL	R. Fulton
		MN	B. West
		OH	N. Bly
1S	R.E. Lee	.	.
1W	W.B. Hickock	AZ	B. Smith
		CA	M. Wesson
	.	.	.
	.	.	.
	.	.	.

Notice that no branch office information is printed for REG.CODE = 1S, due to the screening out of branch records with B.QUOTA less than or equal to 100. The fact that the regional manager's name is printed illustrates an effect of using two verb phrases, i.e., the screening **IF** phrase affects only the verb phrase that precedes it.

Since the two files are **JOIN**ed, this particular dual request can also be written with a single verb, as:

```
C>PRINT REG.MANAGER STATE BRANCH.MANAGER
R>AS 'BRANCH MGR' BY CODE SKIP BY STATE NOPRINT,
R>IF BQUOTA GT 100.


REGION   REGION       BRANCH
CODE     MANAGER      STATE    BRANCH MGR

1E       B. Franklin  DC       R. Cody
                      MD       J. Hopkins
                      PA       W. Lemmon
                      PA       A. Mellon

1N       J.R. Adams   IL       R. Fulton
                      MN       B. West
                      OH       N. Bly

1W       W.B. Hickock CA       C. Smith
                .     AZ       M. Wesson
                .        .         .
                .        .         .
                .        .         .
```

The report looks the same, except the 1S line is missing because the **IF** phrase affects the whole request.

COORDINATED REQUESTS WITH NESTED SORT PHRASES

A more interesting report lists three levels of managers, with their goals or sales quotas next to the sum of the quotas for their immediate subordinates. In this example the filenames are abbreviated to DIV, REG, BR, S, and NEW.

```
WRITE DIV.DIRECTOR DIV.GOAL SUM.REG.QUOTA
      BY DVNO;

WRITE REG.MANAGER REG.QUOTA SUM.BR.QUOTA
      BY DVNO BY CODE SKIP;

WRITE  BR.MANAGER  BR.QUOTA  SUM.S.QUOTA
      BY DVNO BY CODE BY BRNBR.
```

The factor that ensures these requests are correctly coordinated is the nesting of the **BY** phrases. That is, each request in order includes the **BY** phrases of the request before it. Each request may be thought of as summarizing the quota values from the records in the next lower level of the hierarchy, as shown in the block diagram.

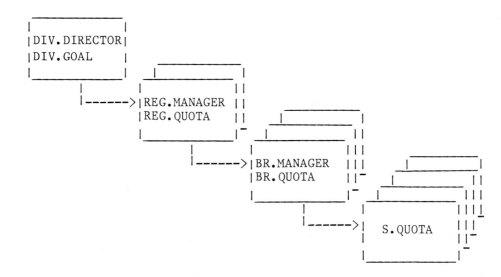

BY-fld1 <------First Verb Phrase------>|
BY-fld1 --------------------------------|BY-fld2 <----Second Verb Phrase---->|
BY-fld1 --------------------------------|BY-fld2 ----------------------------|BY-fld3 <----Third Verb Phrase----->

DIVISION DVNO	DIVISION DIRECTOR	DIVISION GOAL (000)	SUM REGION QUOTA	REGION CODE	REGION MANAGER	REGION QUOTA	SUM BRANCH QUOTA	BRANCH BRNBR	BRANCH MANAGER	BRANCH QUOTA	SUM SALESMAN QUOTA
1	A.J. MacLee	5000	5075	1N	J.R. Adams	1210	1335	49	R. Fulton	505	560
								51	B. West	300	328
				1E	B. Franklin	1240	1350	57	N. Bly	405	442
								63	J. Smith	261	288
								64	U.S. Grant	240	265
								.	.	.	.
								.	.	.	.
								.	.	.	.

This report provides comparisons of a manager's quota with the sum of the individual quotas of those working for him. The three sections of the report result from the three verb phrases, as indicated. Each column is associated with the BY-fld columns to the left.

Another coordinated report could compare the average quota for a salesperson, where the averages are first computed companywide, next by division, then by region, and finally by branch.

```
C>WRITE AVE.S.QUOTA;
R>WRITE AVE.S.QUOTA BY DVNO;
R>WRITE AVE.S.QUOTA BY DVNO BY CODE;
R>WRITE AVE.S.QUOTA BR.MANAGER BY DVNO BY CODE BY BRNBR.
```

AVE SALES QUOTA	DIVISION DVNO	AVE SALES QUOTA	REGION CODE	AVE SALES QUOTA	BRANCH BRNBR	AVE SALES QUOTA	BRANCH MANAGER
143	1	165	1N	188	49	187	R. Fulton
						192	B. Weiss
						181	N. Bly
			1E	81	63	72	J. Smith
						66	U.S. Grant
						.	.
						.	.
						.	.

```
|vobj1|        |      |     |      |    |     |     |
|-----|BYfld 1 |vobj2|     |      |    |     |     |
| --- |BYfld 1 |-----|BYfld2|vobj3|    |     |     |
| --- |BYfld 1 |-----|BYfld2|-----|BYfld3|vobj4|  vobj 5
```

In this case the first request segment averages quotas over the whole file. Each request segment moves down the hierarchy by one level but at each level the data is drawn from the salesperson quota field, as you can see from the column headings. You may prefer to use AS phrases to differentiate among the four averages.

RULES FOR COORDINATED REPORT REQUESTS

1. Each request segment must include as **BY** fields at least those **BY** fields of the prior request segment, in the same order; additional **BY** fields, if any, must follow.
2. All primary verbs (**SUM, WRITE, COUNT,** and **PRINT**) are allowed, but in the case of **PRINT**, the last **BY** field in the request segment and the verb objects to be **PRINT**ed must reside in the same **FILE**.

3. The verb phrase of each request segment precedes the related **BY** and **IF** phrases.

4. **IF** phrases (including group tests) have no effect upon preceding request segments, and they have a cumulative screening effect upon subsequent request segments.

The first rule is illustrated by the nesting of **BY** fields in the last two examples. A variant on this rule is discussed later.

The second rule is illustrated by the first example of coordinated requests, i.e., the listing of regional and branch managers' names. The rule ensures the **PRINT**ed segment has report lines which are sorted in the same order as the subsequent request segment. This condition is so because the next request segment must include the same **BY** field, in accord with Rule #1.

Rule #3 restricts your freedom to place the **BY** and **IF** phrases before the verb phrase. With multiple verbs in a report request the rule is necessary to avoid ambiguity in relating **BY** phrases to verbs. Punctuation may be used to help the reader, but the computer recognizes each new verb as the beginning of a new request segment.

The fourth rule introduces a new factor in multisegment reports; one that offers an extra dimension in arranging and analyzing data which is discussed in detail in the following sections.

SCREEN AND GROUP TESTS IN MULTIVERB REQUESTS

Look at the last example report request, and consider the effect of inserting a single **IF** phrase at the end of one of the four segments. Let the **IF** phrase restrict records to branch offices located in a certain set of states.

- If the screen is placed on the first line, it affects all four segments uniformly, and the result is the same as if only the records of the desired states were in the database.

- If the screen appears only on the second line, the result is as just stated except that the number in the first column and row is the average for the whole corporation, i.e., 143 (x $1000), rather than for just the offices in the selected states.

- If you move the sreening **IF** phrase down one line, the AVE.SALESPERSON.QUOTA for the divisions (i.e., 165) retains its companywide character, while all figures to the right are restricted to certain states.

- When placed on the fourth line the screen has the effect of printing only part of the full report (as defined in the foregoing example)—just for those branch offices in the desired states.

Now, let's insert a screen which will let us compare company and division average quotas per salesperson with branch and regional averages, but only for those regions with a *minimum* quota (among all the salespeople in the region) greater than $75,000. To accomplish this, insert this phrase at the end of the third line to screen out certain regions:

```
IF MIN.S.QUOTA GT 75
```

Then regions failing this group test are not available to the request segment on the fourth line.

Group tests of this kind are designed to exclude clusters of records, where the clustering is defined by the **BY** field of the particular request segment. The field appearing in the group test, such as, **MAX.S.QUOTA**, **SUM.NEW.QTY**, or **AVE.NEW.AMOUNT**, must reside in a file that is lower in the hierarchy than each of the **BY** fields that define the cluster.

REQUEST SEGMENTS IN REVERSE ORDER

We now present a variant of Rule #1, by rewriting the earlier example with the request segments in the reverse order, and with a group test:

```
C>WRITE AVE.S.QUOTA AS BAVG BR.MANAGER
R>     BY DVNO BY REG.CODE BY BRNBR;
R>WRITE AVE.S.QUOTA AS RAVG
R>     BY DVNO BY REG.CODE SKIP
R>IF MIN.BAVG GT 99;
R>WRITE AVE.S.QUOTA AS DAVG
R>     BY DVNO;
R>WRITE AVE.S.QUOTA.
```

With this reversal two things happen. The layout of the report is quite different, yet no more so than would be expected from the sequence of the request elements. More important, however, is that the earlier request segments define report lines which, like records, are clustered by the **BY** fields of later request segments, and hence may appear in screens of the later segments. This is illustrated with the variable labelled BAVG (branch office average quota) which is formed in the first request segment. In the second segment, for each region (REG.CODE) there are several values of BAVG, and the minimum value of that set of values is used in a group test of each region. Regions failing the test are not included in the division and corporate averages that follow in the last segments.

The report appears as follows, where the regional, divisional, and corporate summary figures are printed to the right and *below* the rows of detailed branch data.

DIVISION DVNO	REGION CODE	BRANCH BRNBR	BAVG	BRANCH MANAGER	RAVG	AVE DAVG	SALESPERSON QUOTA
1	1E	63	101	J. Smith			
		64	107	U.S. Grant			
		65	117	W. Lemmon			
		66	112	A. Mellon			
		67	120	S. Cody			
		71	115	J. Hopkins	109		
	1N	49	121	R. Fulton			
		51	95	B. West			
		57	117	N. Bly	.		
	1S	72	107	T. Mix			
		74	123	C. Laplace			
		76	132	A. Smead			
		78	116	W. Hood	119		
	1W	81	102	S. Johnson	184	161	
		83	104	P. McDowel			
		84	116	B. Hill			
		86	98	B. Marshal			
		92	140	M. Davis			
		95	122	N. Fleury	118	115	
2	2E	63	93	R. Dallas			
		64	122	A. Bean	.		
	2N	43	141	F. Heinz			
		45	92	A. Howard			
		49	106	P. Frank			
.	.	.	.	.	151	149	
.	.	.	.	.			
4	4W	17	115	R. Abel			
		32	107	Q. Bronski			
		42	98	B. Robert			
		46	102	N. Lloyd			
		55	96	L. Gomez	.	137	128

Rules for Coordinated Report Requests are now restated as follows:

1. A set of report request segments have an order based upon the nesting of common **BY** fields. The number of **BY** fields in successive segments may either increase or decrease from segment to segment, but not both. Each segment must include at least those **BY** fields found in an adjacent segment, in the same order. Adjacent segments may have the same **BY** fields.

2. When the **PRINT** verb is used, the last **BY** field and the verb objects must reside in the same **FILE**.

3. Each primary verb begins a new request segment.

4. **IF** phrases do not affect preceding segments.

5. **AS** phrase labels on verb objects may be referenced from **IF** phrases and **COMPUTE** phrases in later request segments.

FETCHING AND SELECTIVE DISPLAY OF DATA

In the last example, the right-most columns of the report contain summary information about divisions and the corporation based upon selective constraints applied to a lower level of the file hierarchy. That is, for a regional office to qualify, *all* of its branch offices must have an average quota per salesperson greater than $99,000. In many cases, only the summary information is desired, and the long printed report is found to be confusing and unnecessary. To suppress the columns of detail, you may use the **NOPRINT** option in the early request segment. There is another option which may be neater, and that is the verb **FETCH** as an alternative to **WRITE**.

Throughout the book all primary verbs implicitly have been assigned two, if not three, tasks:

- Fetch the verb objects from the file

- Count the records or sum numeric items

- Display the results

It is the last task that sometimes we suppress with the keyword **NOPRINT**. The keyword **FETCH** has all the attributes of the keyword **WRITE**, save one— it does not display the results. In the example, **FETCH** could replace the first two verbs, and the result would be a short summary report of divisional and corporate level data.

The next example is to prepare a report on those regional offices whose branches have all met a six-months performance criterion. A new variable called PERF% is to be computed using this definition:

```
PERF% = 100 * (SUM.AMOUNT - 0.5 * BRANCH.QUOTA)/0.5
               * BRANCH.QUOTA
```

This expression gives the percentage by which the sum of all new orders exceeds the sales quota for the first half year.

The full statement of the requirements for the summary report is as follows:

Report on current new orders and the average and maximum performance of the branch offices, for each regional manager with all of his branches performing above 10 percent over quota where branches with three or fewer salespeople are not counted and where new salespeople and salespeople handling government accounts are excluded from consideration.

We will regard government accounts as meaning product codes of G45, A70, and B70. Then salespeople with new orders of these products are to be excluded. Also new salespeople with a total quantity of units sold less than 50 are to be screened out.

The first request segment in the example below fetches the records for the salespeople that qualify. The second segment qualifies the branch offices with more than three salespeople and computes the performance figure for each branch. Finally, the third segment, which writes the report, selects only those regions for which *all* branches have met the desired 10 percent-over-quota criterion.

```
GETFILES SALES
HEADING "<14REGIONS WITH ALL BRANCH OFFICES EXCEEDING 10% OVER QUOTA"
             "<31 1981, FIRST SIX MONTHS"
  *
  * This segment qualifies salespeople
FETCH SUM.NEW.UNITS BY DVNO
   BY REG.CODE BY BRNBR BY SALESPERSON
   IF SUM.NEW.UNITS GT 50
   IF ALL.PRODUCT NE G45 NOR A70 NOR B70;
  *
  * This segment qualifies branches
FETCH BR.QUOTA SUM.AMT
   ANDCOMPUTE PERF%= 100*(SUM.AMT- 0.5*BR.QUOTA)/0.5*BR.QUOTA
   BY DVNO BY REG.CODE BY BRNBR
   IF CNT.S.NAME GT 3;

  *
  * This segment writes summary data by region

WRITE REGION.NAME REGION.MANAGER
    RQUOTA AVE.PERF MAX.PERF SUM.AMT AS 'NEW ORDERS'
    BY DVNO AS DIV BY REG.CODE
    IF MIN.PERF GT 10.
```

      REGIONS WITH ALL BRANCH OFFICES EXCEEDING 10% OVER QUOTA
                      1981, FIRST SIX MONTHS

				AVE REGION QUOTA	MAX BRANCH PERF%	BRANCH PERF%	
DIV	REGION	REGION NAME	REGION MANAGER				NEW ORDERS
1	1E	Md Atl	B. Franklin	1240	15.35	22.50	$705,532.50
	1S	So&SW	R.E. Lee	1212	12.12	18.75	$650,544.32
2	2N	No Cen	H. Ford	1406	11.75	21.22	$780,332.17
	.						.
	.						.
	.						.

To summarize, the device of sorting records by nonunique codes in order to form clusters of records with various properties is more than a means for arranging the format of a report. With the options presented in this chapter, a nonprocedural request can include several levels of selection logic without requiring the holding of intermediate results in a temporary file.

This chapter presented the following keywords:

ALL	• a verb object prefix
ANY	• a group test prefix
ALL	• a group test prefix
FETCH	• a primary verb

SECTION **THREE**

LANGUAGE REFERENCE
SECTION

REFERENCE SECTION

This section contains complete definitions of all NPL keywords and all master file attribute names. See also the definitions and explanations under these headings:

Back-space Key	Names
Conversion	Over-ride Key
Exit Key	Period
Keyword	Prefix
Limits	Reset
Literals	Rules
Mask	Tab Key
Modifiers	Terms

ABS

```
ABS(numeric identifier or expression)
```

An arithmetic function which finds the absolute value of a number. Thus, negative values are made positive. Used in DEFINE and COMPUTE expressions.

ACROSS

```
WRITE AMOUNT ACROSS DEPT BY ACCOUNT
```

A sort phrase option to format the report as a two-way table or matrix report. The word ACROSS replaces the word BY in one of the BY phrases. The values of the ACROSS field become column headings.

ACTUAL

ACTUAL is a required master file attribute, an alias for FILE_FMT, which specifies the format in which the data is actually stored on disk. Alphanumeric codes, An, specify n characters of space. The code I2 indicates a two-byte binary integer, and the code F4 indicates a four-byte binary real number. Sn and

Ln indicate string and long integer formats that are available only in UCSD and Apple Pascal Systems.

ALIAS

An ALIAS is an alternative name for a field, appearing in a master file definition of a record. An ALIAS may be any twelve printable characters, except a comma. Good usage dictates a letter for the first character and the use of only letters, 0 to 9, colon, hyphen, and #. Lowercase is not distinguished from uppercase. See NAMES.

ALL.
ANY.

```
IF ALL.AGE GT 30
IF ANY.COLOR EQ BLUE OR GREEN
```

Both are prefix operators used in group tests for determining whether a cluster of records includes or excludes specific field values.

AND

The word AND may appear between report phrases and between verb objects in an NPL request to improve clarity, but it is not required. The logical AND function is not allowed in IF phrases or IF. . .THEN. . .ELSE statements. In screening, the logical AND function is achieved by two or more IF phrases.

APPEND

APPEND is the DATA-FORM command to change from editing to the appending option. It is an alternative to RUN, to initiate the DATA-FORM with the screen empty of data, ready to accept new records.

```
M>APPEND PROMPT fn1.fld1,...END
M>APPEND fn1.fld = fn2.fld,...END
```

A request in Modify mode to append a new record to the file named "fn1", with data values obtained by prompting the operator or from file "fn2."

ARRAY

ARRAY is a master file attribute which is used in lieu of FIELDNAME when a set of data items are to be recognized as related and to be named as a single array variable. The number of items in the array is specified as a leading integer in the PRINTING_FMT. For example, a list of monthly sales figures is defined as an array of twelve items of F6 format:

```
ARRAY = SALES,SLS,12F6.2,A72,SUBSCRIPT=MTH,$
```

The FILE_FMT reserves 6 x 12 = 72 characters of storage. MTH is an integer variable from 1 to 12.

AS

```
AS 'column hdg'
```

The AS phrase modifies identifiers (i.e., verb objects, BY field names, and COMPUTE phrases) to specify a column heading for reports. Any printable characters (and the space) may appear between the quote marks, up to twelve characters. The quotes are not required if no embedded spaces are used. AS-phrase titles are retained in a HOLD master file in lieu of fieldnames.

```
HOLD AS filename
```

A phrase modifying the HOLD command to change the naming of the HOLD.M and HOLD.D files. "Filename" may have up to eight characters, with a leading letter, and may be prefixed by a volume identifier. For example:

```
HOLD AS B4/SALES
```

creates two files called SALES.M. and SALES.D. on the disk volume named B4. "Filename" may also specify different names for the master and datafiles with the form used in the GETFILE command, i.e.:

```
HOLD AS (dfile) mfile.
```

```
GRAPH AS filename
```

A phrase following the GRAPH command. The same rules apply as for HOLD.

ASQ

```
ASQ.fld
```

A prefix to a verb object, to request the calculation of the Average-Sum-of-the-Squares of the values of a numeric variable, for a group of records. Must occur in a SUM, COUNT, or WRITE phrase. "fld" is any valid fieldname, alias, defined name, or unique truncation. ASQ and the name may be separated by either an asterisk or a period. The variance of X (which is the square of the standard deviation) is equal to $(ASQ.X - (AVE.X)*(AVE.X))*N/(N-1)$. For large values of N and a zero mean, the variance is equal to $ASQ.X$.

Attribute

Attributes are a special class of NPL words which appear in master files and are recognized by NPL only in CREATE mode. Attributes are the values that define a database.

AVE

AVE.fld

A prefix to a verb object, to request the calculation of the average (mean) value of the values of a numeric variable, for a group of records. Must appear in a SUM, COUNT, or WRITE phrase. "fld" is any valid fieldname, alias, defined name, or unique truncation. AVE and the name may be separated by either an asterisk or a period. The prefixes AVG. and AVERAGE. are synonyms for AVE.

AVG

AVG.fld

A prefix to a verb object, to request the calculation of the average (mean) value of the values of a numeric variable, for a group of records. Must appear in a SUM, COUNT, or WRITE phrase. "fld" is any valid fieldname, alias, defined name, or unique truncation. AVG and the name may be separated by either an asterisk or a period. The prefixes AVE. and AVERAGE. are synonyms for AVG.

Back-space Key

A name used in NPL manuals to refer to the key to be pressed, in DATA-FORM mode, to cause the cursor to move to the left one space at a time (within a field), or to jump back and/or up the screen from field to field (when the cursor is in the first character position in a field). The actual key may be marked BS, RUBOUT, or DEL. Often the *left-arrow* key is used as well. See Appendix D.

BINARY

```
R>...HOLD BINARY AS filename
C>PRINT ACNT...AMOUNT BINARY, HOLD.
```

A keyword which modifies the HOLD phrase or selected numeric verb objects (when HOLD is present) to avoid converting one or more numeric fields to alphanumeric characters (A format) when a HOLD datafile is created. See HOLD.

BOTTOM

```
M>BOTTOM
```

A DATA-FORM command to change the current position to the end of the file. If an INDEX exists the current position becomes the last record according to the INDEX file.

```
FOOTING BOTTOM "text..."
```

A modifier in a FOOTING phrase to cause the text to be placed at the bottom of the page of paper rather than just below the last report row.

BY

```
BY fld
BY HIGHEST fld
BY fld modifiers
```

A BY phrase designates a variable as a sort key. "fld" is any valid fieldname, alias, defined name, or unique truncation, though not a COMPUTEd variable. The optional modifiers may be one or more of these keywords: FOLD, PAGE, RESET#, SKIP n, and SUBTOTAL. The modifiers specify actions to take effect whenever the "fld" value changes. SKIP may optionally be followed by an integer. FOLD affects the column formatting of a report.

"fld" may also be modified by a field modifier NOPRINT, BINARY, or an AS phrase, which must precede the BY field modifiers. NOPRINT suppresses printing of the sort field. NOPRINT and AS must appear before the options of the paragraph above. BY acts as a command to enter the Report mode. See HIGHEST.

CENTER

```
HEADING CENTER "text..."
```

A modifier on a HEADING or FOOTING phrase to cause the text to be centered with respect to the report width. Tab controls, in the form <n, override the effect of CENTER, for the text following the tab.

CLEAR

```
C>CLEAR DEFINE
C>CLEAR SELECT
```

The first form clears all stored definitions. The second form clears the stored SELECT condition.

```
M>CLEAR
```

In the DATA-FORM mode the SELECT condition is cleared.

CLIP

```
CLIP(alphanumeric identifier)
```

A string function which clips all space characters from the right-hand end of an alphanumeric variable. Used in DEFINE and COMPUTE expressions. Often followed by the plus sign, for concatenation of other strings of characters. A common use is to form a name from fixed length fields, e.g.

```
FULLNAME/A30=CLIP(FIRSTNAME) + ' ' + LASTNAME.
```

CNT

```
CNT.fld
```

A prefix to a verb object to request the count of records in a group, as determined by the BY fields. "fld" may refer to any field or defined variable with the same effect. Only used in SUM or WRITE phrase.

```
WRITE CNT.X BY Y
```

```
is equivalent to:    COUNT X BY Y
```

COLUMNTOTAL

COLUMNTOTAL is a one-word report phrase, which causes printing of a grand total for all numeric verb objects in a report, except those followed by NOTOTAL. The Printing formats of verb objects must be wide enough to accommodate grand totals.

COMPUTE

    COMPUTE   name/format=expression

A secondary verb used to name and specify a new verb object in a Report mode verb phrase. The slash and "format" are optional when the variable is numeric. If omitted a format of F10.2 is assigned.

"name" is up to twelve characters, restricted to letters, 0 to 9, colon, hyphen, and #. Names beginning with 0 to 9 or containing a hyphen may not appear in subsequent COMPUTE expressions. Variables appearing in "expression" must also appear as preceding verb objects. May be followed by a field option (NOPRINT, NOTOTAL, BINARY, or an AS phrase).

CONSOLE:

    C>CONSOLE:

A command to reverse the effect of PRINTER: and REMOUT: by directing reports to the console screen.

CONTAINS

    IF fld CONTAINS value   ...OR value...

A relational operator in a screening IF phrase. "fld" is any fieldname, alias, defined name (or unique trucation), of an alphanumeric variable. "value" is a literal string of characters to be searched for within the length of the field. OR phrases are optional.

    IF fld CONTAINS 'value' THEN...ELSE...

A relational operator in DEFINE or COMPUTE statements. "fld" is any fieldname, alias, defined name (or unique truncation), of an alphanumeric variable; "value" is a literal string of characters to be searched for within the length of the field and must be within quotes. "value" may be repeated with OR phrases.

    IF expr1 CONTAINS expr2 THEN...ELSE...

In the general form expr1 and expr2 are alphanumeric expressions, such as: MONTH+DAY+YR, which concatenates alphanumeric characters.

    IF fld CONTAINS $$cc$c...   ...OR...

321

Dollar signs and "c" (any printable character except ampersand and quotes) form a string of characters which is used as a mask in the screening IF phrase. If a period or space character appears in the string, surrounding quotes are required. The mask has a length equal to or less than the length of "fld," an alphanumeric variable. OR phrases of masks or literal alphanumeric strings are optional.

When mask length equals "fld" length, a match is sought for the non-$ characters; e.g.,

```
IF ZIP CONTAINS 01$$$
```

will match ZIP codes with 01 in the first two positions.

When mask length is shorter than "fld," the mask is moved across "fld" looking for a pattern match, within the length of "fld," while ignoring the $ positions. For example:

```
IF fld CONTAINS $TON$
```

will find STONES, but not TONNAGE or APPLETON.

Upper- and lowercase differences are significant. Masks are used only with the CONTAINS relational operator.

Conversion

```
alphafield/A4 = numericfield
numericfield/fmt = numericfield
numericfield/fmt = alphafield
```

Conversion of data formats is accomplished in DEFINEs and COMPUTEs. Numbers stored in any of the numeric formats may be changed into numbers stored in alphanumeric format or other numeric formats, and vice versa. In the latter case, the format of the receiving numeric field must conform to the contents of the alphanumeric field. If the receiving field is integer, the alphanumeric field must contain only digits and a plus or minus sign. If the receiving field is real, the alphanumeric field may also contain a decimal point. If the receiving field is extended precision, the alphanumeric field may additionally contain a dollar sign and commas. This function makes possible string editing operations with numeric data, and arithmetic operations with alphanumeric data.

COPYFILE

```
C>COPYFILE filename1 TO filename2
```

A command to copy any datafile to a new file. NPL affixes the .D suffix to the filenames given. Two or more files may be concatenated using this form:

```
C>COPYFILE fn1 + fn2 + fn3 TO fn4
```

A master file must exist for the target filename (fn4, in the example), or a master file for one of the input files must be specified (using the (dfile)mfile form; see GETFILE) as follows:

```
C>COPYFILE fn1 + fn2 + fn3 TO (fn4)fn2
```

Files not on the same disk with the master file require a volume name. COPYFILE may be abbreviated as COPY.

COUNT

```
COUNT fld
```

A primary verb which requests a count of the records in a group, as determined by the BY fields, independent of "fld." "fld" is a dummy verb object; COUNT "records" is implied. COUNT acts as a command to enter Report mode. It may appear with verb prefixes as in:

```
COUNT ORDERS MAX.ORDER AND SUM.SALES BY MONTH.
```

CREATE

```
C>CREATE filename
```

A command which executes a special DATA-FORM program for building a new master file. "Filename" may have up to eight characters, with a leading letter, and may be prefixed by a volume name.

DATA>TEXT

A utility program, available only in UCSD and Apple Pascal systems, to convert a datafile (e.g, SALES.D.DATA) into a format (SALES.D.TEXT) suitable for use with the Edit mode. A Master file must exist. The Program requests the name of the DATAfile with D> as the prompt. The reply may specify both the datafile and the master file, using the rules from the GETFILE command. For example:

```
Enter Filename D> (.D2/SALES82) SALES
```

DEFINE

```
C>DEFINE name/format = expression...
```

A command to enter the DEFINE mode, which is followed by one or more definitions. A period or END terminates the mode. The new variables are associated with the current file.

"name" is up to twelve characters, restricted to letters, 0 to 9, colon, hyphen, and #. The first character must be a letter. Names containing a hyphen may not appear in DEFINE or COMPUTE expressions.

The slash and "format" are optional when the variable is numeric. If omitted a format of F10.2 is assigned.

A one-line DEFINE statement for defining a new variable called CLASS might appear as:

```
DEFINE CLASS/A4='19' + YEAR.
```

"expression" is any combination of functions (as IF...THEN...ELSE, CLIP, ABS), arithmetic operators, and fieldnames, aliases, other defined names, or unique truncations.

DEFINE statements are evaluated as each record is retrieved from the file, after IF phrase screening, except when the variable in a screening IF phrase is itself a DEFINEd variable. In this case all definitions are evaluated before the IF phrases are evaluated.

Successive DEFINE commands add new definitions to the list of active definitions. This list is associated with a particular file, hence changing the active master file with GETFILE clears the definitions, as does

```
C>CLEAR DEFINE
```

"name" must be unique among all active names (fields and DEFINEs). An attempt to establish a definition with a name already in use is rejected, without error messages. This occurs routinely when an Exec program is run a second time. The existing definitions are retained.

When an existing definition is to be replaced by a new definition for the same name the REPLACE command is used to enter the DEFINE mode rather than the DEFINE command.

DEFINE is an optional master file attribute, with alias EXPRESSN, which is the first word of an NPL DEFINE statement as stored in a master file. The form of the statement is the same as used elsewhere for a single variable DEFINE. DEFINE statements follow FIELD and ARRAY statements for each FILE.

DELETE

M>DELETE

A single word command in the DATA-FORM mode which marks one record to be deleted as the file is copied to a revised file upon leaving the DATA-FORM mode, at which point all deletions may be aborted.

M>DELETE FROM fnl IF condition, IF...END
M>DELETE FROM fnl IF fn2.fld EQ fnl.keyfld, IF...END

A request in Modify mode to delete a record by searching until certain conditions are met, or by matching values of a keyfield with values in file "fn2."

DELETEFILE

C>DELETEFILE filename

A command to delete a file. "filename" may contain the volume name as a prefix and must include a filetype suffix, like .D or .M. NPL requests verification from the operator, except when the command is used in an Exec program.

DIRECTORY

C>DIRECTORY
C>DIR

A command to display the name of available NPL files (all files with names including .E, .M, .D, or .I) as well as GRAPH files (names with .P) with UCSD operating systems.

DISK:

C>DISK: filename

A command to direct the next Report to a file on disk. Output reverts to the CONSOLE: after the report is written. DISK: may also precede the "FILE?" and DIRECTORY commands, and the TYPEFILE command, which then copies files from one disk to another.

ECHO

C>ECHO ON   (or OFF or ALL or *)

A command with four options for controlling the display of Exec file commands. When ALL, the lines of an exec file are displayed as each line is read by NPL. The ON mode, useful for testing a new exec program, displays all NPL request lines, but not the comment lines with an asterisk in the second character position. The * mode causes display of only those exec file lines with an asterisk in the first character position. The latter is used to display a menu of options. The first mode to be set, ON, ALL, or *, remains set until reset by ECHO OFF. Thus ECHO ON, before running an Exec program, overrides ECHO * within the program.

Edit

Edit is the name of a command (E) in UCSD and Apple Pascal operating systems. Type E to enter the Edit mode.

END

END completes a Report mode request (synonym of the period), and it completes a DEFINE mode group of statements.

EQ

IF fld EQ value   ...OR value...

EQ is a relational operator used to test the equality of two numbers or two alphanumerics.

In a screening IF phrase "fld" is any fieldname, alias or defined name, or unique truncation; OR phrases are optional.

IF expression1 EQ expression2 THEN...ELSE...

In DEFINE and COMPUTE statements, both "expressions" may be, or may contain, any valid identifier or a literal value, as 143 or '07463' or 'F.' Alphanumeric literals must be enclosed in quotes. EQ and IS are synonymous.

Escape

ESCape is the name of a key on some keyboards, which is marked: ESC. It is used as the Exit key in Apple II and III systems.

As the Exit key it is used to "escape" from one mode to a less restrictive mode, usually the Command mode. In DATA-FORM mode, ESC (within a field) discards the current value; (at beginning of field) ends the current record; (at top of screen) discards the current record and continues; (at beginning of first field) quits the data entry mode; (at M>) terminates the DATA-FORM session.

On the Apple II, the ESC key also acts as an *interrupt* or *break* key during NPL execution of a Report mode request or a search in the DATA-FORM mode. Partial HOLD files (but not GRAPH files) are saved. See Exit Key.

EXCEEDS

```
IF fld EXCEEDS value
```

A relational operator used to compare two numbers or two alphanumerics. Synonymous with GT (greater than); with alphanumerics this means "sorts after," using the ASCII character set. In a screening IF phrase "fld" is any fieldname, alias or defined name, or unique truncation.

```
IF expression1 exceeds expression2 THEN...ELSE...
```

In DEFINE and COMPUTE statements, both "expressions" may be, or may contain, any valid identifier or a literal value, as 143 or '07463' or 'F.' Alphanumeric literals must be enclosed in quotes.

Exchange

Exchange (X) is the command in UCSD and Apple Pascal Edit mode used to replace characters in a .TEXT file with new characters. Type X to enter the Exchange mode.

EXEC

```
C>EXEC filename
```

An NPL command, which may be abbreviated as EX, to call upon a file of NPL commands to be executed. "filcname" is up to eight alphanumerics beginning with a letter. The actual full name of the file is /vol/filename.E.TEXT where the .E designates the Exec type file. The EXEC command may be the last command in an Exec program. May be abbreviated as EX.

Exit Key

A name used in NPL manuals to refer to the key to be pressed to quit an NPL mode, on the Apple II and CP/M systems to end the printing of a long report, or to escape from various conditions in the DATA-FORM mode. The actual key used varies from one computer keyboard to another. The "Control-X" code is used on most computers, yet special keys may be assigned. On Apple II and III computers the "ESC" key is the Exit key.

FETCH

```
FETCH fld1 fld2...BY sortfld...
```

A primary verb with all the attributes of the WRITE verb, save one— FETCH retrieves and stores data temporarily but does not display the results. In a multisegment (multiverb) request, the early verb phrases may use FETCH and the last one is usually a WRITE or PRINT phrase.

FIELD

FIELDNAME, or FIELD, is the name of the first element in a master file record. Every data item in a data record has a FIELDNAME, which may be any twelve printable characters, except comma, including the space character. Lowercase is treated as uppercase.

FIELDNAME

FIELDNAME, or FIELD, is a master file attribute, which names a data item with up to twelve alphanumeric characters. See *NAMES*.

FIELDTYPE

FIELDTYPE is an optional master file attribute which indicates if an item uniquely defines each record (FIELDTYPE = UNIQUE), is an ARRAY variable which is used as a SUBSCRIPT for other ARRAYS (FIELDTYPE = SUBS), or is a subscript relation array (FIELDTYPE = SUBSREL).

FILE_FMT

FILE_FMT is a required master file attribute, with alias ACTUAL, which specifies the format in which the data is actually stored on disk. Codes of the form An indicate that the data field requires space on the disk for n alphanumeric characters. I2 designates a two-character-wide field for storing a 16-bit integer. F4 provides space for a 32-bit floating point number, and D6 provides for a 40-bit integer.

Ln designates a field for an Apple Pascal long integer (n is the largest number of digits allowed). The actual field width is two greater than n divided by two and rounded up to an even integer.

328

Sn designates a field for an Apple Pascal string variable (n is the maximum length of the string). The actual field width is the next even number larger than n.

FILENAME
FILE

FILENAME, or FILE, is a required master file attribute, with alias FN, which is the name of a set of field and segment descriptions and of a set of data records. The name must begin with a letter and may contain up to six (or eight, depending upon the operating system) characters, limited to letters and 0 to 9.

FILE?
FILES?

C>FILE?

A command to display information about the currently active file like fieldnames, alias, Printing formats, defined names and formats, and the active INDEX files. It may be used with PRINTER:, DISK:, and REMOUT: commands. "FILES?" is a synonym.

FINISH

FINISH is a command to terminate the NPL session and return to the Operating System level. May be abbreviated as FIN.

FOLD

BY fld FOLD

FOLD is a BY field modifier used to reduce the page width of a report, by "folding" the data columns to the left and under the sort field values. FOLD may appear after one or more BY fields. In each case, after the BY field value is printed the print position moves down one line and to the left by the width of the BY field less two character positions.

FOOTING

```
FOOTING "...text..."
" "
"</n text...<+m  <fld  <p  text"
```

A report phrase, to specify the printing of text at the bottom of each report page. Any number of lines of free text within pairs of quotes (single or double) may be used. The second sample line above is a null line and results in a blank line in the report footing. Four special controls are allowed between the quotes: </n moves down n blank lines; <+m causes m blank spaces to be written; <p positions the printer at column p (which makes overprinting possible); and <fld prints the current value of the variable, "fld," in the FOOTING.

"fld" is any fieldname, alias, defined or computed name, unique truncation, or prefixed name. "fld" is a verb object. If no explicit verb exists, the implicit verb is WRITE.

Single quotes within a double-quote pair are treated as text characters, and vice versa. Text lines may be up to 130 characters long; the RETURN character in the program file is treated as a space character in the text line, hence a long text line may appear on more than one line in the Exec file.

FOR...ELSE...ENDFOR

```
FOR expression rel-oper  value1 :            statements
                         value2 :  value3 :  statements
               ...ELSE                       statements
               ENDFOR
```

A procedural command to select, for execution, a single group from among one or more groups of statements, depending upon the value of the expression. Upon completion of the selected group of statements the next command read by NPL is the one following the keyword ENDFOR. Any expression or variable (including an amper variable) may be compared by *rel-oper*, a relational operator, to literal *values*. Each *value* must be followed by a colon. Values that are alphanumeric codes must be enclosed in quote marks. More than one *value* may select a group of statements. A group may have any number of commands, Report mode requests, and Modify mode requests.

FORM

```
FORM
"... text  ...  <fld  ...
  ...  <fld  ...  text  ...
             .
             .
             .
  ... text   ...      <fld..."
```

A keyword in DATA-FORM mode, to indicate that information follows for formatting the screen for data entry. Up to twenty-three lines of seventy-eight characters each are allowed. The entire FORM or screen picture is enclosed between a pair of quotes. "fld" is any fieldname, alias, or unique truncation. "<fld" is called a field marker; it reserves a blank space for entry of values for "fld."

All text and field markers appear on the monitor in exactly the same position as when the Exec program file is viewed in the Edit mode.

Each data entry field begins at the "<" character and extends to the right the length (according to the FILE format) of the field. When data is being entered the cursor moves from left to right, top to bottom, except when a PROMPT statement specifies a different sequence.

FST

FST.fld

A prefix to a verb object, to select the first value retrieved among the values of "fld" in a group of records. Must appear in a SUM, WRITE, or COUNT phrase. "fld" is any valid fieldname, alias, defined name, or unique truncation. FST and the name may be separated by either an asterisk or a period.

GE

IF fld GE value

A relational operator, short for Greater-Than-or-Equal-To, used to compare two numbers or two alphanumerics. In the latter case, "greater" means "sorts after," using the ASCII character set. In a screening IF phrase "fld" is any fieldname, alias, defined name, or a unique truncation; "value" is a numeric or alphanumeric literal; quotes are needed only when spaces are embedded.

IF expression1 GE expression2 THEN...ELSE...

IF...THEN...ELSE phrases arc uscd only in DEFINE and COMPUTE statements; both "expressions" may be, or may contain, any valid identifier or a literal value, such as 143 or '07463' or 'F.' Alphanumeric literals must be enclosed in quotes.

GETFILE
GETFILES

C>GETFILE (dfile) mfile

331

GETFILE is a command which specifies the files to be used by subsequent NPL requests. Both a master file and a datafile are identified. The selected files remain active until a new GETFILE command is given. In the usual case, the simple form, for example:

```
C>GETFILE ACCOUNTS
```

selects both files, ACCOUNTS.M and ACCOUNTS.D, with a single filename.

NPL searches the disk directories for the master filename (mfile). If the same "mfile" exists on more than one disk, NPL uses the first file found.

The volume name may be used to specify a pair of files on a particular disk, as in:

```
C>GETFILE .D3/ACCOUNTS
```

Several datafiles (ACCNTS79.D, ACCNTS80.D, ACCNTS81.D) may be associated with one ACCOUNTS.M master file, though only one such datafile may be active at a time. The general form of the GETFILE command shown above includes the parenthetic item (dfile) as an option. Thus the following examples are used to select one of the datafiles (using Apple III notation):

```
C>GETFILE (ACCNTS81) ACCOUNTS
C>GETFILE (.D3/ACCNTS79) ACCOUNTS
C>GETFILE (ACCNTS79) .D3/ACCOUNTS
```

NPL first locates the master file and takes the datafile from the same disk, unless a different volume name is given.

A filename may have up to six (or eight, depending upon the operating system) characters beginning with a letter. The suffix .M or .D is not used.

When GETFILE changes the active master file all stored DEFINEs are cleared. GETFILE may be abbreviated as GET. GETFILES is a synonym.

GRAPH

```
GRAPH AS filename
```

A report phrase, for use in UCSD and Apple Pascal systems, which creates a datafile of two data fields in the format of a POINTS file for the Apple Business Graphics System. "Filename" may contain up to eight characters with a leading letter. The new file is named filename.P.DATA, or if there is no AS phrase, GRAPH.P.DATA.

GT

```
IF fld GT value
```

A relational operator, short for Greater-Than, used to compare two numbers or two alphanumerics. In the latter case, "greater" means "sorts after," using the ASCII character set. In a screening IF phrase "fld" is any fieldname, alias, defined name, or unique truncation; "value" is a numeric or alphanumeric literal. Quotes are needed only when spaces are embedded.

```
IF expression1 GT expression2   THEN...ELSE...
```

IF...THEN...ELSE phrases are used only in DEFINE and COMPUTE statements; both "expressions" may be, or may contain, any valid identifier or a literal value, as 143 or '07463' or 'F.' Alphanumeric literals must be enclosed in quotes. GT, IS-MORE-THAN, and EXCEEDS are synonyms.

HEADING

```
HEADING "  ...text...  "
" "
"</n text...<+m  <fld  <p  text"
```

A report phrase, to specify the printing of text at the head of each report page. Any number of lines of free text within pairs of quotes (single or double) may be used. The second sample line above is a null line and results in a blank line in the report heading. Four special controls are allowed between the quotes: </n inserts n blank lines; <+m causes m blank spaces to be written; <p positions the printer at column p (which makes overprinting possible); and <fld prints the current value of the variable, "fld", in the HEADING.

"fld" is any fieldname, alias, defined or computed name, or unique truncation, or a prefixed name. "fld" is a verb object. If no explicit verb exists, the implicit verb is WRITE.

Single quotes within a double quote pair are treated as text characters, and vice versa. Text lines may be up to 130 characters long; the RETURN character in the program file is treated as a space character in the text line, hence a long text line may appear on more than one line in the Exec file.

HI

```
C>SELECT keyfld = value THRU HI.
```

HI is a keyword, meaning the highest value (numeric or alphanumeric) of a keyfield. Used only in the SELECT command.

HIGHEST

```
BY HIGHEST fld
```

A BY field modifier to cause sorting in descending order, i.e., high-to-low or Z-to-A.

HOLD

```
HOLD AS filename
HOLD BINARY AS filename
```

A report phrase, which suppresses the report and creates two files, HOLD.M and HOLD.D, of the fields that otherwise would have been printed. The AS phrase substitutes "filename" for "HOLD" in the two names. "filename" may have up to eight characters; the first must be a letter; and it may have a volume name prefix. HOLD may appear first, last, or between phrases. HOLD also acts as a command to enter the Report mode.

The new master file has fieldnames, aliases, and PRINTING formats which are taken from the original master file, or from AS phrases, if any. When verb objects are prefixed by MAX., MIN., AVE., etc., the HOLD file fieldnames are prefixed by MAX:, MIN:, AVE:, etc., and truncated on the right at twelve characters, if necessary.

When the word BINARY is not present, HOLD master FILE formats are "An," where "n" is the PRINTING format width.

When the word BINARY is present, HOLD master FILE formats are derived from the original PRINTING *and* FILE formats, as follows:

PRINTING	FILE	HOLD BINARY FILE FMT
An	Am	Am
In	Am or I2	I2
Fn	Am or F4	F4
Dn	Am or D6	D6

The standard End-of-Record field is not written in the case of HOLD BINARY.

```
HOLD INTO filename
```

The INTO phrase is an alternative to the AS phrase for naming the new files. If master and datafiles with the specified file name already exist, the AS phrase deletes those files before creating the new files, while the INTO phrase causes the new datafile to be appended to (i.e. written into) the existing datafile. In the latter case, if the record length of the new datafile is not the same as that of the existing datafile, an error message is written and the request is cancelled.

The form used in the GETFILE command for specifying different names and volumes for data and master files may be used in AS and INTO phrases; e.g.:

HOLD AS (dfile) mfile
HOLD INTO (dfile) mfile BINARY

IF

IF condition1

A phrase for screening data records. When "condition1" is true for a retrieved record the record is retained for the report, otherwise it is rejected. "condition1" has the form:

fld relational-operator value   ...OR value...

Where "fld" is any fieldname, alias, defined name or unique truncation (but not a computed variable). When "fld" is a DEFINEd variable, all DEFINEs are evaluated before the IF phrase is evaluated. OR phrases are optional.
"value" is a numeric or alphanumeric literal. Quotes are not required around the literal except when embedded blanks are present.
Relational-operators compare two numeric values (or alphanumeric strings): EQ, LT, LE, GT, GE, NE, and synonyms like IS, IS-NOT, EXCEEDS; and string tests: CONTAINS, OMITS. Range tests have the form:

fld IS   value TO value   ...OR...
fld IS-NOT value TO value   ...NOR...

Multiple tests occur when OR phrases or NOR phrases are appended to specify additional test values and ranges. A long list of test values in a file may be specified with the IN phrase; see IN.

R>IF fn1.fld EQ fn2.fld
M>IF fn1.fld EQ fn2.fld THEN UPDATE...ELSE INSERT...

The matching IF phrase is a special case. The EQ relational operator is followed by a filename and fieldname separated by a period. The two data fields are in different files. The second example is a special form for the Modify mode.
This form of IF may act as a command to enter the Report mode.

IF...THEN...ELSE

IF condition2 THEN expression1 ELSE expression2

An IF. . .THEN. . .ELSE expression, which appears only in DEFINE and COMPUTE statements, has a "value" equal to expression1 or expression2 depending on whether "condition2" is true or false. "condition2" may have the forms of "condition1," excepting range tests and the IN phrase, or the more general form:

```
expression3 relational-operator expression4
```

Literal alphanumeric values require quotes. OR phrases may be used to test several literals.

IN

```
IF fld IN filename    ...OR filename...
```

An IN phrase in a screening IF phrase is a multiple test of equality between the value of a variable, "fld," and a series of values stored in a file. The file must be an NPL Datafile. The file values must have the same format as the field variable and appear as the first field in the record.

Optional OR phrases name additional files to be searched, e.g.:

```
IF SYMBOL IN STOCKS OR BONDS

C>SELECT keyfld IN filename    ...OR...
```

An IN phrase in a SELECT command functions exactly as in an IF phrase, except that values of 'keyfld' are selected through the use of an Index file. The SELECT command is active for all reports until cleared.

IN phrase values are read as a group from the file into computer memory for fast search. A very large group could overload the memory.

INDEX

```
C>INDEX fld
```

A command to create an index file for a particular field. "fld" must be a fieldname, alias, unique truncation, or a DEFINEd variable. Sufficient diskette space for storing the index file must exist on the same volume with the active datafile. The variable "fld" is called a *key*field of the file. It provides a view of the field, sorted by the key. If an Index file is built for a DEFINEd variable, the same DEFINE must be active when the Index is SELECTed.

INDEX is an optional master file attribute, with alias KEY, which names the suffix used in the filename of an INDEX file for a particular FIELD. The INDEX name is usually the same as the ALIAS but may be limited by naming conventions to fewer characters. It must be a unique name. It may not be changed without also changing the filename of the INDEX file.

IN-GROUPS-OF

BY field IN-GROUPS-OF nnn

IN-GROUPS-OF is a modifier in a BY phrase or an ACROSS phrase which defines ranges of sort field values. 'nnn' is an unsigned number. Values of the sort field that fall between consecutive multiples of 'nnn' are considered to be a single value. IN-GROUPS-OF may be used only with numeric sort fields.

INSERT

M>INSERT

A command in the DATA-FORM mode to cause the insertion of a new record just before the current record displayed. The new record is held in a temporary file called, for example, SALES.D.NEW (the filename suffix varies among operating systems), and is inserted when the datafile is copied at the end of the DATA-FORM session.

M>INSERT PROMPT fn1.fld,...END
M>INSERT fn1.fld = fn2.fld,...END

A request in Modify mode to insert a new record in file "fn1" with data values obtained by prompting the operator or from file "fn2".

I)NSERT

INSERT is a command (I) in UCSD and Apple Pascal EDIT mode, used to insert characters and records into a .TEXT file. Type I to enter Insert mode, which is the normal data entry mode for the UCSD Pascal Editor.

Integer

Integer format codes (I) appear in master files and as edit codes in DATA-FORM PROMPT statements. Integer values are limited to the range –32768 to +32767, though PRINTING FORMATs may be as wide as needed, up to 999, to provide wide column spacing.

Integer should be distinguished from numeric codes. In the latter case these groups are in a proper sort order:

    0   00   019   02   1   115   15   2   22   3   4

because sorting is on the left-most character first. Integers are right-justified.

INTO

```
HOLD INTO filename
```

A phrase modifying the HOLD command to append records to an existing datafile. "Filename" may have up to eight characters, with a leading letter, and may be prefixed by a volume identifier. For example:

```
HOLD INTO B4/SALES
```

Stores records at the end of the SALES.D file on the disk volume named B4. "Filename" may also specify different names for the master and datafiles with the form used in the GETFILE command, i.e.:

```
HOLD INTO (dfile) mfile.
```

The INTO phrase is an alternative to the AS phrase. If "filename" does not exist, the result is the same as an AS phrase.

IS
IS-NOT

```
IF fld IS     value    ...OR value...
IF fld IS-NOT value    ...NOR value...
```

A relational operator used to test the equality of two numbers or two alpha-numerics. In a screening IF phrase "fld" is any fieldname, alias, defined name, or unique truncation; OR phrases and NOR phrases are optional. "value" is a numeric or alphanumeric literal; quotes are needed only when spaces are embedded.

```
IF expression1 IS expression2 THEN...ELSE...
IF expression1 IS-NOT expression2 THEN...ELSE...
```

IF...THEN...ELSE phrases are used only in DEFINE and COMPUTE statements, both "expressions" may be, or may contain, any valid identifier or a literal value, as 143 or '07463' or 'F.' Alphanumeric literals must be enclosed in quotes. EQ and IS are synonyms, and NE and IS-NOT are synonyms, except in range tests, where EQ and NE are not used.

```
IF fld IS     value TO value  ...OR...
IF fld IS-NOT value TO value  ...NOR...
```

Range tests define inclusive ranges of numeric, or alphanumeric, values. In the latter case relative values are determined by the sort sequence of ASCII characters. OR/NOR phrases may mix value and range tests.

IS-LESS-THAN
IS-MORE-THAN

IS-MORE-THAN, GT, and EXCEEDS are synonymous relational operators. IS-LESS-THAN and LT are synonymous relational operators.

JOIN

```
C> JOIN fnl.fld TO fn2.fld2
```

JOIN is a command and an optional master file attribute which is assigned a name by NPL when a JOIN command cross-references the field in the first file TO a field in another file. The name assigned is the full name (fn2.fld2) of a field in the other file.

KEY
Keyfield

"Keyfield" describes an indexed field; see INDEX. KEY is an optional master file attribute, an alias for INDEX, which names the suffix used in the filename of an INDEX file for a particular FIELD. The INDEX name is usually the same as the ALIAS but may be limited by naming conventions to fewer characters. It must be a unique name. It may not be changed without also changing the filename of the INDEX file.

Keyword

There are over 110 NPL keywords. These appear on the NPL System Guide and in this reference section.

Conflict can arise when keywords are used as variable identifiers (fieldnames, aliases). NPL resolves the conflict in favor of the keywords. Thus fieldnames called PAGE, BY, and AVERAGE are not recognized as such unless they are abbreviated when used in a report request, e.g., PAG, B, and AVER.

The fieldnames, PAGER, BYM3, and AVERAGE:AGE, which include keywords, may be used, but may not be referred to in the abbreviated forms of PAGE, BY, and AVE. For example, the word PAGE is interpreted as a keyword rather than a truncation of PAGER.

The keywords REC#, ROW#, PAGE# are names of system variables. These names may not be abbrieviated.

LAST

```
LAST fld
```

A prefix to an identifier in DEFINE or COMPUTE statements to cause the term to be evaluated as the previous value of "fld." When used in a DEFINE, LAST refers to the last value retreived. For example, for a sequence of daily records, define:

```
DAY=IF MONTH NE LAST MONTH THEN 1 ELSE LAST DAY+1
```

"LAST MONTH" means the value of the field called MONTH in the last record retrieved and accepted.

DEFINES are evaluated after IF-phrase screens, unless the IF phrase contains a DEFINEd variable. In the latter case, "LAST MONTH" has the values of MONTH in the preceding record in the file, even though that record may not be accepted by the IF phrase.

Used in COMPUTE statements it refers to the last computed, or printed, value. The identifier "fld" is any fieldname, alias, defined name, or unique truncation.

To calculate a running balance for a sequence of transactions, define

```
YTDTOTAL=IF YR NE LAST YR THEN CURRAMOUNT
              ELSE CURRAMOUNT  +  LAST YTDTOTAL
```

LE

```
IF fld LE value
```

A relational operator, short for Less-Than-or-Equal-To, used to compare two numbers or two alphanumerics. In the latter case, "less" means "sorts before," using the ASCII character set. In a screening IF phrase "fld" is any fieldname, alias, defined name, or unique truncation; "value" is a numeric or alphanumeric literal; quotes are needed only when spaces are embedded.

```
IF  expression1  LE  expression2  THEN...ELSE...
```

IF...THEN...ELSE phrases are used only in DEFINE and COMPUTE statements; both "expressions" may be, or may contain, any valid identifier or a literal value, as 143 or '07463' or 'F.' Alphanumeric literals must be enclosed in quotes.

Limits

NPL has limits to certain functions. Some of these (*) vary from one NPL version to another; typical values are shown.

- characters per record limited to 4000 *
- 100 field identifiers *
(Master file, DEFINE, and COMPUTE names)
- 30 verb objects in a request *
- 10 sort keys (BY fields) *
- Total combined length of sort keys limited to 512 bytes.
- 12 characters in an identifier or AS phrase
- 8 characters in an NPL filename
- 160 total number of DATA-FORM value & range checks *
- 23 lines in a FORM, 78 characters wide
- All fields in the master file may be indexed
- Field widths are limited to 999
- Alphanumeric strings are not limited in headings
- Integer values limited to -32768 to $+32767$
- 100 record DELETEs per DATA-FORM session *
- 100 record INSERTs per DATA-FORM session *
- APPENDed records limited only by disk capacity

Literals

A word used by programming texts to refer to a group, or string of characters, that are to be taken literally as data items, rather than as the *name* of a data variable. The numbers 5, 75, and 16000 may be called numeric literals. The strings of characters, '08540,' 'JONES,' '609-924-7111,' and "Harper's Ferry" are alphanumeric literals. The latter are usually embraced by a pair of quote marks. As a convenience, the quote marks may be omitted in a screening IF phrase, provided the string contains no space, quote, or period characters.

LO

```
C>SELECT keyfld = LO THRU value.
```

LO is a keyword, meaning the lowest value of a keyfld. Used only in a SELECT command.

LOG

```
ON MATCH LOG fn.fld...AS fn2
ON NOMATCH LOG fn.fld...AS fn2
```

A request to write data to a file, as part of an UPDATE or DELETE statement in Modify mode depending upon the matching of record value, as specified in a related matching IF phrase.

LST

    LST.fld

A prefix to a verb object, to select the first value retrieved among the values of "fld" in a group of records. Must appear in a SUM, WRITE, or COUNT phrase. "fld" is any valid fieldname, alias, defined name, or unique truncation. LST and the name may be separated by either an asterisk or a period.

LT

    IF fld LT value

A relational operator, short for Less-Than, used to compare two numbers or two alphanumerics. In the latter case, "less" means "sorts before," using the ASCII character set. In a screening IF phrase "fld" is any fieldname, alias, defined name, or unique truncation; "value" is a numeric or alphanumeric literal. Quotes are needed only when spaces are embedded.

    IF expression1 LT expression2   THEN...ELSE...

In DEFINE and COMPUTE statements, both "expressions" may be, or contain, any valid identifier or a literal value, as 143 or '07463' or 'F.' Alphanumeric literals must be enclosed in quotes.

LT and IS-LESS-THAN are synonyms.

Mask

    IF fld CONTAINS $$cc$c...   ...OR...

Dollar signs and "c" (any printable character except ampersand and quotes) form a string of characters which is used as a mask in the screening IF phrase. If a period or space character appears in the string, surrounding quotes are required. The mask has a length equal to or less than the length of "fld," an alphanumeric variable. Or phrases to specify two or more masks or literal strings are optional.

When mask length equals "fld" length, a match is sought for the non-$ characters; e.g.

```
IF ZIP CONTAINS 01$$$
```

will match ZIP codes with 01 in the first two positions.

When mask length is shorter than "fld," the mask is moved across "fld," within the length of "fld," looking for a pattern match while ignoring the $ positions. For example:

```
IF fld CONTAINS $TON$
```

will find STONES but not TONNAGE or APPLETON.

Upper- and lowercase differences are significant. Masks are used only with the CONTAINS relational operator.

MASTER

The word *MASTER* is used in two ways. First, it describes a type of file which contains all the information necessary to define and describe a database. A master file is also known as the *schema* or *dictionary* file.

Second, within the master file, MASTER is a database attribute, having the same meaning as SEGMENT, which is the name of a file segment or record type. Such a name is required only in multisegment file definitions, and then MASTER is used only for the first, or root, segment. The name must begin with a letter and may have up to eight characters, limited to letters and 0 to 9. Case is ignored.

MATCH

```
ON MATCH PRINT fn.fld...
ON MATCH LOG fn.fld...AS fn2
```

An optional phrase in an UPDATE or DELETE statement to write data to the printer, or console, or a file, each time a related matching IF phrase is satisfied.

MAX

```
MAX.fld
```

A prefix to a verb object, to find the highest value of the variable for a group of records. For alphanumeric variables highest refers to the sort sequence. Must appear in a SUM, COUNT, or WRITE phrase. "fld" is any valid fieldname, alias, defined name, or unique truncation. MAX and the name may be separated by either an asterisk or a period. The prefix MAXIMUM is a synonym for MAX.

MEMORY?

C>MEMORY?

A command to display an approximate measure of the memory space available for sorting. MEM? is an abbreviation. See Chapter 13.

MIN

MIN.fld

A prefix to a verb object, to find the lowest value of the variable for a group of records. For alphanumeric variables highest refers to the sort sequence. Must appear in a SUM, COUNT, or WRITE phrase. "fld" is any valid fieldname, alias, defined name, or unique truncation. MIN and the name may be separated by either an asterisk or a period. The prefix MINIMUM is a synonym for MIN.

Modifiers

The following keywords are called field modifiers, and they always follow a fieldname in either a verb phrase or a BY phrase: NOPRINT, NOTOTAL, BINARY, AS phrase.

These keywords are called BY field modifiers: SUBTOTAL, PAGE, SKIP n, FOLD, RESET#. If both kinds of modifiers are present field modifiers come first.

The HOLD modifiers are BINARY, the AS phrase, and the INTO phrase.

Modifiers follow the word they modify, and, when more than one is used, modifiers of the same kind may appear in any order. Field modifiers must precede BY field modifiers if both kinds are used.

MODIFY

C>MODIFY

A command to enter the DATA-FORM mode for adding, deleting and revising records for the current datafile. There must be an active master file; if a datafile does not exist, it is created on the same volume with the master file.

Names

Names for files are limited to six or eight letters or digits (depending upon the computer operating system), beginning with a letter. NPL appends .E, .M, .I, or .D, a filetype suffix, for Exec, Master, Index, and Data files. The POINTS files, available in UCSD and Apple Pascal Systems only, have .P appended to the name (See GRAPH).

Names for master file fields, aliases, and DEFINEd and COMPUTEd variables are called identifiers and consist of up to twelve characters. Identifiers used in NPL phrases and expressions must begin with a letter and contain only letters, 0 to 9, colon, hyphen, or #. Fieldnames and COMPUTE names that only appear as column headings may contain any printable character, except a comma. Identifiers in DEFINE and COMPUTE expressions may not contain hyphens, which cannot be distinguished from the subtraction symbol.

In recognizing identifiers NPL does not distinguish between upper- and lowercase letters. An identifier may be recognized by only the first few characters, provided this truncated form is a unique name among all the possible shortened names for all identifiers.

In conflicts between names and NPL Keywords, NPL recognizes keywords first. If a name is the same as, or contains, a keyword (e.g., COUNT or CLIPPER), a non-keyword spelling must be used to refer to it. For example: COU, CLI, or CLIPP.

NE

```
IF fld NE value      ...NOR value...
```

A relational operator used to test the inequality of two numbers or two alphanumeric variables. In a screening IF phrase "fld" is any fieldname, alias, defined name, or unique truncation; NOR phrases are optional. "value" is a numeric or alphanumeric literal; quotes are needed only when spaces are embedded.

```
IF expression1 NE expression2 THEN...ELSE...
```

IF...THEN...ELSE phrases are used only in DEFINE and COMPUTE statements, both "expressions" may be, or may contain, any valid identifier or a literal value, as 143 or '07463' or 'F.' Alphanumeric literals must be enclosed in quotes. NE and IS-NOT are synonyms. OR is accepted as a synonym for NOR.

NEWRECS

M>NEWRECS

A command in DATA-FORM to locate the first record of the group of new records which were appended to the datafile subsequent to the last building of Index files. NEWRECS is not valid when no Index is active.

NOMATCH

```
ON  NOMATCH  PRINT  fn.fld...
ON  NOMATCH  LOG  fn.fld...AS  filename
```

An optional phrase in an UPDATE or DELETE statement to write data to the printer, the console, or a file, each time a related matching IF phrase is not satisfied.

NOPRINT

```
...fld  NOPRINT...
...BY  fld  NOPRINT...
...COMPUTE  fld  =  expression  NOPRINT
```

A field modifier, which follows a verb object, BY field, or computed variable, causing the variable to be excluded from a printed report or a HOLD or GRAPH file. Such variables are used as temporary variables for use in COMPUTE phrases, or for sorting without displaying the sort key on the left side of the report page. As a field option NOPRINT must precede any BY field options.

NOR

```
...value1  NOR  value2      ...NOR  value3...
...TO  value1  NOR  value2  TO  value3...NOR  value4...
```

A NOR phrase repeats a test in a screening IF phrase. The tests are inequality and omitted range tests. Use OR with equality tests. While NOR more clearly conveys the meaning of repeated inequality tests, OR is accepted as a synonym for NOR.

NOSORT

NOSORT is a one word phrase in a Report request to suppress the actual sorting of the file, while retaining the report formatting effects of the BY phrase. NOSORT is used when the file is known to be in the desired sort sequence.

NOTOTAL

```
verb-object   NOTOTAL
```

NOTOTAL is a field modifier, which is used to suppress the printing of accumulated totals for selected verb objects when COLUMNTOTAL or SUBTOTAL is requested. In the case of COMPUTEd variables NOTOTAL causes the COMPUTE statements to be evaluated with the summary values at each sub- and columntotal line, and to be printed in lieu of the accumulated totals.

In general, NOTOTAL is used when a COMPUTE expression uses division by a variable, or uses ABS or other nonlinear functions. A common example is a percentage variable computed from two other fields. A columntotal of percentages has no meaning, but a total percent can be computed from the totals of the two other fields.

OMITS

```
IF fld OMITS value      ...OR value...
```

A relational operator in a screening IF phrase. "value" is a literal string of characters to be searched for within the length of the field. OR phrases are optional.

```
IF fld OMITS 'value' THEN...ELSE...
```

A relational operator in a DEFINE or COMPUTE statement. "fld" is any fieldname, alias, defined name (or unique truncation) of an alphanumeric variable. "value" is a literal string of characters to be searched for within the length of the field and must be within quotes. "value" may be repeated with OR phrases.

```
IF expr1 OMITS expr2 THEN...ELSE...
```

In the general form expr1 and expr2 are alphanumeric expressions, such as: MON+DAY+YR, which concatenates alphanumeric characters.

OR

```
...value1 OR value2      ...OR value3...
...TO value1 OR value2 TO value3 ...OR value4...
...IN filename1 OR filename2  ...OR filename3...
```

An OR phrase repeats a test in a screening IF phrase. The tests are equality and range tests. The OR phrases also repeat the IN phrase search of a file. Use NOR with inequality tests. All OR and NOR phrases are optional.

OVER

        ...fld1 OVER fld2...

A verb phrase option, which revises the normal columnar format of reports. OVER has the effect of inserting a carriage return and line feed between the printing of "fld1" and "fld2." The two flds are any verb objects (includes COMPUTEd variables). Any number of OVERs may be used. OVER causes the suppression of all column headings on verb objects. AS phrases may be used to print labels to the left of each data value.

Over-ride Key

A name used in the NPL manuals to refer to the key to be pressed, in DATA-FORM mode, to overcome the effect of the edit checks that prevent entry of data items that do not satisfy the character, range, or value criteria. The actual key may vary from one keyboard to another.

OWNER

OWNER is an optional master file attribute, an alias for PARENT, which defines relationships between segments of a file.

PAGE

        BY fld PAGE

A BY field modifier which causes the page of a report to be ejected (go to top of form or screen) whenever "fld" changes value. When the word PAUSE appears in the request, processing is suspended at the bottom of each page until RETURN is pressed, to permit reading of a page or changing of paper.

PAGE#

        HEADING   " Page <PAGE#...   "

The name of a "computed" system variable (with PRINTING Format = I4), which counts from one and is incremented each time the report advances to a new page. The name may not be abbreviated. It may appear in HEADINGs, verb phrases, and COMPUTE expressions.

When the PRINTER: is active and the HEADING phrase is not used, PAGE# is automatically printed at the top right margin of each page. The right margin is determined by SET WIDTH = n.

PARENT

PARENT is an optional master file attribute, with alias OWNER, which defines relationships between segments of a file.

PAUSE

PAUSE is a single-word report phrase which causes the report output to be suspended at the end of each page until the RETURN key is pressed. This permits reading of a page or changing of paper.

PCT.fld

A prefix to a numeric verb object, to calculate the percentage for that variable based on the subtotal for a group of records divided by the total for all records selected by the Report request. The result is available for use in HEADING and COMPUTE phrases. Must appear in a WRITE, COUNT, or SUM phrase. "fld" is any numeric fieldname, alias, defined name, or unique truncation. PCT and the name may be separated by a period or an asterisk. The prefix PERCENT is a synonym for PCT.

Period

The period character (.) has four uses: as a decimal point in real numbers, as punctuation in data and literal values, such as, "C.O.D." (quotes are needed if a literal value includes a period, a space, or a quote mark), as a separator between filename and fieldname, and as a terminator (punctuation) to a Report mode request or to a DEFINE or SELECT mode statement. As punctuation it is always the last character on a line, like the period at the end of a paragraph, e.g.:

```
IF DEPARTMENT.MAIL IS COD.
IF DEPARTMENT.MAIL IS 'C.O.D.'.
SELECT SALES.AMOUNT = 1.50 THRU 75.
```

Prefix

There are verb object prefixes (AVE, MIN, MAX, ASQ, FST, LST, SUM, ROWPCT, TOT, PCT, CNT) which are connected by a period to a verb object name. There are also group test prefixes (including all of the above plus ANY and ALL) which are connected by a period to a fieldname in an IF phrase.

Prefix is the name of a UCSD Pascal operating system variable and of a command (P) in the Filer mode, which allows you to set the Prefix variable to a volume name. When searching for a filename on a diskette the Filer system assumes the "Prefix" volume unless the diskette name is otherwise specified.

PRINT

```
PRINT fld...
```

A primary verb, which causes a line on a report, or a record in a HOLD file, to occur for each record retrieved and accepted. PRINT followed by one or more verb objects, with their modifiers, is a verb phrase. "fld" is any fieldname, alias, defined name, or unique truncation. PRINT acts as a command to enter Report mode.

PRINTER:

```
C>PRINTER:
```

A command to direct reports to the printer. The command CONSOLE: reverses the action.

At the UCSD Pascal Operating System level the volume name assigned to volume #6: is PRINTER:. It is .PRINTER for the Apple III.

PRINTING Format

PRINTING Format is the name of the first format code in each record of a master file. The code carries two pieces of information. A letter, A, I, F, or D, specifies the format of a data item internal to the computer. "A" means alphanumeric characters (ASCII codes). "I" means integer values, from −32768 to +32767. "F" means floating point numbers are processed internally. The letter is followed by an integer which specifies the field width, e.g.:

```
A1, A33, A400,    I1, I9, I21,    F12.9, F3.1, F12.0
D15, D14.2CL, D14CRB
```

In F format the digit following the decimal point specifies the number of fractional positions—this number must be two less than the width, or smaller, to allow for the sign and decimal point. Apple Pascal prints a maximum of six significant digits. Large numbers that do not fit in a format overflow to the right or are printed in engineering format. To produce fields wider than the data itself, PRINTING Formats may be as large as A999, I999, and F999.9.

D format can accommodate whole numbers to one trillion, with commas (D17C), or dollars and cents to 11 billion dollars, with commas and $ sign (D18.2CL). Only two fractional positions or none are allowed. The options are given by C for commas at every third position, L or R for $ sign in the left or right-most leading position, and B for brackets to indicate negative values.

PRINTING_FMT

PRINTING_FMT is a required master file attribute, with alias USAGE, which defines the type of variable (Integer, Real, Double, or Alphanumeric) and the display format to be used for reports.

PROFILE

A file with the name PROFILE.E is called the Profile Exec. It may contain any NPL program statements. It is executed each time the NPL system is initiated. The Profile Exec usually presents a list of options, prompts for a response, and calls another exec program, as in this simple example:

```
ECHO *
*   CHOOSE ONE: JOB1, JOB2, OR JOB3
ECHO OFF
EXEC &CHOICE
```

The word "profile" is also used to refer to a particular datafile and the data items in it. The datafile named PROFILE.D (in the master file, FILE= PROFILE), contains fields which are called "profile variables." The datafile is unique in that it has only one record, and hence the profile variables are single valued. Profile variables may be accessed at any time, by commands or by requests, and may be assigned to exec variables. The filename prefix for a profile variable is simply the period character.

PROMPT

```
PROMPT fld1 fld2...
```

A command in DATA-FORM mode, to specify which fields, and in what order, are to be prompted for input values. "fld" is a fieldname, alias, or unique truncation. When used with the FORM command, the sequence of the list of "flds" determines the movement of the cursor across the FORM. If a "fld" appears in the FORM statement but not the PROMPT statement, or vice versa, an error message is displayed.

```
PROMPT fld1 optionlist, fld2 optionlist,...
```

Validation criteria may be specified for each field with an "optionlist." The commas are optional. An "optionlist" may contain up to five edit option codes, in any order. The codes specify how characters being entered as data should be accepted or rejected. The edit option codes are:

REQ   Data is REQUIRED for this field.

351

FIL	The full width of this A format field must be FIL-LED.
LTR	Only letters (and / . - ,) are accepted in this A format field.
NBR	Only numbers (and / . - ,) are accepted in this A format field.
NOC	No change is allowed to this field after the record is first created.
VAL(list)	Only values on the list of numeric or alphanumeric literals are accepted in this field with formats of A, I, F, or D.

"list" items are separated by spaces, and an item may also specify a range, as in (1..16 65..80) and (AL..DE MO..WY). Alphanumeric literals containing spaces, periods, or quote marks must be surrounded by quotes.

Examples are:

```
PROMPT
   CODE       LTR VAL (USA 'U.S.A.' 'C.O.D.' RFD
                            'SPECIAL DELIVERY')
   TIME       REQ FIL NBR VAL (0000..2400)
   WEEKDAY    REQ FIL LTR VAL (MON TUE WED THU FRI)
   CITY       REQ LTR
   ZIPCODE    FIL REQ NBR
   PRICE      VAL (100..350 395 495) REQ
   DISCOUNT   VAL (0.1..0.25)
   SSN        NOC NBR FIL
   ODDNBRS    VAL (1 3 5 7 9 11 13)
```

The five edit option codes may appear in any combination. The codes may be abbreviated to their first letter. If the field has a Printing Format type of I, F, or D, that is, a numeric field, only the digits, 0 to 9, the minus sign, and the decimal point are accepted. However, commas are tolerated (but ignored), and the minus sign (hyphen) may be entered as the leading or the trailing character.

The VALIDATE statement is an alternative to the PROMPT statement. The statement form is the same, but the "optionlist" of edit codes is required. The sequence of the list of "flds" is arbitrary and does not affect the prompting sequence. If FORM is present, PROMPT must precede it, while VALIDATE follows a FORM statement.

QUIT

QUIT is a command available in Report and DEFINE modes, to cause return to the Command mode. QUIT usually abandons any partially complete activity. QUIT and the Exit key have the same effect in Report and DEFINE modes. In DEFINE mode QUIT abandons definitions just typed.

Quotes

Single and double quote marks may be used interchangably (in pairs) for heading text, for AS phrases with embedded spaces, for literal strings, and for text following the FORM command in the DATA-FORM mode. Single quotes between double quotes are treated as text characters, and vice versa. Verb object names may not appear within quotes. Alphanumeric literal strings generally are embraced by a pair of quote marks. As a convenience the quote marks may be omitted in a screening IF phrase, provided the string contains no space, quote, or period characters.

REC#

The "fieldname" of a system variable (with PRINTING Format = I4), which is the physical sequence number of the records of the currently active file. The name may not be abbreviated. The fieldname may appear in HEAD-INGs, verb phrases, in SELECT, DEFINE and COMPUTE statements, and in IF phrases. For example:

```
SELECT REC# = LO THRU 20.
```

This phrase may be used to limit the number of records retrieved.

RECODE

```
newname/fmt=RECODE codename (code1 new1, code2 new2,...
                                    ..., ELSE new;)
```

A function used in DEFINE and COMPUTE statements to substitute one set of values for another. The list of value pairs appear within parentheses. The commas and the ELSE phrase are optional.

```
fileA.new/fmt=RECODE fileA.code (fileB.code, fileB.new)
```

The list of value pairs may be two fields in another file, e.g. fileB.code and fileB.new; RECODE performs the table lookup function within the second file.

RECTYPE

A keyword which is used only in a master file as a special fieldname and is associated with an alphanumeric code value, which is recorded as the alias. The code identifies particular record types.

REMOUT:

```
C>REMOUT:
```

A command to direct reports to the remote output channel. In UCSD and Pascal operating systems .RS232 or REMOUT: is the volume name assigned to the serial input/output port.

REPEAT:...UNTIL

```
C>REPEAT:
<>statement(s)
<>UNTIL logical-expression
C>
```

REPEAT: is a command to direct that a group of NPL statements be performed one or more times, UNTIL a particular test condition is satisfied. The test condition is a logical expression of the same form used in any IF. . .THEN. . .ELSE expression. The group of statements may contain any NPL command, Report request, DEFINE statement, EXEC statement, or file maintenance statement—or any combination thereof. Other RE-PEAT:. . .UNTIL statements may be included as well.

REPLACE

```
C>REPLACE name/format = expression...
```

p A command to enter the DEFINE mode, which is followed by one or more definitions. A period or END terminates the mode.

REPLACE differs from the DEFINE command in that "name" must exist as a DEFINEd variable, and "expression" and "format" are *replaced* by the new definition.

"name" must not be the same as a master file fieldname or alias. "name" must be the full spelling of the defined variable to be replaced. Type "FILE?" first to verify names.

REPLACE is used to correct or revise an existing definition or format. Only the numeric part of the format code may be changed. If the A, F, or I code is also changed the results are unpredictable.

RESET

RESET is a button on some computer keyboards to be used as a last resort in recovering from an error situation. The CONTROL key must be held down when RESET is pressed. RESET restarts the Apple Pascal Operating System. Press X and then type NPL/NPL to reenter NPL.

RESET#

```
BY fld RESET#
```

RESET# is a BY field modifier, which follows a BY fld to reset the line counter ROW#. See ROW#.

RETURN

RETURN is the name of a button on the keyboard which usually has the effect of a typewriter carriage return lever. An automatic line advance is assumed. In HEADING text a carriage return character is treated as a space character. In DATA-FORM Mode the RETURN key also causes the cursor to advance to the next field. In DATA-FORM mode the RETURN key causes (a) a new data item to be accepted from the keyboard, or (b) a new or revised record to be written to disk storage, or (c) the next record to be selected. In HEADING text the RETURN character is treated as a space.

ROW#

```
PRINT fld...ROW#     AS name...
```

The name of a "computed" system variable (with PRINTING format=I4) which counts the lines printed on a report and is displayed as a column according to its verb object position. The name must not be abbreviated. ROW# may appear in HEADINGs, verb phrases, and COMPUTE expressions. An AS phrase is optional, to specify a column heading.

The ROW# counter is reset to 1 when the value of "fld" changes, in the following BY phrase:

```
:..BY fld RESET#
```

ROWPCT
ROWTOTAL

ROWPCT is a verb object prefix to calculate the percent one verb object is of the ROWTOTAL value.
ROWTOTAL is a report mode option which acts like a verb object to create a column containing the sum of the numeric verb objects on each line.

Rules

• Report phrases may appear in any order in a Report request.

• Field modifiers (NOPRINT, NOTOTAL, AS, and BINARY) must precede BY field modifiers (SUBTOTAL, PAGE, UNDERLINE, SKIP n, FOLD, RESET#, IN-GROUPS-OF) in a BY phrase.

355

- The Exit key is used to escape from the current mode or special conditions (data entry, error status...) and to cancel long unwanted reports and searches.

- When in doubt about the current NPL Mode press RETURN key to see the prompt character.

- Commas, semicolons, and the word AND are optional, and may be used in Report requests to separate phrases and verb objects, as in English, to improve the clarity of the text. In addition commas or semicolons may separate BY field modifiers, SELECT statement values, and fieldnames in VALIDATE and PROMPT statements.

- Alias names should begin with a letter, have no embedded blanks, be limited to letters, 0 to 9, colon, #, and for convenience be short.

- Formats for real numbers must provide for the decimal point and a sign; hence, the two-format numbers should differ by at least 2; e.g., F8.2, F4.2, F9.7, F12.9, but not F9.8, F3.2, F2.1.

- NPL evaluates IF phrases first, unless the IF-phrase field is a DEFINEd variable; then it evaluates all of the DEFINE statements first.

- 'LAST fld' in a DEFINE is the value of fld in the last record accepted. (The prefix + verb object, 'LST.fld,' are not related to the above).

- 'LAST fld' in a COMPUTE is the value of fld in the last line printed.

- COUNT fld and CNT.fld produce the same result, the number of records retrieved and accepted. The choice of fld does not affect the count.

- ROW# counts lines, or rows, printed. ROW# can be reset to 1 with 'BY fld RESET#.' REC#, ROW# and PAGE# are available for COMPUTEs. REC# may also be used in DEFINE and SELECT statements.

- Alphanumeric literals which include a period, a space, or a quote mark must be enclosed in quotes.

- A PRINTING format of F10.2 is assigned if none is specified in a DEFINE or COMPUTE statement.

• Fieldnames that are NPL keywords must be referred to by an abbreviated form to be recognized as names. The names of the system variables ROW#, REC#, and PAGE# may not be abbreviated.

RUN

RUN is a command in DATA-FORM mode. It signals the end of the DATA-FORM request and initiates the building of the formatted screen, in which the first record of the file is displayed. Alternatively APPEND prepares an empty screen, ready for entry of new records. When no datafile exists, RUN and APPEND have the same effect. In Report mode RUN is a synonym for END and the terminating "period."

SEGMENT

SEGMENT is an optional master file attribute which names a set of field descriptions. Segment is used to describe files with several record formats that may be distinguished by a RECTYPE code.

SELECT

```
C>SELECT keyfield = values.
C>SELECT keyfield IN filename.
C>SELECT keyfield.
M>SELECT keyfield.
```

A command to enter the SELECT mode and to specify a subfile, and an indexed view of the currently active datafile. For a field to be a "keyfld" an Index file for that field must exist. SELECT stores a single selection condition, automatically clearing any previous condition. END or period must follow the "values". With the second form a list of test values may be read from a file. See IN.

The last two forms select a sorted view of the file, via the indexed "keyfield," from Command mode and from within the DATA-FORM mode. The subfile feature of the first two examples is not available in DATA-FORM mode; if selected the subfile condition is ignored.

```
M>SELECT REC#
C>SELECT REC# = values.
```

These are special cases which select records according to their physical position numbers.

Subsequent operations in Report mode and in DATA-FORM mode are affected by the selection of an Index file. Searching the file is performed in the sort sequence of the Index file. Report mode requests operate upon only those records that satisfy the selection conditions. Only those records are read from the file. Very rapid retrieval is achieved by direct access to the disk using an Index file.

"keyfield" is a fieldname, alias, or unique truncation, for which there exists an Index file. "values" in the first form above is any combination of these phrases ("value" is a numeric or alphanumeric literal), e.g.:

```
value   value   value...
LO THRU value
value THRU value    value THRU value
value THRU HI
```

Commas or spaces may separate these phrases in a sequence, on one or more lines. LO and HI mean the lowest and highest values in the file.

The order of the sequence of "values" determines the order of selection and retrieval.

Repeated values result in selection of duplicate records. The order of records within a range is the sort order of "keyfld."

A selection condition is associated with a particular datafile, hence it is cleared when GETFILE changes the active datafile, or by the command:

```
C>CLEAR SELECT
```

SET

```
C>SET name/format = expression...
```

A command to enter the SET mode to assign values to one or more SET variables. A period or END terminates the mode. The SET variables may appear in DEFINE expressions, other SET statements, and Report requests.

"Name" is up to twelve characters, restricted to letters, 0 to 9, colon, hyphen, and #. The first character must be a letter. Names containing a hyphen may not appear in DEFINE, COMPUTE, or SET expressions.

The slash and "format" are optional when the variable is numeric. If omitted, a format of F10.2 is assigned.

A one-line SET statement for defining a new variable or for assigning a new value to an existing variable called CLASS might appear as:

```
SET CLASS/A4='19' + YEAR.
```

A new value for CLASS is formed from the current value of YEAR.

"Expression" is any combination of constants, functions (such as IF...THEN...ELSE, CLIP, ABS), arithmetic operators, and fieldnames (aliases, other defined names, or unique truncations).

SET statements are evaluated immediately and only once (except in a RE-PEAT loop). Succesive SET commands add new variables to the list of active SET variables.

"Name" must be unique among all active names (fields, SETs, and DE-FINEs). An existing "expression" (and "format") may be replaced by an new definition for the same name.

```
C>SET LENGTH = n
C>SET WIDTH = m
```

Special commands for changing and for reading the stored values of certain system parameters, like page length and page width. The initial settings are: n = 58 lines, m = 132 columns. The LENGTH setting limits the number of lines which appear on a page, including headings and blank lines between data lines. When a report exceeds the LENGTH limit, HEADINGs are repeated. If the PAUSE phrase is in the request, printing pauses before each new page. The WIDTH setting determines the position of the page number when PRINTER: is active and HEADING is *not* used. WIDTH also determines CENTER if requested in HEADING or FOOTING phrases.

SET?

```
C>SET?
```

A command to cause the display of all current settings.

SKIP

```
SKIP n
BY fld SKIP n
```

A one word phrase, in Report mode, with an optional integer modifier. If the integer n is missing, a value of one is assumed. SKIP causes extra blank lines after each row printed. As a BY field modifier the extra lines occur only when "fld" changes value. The two forms may be used concurrently in one report request.

SQRT

```
SQRT(numeric identifier or expression)
```

An arithmetic function to calculate the square root of a variable; used in DEFINE and COMPUTE statements.

SUBS

SUBS is a FIELDTYPE attribute value which is assigned by NPL to array variables which are used as subscripts of other arrays.

SUBSCRIPT

SUBSCRIPT is an optional master file attribute of an ARRAY variable which is the name of another ARRAY variable used to select among the data items of the first ARRAY.

SUBTOTAL

        BY fld SUBTOTAL

A BY field modifier to accumulate running totals for the numeric verb objects and to print group subtotals for each value of "fld." SUBTOTAL may follow each of several BY fields to produce nested sets of running subtotals. Has no effect upon alphanumeric fields. Verb objects followed by NOTOTAL are not accumulated, but if they are computed variables the COMPUTE statements are evaluated with the subtotal values.

SUM

        SUM   fld...

SUM is a synonym for WRITE, a primary verb, which causes the accumulation of numeric verb object values for a group of records, as determined by constant values of the BY fields. The accumulated sums are printed on one line in a report (or in one record in a HOLD file). In the absence of BY phrases the group is all records selected from the file, and the report has one line. SUM followed by one or more verb objects (including COMPUTE phrases) is a verb phrase. "fld" is a fieldname, alias, defined name, or unique truncation. SUM acts as a command to enter Report mode.

        SUM.fld

A prefix to a verb object, which is used to accumulate (as above) in a COUNT n WRITE phrase for a group of records, as in: COUNT SSN AND SUM.HOURS. "fld" is defined as above. SUM and the name may be separated by either an asterisk or a period.

Tab Key

A name used in NPL manuals to refer to the key to be pressed, in DATA-FORM mode, to cause the cursor to advance from field to field. The actual key may vary from one keyboard to another, but generally the key marked "TAB" performs this function, and sometimes the *right-arrow* key is used as well.

Terms

Terminology used in NPL documents include:

- A report phrase is any of the following: verb phrase, IF phrase, BY phrase, HOLD phrase, HEADING, SKIP n, NOSORT, PAUSE, COLUMNTOTAL, AND. The last keyword, AND, is a "do nothing" keyword which may appear between other report phrases to improve the readability of the report request.

- Field modifiers are keywords (NOPRINT, NOTOTAL, AS, BINARY) which follow a field identifier in verb and BY phrases.

- BY field modifiers are keywords (SUBTOTAL, PAGE, UNDERLINE, SKIP n, FOLD, RESET#, IN-GROUPS-OF) which follow a BY field (or its field modifier, if any). One or more may be used concurrently.

- The HOLD modifiers are BINARY, the AS phrase, and the INTO phrase.

- An identifier is a fieldname, or alias from a master file, or a DEFINEd or COMPUTEd variable name or a unique truncation thereof.

- An NPL filename is a six or eight character string, depending upon the particular computer and operating system, followed by a suffix that specifies the type of file, as in: string.M.TEXT and string.D.DATA for Apple III, or string/M.TEXT and string/D.DATA for Apple II, or string.MAS and string.DAT for other computers.

- A volume name is an operating system identifier for a diskette, or certain input or output devices like .PRINTER.

- In this Reference Section three dots . . . (called an ellipsis), denote an optional repeating item or a continuing sequence.

- The characters C>, R>, S>, M>, D> refer to the prompt message which is displayed by NPL in the Command, Report, Select, Modify (i.e., DATA-FORM) and Define modes, respectively. F> appears when a FORM statement is typed directly, rather than in an Exec file. S> also signals an incomplete SET command.

• Numeric means integer or real number variables

• The terms real number and floating point number are used interchangeably.

• Numbers or digits sometimes refer simply to the 0 to 9 characters in a alphanumeric field, which are not numeric, just as zip codes and telephone numbers are not numeric quantities.

• Alphanumeric usually means all printable characters including the space character. Sometimes it means all letters and digits.

• Variables: There are file variables, profile variables, &variables, and exec variables.

TEXT>DATA

A utility program available only in UCSD Apple Pascal operating systems, to convert a TEXT file (e.g., SALES.D.TEXT) into a normal NPL datafile (SALES.D.DATA) consistent with a master file (SALES.M). The program requests the name of the TEXT file with T> as the prompt. The reply may specify both the datafile and the master file, using the rules from the GETFILE command. For example:

```
Enter Filename T> (.D2/SALES82) SALES
```

THRU

```
value1 THRU value2
LO THRU value
value THRU HI
```

Used in SELECT statements to specify an inclusive range of values, numeric or alphanumeric. LO and HI are keywords meaning the lowest and highest values present in the file.

TO

```
IF fld IS value TO value    ...OR value TO value...
```

The word TO is used with IS and IS-NOT to define a range of numeric or alphanumeric values (including the end values) in a screening IF phrase. OR phrases with ranges are optional and may be mixed with single-value OR phrases.

TOP

```
M>TOP
```

A command in the DATA-FORM mode, which moves the current position to the beginning of the file. If an Index is active the current position becomes the record with the lowest value of the Indexed field.

TOT.fld

A prefix to a numeric verb object, to calculate the total of that variable for all records selected by the Report request. The result is available for use in HEADING and COMPUTE phrases. It must appear in a WRITE, COUNT, or SUM phrase. "fld" is any numeric fieldname, alias, defined name, or unique truncation. TOT and the name may be separated by a period or an asterisk. The prefix TOTAL is a synonym for TOT.

Transfer

Transfer is the name of a command (T) in UCSD and Apple Pascal operating systems in the Filer mode used to copy a file to the CONSOLE:, the PRINTER:, REMOUT:, or to another diskette. Press T and type

```
/oldvolume-id/oldfilename,/newvolume-id/newfilename
```

TYPEFILE

```
C>TYPEFILE filename
```

A command which displays a file, or prints it if PRINTER: is active. The full NPL filename must be specified (e.g. CLIENTS.D or CENSUS.E), and volume id may be typed to save search time.

UNDERLINE

```
BY-field UNDERLINE
```

UNDERLINE is a BY-phrase modifier to print a line across the report at the change of the sort field.

UP

```
M>UP
```

A command in the DATA-FORM mode to move the current postion toward the TOP of the file by one record. If an Index is active, UP is not available; selection by key value is used. Pressing the RETURN key steps "down" the file one record at a time.

UPDATE

```
M>UPDATE fnl.fld WITH expression,...END
M>UPDATE fnl.fld WITH fn2.fld,...END
```

A request in Modify mode to change the value of one or more fields, with a completed value from another file.

USAGE

USAGE is a required master file attribute, with alias PRINTING_FMT, which defines the type of variable (Integer, Real, Double, or Alphanumeric) and the display format to be used for reports.

VALIDATE

```
VALIDATE fldl optionlist, fld2 optionlist...
```

A command in DATA-FORM mode, to specify validation criteria for accepting new data values. "fld" is a fieldname, alias, or unique truncation. The commas are optional. Any or all fields may be included.

Validation criteria are specified for each field with an "optionlist." The commas are optional. An "optionlist" may contain one to five edit option codes, in any order. The codes specify how characters being entered as data should be accepted or rejected. The edit option codes are:

REQ	Data is REQUIRED for this field.
FIL	The full width of this A format field must be FILLED.
LTR	Only letters (and / . - ,) are accepted in this A format field.
NBR	Only numbers (and / . - ,) are accepted in this A format field.

NOC

No change is allowed to this field, after the record is first created.

VAL(list)

Only values on the list of numeric or alphanumeric literals are accepted in this field with formats of A, I, F, or D.

"list" items are separated by spaces, and an item may also specify a range, as in (1..16 65..80) and (AL..DE MO..WY). Alphanumeric literals containing spaces, periods, or quote marks must be surrounded by quotes.

Examples are:

```
VALIDATE
   CODE       LTR VAL (USA 'U.S.A.' 'C.O.D.' RFD
                          'SPECIAL DELIVERY')
   TIME       REQ FIL NBR VAL (0000..2400)
   WEEKDAY    REQ FIL LTR VAL (MON TUE WED THU FRI)
   CITY       REQ LTR
   ZIPCODE    FIL REQ NBR
   PRICE      VAL (100..350 395 495) REQ
   DISCOUNT   VAL (0.1..0.25)
   SSN        NOC NBR FIL
   ODDNBRS    VAL (1 3 5 7 9 11 13)
```

The five edit option codes may appear in any combination. The codes may be abbreviated to their first letter. If the field has a Printing format type of I, F, or D, that is, a numeric field, only the digits, 0 to 9, the minus sign, and the decimal point are accepted. However, commas are tolerated (but ignored), and the minus sign (hyphen) may be entered as the leading or the trailing character.

The PROMPT statement is an alternative to the VALIDATE statement. The statement form is the same, but the PROMPT list determines which fields are used for input and in what sequence. If FORM is present, VALIDATE follows. PROMPT must precede a FORM statement.

Volume
VOLID

Volume refers generally to a diskette or to other disk storage units. VOLID is the name or identifying label of a volume. A VOLID is used as a prefix to filename, separated by a slash, a colon, a period, or another character, depending upon the operating system.

WRITE

WRITE fld...

A primary verb, which causes a line on a report, or a record in a HOLD file, to occur for a group of records, as determined by constant values of the BY fields. In the absence of BY phrases the group is all records selected from the file, and the report has one line. WRITE followed by one or more verb objects (including COMPUTE phrases) is a verb phrase. "fld" is any fieldname, alias, defined name, or unique truncation. WRITE acts as a command to enter Report mode. WRITE and SUM are synonyms. WRITE sounds better than SUM when MAX, MIN, AVE, LST prefixes are used.

&variable

&variable

A string of characters (up to seventy-two) preceded by an ampersand (&) in an Exec file is treated as a run-time variable (also called an "amper-variable"). The string is displayed on the console, as a prompt to the operator. The operator's reply replaces the &variable before the Exec file is executed. If an &variable appears more than once the prompting occurs for each appearance.

An &variable may be embedded in a word, with its end determined by the first space, quote character, parenthesis, period, or another ampersand. The &variable may contain any other printable character. If the period character terminates the &variable, the period is removed from the text upon replacement of the &variable with the operator's reply.

&string(a,b,c,...)

A list of values, within parentheses, may follow an amper-variable string, with no intervening space. The values are separated by commas or spaces, and they must be within quote marks if the alphanumeric values themselves contain spaces, commas, parentheses, or quote marks. The values are used to test the response by the operator to an amper-variable prompt. Only values on the list are accepted. The operator's only other option is to press the Exit key.

*

An asterisk in column one or two (or both) of an exec file marks the line as a comment line. When ECHO * mode is set, an asterisk in column one causes the line to be displayed on the console, to provide the text for a "menu" of options. See ECHO.

The asterisk is the multiplication operator in DEFINE and COMPUTE statements.

+ - / * ( )

The characters + - / * ( ) have their usual functions in arithmetic expressions. To avoid confusion with the minus sign, the hyphen character may not be used with identifiers that appear in DEFINE and COMPUTE expressions.

The plus sign is also used for concatenation of string variables.

Parenthesis are used in the arithmetic expressions which may be in the logical condition of an IF statement (IF condition THEN. . .ELSE. . .), but they are not allowed around the entire "condition."

<n

A control device in a HEADING phrase. "n" is an integer. When printing the HEADING text the print head is moved to the nth column position. Overprinting is possible.

<+n

The print head tabs n positions to the right.

</n

The print head moves n lines down the page.

<fieldname

The current value (at the top line of the page) of a field marker is written into the HEADING beginning at the bracket character. "fieldname" is any valid verb object, including a prefix, or BY-field name. If no explicit verb exists, the implicit verb is WRITE.

AN NPL TUTORIAL FOR THE APPLE II COMPUTER

CONTENTS

Introduction 373
   Equipment and Materials 376

Lesson I: Report Writing 377
   Starting Up 377
   Using NPL 379
   Writing NPL Reports 382
   Screening 384
   Printing 388
   Headings 388
   APPLE PASCAL System 389
   Writing More Reports 392
      Sorting 393
      Counting 397
      Totals 398
      Summing 398
   Summing Up 400

Lesson II: Data Entry 403
   Mailing List Entry 403
   Using DATA-FORMs 406
   Correcting Entry Errors 407
   A Complex DATA-FORM 407
   Report Writing 409
      PRINT 410
      BY 410
      OVER 411
      NOPRINT 412

Lesson III: Creating DATA-FORMs 415
   Master Files 415
   Data Record Format 416
      Fieldnames 416
      Alias 416
      Printing Format 416
      File Format 416
   Creating a Master File 417
   Data Entry 421
   Using the Printer 423
   Report Writing 425
   DATA-FORM Mode 427
      Formatting the Screen 427
   Summary 429
   Screens in Apple PASCAL Editor 429

CONTENTS

Using Screens in NPL.. 434
Special Keys 436

INTRODUCTION

The three self-teaching lessons in this *Tutorial* will introduce you to NPL. You may practice the basic functions of NPL with the sample datafiles provided on the diskettes that accompany this *Tutorial*. You should read the *Tutorial* and try the examples before going to the *NPL User's Guide*.

NPL expects from you instructions on what data to use and what the final report format should look like. NPL figures out the step-by-step process needed to produce your desired report. This is the essence of a nonprocedural language; you tell the system what you want, and the system determines how to fulfill your request.

Lesson I teaches basic report-writing features and commands of NPL. You learn the structure of an NPL request, how to write NPL report requests, and how to send the reports to the screen and to a printer.

Lesson II demonstrates how to use a DATA-FORM screen for entering new data items. By executing a sample DATA-FORM program, you may practice building a datafile.

Lesson III shows you how to prepare DATA-FORM pictures to be used for data entry, editing of datafiles, and file maintenance. It teaches the creation of datafiles and the so-called Master files, which describe the record formats used in the datafile. It also demonstrates techniques of creating stored program files, which are used for writing reports and displaying DATA-FORM screens.

If the data that seems to confound your life—like tax receipts, bills, appointments, travel expenses, budgets, etc.—resides on paper forms stacked in the corner of your office, and if you wish to analyze it and put it to work for you, the steps in the process are the following:

1. Examine the data to see which **data items** cluster together naturally by subject matter. Then describe a **record format** for each such cluster.
2. **Capture**, that is, enter the data items into **data records** using your personal computer, forming for each subject a **datafile**, which is stored on magnetic diskettes.
3. **Query**, that is, interrogate the resultant datafiles of records using NPL.
4. **Sift**, **reorder**, and **coordinate** these records, and print tabulations with the same language.

These are the steps that you can take, with the help of NPL and without the need of a computer programmer. You can indeed take charge of your own data collections and be master rather than slave.

Steps 1, 2, and 3 are discussed in Lesson II: Data Entry and Lesson III: Creating DATA-FORMs. Steps 3 and 4 are the subject of Lesson I: Report Writing.

On this page, the NPL System Guide is displayed. This chart appears in the *NPL User's Guide* as a convenient reference to all the words of the NPL user's vocabulary. The full vocabulary can be grouped conveniently according to various NPL modes. The modes are illustrated here, but without the words. As you read about and learn to use these NPL *keywords*, the chart reappears in this *Tutorial* with the words presented in each lesson.

The NPL™ System Guide

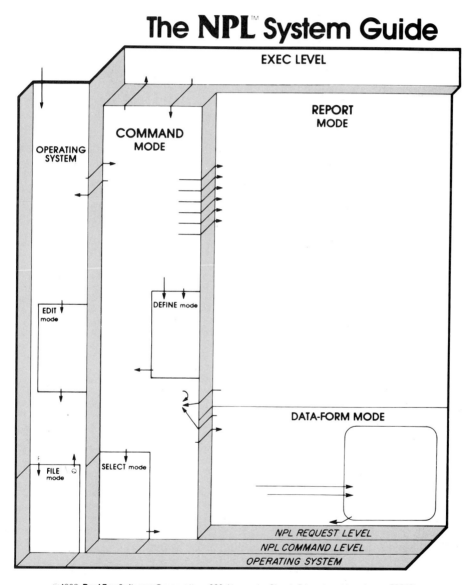

Think of the NPL system as a house with several rooms. Different activities take place in each room, and a different vocabulary is used. Upon turning the Apple on, you will be in the Operating System room, or mode. This mode has a Filer and an Editor room, which are discussed in Lessons I and III. From the Operating System room you enter the COMMAND room, or mode, of NPL. In the COMMAND room you can activate the printer and then type the contents of various files. Also, you can enter the REPORT room (mode), the DATA-FORM mode, the SELECT mode, and the DEFINE mode.

The first two of these modes within NPL are presented in this *Tutorial*. The SELECT mode and the DEFINE mode are discussed in the *NPL User's Guide*.

Lesson I takes you from the COMMAND room into the REPORT room and lets you practice with some of the words that are spoken there.

Lesson II and Lesson III take you from the COMMAND room to the EXEC Level and then into the DATA-FORM room where the basic DATA-FORM control words are introduced.

After each lesson the NPL System Guide is displayed with the new words you have learned.

EQUIPMENT AND MATERIALS REQUIRED

To use NPL you need an Apple II computer with the following features and software:

Apple II or II plus with 48K RAM

Apple Language Card (includes 16K RAM additional)

Black & white or color monitor

Two Disk Drives (a minimum)

A printer (optional)

An **APPLE1:** diskette

An **NPL:** diskette (contains the NPL Software System with demonstration files)

Note: NPL does *not* require other Apple software products such as APPLESOFT, INTEGER BASIC, and DOS 3.3.

The NPL System is run on the Apple II computer in conjunction with, or under the control of, the standard Apple Pascal System.

REPORT WRITING

The purpose of Lesson I is to give you first-hand experience with NPL on an Apple—sorting, screening, and selecting data, and then seeing the printed results. You can try NPL now, with no other preparation, using demonstration datafiles available on the diskette that comes with the NPL package.

STARTING UP YOUR APPLE WITH NPL

Turn on the monitor. Then, before turning on the Apple, insert the two diskettes into the disk drives as illustrated—the one labelled **APPLE1:** into Drive 1 and the one named **NPL:** into Drive 2. Do not touch the magnetic surfaces and do not touch the diskettes in the drives while the red light is on. Place each diskette into the drive with the label side up.

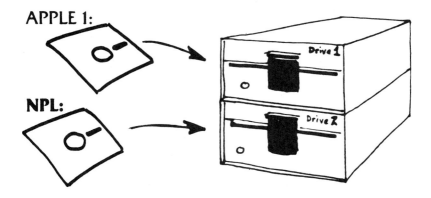

Before you actually turn on the Apple, you must learn some simple terminology.

The Apple Pascal Operating System, for reasons known only to wizards, refers to Disk Drive 1 by the name #4: and Disk Drive 2 by #5:. However, we have little use for these names because the so-called volume names of the diskettes are equivalent to the names of the drives in which they are inserted. Thus,

APPLE1:   means the same as #4:

NPL: means the same as #5:

These volume names appear as prefixes to filenames. For example, the CLIENT datafile on the **NPL:** diskette has the full name of

NPL:CLIENTS/D.DATA

If the word "volume" seems strange as a name for a diskette, you might think of each diskette as a book containing many chapters (called files). Librarians refer to books as volumes. Books and **diskettes** are portable and contain multiple chapters or **files**. These, in turn, contain multiple pages or **records**. The records contain words or **data items** consisting of characters (also called bytes). It is a useful analogy:

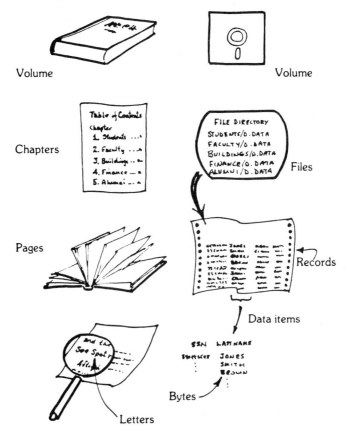

USING NPL

First look at the NPL System Guide in the Appendix. It shows a diagram of different rooms, or modes, through which you will move when using NPL. In each room you use a different vocabulary for instructing the computer, and NPL will perform different functions. Lesson I is concerned with teaching you the vocabulary of the Report mode room.

Now turn on the power to the computer and you will be welcomed to Apple Pascal. If you have an eighty-column display, the screen will look similar to this:

```
|COMMAND:E)dit,R)un,F)ile,C)omp,L)ink,X)ecute,A)ssem,D)ebug,?[1.1]|
|                                                                 |
|                                                                 |
|                                                                 |
|Welcome APPLE1:, to APPLE II Pascal 1.1                          |
|                                                                 |
|Based on UCSD Pascal II.1                                        |
|                                                                 |
|Current date is   1-May-81                                       |
|                                                                 |
|                                                                 |
|                                                                 |
|(C) Apple Computer Inc. 1979, 1980                               |
|(C) U.C. Regents 1979                                            |
|                                                                 |
|_____|
```

First, look carefully at the line of text on the top of the screen. When this text is displayed, you know you are in the first room, called Operating System, on the **NPL System Guide**. Here there are many commands you may give the computer, and all of them require only one letter. Some of the options are displayed at the top of the screen. For example,

   X to execute the **NPL** program

   F to enter the **FILER** mode

   E to enter the **EDITOR** mode

WARNING! Careless pressing of keys can lead to surprising results. If you find yourself in a strange mode, which you had not intended, read the instructions at the top of the screen. Usually pressing the **RETURN** or **ESCAPE** (**ESC**) key will return you to the Apple Pascal Operating System mode.

These options are discussed later in the *Tutorial*. First you should enter the NPL Command mode and try it out.

Press: **X**   and the computer asks:

EXECUTE WHAT FILE?

You type, **NPL:NPL**   and press the **RETURN** key.

The computer will go looking for the NPL program and find it on the **NPL:** diskette in the second disk drive. You will see the red lights go on and off while it is searching for NPL.

Now you have entered the NPL Command mode. English is spoken here— for the most part, anyway. There are no one letter commands; rather, there are words like **DIRECTORY**, **GETFILE**, **DEFINE**, **TYPEFILE**. The options are listed on the NPL System Guide.

The best way to learn to use these commands is to try them. So come along and type the boldfaced lines which follow, ending each line with the **RETURN** key. Use the **LEFT-ARROW** key to back-space over errors.

Do not begin typing until you see this symbol, > , called a prompt character. The computer is **prompting** you to speak next. The letter preceding the prompt character identifies the room you are in. When in the NPL Command mode, the prompt is **C>**. It is **R>** in the Report mode. If you are uncertain which mode you are in, press **RETURN** to see the prompt characters and then refer to the NPL System Guide. Press **RETURN** several times, now, to see what happens.

Practice Commands (press **RETURN** after each line)	**Comments**
Type: **DIRECTORY** Press: **RETURN**	Remember: you type whatever is in **boldfaced** type. Note the **C>** prompt. NPL will display the prompt; you should not type it.
	The result is a listing of filenames, file sizes, and creation dates of files with names containing the slash character, /. These are NPL files and are the only files you should need.

Each diskette directory is listed. Notice that there may be no NPL files on the APPLE1: diskette. There may, however, be some free disk space available. The following is an example of a possible **DIRECTORY** listing.

```
APPLE1:
0 FILES OUT OF 10
170 USED BLOCKS, 110 FREE BLOCKS
110 BLOCKS IN LARGEST CONTIGOUS GROUP.

SPACE TO CONTINUE, ESC TO QUIT
```

Press: **SPACE BAR**

```
NPL:
MAILIST/M.TEXT       4 BLOCKS,   9/17/81
MAILIST/E.TEXT       4 BLOCKS,   9/17/81
MAILIST/D.DATA       2 BLOCKS,   10/23/81
NUCLIENT/E.TEXT      6 BLOCKS,   12/1/81
CLIENT/M.TEXT        4 BLOCKS,   11/12/81
    .
    .
    .
9 FILES OUT OF 18
240 USED BLOCKS, 38 FREE BLOCKS,
38 BLOCKS IN LARGEST CONTIGOUS GROUP.

SPACE TO CONTINUE, ESC TO QUIT
```

Pressing the **SPACE BAR** will continue the **DIRECTORY** listing of any other disk drives. After the **NPL:** listing, press the **ESC** key to quit the **DIRECTORY**.

Next, look at the following list. The display is a list of names and nicknames (i.e., aliases) for data items in the CLIENTS file. Using these names and aliases together with NPL commands, you can begin writing NPL Reports. Notice that the aliases are convenient when typing Report requests.

CLIENTS WORDS

FIELDNAME		ALIAS
TITLE	=	PREFX
FIRST	=	FN
MIDDLE	=	MI
LASTNAME	=	LN
SUFFIX	=	SUFX
SSN	=	SSN
STREET	=	STR
CITY	=	CTY
STATE	=	ST
ZIPCODE	=	ZP
TELEPHONE	=	PHONE
AGE	=	AGE
SEX	=	SEX
DEPENDENTS	=	DEPS
YRS EDUC	=	EDYRS
YRS EMPLOYED	=	WRKYRS
EMPLOYER	=	EMP
INCOME(000)	=	INC
ACCOUNT	=	ACNO
ACCOUNTYPE	=	TYP
AMOUNT(000)	=	SIZE

WRITING NPL REPORTS

Next, follow the directions and learn to write NPL requests.

Type: **GETFILE CLIENTS**

Press: **RETURN**

The **GETFILE** command indentifies the particular file you want. In this case, you instruct the computer to get the CLIENTS file.

Wait for the **C>** prompt and then type:

PRINT LASTNAME AGE EMPLOYER.

The **PRINT** command tells NPL to display the data items requested. Note the period. It is needed to complete the NPL request.

Press: **RETURN**

Note this request is on two lines. Press the **RETURN** after the first line. NPL displays an **R>** prompt, denoting the Report mode, which means the Report request is not yet complete.

The screen displays:

LASTNAME	AGE	EMPLOYER
WALTERS	29	WAYNE OIL CO
FREEDMAN	29	INNOVATIONS INC.
HURLBUTT	36	RED BALLOON INC.
MOREY	24	CENTER SPORTS
BARNES	28	SIMI RESEARCH
WARD	46	PICKWICK PAPER
HENDERSON	34	PRIME SERVICE
SOLOMON	38	OHIO LIFE
SCHANKLE	41	FRANKLIN MINT
ROZICS	37	TAKOMA HIFI
CORRIGAN	47	CHARLIE CHIP CO
.		
.		
.		

The last line you typed, **PRINT LASTNAME AGE EMPLOYER.**, is a **complete NPL request**, that is, a query of the CLIENTS datafile. The NPL response to the query is a table of data or a report.

Notice these facts:

- The request consists of the verb **PRINT**, three verb objects, and a period.

- The words LASTNAME, AGE, and EMPLOYER appear as column headings in the report in the same order you typed them in the request.

- There is one line in the table for each record in the datafile.

Type: **PRINT LN AGE EMP.**

Do not forget to press **RETURN**. Now the result is the same as above. The same fields have been selected; yet the first and third verb objects in the request, namely LN and EMP, appear to be different.

If you look back at the CLIENTS word list, you can see that each data field has two names. The first is the fieldname; the second is called the alias. The alias names are simply a convenience that make it possible for you to type a short nickname for each field. Thus LN stands for last name. You might ask how the computer knows about these names. The answer is discussed later in connection with the CLIENTS Master file.

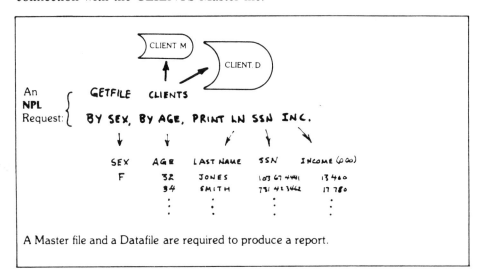

An NPL Request:

GETFILE CLIENTS

BY SEX, BY AGE, PRINT LN SSN INC.

SEX	AGE	LAST NAME	SSN	INCOME (000)
F	32	JONES	103 67 4441	13 460
	34	SMITH	731 41 3442	17 780
⋮	⋮	⋮	⋮	⋮

A Master file and a Datafile are required to produce a report.

Type:
IF AGE GT 30,
PRINT LN SEX AGE ED.
Press: **RETURN**   after each line.

This line is mostly English language, if you'll forgive the use of **GT** as an abbreviation for **Greater Than**. The result is:

LASTNAME	SEX	AGE	YRS EDUC
HURLBUTT	M	36	16
WARD	M	46	18
HENDERSON	F	34	14
SOLOMON	F	38	16
SCHANKLE	M	41	18
ROZICS	M	37	16
CORRIGAN	M	47	14

Notice that the records of people 30 and younger are not included in the list. This is because the request has an **IF** phrase which asks NPL to select or

screen only the records of people older than 30. There are several abbreviations which you will want to remember for regular use in **IF** phrases.
They are:

equals	**EQ**
equals	**IS**
less than	**LT**
less than or equal	**LE**
greater than	**GT**
greater than or equal	**GE**
not equal	**NE**
not equal	**IS-NOT**

IF phrases always have a single fieldname, or alias, followed by a *relational operator*, like the above, followed by a constant value—numbers or letters.

Other examples are:

```
IF  AGE  LE  20
IF  AGE  IS  15  TO  25
IF  EDYRS  EQ  8  OR  12  OR  16
IF  SEX  EQ  F
IF  SEX  IS  F
IF  LN  IS  JONES  OR  SMITH
```

Before going on, a remark about APPLE monitors (also called CRT screens) is needed here. The Apple's screen is only forty characters wide (unless you have an eighty-column board installed, in which case you should skip this section). The Apple Pascal Operating System actually displays eighty characters on a line. Moreover, NPL will print tables as wide as 130 characters. In fact, it will print however wide the capability of your printer permits. But remember that you can see only forty characters at a time on your monitor screen.

Visualize the other half of the eighty-column image as an imaginary panel off to the right of your screen.

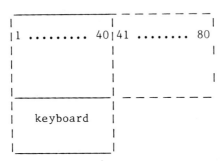

If you have a forty-column screen, try the following: hold the **CONTROL** key down and press A; columns forty-one to eighty are displayed. Press **CONTROL-A** again and the screen returns to normal.

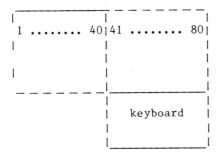

Thus, you can make an NPL request longer than forty columns and get a wider report even if you have to use the **CONTROL-A** toggle switch to see it.

Press: **CONTROL-A**   when you get to the screen edge, and continue. Remember, don't use **CONTROL-A** if you have an eighty-column card.

Type:
**PRINT FN LN SSN AGE SEX EMP
EDYRS IF SEX IS F
IF EDYRS GT 12 END**

Press: **RETURN**

Note this request is on three lines. Press the **RETURN** after the first line. NPL displays an **R>** prompt, denoting the Report mode, which means the Report request is not yet complete.

The **period** or **END** completes the NPL request and causes NPL to process the request and then return to Command mode, **C>**. The word **END** and the **period** are equivalent.

Using two **IF** phrases reduces the number of records selected, since both test conditions must be satisfied.

Try the **CONTROL-A** toggle switch.

Now make up a request of your own, like the long one above. But to save you the inconvenience of switching screen panels for a long request, first press **CONTROL-Z**; that is, hold the **CONTROL** key down and press the letter **Z**. Nothing happens until you type past column forty. Try it and see what **CONTROL-Z** does for you. You may still use **CONTROL-A** to switch panels as well.

INTERACTIVE ERROR CORRECTION

If NPL does not recognize a word in your request, it asks for a correction. Try misspelling some of the words in the examples. For instance, try misspelling the word FIRST. NPL responds with

    UNKNOWN NAME: FISRT
    PLEASE REPLACE:

At this point you may do the following:
  a) press **RETURN** to replace the unknown word with a blank (i.e., to erase the word, which perhaps was caused by a mistaken key stroke); or
  b) type the intended word correctly and press **RETURN**; or
  c) type several words which will be substituted for the unknown word; or
  d) type **QUIT**, or press the **ESC** key, to return to the NPL Command mode.
If the spelling error is in the first word following the Command mode prompt, for example,

    C>PRNIT LASTNAME BY AGE .

NPL responds with this statement:

    INVALID COMMAND:PRNIT

Retype the whole request again, spelling **PRINT** correctly.

USING THE PRINTER

Next, you may send NPL requests to the printer.

Type: **PRINTER:**

Press: **RETURN**

This command (which includes the colon) tells NPL to direct future display information to the printer rather than to the console or monitor. To print a report on paper, be sure the printer power is on.

Now, type:
PRINT LN FN AND SSN.

The report should appear on the printer. Now try a fancier report. Use **CONTROL-Z** or press **RETURN** as needed for your convenience. You may use any number of lines for an NPL request. The **period**, or **END**, tells NPL when you have completed the request. Until that point the prompt on each line is **R>** to remind you that you are still in Report mode.

AND is a new keyword used to separate verb objects and NPL phrases for easier reading. **AND** does not affect the report.

Type:
HEADING "CLIENTS WITH COLLEGE DEGREES"
"EMPLOYER DEPENDENTS"
PRINT FN LN SSN EMPLOYER DEPS
AND COLUMNTOTAL
IF EDYRS GE 16 END

The word **HEADING** takes you into Report mode. The text of the heading is entered next, starting and ending with double or single quotation marks. The number of **HEADING** lines is limited only by the size of the page.

Notice that the columntotal applies only to the dependents field, for it is the only numeric field. The SSN field contains all digits, 0 thru 9, but it is really only a code and does not contain numeric data.

Type: **CONSOLE:**

Press: **RETURN**

This command reverses the effect of the **PRINTER:** command. NPL is now said to be printing *on-line* to the console screen, whereas previously NPL was in the *off-line* mode.

Type: **FINISH**

This command takes you out of NPL into the Apple Pascal Operating System, Command level. You can recognize this mode from the line of information at the top of the screen. We have entered the Operating System to demonstrate another way to send information to the printer.

Now press **F** to enter the small room called the **FILER**. **FILER** is a short name for File Directory. In this mode you have another prompt list of command options, and again they are one-letter commands. For the present we use only these options:

```
L    to list the directory of files
V    to show all the volumes that are active
T    to transfer files and to display them on the screen
```

Press: **V** and wait for a display of the volumes on-line. While waiting, notice that the red lights of the disk drives go on momentarily while the computer reads the volume name of each disk. You will hear a buzz if the disk drive is empty.

The display may look like this:

```
VOLS ON-LINE:

1   CONSOLE:
2   SYSTERM:
4 # APPLE1:
5 #    NPL:
6   PRINTER:
7   REMIN:
8   REMOUT:


ROOT VOL IS  - APPLE1:
PREFIX IS    - APPLE1:
```

Why are the console and printer also referred to as volumes? There is no particularly good reason except that within the computer any destination to which a file can be sent is given a volume name. All volume names end with a colon.

Press: **L** to list a directory on the named disk.
The computer asks:
DIR LISTING OF ?:
Type: **NPL:**
Press: **RETURN**

Note: if you mistype, use the **LEFT-ARROW** key as a back-space key to correct the error.

The names, sizes, and dates are listed for all files on the **NPL:** diskette (not just NPL files).

```
NPL:

CLIENTS/M.TEXT      4   12-NOV-81
CLIENTS/D.DATA      6    1-DEC-81
CLIENT40/E.TEXT     6   23-FEB-82
MAILIST/M.TEXT      4   17-SEP-81
MAILIST/E.TEXT      4    1-FEB-82
MAILIST/D.DATA      2   23-OCT-81
CLIENT80/E.TEXT     6    1-FEB-82
  .
  .
  .
```

You may need to press the space bar to see the second page of this list. Notice the various types of filenames. Filename types are discussed in the *NPL User's Guide*, but note that all NPL files have names which contain /D, /M, /I, or /E. These letters stand for **D**atafile, **M**aster file, **I**ndex file, and **E**xec file.

Next, press: **T**   to transfer a file.
The computer asks:
TRANSFER?   which means, "transfer what file?"
Type: **NPL:CLIENTS/M.TEXT**
Press: **RETURN**
The computer asks:
TO WHERE?
You type: **CONSOLE:**
Press: **RETURN**

Then the file called CLIENTS Master file is displayed on the screen (Master files are discussed in Lesson III). Repeat the sequence above, but answer "TO WHERE ?" with **PRINTER:** (be sure your printer is turned on), and press **RETURN**.

You should practice transferring other files to the **CONSOLE:** for display and to the **PRINTER:** for printed copies. Files with names ending in .DATA do not always print in a readable display. Files with .TEXT in the name are always readable. To halt the rapid motion of the display of long files in order to read the records on the screen, hold the **CONTROL** key down and press **S**. The transferring of the file continues when you press **CONTROL-S** again.

The previous discussion demonstrates that there are two ways to send information to the printer. In the Apple Pascal Filer mode you press **T** to transfer

391

whole files to the **PRINTER:**. In the NPL Command mode, you use the **PRINTER:** and **TYPEFILE** commands.

WRITING MORE REPORTS

Next try some more reports.

Press: **Q**   to **Q**uit the Filer.
Press: **X**
Then type: **NPL:NPL**   to enter the NPL Command mode
                                           again.

Press: **RETURN**

Remember to wait for the C>
prompt before typing.

Type: **GETFILE CLIENTS**   to specify the CLIENTS file. You
                                           must press **RETURN** to end each line
                                           when in NPL. Only in the FILER
                                           mode can you give one-character
                                           commands without the **RETURN**
                                           key.

Write a few requests of your own using **IF** phrases like these:

IF EMPLOYER CONTAINS RED

IF EDYRS IS-NOT 16

IF AGE IS 17 TO 19 OR 22 TO 26

**IF INCOME IS-NOT 8 TO 10 NOR
16 TO 18**

Then verify the results against the
datafile printed in the previous sequence.

Next type:
**BY EDYRS, PRINT LN EMP
AND DEPS.**

Press: **RETURN**

BY EDYRS means **sort by education**. Note the position of YRS EDUC in the report and that each value of YRS EDUC is printed only once. YRS EDUC (the alias name is EDYRS) is called a **BY field**; it is also known as a **sort key**.

YRS EDUC	LASTNAME	EMPLOYER	DEPENDENTS
12	KINGFISH	OCEAN SEAFOOD	0
	ROSER	GREYS MARKET	0
	GREEN	MAGIC MOTION	0
	KELSEY	MEDICAL CENTER	0
	HUGHES	UPLAND REALTORS	0
14	FREEDMAN	INNOVATIONS INC	1
	HENDERSON	PRIME SERVICE	3
	CORRIGAN	CHARLIE CHIP CO	6
	MOORE	COUNTRY CRUMPET	0
16	WALTERS	WAYNE OIL CO	1
	HURLBUTT	RED BALLOON INC	3
	MOREY	CENTER SPORTS	1
	SOLOMON	OHIO LIFE	4
	ROZICS	TAKOMA HIFI	1
	HAYES	PUBLIC LIBRARY	3
	SMITH	APPLE TOURS	0
	FARRELL	BTA COMPUTING	0
18	BARNES	SIMI RESEARCH	1
	WARD	PICKWICK PAPER	4
	SCHANKLE	FRANKLIN MINT	4

Try two **BY** fields in one request:
BY EDYRS BY AGE, PRINT DEPS.
Press: **RETURN**

YRS EDUC	AGE	DEPENDENTS
12	18	0
	19	0
		0
	21	0
	22	0
14	21	0
	29	1
	34	3
	47	6
16	24	1
	25	0
		0
	28	3
	29	1
	36	3
	37	1
	38	4
18	28	1
	41	4
	46	4

Note the column positions. The **BY** fields always appear on the left side of the table, even when the **BY** phrases are typed after the **PRINT** phrase. Notice that with sorting the computer takes longer to respond. Watch the red light on Disk Drive 2. NPL reads the file once to find the sort key values and again while writing the requested report.

Type:
PRINT AGE, BY LN BY FN, IF SEX IS M END
Press: **RETURN**

This request has three kinds of
phrases: **verb**, **BY**, and **IF** phrases.

LASTNAME	FIRST	AGE
CORRIGAN	JOHN	47
HAYES	ROBERT	28
HUGHES	MANFRED	18
HURLBUTT	FRED	36
KELSEY	DENNIS	19
MOREY	HENRY	24
ROSER	PETER	21
ROZICS	CHARLES	37
SCHANKLE	ROGER	41
SMITH	JOE	25
WALTERS	PHILIP	29
WARD	WILLIAM	46

In summary, these are the principal elements of NPL requests:

- All NPL requests have a verb phrase with verb objects.

- Most requests have at least one **IF** or **BY** phrase, or both.

- The three types of phrases may be arranged in any order.

All **BY** fields appear at the left of the table in the order presented in the request. A request may be typed on one or more lines. A line may begin between
any pair of words, but a word may not be hyphenated at the end of a line.

Type:
IF AGE LT 46
BY DEPS BY SEX
BY EDYRS BY LN
PRINT EMPLOYER.
Press: **RETURN**   after each line.

DEPENDENTS	SEX	YRS EDUC	LASTNAME	EMPLOYER
0	F	12	GREEN	MAGIC MOTION
			KINGFISH	OCEAN SEAFOOD
		14	MOORE	COUNTRY CRUMPET
		16	FARRELL	BTA COMPUTING
	M	12	HUGHES	UPLAND REALTORS
			KELSEY	MEDICAL CENTER
			ROSER	GREYS MARKET
		16	SMITH	APPLE TOURS
1	F	14	FREEDMAN	INNOVATIONS INC
		18	BARNES	SIMI RESEARCH
	M	16	MOREY	CENTER SPORTS
			ROZICS	TAKOMA HIFI
			WALTERS	WAYNE OIL CO
3	F	14	HENDERSON	PRIME SERVICE
	M	16	HAYES	PUBLIC LIBRARY
			HURLBUTT	RED BALLOON INC
4	F	16	SOLOMON	OHIO LIFE
	M	18	SCANKLE	FRANKLIN MINT

Notice in this example that the verb phrase appears last and includes only one verb object, and that there are four **BY** phrases.

Type:
COUNT SSN BY DEPS.

Note the new verb **COUNT**. It counts the records as grouped by the number of DEPENDENTS. The verb **COUNT** must have an object, so choose a fieldname, like SSN, to make the sentence have the right meaning. Actually, any fieldname would yield the same results as SSN for the verb object—only the records are counted.

DEPENDENTS	COUNT
0	8
1	5
3	3
4	3
6	1

Type:
**COUNT LN BY DEPS
SKIP BY SEX.**

Press: **RETURN**

The **BY** phrase option, **SKIP**, follows the **BY** field. It means: upon each change in value of the **BY** field, skip a line in the report.

DEPENDENTS	SEX	COUNT
0	F	4
	M	4
1	F	2
	M	3
3	F	1
	M	2
4	F	1
	M	2
6	M	1

Any **BY** phrase may also be modified by the keywords **PAGE** and **SUB-TOTAL**. In the example above, if you replace **SKIP** with **PAGE**, then

BY DEPS **PAGE**   starts a new page after every two lines, or

BY DEPS **SUBTOTAL**   prints subtotals of numeric fields for each value of DEPENDENTS.

Finally the verb **SUM** allows you to prepare reports to group records according to a particular field, like AGE, and then to write only one line for each age group, summing up the number of dependents.

Type: **SUM DEPS BY AGE.**   Note the new verb **SUM**.

Press: **RETURN**

AGE	DEPENDENTS
18	0
19	0
21	0
22	0
24	1
25	0
28	4
29	2
34	3
36	3
37	1
38	4
41	4
46	4
47	6

Instead of counting the number of records in each age group, the **SUM** verbs tells NPL to add together the values of the DEPS field in each record and each age group. Then each line in the report is the total number of dependents for the clients of a particular age (e.g., a total of four dependents for all clients of age 28).

Type: **SUM DEPS.**   Yields a total for all records.
Press: **RETURN**

DEPENDENTS
32

Type: **SUM DEPS AND COLUMNTOTAL BY EDYRS.**

Press: **RETURN**

The grand total should agree with the previous report.

YRS EDUC	DEPENDENTS
12	0
14	10
16	13
18	9
	32

Type:
**SUM DEPS AND
COLUMNTOTAL,
BY EDYRS SUBTOTAL,
BY SEX SUBTOTAL,
BY AGE IF EDYRS GT 14 END**

Press: **RETURN**

For two levels of summarization of the data.

YRS EDUC	SEX	AGE	DEPENDENTS	
16	F	25	0	
		38	4	
			4	Female subtotal
	M	24	1	
		25	0	
		28	3	
		29	1	
		36	3	
		37	1	
			9	Male subtotal
			13	EDYRS=16 subtotal
18	F	28	1	
			1	Female subtotal
	M	41	4	
		46	4	
			8	Male subtotal
			9	EDYRS=18 subtotal
			22	Columntotal

SUMMING UP

You have completed the first lesson in using NPL on the Apple II computer. You should remember that the key functions are

- Screening   (**IF**...)

- Sorting   (**BY**...)

- **PRINT**ing   particular data items

- **SUM**ming   numeric data items

- **COUNT**ing   data records

You have used these keywords:
GETFILE, DIRECTORY, IF, BY, PRINT, SUM, COUNT, CONSOLE:, PRINTER:, IS. . .TO, OR, HEADING, COLUMNTOTAL, SKIP, PAGE, SUBTOTAL, TYPEFILE, GE, GT, EQ, LT, LE, IS, IS-NOT, FIN, AND, END, and the **period .**

With these few keywords in mind you can readily search your files and print useful reports for most applications. This is a new skill which should serve you well in sifting, sorting, and probing your various collections of data items, and in turning them into useful, **information-rich** reports.

The writing of reports is certainly the most satisfying use of NPL. You can see from the NPL System Guide that in this lesson you have tried only a few of the many features of the NPL Report mode.

A few hours of practice with demonstration files like the Clients file should leave you with a practical understanding of most of the Report mode options. With this background you are ready to consider building your own data and Master files.

On the next page, the NPL System Guide is displayed showing the keywords presented in this lesson.

The **NPL**™ System Guide

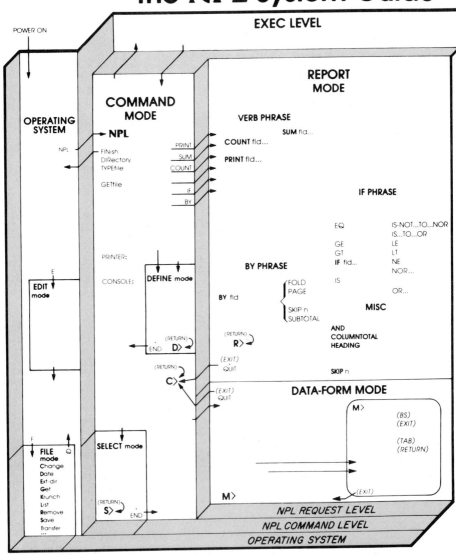

Release 1.1

LESSON II

DATA ENTRY

In Lesson I, you told NPL what you wanted, and NPL replied by displaying columns of data items drawn from many records. Lesson II offers you some practice in the use of a DATA-FORM screen to enter new data items into new records on a diskette.

In the DATA-FORM mode, NPL displays on the Apple's screen a picture resembling a paper form, which might be like one used in your office. Data items are entered into blank spaces on the screen, checked for accuracy, and then stored on a magnetic diskette in a datafile.

This lesson begins with instructions on how to enter data into a simple form. The second section explains how to enter data into a more complex form. The third section reviews some of the report-writing features you learned in Lesson I.

By using the demonstration files on the NPL diskette and following the instructions below, you can enter data and report on it right away.

The best way to learn to use these commands is to try them—so come along and type the boldfaced lines which follow, ending each line with the **RETURN** key. Use the **LEFT-ARROW** key to back-space over errors.

Do not begin typing until you see this symbol, > , called a prompt character. The computer is **prompting** you to speak next. The letter preceding the prompt character identifies the room you are in; see the NPL System Guide. When in the NPL Command mode, the prompt is **C>**, and it is **R>** in the Report mode. If you are uncertain which mode you are in, press **RETURN** to see the prompt characters and then refer to the NPL System Guide.

MAILIST : A DATA-FORM PROGRAM

A popular use of NPL is the maintenance of mailing lists; so for the next practice session you will create a mailing list of your own.

After entering the NPL Command mode, type the following statements (type only the **bold** characters):

Type: **EXEC MAILIST**

This request tells NPL to display the DATA-FORM associated with the MAILIST file. After several seconds a form appears on the screen.

Press: **RETURN**

```
 _____
|                                            |
|          MAILING LIST FORM                 |
|                                            |
|FIRST NAME:_____                       |
| LAST NAME:_____                       |
|    STREET:_____                 |
|      CITY:_____                   |
|     STATE:__                               |
|  ZIP CODE:_____                            |
|_____|
```

When the computer is ready for you to enter the information requested, you will hear a beep, and a small white box (called the cursor) will appear next to FIRST NAME:.

Type a name in the space, up to ten characters long.

For example: **ANNE**   (four characters).

To move the cursor to the next question, LAST NAME,

Press: **RETURN**

This key tells NPL to accept the FIRST NAME value and moves the cursor to the next line. If you fill all the spaces, the cursor moves down automatically.

Typing and spelling errors may be corrected by back-spacing with the **LEFT-ARROW** key. When the cursor is at the beginning of a line and you press the **LEFT-ARROW** key, the cursor jumps back to the beginning of the last question, allowing you to reenter information.

Continue entering each line of requested information, using the **RETURN** key to accept each item and to move the cursor, if necessary, until all the lines of the form are filled. Below is a completed form. You may use this example or enter names of your own.

```
|                    RETURN or  ESC >        |
|                                            |
|           MAILING LIST FORM                |
|                                            |
|FIRST NAME:ANNE                             |
| LAST NAME:PETERSON                         |
|    STREET:43 MAPLE AVE                      |
|      CITY:WILMINGTON                        |
|     STATE:OH                               |
|  ZIP CODE:45177                            |
|_____|
```

Upon entering the ZIP CODE (which is five characters in length and fills the allocated space), the cursor jumps to the top right-hand corner, next to the message seen in bold in the picture above.

Press: **RETURN**

All the data you have just typed is stored on the diskette as each item disappears from the screen. The blank form remains on the screen. You should continue entering several more names and addresses to get the feel of this operation.

Pressing the **ESC** key (instead of **RETURN**) causes NPL to erase the data items *without* storing them on diskette.

When a blank form is displayed on the screen and the cursor is at the FIRST NAME position, press:

ESC key *twice*

NPL asks the following question:

MAKE FILE CHANGES PERMANENT? Y/N >

Type: **Y**

Y tells NPL to append the new data records to the existing file or to open a new datafile. **N** leaves the datafile as it was before you ran the program called MAILIST.

After you have saved your new file (by answering **Y** to the last question), the form disappears and **C>** appears. You have reentered the NPL Command mode and the MAILIST datafile has been placed on the diskette.

C>

The MAILIST DATA-FORM screen is a very simple form. For additional practice with a more complex DATA-FORM screen,

Type: **EXEC CLIENT40**   A new screen appears after a short
Press: **RETURN**   wait. If you have an eighty-column
                                              card, type **EXEC CLIENT80** instead.

DATA ENTRY RULES

Before using this DATA-FORM, read the following rules for entering data.

a) Begin typing at the cursor, entering the requested data into the appropriate field.

b) When a data field is filled, the cursor jumps automatically to the next field. If filling the field is not required and the field length is more than ten characters, a tone sounds as the last three characters in the field are entered. The tone, like the bell on a typewriter, warns you of the approaching end of the field. The pitch of the third tone is lower than the others to indicate the cursor has moved to the next field.

c) To have a data item accepted and advance the cursor to the next field when not filling a field, press the **RETURN** key.

d) A field may be filled with the value entered in the *previous record* by pressing the **RIGHT-ARROW** key.

e) If NPL detects that the data entered is in violation of an edit test specified in the DATA-FORM program, a beep sounds and a message is displayed on the top line of the screen.

f) When the data item in the last field is accepted, either by your filling the field or pressing the **RETURN** key, the cursor jumps to the top of the screen. You now must press **RETURN** or **ESC**. If **ESC** is used, the record is discarded rather than stored. If you press **RETURN**, the record is added to the datafile, the screen is cleared, and the cursor moves to the first field. A tone signals when to begin typing data for the next record.

g) After entering your last record, press the **ESC** key when the cursor is at the beginning of the next blank form. NPL responds with the **MODIFY** mode prompt **M>**. A second **ESC** (or the word **QUIT**) ends the session.

h) After a session, NPL asks: MAKE FILE CHANGES PERMANENT? Y/N >. Pressing **Y** appends the new data records to the existing file, or it creates a new file if none exists. Pressing **N** discards the new records, leaving the datafile the same as before the session.

After answering the above question, you are returned to the NPL Command mode.

CORRECTING ENTRY ERRORS

NPL provides commands to allow you to correct typing errors. The rules are as follows:

a) The **LEFT-ARROW**, i.e., back-spacing, key erases the characters that have been typed into a field.

b) Pressing **ESC** after several characters have been typed into a new field erases all characters in the field and places the cursor back at the beginning of that field.

c) Pressing **LEFT-ARROW** at the beginning of a field moves the cursor to the beginning of the previous field. The data is not erased. A corrected entry is entered for the field by typing the new value and then pressing **RETURN**. **RIGHT-ARROW** is used to advance the cursor across the fields which have been entered.

A COMPLEX DATA-FORM

Now, look at your monitor and you should see the **CLIENT40** screen.

```
 _____
|                                          |
|                                          |
|......... CLIENT   INFORMATION .......... |
|                                          |
| NAME:                                    |
|                                          |
|-------  ----------------  -  -------------|
| MR,MRS,MS                                |
|                   ------ (JR,ESQ,PHD)    |
| SSN#:            PHONE:                   |
|      ---  --  ----        ---  ---  ----  |
|                                          |
|---------------    ------------ -- ----- |
| STREET ADDRESS    CITY         ST ZIP    |
|                                          |
|        AGE:       ANN INC  :     ,000    |
|        SEX:                 ----         |
| NO. DEPS:         ACCT #   :              |
| YRS EDUC:                   ------        |
| YRS EMPL:         ACCT TYPE:              |
|                             ----         |
| ---------------   ACCT $   :     ,000    |
| EMPLOYER                    ---          |
|                                          |
|_____|
```

Now, enter the information required by the form. NPL beeps at you if you enter an invalid value. When you hear a beep, look at the top of the screen for special instructions. For practice, make various mistakes to see how NPL responds.

After you have filled in all the spaces for your first new record, look at the top of the screen. NPL asks you to press **RETURN** or **ESC**; i.e., to keep or reject the whole record. Press **RETURN**. Now type in a second record.

Another feature of the DATA-FORM mode saves your having to retype data that is repeated on two or more records.

Press: **RIGHT-ARROW**

when a blank form is displayed. Continue pressing it and note that the name and other information you just typed reappears on the screen! As an example, let's say that a client has several ACCOUNT NUMBERs and ACCOUNT TYPEs, but other information on the record remains the same. With the **RIGHT-ARROW** key you can call back onto the screen the name, address, and other items from the last record, enter new ACCOUNT data, and save it all as a new entry.

Press: **RIGHT-ARROW**

until the cursor is sitting on ACCOUNT NUMBER. Enter a new ACCOUNT NUMBER and press a **RETURN**. Then move, using the **RIGHT-ARROW**, to ACCOUNT TYPE and type a new value. Remember to press **RETURN**. After entering several more records:

Press: **ESC** key *twice*

NPL asks the following question:

MAKE FILE CHANGES PERMANENT? Y/N >

Type: **Y**

Y tells NPL to append the new data records to the existing file, or to open a new datafile.

N results in *NO changes* being made to the datafile. All new records created are abandoned or may be saved in a separate file (see *NPL User's Guide*).

Next NPL returns to the Command mode. Note the **C>** prompt message.

REPORT WRITING

Now that you have practiced entering data, the next step is to write some NPL requests.

Type: (only the words in bold type, and
                                         press the **RETURN** after each line)

GETFILE MAILIST
PRINT FIRSTNAME, LASTNAME,
ADDRESS, CITY, STATE, ZIP.

After several seconds a report like this appears:

```
 _____
|                                                                 |
|FIRSTNAME   LASTNAME     ADDRESS       CITY          STATE  ZIPCODE|
|                                                                 |
|ANNE        KINGFISH     10 FISHER     OCEAN         NJ     09820 |
|JOE         SMITH        4 RIVER RD    N.Y.C.        NY     11347 |
|PETER       ROSER        123 BAT DR    BAYSIDE       MD     25321 |
|MARY        GREEN        456 RED HILL  GREYSTOWN     OH     47890 |
|.                                                                |
|.                                                                |
|.                                                                |
|_____|
```

Try another request; type:

PRINT FIRSTNAME, LASTNAME,
ADDRESS, CITY, STATE
BY ZIP.

If you remembered to press **RETURN**, a report appears like this:

```
 _____
|                                                                         |
|ZIPCODE   FIRSTNAME   LASTNAME   ADDRESS        CITY          STATE |
|                                                                         |
|09820     ANNE        KINGFISH   10 FISHER      OCEAN         NJ    |
|11347     JOE         SMITH      4 RIVER RD     N.Y.C.        NY    |
|          COLLEEN     MILLER     26B GREENBAY   N.Y.C.        NY    |
|25321     PETER       ROSER      123 BAT DR     BAYSIDE       MD    |
|29023     GEORGE      ABLE       2367 KING WAY  WALLINGFORD   PA    |
|47890     MARY        GREEN      456 RED HILL   GREYSTOWN     OH    |
|          JEFFREY     DODGER     56 DOGWOOD LN  GREYSTOWN     OH    |
|          TERRY       DAISY      981 PETAL LN   GREYSTOWN     OH    |
|56023     BILL        BEAR       4 HONEY DR     DARK CAVE     IL    |
|63067     ALICE       DODGER     212 SHERWOOD   KINGSVILLE    TX    |
|99880     ANNE        FIELD      128 PLOW       FARMER        WA    |
|.                                                                        |
|.                                                                        |
|.                                                                        |
|_____|
```

This report was sorted by the zip codes. Notice that when a zip code repeats, it
is not printed for subsequent records.

NPL sorts the data in any order you request. As you learned in Lesson I, simply place the word **BY** before the field that is to control the sorting of lines on the report.

In the following example, sorting is by last name:

Type:
PRINT FIRSTNAME,
ADDRESS, CITY,
BY LASTNAME.
Press: **RETURN**

LASTNAME	FIRSTNAME	ADDRESS	CITY
ABLE	GEORGE	2367 KING WAY	WALLINGFORD
BEAR	BILL	4 HONEY DR	DARK CAVE
DAISY	TERRY	981 PETAL LN	GREYSTOWN
DODGER	JEFFREY	56 DOGWOOD LN	GREYSTOWN
	ALICE	212 SHERWOOD	KINGSVILLE
FIELD	ANNE	128 PLOW	FARMER
GREEN	MARY	456 RED HILL	GREYSTOWN
KINGFISH	ANNE	10 FISHER	OCEAN
MILLER	COLLEEN	26B GREENBAY DR	N.Y.C.
.			
.			
.			

The records for Jeffrey and Alice appear in the order in which they reside in the file. FIRSTNAME is not a sort field in the request.

The next request produces a mailing list which could be printed on labels.

Type:
PRINT FIRSTNAME LASTNAME
OVER STREET
OVER CITY STATE ZIPCODE
SKIP.
Press: **RETURN**   after each line.

The request tells the computer to print the fields, FIRSTNAME and LASTNAME, **OVER** the address lines. The word **OVER** is an NPL keyword which causes a new line to be started. **SKIP** means to skip a line between each record.

411

This request produces:

```
| ANNE           KINGFISH                                           |
| 10 FISHER                                                         |
| OCEAN          NJ    09820                                        |
|                                                                   |
| JOE            SMITH                                              |
| 4 RIVER RD                                                        |
| N.Y.C          NY    11347                                        |
|                                                                   |
| PETER          ROSER                                              |
| 123 BAT DR                                                        |
| BAYSIDE        MD    25321                                        |
|                                                                   |
| MARY           GREEN                                              |
| 456 RED HILL                                                      |
| GREYSTOWN      OH    47890                                        |
| .                                                                 |
| .                                                                 |
| .                                                                 |
| C>                                                                |
|_____|
```

The file, as stored on the diskette, is sorted by ZIP CODE. It could be sorted by LASTNAME to provide a different kind of a list.

Type:
PRINT FIRSTNAME LASTNAME
OVER STREET
OVER CITY STATE ZIPCODE,
SKIP
BY LASTNAME NOPRINT.

Press: **RETURN**   after each line.

The word **NOPRINT** suppresses the printing of the second occurrence of the field LASTNAME.

```
GEORGE        ABLE
2367 KING WAY
WALINGFORD     PA   29023

BILL          BEAR
4 HONEY DR
DARK CAVE      IL   56023

TERRY         DAISY
981 PETAL LN
GREYSTOWN      OH   47870

JEFFERY       DODGER
56 DOGWOOD LN
GREYSTOWN      OH   47870

ALICE         DODGER
212 SHERWOOD
KINGSVILLE     TX   63067
.
.
.
C>
```

Lesson II provided practice in entering data through the use of NPL DATA-FORMs—first, with the simple MAILIST form, and second, with a complex form, CLIENT40 (or CLIENT80 for an eighty-column card).

Lesson II also introduced the use of the **ESC**, **LEFT-ARROW**, and **RIGHT-ARROW** keys, as well as these new keywords: **EXEC**, **OVER**, and **NOPRINT**. On the next page the NPL System Guide displays the new keywords and those presented in Lesson I.

The NPL™ System Guide

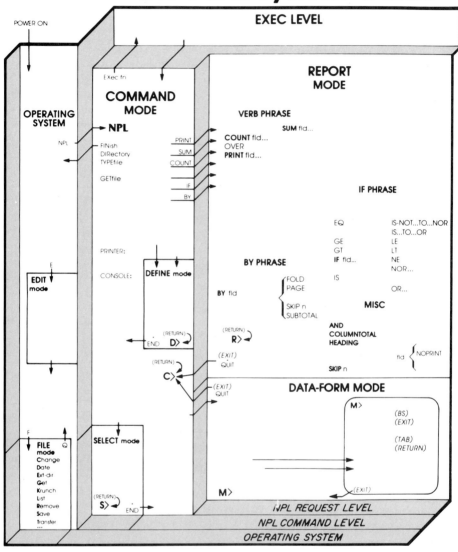

©1982 **DeskTop** Software Corporation 228 Alexander Street Princeton, New Jersey 08540

Release 1.1

CREATING DATA-FORMS

Lesson III gives you an introduction to NPL **Master** files, the Apple Pascal Edit mode, and the *preparation* of simple DATA-FORM programs.

THE STARTING POINT : DEFINING THE DATA RECORD FORMAT

Before attempting to create a new datafile, you must look carefully at the form of your data and then describe it to the computer. You do this by creating a **Master** file.

Imagine that the following is a paper form found on your desk.

```
|                                                                      |
|                    CLIENT INFORMATION FORM                           |
|                                                                      |
|   FIRST NAME:Jane              MIDDLE:D                               |
|    LAST NAME:Smith              TITLE:MS                              |
|                                                                      |
|   STREET:132 Springvalley Street                                     |
|   CITY:Rivertown   STATE:PA   ZIP:09876                              |
|                                                                      |
|   SOC SEC NBR:135-38-5432   AGE:25   SEX:F                            |
|                                                                      |
|      EMPLOYER:Red Balloon Company                                    |
|                                                                      |
|   NO OF DEPENDENTS:   0                                               |
|                                                                      |
|   YRS OF EDUCATION:  16                                               |
|                                                                      |
|      YRS EMPLOYED:   3                                                |
|                                                                      |
|   ANNUAL INCOME:$ 12000                                              |
|                                                                      |
|_____|
```

The first step in entering data into a computer is to describe the data items in a form that the computer understands.

The groups of letters and numbers that are underlined on this form are **data items**, and each appears in a **data field** on the form. Each data field is described by a **fieldname**, like TITLE, ZIP, and AGE.

To place data items on a diskette, the computer must reserve space (i.e., a **data field**) on the magnetic diskette for each item. Each location on the diskette is identified by a fieldname and by a format code, like **A6** or **A30**.

The fieldnames and format codes for all of the sixteen items on the "Client Information Form" are themselves stored on the diskette in a file called a **MASTER FILE**. The subject of **MASTER** files is presented fully in the *NPL User's Guide*. In this lesson we introduce only the information you need to create your first NPL file.

Each line within a **MASTER** file describes a data field. Each field is described by four items: two names and two format codes. Here is a sample data record.

```
FIELDNAME        = FIRST
ALIAS            = FN
PRINTING FORMAT  = A15
FILE FORMAT      = A15
```

The first item is the **FIELDNAME**, such as FIRST, for first name.

The second item is a convenient abbreviation, or nickname, called an **ALIAS**; for example, FN stands for "first name."

The third item is the **PRINTING FORMAT** code. It shows the number of spaces alotted a given field on printed reports, and whether the data field will contain alphabetic characters, integers, or fractions. When the code starts with the letter **A**, any printable character may appear on the report. When it starts with an **I**, it indicates an integer value between –32,767 and +32,768. Starting with an **F**, the code indicates a fractional or decimal number, up to 10 raised to the 40th power, with precision to six decimal places.

Example: The **PRINTING FORMAT** for AGE should be I3. People's ages are not over 999 years; however, they may be over 100 years. Thus, you may need to use a field width of 3. It is necessary to use I for numeric items which we might want to add, average, or use in some other kind of mathematical calculation. Thus, I3 is preferable to A3 for age.

```
FIELDNAME        = AGE
ALIAS            = AGE
PRINTING FORMAT  = I3
FILE FORMAT      = A3
```

The fourth item is the **FILE FORMAT** code. The **FILE FORMAT** code specifies the number of spaces reserved on a disk for a field. The format is always **A**, followed by the number of character spaces to be reserved. In the above example the **FILE FORMAT** code is A3, which is wide enough for the largest possible value of AGE.

To summarize:

1. **MASTER** files consist of records, each of which decribes one field in a datafile.
2. Each record includes four items: two names and two formats. The first item is the **FIELDNAME**, the second is the **ALIAS**, the third is the **PRINTING FORMAT** code, and the fourth is the **FILE FORMAT** code.

When displayed on the screen, a **MASTER** file has the form shown below, where the four items appear in a list on a single line, one for each field.

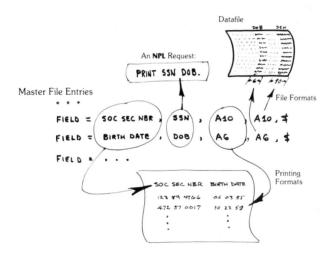

CREATING YOUR OWN MASTER FILE

Starting from the NPL Command mode, follow the commands below to create a small **Master** file called FRIENDS. The FRIENDS **Master** file might include fields like LASTNAME, FIRSTNAME, PHONE#, and BIRTHDATE, thus enabling you to build a small database about your friends.

Type:
CREATE FRIENDS
Press: **RETURN**

The **CREATE** command calls a special DATA-FORM program to help you build a **Master** file.

FRIENDS is called a **FILENAME**. The **FILENAME** must begin with a letter and can be up to eight characters long. Next, the computer displays a data entry form for you to enter the **FIELDNAME**s, **ALIAS**es, **PRINTING FOR-MAT**s, and **FILE FORMAT**s of the new file.

The form looks like this:

```
            CREATING A MASTER FILE

        FIELDNAME:
            ALIAS:
  PRINTING FORMAT:
      FILE FORMAT:
```

The small white rectangle (called the cursor) appears next to **FIELDNAME:** as soon as the computer is ready to accept the first item.

You may type up to twelve characters for a **FIELDNAME**.

Type: **FIRSTNAME** Use the **LEFT-ARROW** key to back-space if needed for corrections.

```
    FIELDNAME: FIRSTNAME
```

Since FIRSTNAME is only nine letters long, type three spaces or press the **RETURN** key, and the cursor will jump down and sit next to **ALIAS**. The **ALIAS** may also be twelve letters long, but usually an abbreviated name is more convenient for writing reports. It is best if an **ALIAS** begins with a letter and contains no embedded spaces.

Type: **FN**

```
    ALIAS: FN
```

Since this uses only two out of the twelve available spaces, press the **RE-TURN** key to make the cursor move down to **PRINTING FORMAT**.

Now type: **A15**

Press: **RETURN**

PRINTING FORMAT: **A15**

The **PRINTING FORMAT** is a code to specify how a data item is displayed in reports. The number is the width of the field in characters.

PRINTING FORMAT	Examples
A11	for a field wide enough for a Social Security number with dashes
A5	for a zip code
A20	for a name
I2	for an integer 0 to 99 (for age)
A1	for M or F (male or female)
I4	for a year (1981)
F6.2	for a decimal value between –99.99 and 999.99
A6	for a date in YYMMDD format (810715)

Remember to enter a letter *and* a number. The letter indicates the kind of data and the number specifies the number of spaces allocated for the **FIELDNAME**. Use the **RETURN** key to move the cursor to the **FILE FORMAT**. If you change your mind and wish to move the cursor up the screen to retype an item, press the **LEFT-ARROW** key.

Next type: **A15**

FILE FORMAT: **A15**

The **FILE FORMAT** specifies the amount of space reserved on the diskette for this data item. The **A** stands for alphanumeric. The number is the width of the field in characters, usually the same number as in the **PRINTING FORMAT**.

Press: **RETURN**   The last item is accepted, and the cursor moves to the top of the screen.

419

Your screen should look like this:

```
                              RETURN  or  ESC  >

              CREATING  A  MASTER  FILE


         FIELDNAME:  FIRSTNAME

            ALIAS:  FN

   PRINTING  FORMAT:  A15

      FILE  FORMAT:  A15
```

Check the entries for errors. If corrections are needed, press the **RIGHT-ARROW** key to move off the top line, and

- use the **RIGHT-ARROW** key to skip forward one field at a time;

- use the **LEFT-ARROW** key to back-space and to move the cursor back field-by-field;

- after positioning the cursor, retype the field;

- press the **RETURN** key to accept a data item that does not fill the twelve-character field.

Also,

- *if the cursor is in the first position of a field*, and you notice an error in the previous field, you may hold the **CONTROL** key down while pressing the **B** key to back across the screen, erasing a field with each step.

You should try each of these control keys.

After making corrections, press the **ESC** key to send the cursor to the top of the screen again. Then press the **RETURN** key to write the record on the diskette. The fields are emptied to prepare for the next FIELD.

Continue entering the fieldnames and formats, such as LASTNAME, LN, A15, A15 and TELEPHONE, PH, A12, A12, until all the information you wish for all fields has been entered for this **Master** file. Remember to press **RETURN** when the cursor reaches the top of the screen to tell the computer you have completed the item description.

Upon writing the last field description to the diskette for this Master file,

Press: **ESC** key *twice*   to **ESC**ape from the DATA-FORM
                                               mode.
The DATA-FORM disappears, and NPL asks:

MAKE FILE CHANGES PERMANENT? Y/N>

Type: **Y**

After answering, **C>** appears on the left side of the screen. The **C>** prompt
indicates the NPL Command mode.
    The name of your new file is FRIENDS/M. The **/M** designates it as a Master file.
Now ask the computer to type the Master file for FRIENDS.

Type: **TYPEFILE FRIENDS/M**

Your FRIENDS Master file might look like the following:

```
I                                                                        I
I         FIELD=FIRSTNAME   ,FN      ,A15  ,A15  ,$                       I
I         FIELD=LASTNAME    ,LN      ,A15  ,A15  ,$                       I
I         FIELD=TELEPHONE   ,PH      ,A12  ,A12  ,$                       I
I         FIELD=BIRTHDATE   ,BD      ,A6   ,A6   ,$                       I
I         FIELD=           ,...     ,     ,A1   ,$ END--OF--RECORD|
I_____I
```

    The computer has taken the information you entered in the DATA-FORM
mode and created a file in the standard format for Master files. The last line in
the Master file is a special field which NPL adds to every Master file. See the
NPL User's Guide for an explanation. In Appendix A you can see other typical
Master files.

PRACTICING DATA ENTRY

    Since the FRIENDS Master file does not have a datafile associated with it at
this time, you obviously are unable to generate reports. The quickest way to
create a *data*file is to move to the DATA-FORM mode. On the NPL System
Guide you see the command **MODIFY** moves you from Command mode to
DATA-FORM mode. To create the FRIENDS/D.DATA file

Type: **GETFILE FRIENDS**
Press: **RETURN**
Type: **MODIFY APPEND**
Press: **RETURN**

MODIFY APPEND is the simplest command you can give to call for the DATA-FORM screen below. Many other options are presented in the *NPL User's Guide.*

```
FIRSTNAME  :
LASTNAME   :
TELEPHONE  :
BIRTHDATE  :
```

Now, enter as many records as you wish. If the cursor does not move to the next item itself, press the **RETURN** key. Back up to make changes with the **LEFT-ARROW** key. At the end of each record when the cursor moves to the top of the screen, press **RETURN** to write the record into the datafile.

After you have entered the last record and the cursor is at the FIRSTNAME position of a blank record,

Press: **ESC** *twice*   to end the data entry session.

Before returning to the Command mode, NPL asks:

MAKE FILE CHANGES PERMANENT? Y/N>

Type: **Y**

You type **Y** to append the new data records to an existing datafile, or, as in this case, to open a new datafile. There may be times when you may not wish to append the new data records to the existing files. If this is the case you type **N**. The new data records are not appended, and your datafile is not opened.

Now type:
PRINT FN LN PH BD.   to display the data you have just entered.
Press: **RETURN**

Next, type the command that displays the names of all NPL files on all disks (as well as the amount of blocks available on each disk):
DIRECTORY
Press: **RETURN**

From this listing of filenames, you can verify that the new files were indeed created and stored on the proper diskette. The directory listing also shows the size of each file, measured in blocks of 512 characters. Thus a size of 4 is roughly 2000 characters. One diskette holds 280 blocks or about 140,000 thousand characters of data.

In review, the simplest method of data capture uses the following steps:

CREATE FRIENDS   to create a Master file
followed by entry of Master file
information, (press **(ESC)** *twice* to
end)

TYPEFILE FRIENDS/M   to verify Master file information

GETFILE FRIENDS   to specify the file

MODIFY APPEND   to enter data into the file

followed by entry of data (press
(ESC) *twice* to end)

PRINT FN LN PH BD.   to verify data

DIRECTORY   to check on the location of the new
                                     files

More complex methods of data capture are presented in the following pages and in Chapter 11 of the *NPL User's Guide*.

USING THE PRINTER

Now that you have had practice with a small Master file, you can try to create a DATA-FORM to enter information for the CLIENTS Master file; but first use the **TYPEFILE** command to display the contents of the CLIENTS Master file.

Type:
TYPEFILE CLIENTS/M

```
FIELD=TITLE         ,PREFX   ,A6    ,A6    ,$
FIELD=FIRST         ,FN      ,A15   ,A15   ,$
FIELD=MIDDLE        ,MI      ,A1    ,A1    ,$
FIELD=LASTNAME      ,LN      ,A15   ,A15   ,$
FIELD=SUFFIX        ,SUFX    ,A6    ,A6    ,$
FIELD=SSN           ,SSN     ,A11   ,A11   ,$
FIELD=STREET        ,STR     ,A15   ,A15   ,$
FIELD=CITY          ,CTY     ,A12   ,A12   ,$
FIELD=STATE         ,ST      ,A2    ,A2    ,$
FIELD=ZIPCODE       ,ZP      ,A5    ,A5    ,$
FIELD=TELEPHONE     ,PHONE   ,A12   ,A12   ,$
FIELD=AGE           ,AGE     ,I3    ,A3    ,$
FIELD=SEX           ,SEX     ,A1    ,A1    ,$
FIELD=DEPENDENTS    ,DEPS    ,I2    ,A2    ,$
FIELD=YRS EDUC      ,EDYRS   ,I3    ,A3    ,$
FIELD=YRS EMPLOYED  ,WRKYRS  ,I3    ,A3    ,$
FIELD=EMPLOYER      ,EMP     ,A15   ,A15   ,$
FIELD=INCOME(000)   ,INC     ,I6    ,A6    ,$
FIELD=ACCOUNT       ,ACNO    ,A6    ,A6    ,$
FIELD=ACCOUNTYPE    ,TYP     ,A4    ,A4    ,$
FIELD=AMOUNT(000)   ,SIZE    ,I6    ,A6    ,$
FIELD=              ,...     ,I2    ,A1    ,$ END-OF-RECORD
```

To make a paper copy of these names for your reference, turn on the power switch of your printer and

Type: **PRINTER:**
Press: **RETURN**
Type: **TYPEFILE CLIENTS/M**
Press: **RETURN**   The same file is now printed on paper.

To print the data you have entered for FRIENDS,

Type: **PRINT FN LN PH BD.**   You now have a paper copy of your file. Remember to press **RETURN**.

Type: **CONSOLE:**   This command redirects reports to the Apple monitor.

Press: **RETURN**

Next, type a report from the file:

GETFILE CLIENTS
PRINT FIRST, LASTNAME, AGE, SEX.
Press: **RETURN**   after each line.

After a brief pause you should see a list of clients like this:

FIRST	LASTNAME	AGE	SEX
PHILIP	WALTERS	29	M
ELAINE	FREEDMAN	29	F
FRED	HURLBUTT	36	M
HENRY	MOREY	24	M
PATRICIA	BARNES	28	F
WILLIAM	WARD	46	M
ELLA	HENDERSON	34	F
LAURA	SOLOMON	38	F
ROGER	SCHANKLE	41	M
CHARLES	ROZICS	37	M
JOHN	CORRIGAN	47	M
ROBERT	HAYES	28	M
ELLEN	KINGFISH	19	F
PETER	ROSER	21	M
SUSAN	GREEN	22	F
DENNIS	KELSEY	19	M
MANFRED	HUGHES	18	M
LINDA	MOORE	21	F
JOE	SMITH	25	M
EVELYN	FARRELL	25	F

For a second request, type:
PRINT LASTNAME,
EMPLOYER, SEX
BY INCOME BY AGE.
Press: **RETURN**   after each line.

INCOME(000)	AGE	LASTNAME	EMPLOYER	SEX
9	21	ROSER	GREYS MARKET	M
	22	GREEN	MAGIC MOTION	F
10	18	HUGHES	UPLAND REALTORS	M
	19	KINGFISH	OCEAN SEAFOOD	F
	21	MOORE	COUNTRY CRUMPET	F
11	19	KELSEY	MEDICAL CENTER	M
14	25	SMITH	APPLE TOURS	M
16	28	HAYES	PUBLIC LIBRARY	M
17	24	MOREY	CENTER SPORTS	M
	29	FREEDMAN	INNOVATIONS INC	F
18	34	HENDERSON	PRIME SERVICE	F
19	37	ROZICS	TAKOMA HIFI	M
	38	SOLOMON	OHIO LIFE	F
22	25	FARRELL	BTA COMPUTING	F
	29	WALTERS	WAYNE OIL CO	M
28	28	BARNES	SIMI RESEARCH	F
	36	HURLBUTT	RED BALLOON INC	M
29	46	WARD	PICKWICK PAPER	M
32	41	SCHANKLE	FRANKLIN MINT	M
35	47	CORRIGAN	CHARLIE CHIP CO	M

Now that you know how to define a new file with the **CREATE** command, let's try the NPL requests that are used for capturing data. The next section presents several methods for entering data.

BRIEF FORMS

The simplest request is one that prompts the operator for the full list of fieldnames in the Master file:

MODIFY APPEND

This request prompts for data until the operator presses the **ESC** key *twice*. Each set of data forms a record, and each record is appended to the datafile.

You may specify fewer fields from the Master file to correspond, say, with a particular paper form of the raw data—other data elements being added later. Thus, your friends' records might be created with the request,

    C>**GETFILE FRIENDS**
    C>**MODIFY, PROMPT LN FN PH, APPEND**

This screen would then appear:

```
LASTNAME
    FIRST
TELEPHONE
```

The sequence on the screen is determined by the order of the names following the keyword **PROMPT** and may be different from the order in the Master file. The names in a **PROMPT** phrase must appear in the Master file.

In this case, blanks are placed in the unmentioned field, BIRTHDATE, so that the records appended to the file have the same total number of characters specified in the Master file.

FORMATTING THE DATA ENTRY SCREEN

In the previous examples the screen format is automatically determined by NPL to be a list of fieldnames from the Master file. You may, however, override this format and create your own display.

The keyword **FORM** is like the keyword **HEADING** in the Report mode. It allows you to arrange text in any format you choose. For example, using the FRIENDS file, you could create the following form:

```
GETFILE FRIENDS
MODIFY
FORM

"   PERSONAL PHONE BOOK

 FIRST NAME: <FN    LAST NAME: <LN

         TELEPHONE: <PH

   BIRTH DATE: <BD                      "

APPEND
```

The shaded area marks the part which will appear on your screen. The general form is:

```
GETFILE filename
MODIFY
FORM

"              text...

   text <field      text <field

                  text <field

      text...                  "

APPEND
```

The text begins and ends with quote marks and is arranged to fill part or all of a 78x23 screen. The spotmarkers, <**field**, show where the operator is to enter the data. When entering data the operator moves the cursor from spotmarker to spotmarker.

When both **PROMPT** and **FORM** statements are used, the **PROMPT** phrase determines the sequence of the data items requested, while the **FORM** phrase specifies where on the screen they appear. Since the fieldnames appear in both phrases, you must ensure that the two lists of names are the same. If they differ, NPL will complain. Ordinarily, DATA-FORM programs are not entered directly in NPL. Rather, they are first stored in a file called an "EXEC file." When this file is executed by NPL, each DATA-FORM phrase is read and tested for correctness; then the screen display is created.

SUMMARY

As shown below, the general form of a **MODIFY** request for data capture contains the four keywords— **MODIFY, PROMPT, FORM,** and **APPEND.**

```
GETFILE filename

MODIFY

   PROMPT  SSN
           YEAR
             .
             .
             .
           alias


   FORM

      "          text

            Soc Sec Nbr:<SSN
      Year:<YEAR                 text <alias
        .
        .
        .
                                 text <alias      "
   APPEND
```

CREATING SCREENS IN THE APPLE PASCAL EDITOR

The next step is for you to create a DATA-FORM and try it out. To do so, you must use the Apple Pascal Editor (see the NPL System Guide). To exit NPL and use the Apple Pascal Editor, type the words below appearing in **boldface.**

First type **FIN** to leave the NPL Command Level. The following apppears on the screen

```
| COMMAND E(DIT, R(UN, F(ILE,  C(OMP, L(INK ,X(ECUTE, A(SSEM,...   |
|        ... D(EBUG? [1.1]                                         |
|_____|
```

429

Next, press: **E**   to select the Editor

Assuming you have an eighty-column display, the following appears

```
|>EDIT:                                                              |
|NO WORKFILE IS PRESENT. FILE? (<RET> FOR NO FILE<ESC-RET> TO EXIT) |
|_____|
```

Press: **RETURN**   to create a new file

Then, again assuming eighty columns, the following line appears

```
|EDIT A(DJST C(PY D(LETE F(IND I(NSRT J(MP R(PLACE Q(UIT X(CHNG Z(AP|
|_____|
```

Press: **I**   to select INSERT mode

```
|>INSERT: TEXT [<BS> A CHAR, <DEL> A LINE][<ETX>ACCEPTS,<ESC>ESCAPES]|
|_____|
```

Now you are in the INSERT mode and the keyboard reacts very much like a typewriter. Everything you type, errors and all, is accepted and recorded on the screen (and in a file in the computer).

Just for practice now, type your name and address on several lines of the screen. Use the **LEFT-ARROW** key to back-space over errors. After you have typed a few lines, hold the **CONTROL** key down and press the letter **C** to leave the INSERT mode and save what you typed. At this point what you just typed in is saved in an Edit mode buffer but is not yet stored on the diskette. Now, move the cursor around the screen with the following characters.

RIGHT-ARROW key: move right
LEFT-ARROW key: move left
RETURN key: move down
CONTROL-O keys: move up
                                    (hold **CONTROL** down and press
                                    O)

If the **CONTROL-O** key seems awkward, a different way to control the up and down motion is to switch the direction of the small arrow in the upper-left corner of the screen. The arrow is an angle-bracket (also called a caret), and its direction may be changed by the two angle-bracket keys. Try pressing the < and > keys alternately and watch the arrow (the shift key is not needed).

With the arrow pointing left, press **RETURN**. The cursor goes up one line! When it points to the right, the **RETURN** key behaves normally. Be careful, it can lead to confusion. Always leave the arrow pointing to the right.

You will have more practice moving the cursor and entering data when you type in a full set of NPL instructions for creating a DATA-FORM screen. First it is necessary to erase the lines now on the Editor screen.

Start with the cursor on the top line, left end;

Press: **D**	to select the **DELETE** mode
Press: **RETURN**	to erase each line. At the last line
Press: **RIGHT-ARROW**	to erase each character. Finally
Press: **CONTROL-C**	to leave the **DELETE** mode.

Now, begin entering the DATA-FORM program that follows on the next page.

Press: **I**   for INSERT.

Remember, while in the INSERT mode, mistakes are corrected by back spacing with the **LEFT-ARROW** key while on the current line. Errors on earlier lines are corrected after leaving the INSERT mode (examples are given below).

The DATA-FORM program we will now build is for the **CLIENTS** file. We use only the **FORM** statement. Enter the following **bold** lines after entering the INSERT mode.

GETFILE CLIENTS	Identifies the file to be modified.
MODIFY	Enters the DATA-FORM mode.
FORM	Defines the screen format.

```
     "        CLIENT INFORMATION FORM

   FIRST NAME:<FN............ MIDDLE:<MI
   LAST NAME:<LN............ TITLE:<TITLE

   STREET:<STR
   CITY:<CTY........  STATE:<ST ZIP:<ZP

   SOC SEC NBR:<SSN....... AGE:<AGE SEX:<SEX

     EMPLOYER:<EMP

  NO OF DEPENDENTS:<DEPS

  YRS OF EDUCATION:<EDYRS

      YRS EMPLOYED:<WRKYRS

    ANNUAL INCOME:$<INC ,000
```

"   terminates the
FORM statement

APPEND	Causes NPL to act upon all of the above

Within the quote marks the text can say anything you wish. Preceding each fieldname (or alias) there must be a bracket, <. Use the alias when a fieldname contains a space, as with EDYRS and WRKYRS. In the **FORM** there may be a maximum of twenty-three lines.

APPEND is a DATA-FORM command to initiate the data entry session.

After typing the word **APPEND**, hold the **CONTROL** key and press the letter **C**. This takes you out of the INSERT mode and returns you to the EDITOR mode.

Use the cursor moving keys (**LEFT-ARROW**, **RIGHT-ARROW**, and **RETURN**, with the carets for changing direction) to move the cursor to any spelling and typing errors. To correct them, enter the INSERT and DELETE modes as needed.

Use the following commands to make changes. First place the cursor on the incorrect letter or word.

Press: **D**

Use Right-Arrow key to delete text

Press: **CONTROL-C**

Places you in the **DELETE** mode. The Editor **D**eletes the text as you move the cursor across it using the **RIGHT-ARROW** key. The original characters can be made to re-appear by moving the cursor in the opposite direction. **CONTROL-C** saves the changes and returns to the Editor mode.

Press: **X**

Enter text to be replaced

Press: **CONTROL-C**

Places you in the **EXCHANGE** mode. Type a new character to re-place what is already there. Notice the computer writes over the original character. Press the **LEFT-ARROW** key and the original characters reappear. After eXchanging, **CONTROL-C** saves the changes, leaves the **EXCHANGE** mode, and returns to the **Editor mode.**

Press: **I**

Enter text to be replaced

Press: **CONTROL-O**

INSERT can be used at any time during an editing session. If you forget a letter or a word, place the cursor just after the desired insertion point, and then press **I**, followed by what you want to enter. If you wish to add a line, place the cursor at the beginning of the line that will follow the new line. Press **I**, type in the new line, and press **RETURN**. Then press **CONTROL-C** to save the changes, leave **INSERT**, and return to the Editor mode.

Press: **ESC**

When in the INSERT, DELETE, or EXCHANGE modes the (**ESC**) key cancels any action taken and causes you to **ESC**ape from the mode with no change to the file.

After checking the form and making all corrections

Press: **Q**   to **QUIT** the Edit mode.

The screen looks like this:

```
>QUIT:
            U(PDATE THE WORKFILE AND LEAVE
            E(XIT WITHOUT UPDATING
            R(ETURN TO THE EDITOR WITHOUT UPDATING
            W(RITE TO A FILENAME AND RETURN
            S(AVE WITH SAME NAME AND RETURN
```

To store the **MODIFY** request you just created, you need to give it a filename. You may have Report requests and **MODIFY** requests that you will run many times. Each should be stored in a file with its own **EXEC** filename to avoid the trouble of retyping the requests each time. To assign a name to the new file:

Press: **W**

```
>QUIT
 NAME OF OUTPUT FILE (<CR> TO RETURN)
```

Type: **CLIENTS/E**   The /E designates an **EXEC** file.
Press: **RETURN**

```
>QUIT
 WRITING...
 YOUR FILE IS 418 BYTES LONG
 DO YOU WANT TO E(XIT FROM OR R(ETURN TO THE EDITOR?
```

Type: **E**   to Exit the Editor and return to the
                                       Apple Pascal Operating System
                                       Mode.

To run this CLIENTS form, enter NPL.

Press: **X**

The computer asks: EXECUTE WHAT FILE?
Type: **NPL:NPL**
Press: **RETURN**

You have now entered the NPL Command mode, and a **C>** prompt appears.

Type: **ECHO ON**	This establishes a special condition which displays each line in the **EXEC** file as the computer is processing it. The **ECHO** feature can be helpful when running a new **EXEC** file. If error messages appear, they are displayed after the echo of the request line that may be in error.
On the next line, after the prompt,	
Type: **EXEC CLIENTS**	This means **EXEC**ute the file called CLIENTS/E.

At this point there are two possibilities:
1. After a brief wait, a CLIENTS Information Form appears on the screen. You can then enter information just as you entered it when you used the MAILIST form.
2. One or more error messages appear on the monitor as NPL examines the CLIENTS/E file in detail. With **ECHO** set **ON**, a message appears below the line being examined. After each message you may press **RETURN** to continue processing or press **ESC** to enter the Command mode. Continuing lets you see all the error messages so that you may have to revise the CLIENTS/E file only once.

The possible messages are:
- **NAME NOT IN MASTER FILE:**   Misspelled fieldname or alias
- **FIELD ALREADY ENTERED IN FORM:**   A duplicate use of a field in a FORM statement
- **FORM TOO WIDE:**   FORM width exceeds seventy-eight columns
- **TOO MANY LINES IN FORM:**   FORM length exceeds twenty-three lines

If you allow the processing to run to completion, NPL will attempt to bring up a DATA-FORM screen display, notwithstanding the errors. Sometimes this helps you to discover what is wrong in the **EXEC** file. In any case, NPL does not allow you to proceed in filling the screen if errors have been found, for the resultant DATA-FORM might damage the datafile. You must correct the **EXEC** file first, and then try to execute it.

435

To leave NPL to correct any mistakes,
Type: **FIN**
Then type: **E**   to enter the EDIT mode.
In response to the **EDITOR** question,
Type: **CLIENTS/E**   to get to your file.

Now, compare your **MODIFY** request with the one displayed in this manual, *in every detail*, and correct all differences.

For further practice creating screens, create a DATA-FORM screen for the Master file FRIENDS.

SPECIAL KEYS

In summary, the special control keys are:

RETURN	• to accept new data from keyboard and advance cursor to the next field
	• (at top of screen) to accept new record
RIGHT-ARROW	• to show codes—tab forward—copy previous values
LEFT-ARROW	• to back-space—tab back
CONTROL-B	• to tab back and erase previous field
(ESC)	• (within a field) to discard current value
	• (at beginning of a field) to end current record
	• (at top of screen) to discard current record and continue
	• (at beginning of the first field) to quit data entry mode
	• (at M>) to terminate DATA-FORM session

In this lesson you have learned:

   • to use the **CREATE** command to produce a new Master file;

   • to use the **MODIFY**, **PROMPT**, **FORM**, and **APPEND** commands to build your own EXEC programs for capturing data;

   • to use the new DATA-FORM exec program for entering new records.

On the following page, the NPL System Guide is displayed with all the keywords presented in this *Tutorial*.

The NPL™ System Guide

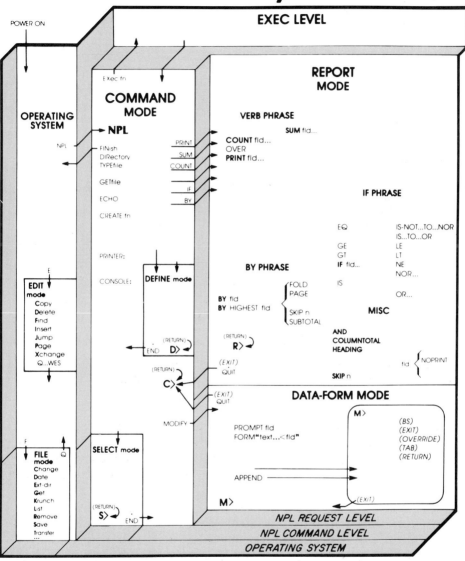

EXEC LEVEL

POWER ON

EXEC fn

COMMAND MODE

REPORT MODE

OPERATING SYSTEM

NPL

NPL

FINish
DIRectory
TYPEfile

GETfile

ECHO

CREATE fn

PRINTER:

CONSOLE:

PRINT
SUM
COUNT
IF
BY

VERB PHRASE

SUM fld...

COUNT fld...
OVER
PRINT fld...

IF PHRASE

EQ   IS-NOT...TO...NOR
            IS...TO...OR
GE   LE
GT   LT
IF fld...   NE
            NOR...

IS   OR...

DEFINE mode

BY PHRASE

BY fld
BY HIGHEST fld

FOLD
PAGE
SKIP n
SUBTOTAL

MISC

AND
COLUMNTOTAL
HEADING

fld   NOPRINT

EDIT mode
Copy
Delete
Find
Insert
Jump
Page
Xchange
Q...WES

E

(RETURN)
END   **D>**

(RETURN)
R>

(RETURN)
C>

(EXIT)
QUIT

SKIP n

(EXIT)
QUIT

DATA-FORM MODE

MODIFY

M>

(BS)
(EXIT)
(OVERRIDE)
(TAB)
(RETURN)

FILE mode
Change
Date
Ext-dir
Get
Krunch
List
Remove
Save
Transfer
...

F   Q

SELECT mode

PROMPT fld
FORM"text...<fld"

APPEND

M>

(EXIT)

(RETURN)
S>   END

NPL REQUEST LEVEL
NPL COMMAND LEVEL
OPERATING SYSTEM

Release 1.1

You are now ready to apply these simple techniques to new situations. Also, you should read the *NPL User's Guide*, for there are many other features of NPL to aid you in organizing and analyzing your data. With a little practice, you can create order where chaos has prevailed, by transferring jumbles of data into useful **information**!

SECTION **FIVE**

APPENDIXES

NONPROCEDURAL SYSTEMS FOR IBM 370 COMPUTERS

There are quite a few nonprocedural language systems installed throughout the industry, that are used for query and report writing by end users who would not normally be classified as computer programmers. Many of these software systems are available for large scale IBM computers only. Some of the leading products are listed in Figure (A-1). Each system has its band of dedicated users, who have in some cases formed *user groups* to hold conferences for exchanging experience with the product.

The enthusiasm with which the users of these software products report about their successes in rapidly developing new database computer applications is a testimonial to the merit of the nonprocedural language concept. It is difficult to assess the relative merit of the *languages* used by the various software systems. This is so, because:

- competitive analyses and benchmark tests are usually designed to compare speed, throughput, and relative costs, rather than the ease and utility of the user language.

- ease of use is too difficult to measure.

- few people have sufficient experience in preparing real applications in two or more systems (which is needed to make an objective evaluation).

FIGURE (A-1)

Nonprocedural Systems
for IBM 370 Computers

```
1967          RAMIS I
               |                              MARKIV
1969           |              INQUIRE           |
               |                 |              |
1971           |                 |  SYSTEM-R|  EASYTRIEVE   SYSTEM 2000
        ------|-------           |   &          |          |              |
1973    |     |        |         |  SEQUEL      |          |              |
        |     |      NOMAD       |   |          |          |              |
1975  FOCUS   |        |         |   |          |          |              |
        |     |        |         |   |          |          |              |
1977    |  RAMIS II    |         |   |  QBE |   |          |              |
        |     |        |         |   |   |  |   |          |              |
1979    |     |     NOMAD2       |   |   |  |   |          |              |
        |     |        |         |  SQL  V  |   |          |              |
1981    |     |        |         |   |      |   |          |              |
        V     V        V         V   V      V   V          V              V
```

SOURCE

RAMIS	Mathematica, Inc.	Princeton, NJ
FOCUS	Information Builders, Inc.	New York, NY
NOMAD	National CSS, Inc.	Wilton, CT
INQUIRE	Infodata Systems, Inc.	Falls Church, VA
SQL	IBM	White Plains, NY
SEQUEL	IBM Research Laboratory	San Jose, CA
SYSTEM-R	IBM Research Laboratory	San Jose, CA
QBE	IBM	White Plains, NY
MARKIV	Informatics, Inc.	Canoga Park, CA
EASYTRIEVE	Pansophic Systems, Inc.	Oak Brook, IL
SYSTEM 2000	MRI Systems Corporation	Austin, TX

It is the purpose of this appendix to examine only the principal phrases of the nonprocedural languages for similarity, in order to judge the relative ease by which a group of users with experience in one language might use another. More particularly the comparisons are between the host computer languages like RAMIS, FOCUS, NOMAD, INQUIRE, SQL, and the NPL language. The NPL language was designed specifically to function as a microcomputer component in a distributed computing system, where one of the aforementioned is the database query language for the host computer. If an IBM 370/3033 computer with the FOCUS system serves a distributed network of interactive terminal and mini- and micro-computers, the users of the small computers will benefit the more their NPL system is compatible with the FOCUS system.

The design of NPL includes a synonym table for keywords, in order to allow the greatest language compatibility. This book teaches words like WRITE, IF, BY, AVE, yet these synonyms will do as well: SUM, WHERE, SORT BY, AVERAGE. By this means NPL may resemble several nonprocedural languages which do not resemble each other.

The first of these systems to become a commercial success is RAMIS I, which was installed in 1967 by Mathematica, Inc., for an application for Allied Chemical Corporation. Written by Gerald Cohen and associates at Mathematica, RAMIS I incorporated the notion that datafiles need be described only once, for all applications, and in a manner which is independent of the programs reading the files. The separation of data descriptions from program procedures is now a fundamental principle embodied in all database management systems.

RAMIS I also introduced the use of English-like phrases for data retrieval and report writing, in a free format. That is, the *sequence* of phrases specifying selection, sorting, summing, and printing was left to the user. Hence these instructions to the computer were something other than step-by-step procedures. The term nonprocedural was adopted.

In 1977, a team at Mathematica under Bernard Finzi redesigned their product to create the RAMIS II data management system which is now in use at over 600 IBM 370 class installations worldwide.

INQUIRE, another early database management system for IBM 370-class computers, was installed first in 1969 by Infodata Systems, Inc. There were 250 installations in 1979. In addition to a general purpose English-like query language, INQUIRE has a special subsystem for inquiry and retrieval from databases of bibliographic extracts.

A group at National CSS, Inc., which offered RAMIS services on a time-sharing network from 1969 on, decided in 1973 to integrate similar features into the NCSS operating system. This resulted in the NOMAD system, written by Harold Feinleib, Judd Boykin, Nick Pisaro, and Nick Rawlings. This product had been restricted to the NCSS network until 1981 when the NOMAD2 database management system was first offered as a software product to customers like the Bank of America.

Gerald Cohen and Peter Mittelman introduced a new system in 1975 called FOCUS. The same English-like query language was expanded to include new features for transaction processing, financial modelling, graphic displays, and statistical analysis. The FOCUS system has been installed by more than 450 major corporations. At many sites it is the preferred system for developing large on-line applications, i.e., in lieu of the widely used COBOL or FORTRAN languages.

Research projects at IBM in the mid 1970s led to two entries in the nonprocedural software field. The first, in 1978, called QUERY-BY-EXAMPLE or QBE, presents quite a unique tabular display to the user who may design a new report right on the terminal screen. It has been judged very easy to learn and use.

IBM's latest offering, called Structured Query Language, or SQL, was released in 1980. SQL is a successor to the research systems called SEQUEL and SYSTEM R, which are known as *relational* database management systems. The query language features nested requests, as illustrated in section A.4, to achieve complete nonprocedurality.

In 1979 the authors of this book undertook the design of the NPL system to provide full compatibility with the nonprocedural languages in use on large IBM computers. NPL was to function in the dual roles:

- an application development system for micro- and minicomputers

- a component in a distributed computer system where a common nonprocedural language is used both on large host computers and on small peripheral machines.

Sections A.1 through A.5, which follow, present commonly used phrases in each of six nonprocedural languages. In each section, NPL phrases are compared with one of the other languages to illustrate how readily the knowledge of one language may carry over to another language.

APPENDIX A.1

FOCUS Information Management System

FILE SELECTION

NPL

```
        GETFILE SALES
```
FOCUS
```
        SET FILE = SALES
```

444

RECORD SELECTION

NPL

        SELECT DEPT = ENGR SALES

FOCUS

        IF DEPT EQ ENGR OR SALES

NPL

        SELECT ACCOUNT = B370 THRU G800

FOCUS

        IF ACCOUNT FROM B370 TO G800

NPL

        IF LASTNAME CONTAINS SMITH

FOCUS

        IF LASTNAME CONTAINS SMITH

NPL

        IF ACCOUNT OMITS B3

FOCUS

        IF ACCOUNT OMITS B3

NPL

        IF BALANCE LT 500

FOCUS

        IF BALANCE LT 500

NPL

        SELECT DEPT = SALES.
          IF SALARY GT 15000
          IF QUOTA GE 100000

FOCUS

        IF DEPT EQ SALES
        IF SALARY GT 15000
        IF QUOTA GE 100000

REPORT WRITING

NPL
>
> PRINT NAME AGE DEPT SALARY

FOCUS
>
> PRINT NAME AGE DEPT SALARY

NPL
>
> PRINT NAME OVER STREET
>   OVER CITY ST ZIP
>   BY ZIP NOPRINT AND SKIP 3

FOCUS
>
> PRINT NAME AS '' OVER STREET AS ''
> OVER CITY AS '' ST AS '' ZIP AS ''
> BY ZIP SKIP-LINE

NPL
>
> HEADING CENTER "...text...<AMOUNT"

FOCUS
>
> HEADING CENTER "...text...<AMOUNT"

NPL
>
> PRINT AMOUNT AS PRICE

FOCUS
>
> PRINT AMOUNT AS 'PRICE'

NPL
>
> PRINT AMOUNT AS 'COST, OF, SALES'

FOCUS
>
> PRINT AMOUNT AS 'COST, OF, SALES'

SUMMING

NPL
>
> WRITE SUM.WAGE AVG.WAGE MAX.WAGE

FOCUS
>
> WRITE SUM.WAGE AVG.WAGE MAX.WAGE

NPL

WRITE SUM.SALARY BY DEPT

FOCUS

WRITE SUM.SALARY BY DEPT

SORTING

NPL

PRINT NAME TITLE
  BY DEPT BY HIGHEST SALARY

FOCUS

PRINT NAME TITLE
  BY DEPT BY HIGHEST SALARY

CALCULATIONS

NPL

DEFINE NEWPRICE/D15.2LC = PRICE * 1.12

FOCUS

DEFINE NEWPRICE/D15.2MC = PRICE * 1.12;

NPL

COMPUTE RATIO/F4.2 = WOMEN / (MEN + WOMEN)

FOCUS

COMPUTE RATIO/F4.2 = WOMEN / (MEN + WOMEN);

APPENDIX A.2

RAMIS Management System

RECORD SELECTION

NPL

SELECT DEPT = ENGR SALES

RAMIS

IF DEPT EQ ENGR OR SALES

NPL

SELECT ACCOUNT = B370 THRU G800

RAMIS

IF ACCOUNT FROM B370 TO G800

NPL

IF LASTNAME CONTAINS SMITH

RAMIS

IF LASTNAME CONTAINS SMITH

NPL

IF ACCOUNT OMITS B3

RAMIS

IF ACCOUNT OMITS B3

NPL

IF BALANCE LT 500

RAMIS

IF BALANCE LT 500

NPL

SELECT DEPT = SALES.
  IF SALARY GT 15000
  IF QUOTA GE 100000

RAMIS

IF DEPT EQ SALES
IF SALARY GT 15000
IF QUOTA GE 100000

REPORT WRITING

NPL

PRINT NAME AND AGE AND DEPT AND SALARY

RAMIS

PRINT NAME AND AGE AND DEPT AND SALARY

NPL

```
PRINT NAME OVER STREET
   OVER CITY ST ZIP
      BY ZIP NOPRINT AND SKIP 3
```

RAMIS

```
PRINT NAME AS '' OVER STREET AS ''
   OVER CITY AS '' AND ST AS '' AND ZIP AS ''
      BY ZIP NO-PRINT SKIP-LINE 3
```

NPL

```
HEADING CENTER "...text...<AMOUNT"
```

RAMIS

```
CENTER
"...text...!AMOUNT!"
```

NPL

```
PRINT AMOUNT AS PRICE
```

RAMIS

```
PRINT AMOUNT AS 'PRICE'
```

NPL

```
PRINT AMOUNT AS 'COST, OF, SALES'
```

RAMIS

```
PRINT AMOUNT AS 'COST, OF, SALES'
```

SUMMING

NPL

```
WRITE SUM.WAGE AVG.WAGE MAX.WAGE
```

RAMIS

```
WRITE WAGE AND AVE*WAGE AND MAX*WAGE
```

NPL

```
        WRITE  SUM.SALARY  BY  DEPT
```

RAMIS

```
        WRITE  SALARY  BY  DEPT
```

SORTING

NPL

```
        PRINT NAME AND TITLE
          BY DEPT BY HIGHEST SALARY
```

RAMIS

```
        PRINT NAME AND TITLE
          BY DEPT BY HIGHEST SALARY
```

CALCULATIONS

NPL

```
        DEFINE  NEWPRICE/D15.2  =  PRICE  *  1.12
```

RAMIS

```
        DEFINE  NEWPRICE/D15.2  =  PRICE  *  1.12;
```

APPENDIX A.3

The NOMAD2 System

RECORD SELECTION

NPL

```
        SELECT  DEPT  =  ENGR  SALES
```

NOMAD2

```
        SELECT  DEPT  =  'ENGR'  OR  DEPT  =  'SALES'
```

NPL

        SELECT ACCOUNT = B370 THRU G800

NOMAD2

        SELECT ACCOUNT BETWEEN ('B370','G800')

NPL

        IF LASTNAME CONTAINS SMITH

NOMAD2

        IF LASTNAME CONTAINS ('SMITH')

NPL

        IF ACCOUNT OMITS B3

NOMAD2

        IF NONE (ACCOUNT CONTAINS ('B3'))

NPL

        IF BALANCE LT 500

NOMAD2

        IF BALANCE LT 500

NPL

        SELECT DEPT = SALES.
          IF SALARY GT 15000
            AND IF QUOTA GE 100000

NOMAD2

        SELECT DEPT = 'SALES'   -
          AND SALARY GT 15000   -
            AND QUOTA GE 100000

REPORT WRITING

NPL

        PRINT NAME AGE DEPT SALARY

NOMAD2

        LIST NAME AGE DEPT SALARY

NPL

        PRINT NAME OVER STREET
        OVER CITY ST ZIP SKIP 3

NOMAD2

        LIST NAME OVER STREET
        OVER CITY ST ZIP 3

NPL

        HEADING '...text...&var...'

NOMAD2

        TITLE '...text...&var...'

NPL

        PRINT AMOUNT AS PRICE

NOMAD2

        LIST AMOUNT HEADING 'PRICE'

NPL

        PRINT AMOUNT AS 'COST, OF, SALES'

NOMAD2

        LIST AMOUNT HEADING 'COST: OF: SALES'

SUMMING

NPL

        WRITE SUM.WAGE AVG.WAGE MAX.WAGE

NOMAD2

        LIST SUM(WAGE) AVG(WAGE) MAX(WAGE)

NPL

        WRITE SUM.SALARY BY DEPT

NOMAD2

        LIST SUM(SALARY) BY DEPT

SORTING

NPL

      PRINT NAME TITLE
        BY DEPT BY HIGHEST SALARY

NOMAD2

      LIST NAME TITLE   -
        BY DEPT BY SALARY DESC

CALCULATIONS

NPL

      DEFINE NEWPRICE/D15.2LC = PRICE * 1.12

NOMAD2

      DEFINE NEWPRICE AS $999,999,999.99   -
      EXPR = PRICE * 1.12;

NPL

      COMPUTE RATIO/F4.2 = WOMEN / (MEN+WOMEN)

NOMAD2

      (WOMEN / (MEN+WOMEN)) AS 99.99 HEADING
'RATIO'

NPL

      WRITE SUM.SALES SUM.QUOTA
        BY REGION SUBTOTAL BY BRANCH SUBTOTAL
        BY PRODUCT
          COLUMNTOTAL

NOMAD2

      LIST SUM(SALES) SUM(QUOTA)   -
        BY REGION BY BRANCH BY PRODUCT   -
        SUBTOTAL TOTAL

DISJOINT AND COORDINATED REPORTS

NPL

        PRINT DIVNAME BY DIVCODE
        PRINT DIVCODE BY DIVNAME

NOMAD2

        LIST DIVNAME BY DIVCODE   -
        LIST DIVCODE BY DIVNAME

NPL

        WRITE SUM.SALES BY REGION
        WRITE SUM.SALES BY REGION BY PRODUCT

NOMAD2

        LIST BY REGION SUM(SALES)   -
        BY PRODUCT SUM(SALES)

NPL

        WRITE SUM.SALARY BY DEPT
        PRINT NAME SALARY BY DEPT

NOMAD2

        LIST BY DEPT SUM(SALARY)   -
        NAME SALARY

APPENDIX A.4

Structured Query Language (SQL)

FILE SELECTION

NPL

        GETFILES SALE, FINANCE

SQL

        FROM SALES, FINANCE

RECORD SELECTION

NPL

    SELECT DEPT = ENGR SALES

SQL

    WHERE DEPT = ENGR OR DEPT = SALES

NPL

    SELECT ACCOUNT = B370 THRU G800

SQL

    WHERE ACCOUNT BETWEEN 'B370' AND 'G800'

NPL

    SELECT PARTNBR = 565 740 1054

SQL

    WHERE PARTNBR IN (565, 740, 1054)

NPL

    WHERE LASTNAME CONTAINS SMITH

SQL

    WHERE LASTNAME LIKE '%SMITH%'

NPL

    WHERE ACCOUNT OMITS B3

SQL

    WHERE ACCOUNT NOT LIKE '%B3%'

NPL

    WHERE BALANCE LT 500

SQL

    WHERE BALANCE < 500

NPL

```
SELECT DEPT = SALES.
   IF SALARY IS 15000 TO 20000
   AND IF QUOTA GE 100000
```

SQL

```
WHERE DEPT = SALES AND
   SALARY BETWEEN 15000 AND 20000
   AND QUOTA >= 100000
```

REPORT WRITING

NPL

```
PRINT NAME AGE DEPT SALARY
```

SQL

```
SELECT NAME, AGE, DEPT, SALARY
```

NPL

```
PRINT AMOUNT AS PRICE
```

SQL

```
SELECT AMOUNT
   FORMAT COLUMN AMOUNT NAME PRICE
```

TITLES

NPL

```
HEADING '...text...'
FOOTING '...text...'
```

SQL

```
FORMAT TTITLE '...text...'
FORMAT BTITLE '...text...'
```

SUMMING

NPL

    WRITE SUM.WAGE, AVG.WAGE, MAX.WAGE, BY DEPT

SQL

    SELECT DEPT SUM(WAGE), AVG(WAGE), MAX(WAGE)
       GROUP BY DEPT

NPL

    WRITE SUM SALARY BY DEPT

SQL

    SELECT DEPT SUM(SALARY)
       ORDER BY DEPT
          FORMAT GROUP (DEPT)

SORTING

NPL

    PRINT NAME TITLE
       BY DEPT BY HIGHEST SALARY

SQL

    SELECT DEPT SALARY NAME TITLE
       ORDER BY DEPT, SALARY DESC

CALCULATIONS

NPL

    DEFINE NEWPRICE = PRICE * 1.12

SQL

    PRICE * 1.12

MATCHING

NPL

        IF INVENTORY.PARTNO EQ QUOTATIONS.PARTNO

SQL

        WHERE INVENTORY.PARTNO = QUOTATIONS.PARTNO

SUBQUERIES

NPL

        GETFILES INVENTORY, QUOTATIONS, SUPPLIERS
        JOIN I.PARTNO TO Q.PARTNO
        JOIN Q.SUPPNO TO S.SUPPNO
        PRINT DESCRIPTION QONHAND BY PARTNO
          IF S.NAME IS AJAX.

SQL

        SELECT * FROM INVENTORY   -
        WHERE PARTNO IN   -
                 (SELECT PARTNO   -
                  FROM QUOTATIONS   -
                  WHERE SUPPNO =   -
                   (SELECT SUPPNO   -
                   FROM SUPPLIERS   -
                   WHERE NAME = 'AJAX'))   -
        ORDER BY PARTNO

NPL

        GETFILE QUOTATIONS
        FETCH AVG.PRICE BY PARTNO;
        PRINT SUPPNO, PARTNO, PRICE
          IF PRICE LT AVG.PRICE.

SQL

        SELECT SUPPNO, PARTNO, PRICE   -
        FROM QUOTATIONS X   -
        WHERE PRICE <   -
                 (SELECT AVG(PRICE)   -
                  FROM QUOTATIONS   -
                  WHERE PARTNO = X.PARTNO)

NPL

```
GETFILE QUOTATIONS
FETCH MIN.PRICE AS LOWEST
   IF PART EQ 102;
SUM PRICE AND COMPUTE
   PRICEFACTOR = PRICE / LOWEST NOPRINT
   BY SUPPLIER
   IF PRICEFACTOR GT 2.
```

SQL

```
SELECT SUPPLIER, PRICE                    -
FROM QUOTATIONS                           -
WHERE PART = 102 AND PRICE >              -
            (SELECT 2 * MIN(PRICE)        -
             FROM QUOTATIONS              -
             WHERE PART = 102)
```

NPL

```
GETFILES QUOTATIONS, INVENTORY
JOIN I.PART TO Q.PART
PRINT SUPPLIER AND PRICE
   BY Q.PART
   IF I.QUANTITY LT 100.
```

SQL

```
SELECT *                                  -
FROM QUOTATIONS                           -
WHERE PART IN                             -
            (SELECT PA                    -
             FROM INVENTORY               -
             WHERE QUANTITY < 100)
```

NPL

```
        GETFILE QUOTATIONS
        FETCH AVG.PRICE AS AVPRICE
          BY PART
          IF CNT.SUPPLIER GE 3;
        WRITE PRICE AND COMPUTE DIFF = PRICE - AVPR
          BY PART
          BY SUPPLIER
          IF DIFF LT 0.
```

SQL

```
        SELECT SUPPLIER, PART, PRICE          -
        FROM QUOTATIONS X                     -
        WHERE PRICE <                         -
            (SELECT AVG(PRICE)                -
             FROM QUOTATIONS                  -
             WHERE PART = X.PART              -
             AND 3 <=                         -
                 (SELECT COUNT(*)             -
                  FROM QUOTATIONS             -
                  WHERE PART = X.PART))
```

APPENDIX A.5

The INQUIRE System

RECORD SELECTION

NPL
```
        SELECT DEPT = ENGR SALES
```

INQUIRE
```
        FIND DEPT = ENGR OR DEPT = SALES
```

NPL
```
        SELECT ACCOUNT = B370 THRU G800
```

INQUIRE
```
        FIND ACCOUNT = (B370 TO G800)
```

NPL

SELECT REC# = 565 740 1054

INQUIRE

FIND ITEM 565 740 1054

NPL

IF LASTNAME CONTAINS SMITH

INQUIRE

SCAN LASTNAME CONTAINS SMITH

NPL

IF ACCOUNT OMITS B3

INQUIRE

SCAN ACCOUNT EXCLUDES B3

NPL

IF BALANCE LT 500

INQUIRE

SCAN BALANCE LT 500

NPL

SELECT DEPT = SALES.
    IF SALARY GT 15000
        AND IF QUOTA GE 100000

INQUIRE

FIND DEPT = SALES.
    AND SALARY GT 15000
        AND QUOTA GE 100000

REPORT WRITING

NPL
>> PRINT NAME AGE DEPT SALARY

INQUIRE
>> TAB NAME AGE DEPT SALARY

NPL
>> PRINT NAME OVER STREET
>> OVER CITY ST ZIP SKIP 3

INQUIRE
>> TAB NAME / STREET
>> / CITY ST ZIP SPACING 3

NPL
>> HEADING '...text...<AMOUNT'

INQUIRE
>> HEADER '...text...' AMOUNT*

NPL
>> PRINT AMOUNT AS PRICE

INQUIRE
>> TAB AMOUNT, TITLE 'PRICE' AMOUNT

NPL
>> PRINT AMOUNT AS 'COST, OF, SALES'

INQUIRE
>> TAB AMOUNT, TITLE (COST OF SALES) AMOUNT

SUMMING

NPL
>> WRITE SUM.WAGE AVG.WAGE MAX.WAGE
INQUIRE
>> TOTAL WAGE   AVG OF WAGE   MAX OF WAGE

NPL
>   WRITE SUM.SALARY BY DEPT

INQUIRE
>   BREAK AFTER DEPT, TOTAL OF SALARY, TAB

SORTING

NPL
>   PRINT NAME TITLE
>   BY DEPT BY HIGHEST SALARY

INQUIRE
>   TAB DEPT SALARY NAME TITLE
>   SORT DEPT (A) SALARY (D)

CALCULATIONS

NPL
>   DEFINE NEWPRICE/D15.2LC = PRICE * 1.12

INQUIRE
>   COMPUTE NEWPRICE FORMAT($D2 15) (PRICE * 1.12)

NPL
>   COMPUTE RATIO/4.2 = WOMEN / (MEN + WOMEN)

INQUIRE
>   COMPUTE RATIO FORMAT(D2 4)
>   (WOMEN / (MEN + WOMEN))
>   TAB

MASTER FILES USED IN THIS BOOK

CLIENTS MASTER

```
FIELDNAME=TITLE             , PREFX    , A6     , A6  , $
FIELDNAME=FIRST             , FN       , A15    , A15 , $
FIELDNAME=MIDDLE            , MI       , A1     , A1  , $
FIELDNAME=LASTNAME          , LN       , A15    , A15 , $
FIELDNAME=SUFFIX            , SUFX     , A6     , A6  , $
FIELDNAME=SSN               , SSN      , A11    , A11 , $
FIELDNAME=STREET            , STR      , A15    , A15 , $
FIELDNAME=CITY              , CTY      , A12    , A12 , $
FIELDNAME=STATE             , ST       , A2     , A2  , $
FIELDNAME=ZIPCODE           , ZP       , A5     , A5  , $
FIELDNAME=TELEPHONE         , PHONE    , A12    , A12 , $
FIELDNAME=AGE               , AGE      , I3     , A3  , $
FIELDNAME=SEX               , SEX      , A1     , A1  , $
FIELDNAME=DEPENDENTS        , DEPS     , I2     , A2  , $
FIELDNAME=YRS EDUC          , EDYRS    , I3     , A3  , $
FIELDNAME=YRS EMPLOYED      , WRKYRS   , I3     , A3  , $
FIELDNAME=EMPLOYER          , EMP      , A15    , A15 , $
FIELDNAME=INCOME(000)       , INC      , I6     , A6  , $
FIELDNAME=ACCOUNT           , ACNO     , A6     , A6  , $
FIELDNAME=ACCOUNTTYPE       , TYP      , A4     , A4  , $
FIELDNAME=AMOUNT(000)       , SIZE     , I6     , A6  , $
FIELDNAME=                  , ...      ,        , A1  , $ END-OF-RECORD
```

STUDENTS MASTER

```
FIELD=SSN            ,SSN       ,A9      ,A9  ,$
FIELD=FIRST          ,FNAM      ,A12     ,A12,$
FIELD=MIDDLE         ,MI        ,A1      ,A1  ,$
FIELD=LASTNAME       ,LNAM      ,A17     ,A17,$
FIELD=STREET         ,ADDR1     ,A30     ,A30,$
FIELD=TOWN           ,ADDR2     ,A30     ,A30,$
FIELD=STATE          ,ADDR3     ,A30     ,A30,$
FIELD=ZIP            ,ZIP       ,A5      ,A5  ,$
FIELD=PHONE          ,PH        ,A10     ,A10,$
FIELD=SEX            ,SEX       ,A1      ,A1  ,$
FIELD=AGE            ,AGE       ,I3      ,A2  ,$
FIELD=INCOME         ,INC       ,F9.2    ,A9  ,$
FIELD=MARITAL        ,MAR       ,A1      ,A1  ,$
FIELD=MILITARY       ,MIL       ,A1      ,A1  ,$
FIELD=ENROLLMENT     ,ENDATE    ,A4      ,A4  ,$
FIELD=DEGREE         ,DGR       ,A5      ,A5  ,$
FIELD=ADVISOR        ,ADV       ,A17     ,A17,$
FIELD=PROGRAM        ,PROG      ,A20     ,A20,$
FIELD=GRADE-PT-AVE,GPA          ,F7.2    ,A6  ,$
FIELD=CUM CREDITS ,CUM          ,I3      ,A3  ,$
FIELD=FEE PAID       ,FEE       ,F9.2    ,A7  ,$
FIELD=GRAD DATE      ,GRDT      ,A4      ,A4  ,$
FIELD=COURSE         ,COR       ,A30     ,A30,$
FIELD=GRADE          ,GR        ,I3      ,A3  ,$
FIELD=               ,...               ,A1  ,$ END-OF-RECORD
```

FACULTY MASTER

```
FIELD=NAME           ,FLAST     ,A17     ,A17,$
FIELD=FAC CODE       ,FCODE     ,A2      ,A2  ,$
FIELD=SSN            ,SSN       ,A9      ,A9  ,$
FIELD=PROGRAM        ,PCODE     ,A2      ,A2  ,$
FIELD=SEX            ,SEX       ,A1      ,A1  ,$
FIELD=SALARY         ,PAY       ,I6      ,A8  ,$
FIELD=GRANT          ,GRANT     ,I6      ,A8  ,$
FIELD=NDP            ,NDP       ,I2      ,A2  ,$
FIELD=               ,...               ,A1  ,$ END-OF-RECORD
```

FINANCE MASTER

```
FIELD=SSN           , SSN        , A9    , A9  , $
FIELD=LOANDATE      , LOAND      , I6    , A6  , $
FIELD=LOANAMT       , AMT        , I4    , A4  , $
FIELD=FUNDS         , FDS        , F9.2  , A9  , $
FIELD=TUITIONPD     , TUTPD      , I4    , A4  , $
FIELD=GRANTS        , GRANTS     , I4    , A4  , $
FIELD=ROOMBOARD     , RB         , I4    , A4  , $
FIELD=STUDFEES      , FEES       , I4    , A4  , $
FIELD=WORKSTUDY     , WS         , A1    , A1  , $
FIELD=WRKSTAMT      , WSAMT      , I4    , A4  , $
FIELD=               , ...       ,       , A1  , $ END-OF-RECORD
```

COURSE MASTER

```
FIELD=COURSE        , COR        , A30   , A30 , $
FIELD=PROGRAM       , PROG       , A2    , A2  , $
FIELD=PROGNO        , PN         , A3    , A3  , $
FIELD=COURSENO      , CN         , A3    , A3  , $
FIELD=FAC-CODE      , FCODE      , A2    , A2  , $
FIELD=CREDITS       , CR         , I3    , A3  , $
FIELD=               , ...       , ?     , A1  , $ END-OF-RECORD
```

MAILIST MASTER

```
FIELD=FIRSTNAME     , FNAME      , A10   , A10 , $
FIELD=LASTNAME      , LNAME      , A10   , A10 , $
FIELD=ADDRESS       , STREET     , A15   , A15 , $
FIELD=CITY          , CTY        , A12   , A12 , $
FIELD=STATE         , ST         , A2    , A2  , $
FIELD=ZIPCODE       , ZIP        , A5    , A5  , $
FIELD=               , ...       ,       , A1  , $ END-OF-RECORD
```

NJ MASTER

```
FIELD=COUNTY         ,CTY      ,A10      ,A10,$
FIELD=MUNICIPALITY,TOWN        ,A20      ,A20,$
FIELD=POPULATION    ,POP       ,F10.0    ,A6 ,$
FIELD=BLACK          ,BL       ,F10.0    ,A6 ,$
FIELD=HISPANIC      ,SPANISH   ,F10.0    ,A6 ,$
FIELD=               ,...               ,A2 ,$ END-OF-RECORD
```

The following three sample master files illustrate the effects of the **HOLD** and **HOLD BINARY** phrases upon the FILE formats. In the first case, **HOLD BINARY** creates the master file BINDATA.M from SALES.M. In the second case, the same request with **HOLD** creates ALFDATA.M from SALES.M.

SALES.M

```
FIELD=CUSTOMER      ,NAME      ,A20      ,A15,$
FIELD=QUANTITY      ,QTY       ,I5       ,A4 ,$
FIELD=UNIT PRICE    ,PRICE     ,F8.2     ,A7 ,$
FIELD=AMOUNT        ,AMT       ,D15.2LC  ,A12,$
FIELD=               ,...               ,A2 ,$ END-OF-RECORD
```

```
GETFILE SALES

WRITE MAX.QTY AVE.QTY NOPRINT
AVE.AMOUNT AS 'SALES AVERAG'
COMPUTE RATIO=MAX.QTY/AVE.QTY
BY NAME
AND HOLD BINARY AS BINDATA.
```

BINDATA.M

```
FIELD=CUSTOMER      ,NAME          ,A20       ,A20,$
FIELD=MAX:QUANTITY,QTY             ,I5        ,I2 ,$
FIELD=AVE:UNIT PRI,PRICE           ,F8.2      ,F4 ,$
FIELD=SALES AVERAG,AMT             ,D15.2LC   ,D6 ,$
FIELD=RATIO        ,               ,F10.2     ,F4 ,$
```

```
        GETFILE SALES

WRITE MAX.QTY AVE.QTY NOPRINT
AVE.AMOUNT AS 'SALES AVERAG'
COMPUTE RATIO=MAX.QTY/AVE.QTY
BY NAME
AND HOLD AS ALFDATA.
```

ALFDATA.M

```
FIELD=CUSTOMER      ,NAME          ,A20       ,A20,$
FIELD=MAX:QUANTITY,QTY             ,I5        ,A5 ,$
FIELD=AVE:UNIT PRI,PRICE           ,F8.2      ,A8 ,$
FIELD=SALES AVERAG,AMT             ,D15.2LC   ,A15,$
FIELD=RATIO        ,               ,F10.2     ,A10,$
FIELD=              ,...           ,          ,A2 ,$ END-OF-RECORD
```

APPENDIX C

NPL SYSTEM GUIDE CARD

The NPL™ System Guide

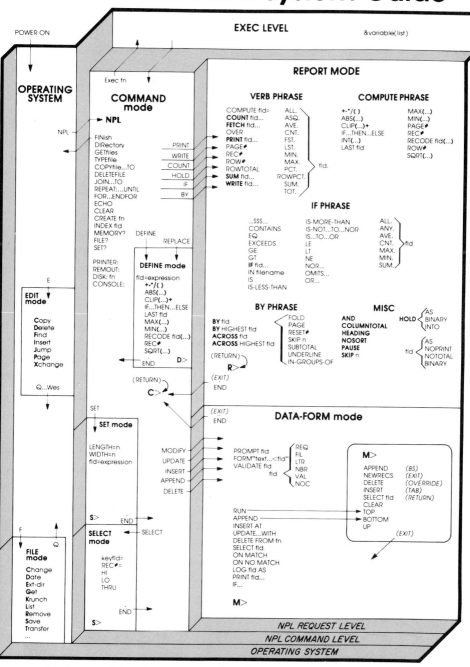

11/82

NPL MICROCOMPUTER CHARACTERISTICS

While the NPL system as seen by the user is virtually the same, irrespective of the make of the microcomputer employed, there are a *few* differences that one must know about. Some are simply a matter of performance and capacity, i.e., sorting and response times, and disk storage capacity. Other differences affect your Exec programs, and others may affect what you type at the keyboard.

PROGRAM PORTABILITY

NPL programs developed on one computer should run on any other computer that has an NPL system, with these possible exeptions:

- The file-naming conventions may not be compatible.

- The disk-naming conventions may not be compatible.

- The D, L, and S data formats may not exist in a particular NPL system for an 8-bit computer.

- If the second computer has less RAM memory, a large NPL program may have to be divided into stages using the **HOLD** feature.

- Disk storage may not be sufficient for a given set of files, even though the NPL program functions.

Filenames

NPL filenames consist of a name and a suffix to specify a filetype (.D, .M, .E, etc.). Most operating systems also use a name and a suffix which are connected by a period. Here are some examples of filename suffixes. Notice that the UCSD and Apple systems have both an NPL suffix and an operating system suffix.

Filetype:	Apple II Pascal & UCSD p-System	Apple III Pascal	RT11	IBM/PC DOS & CP/M
NPL master file	name/M.TEXT	name.M.TEXT	name.MAS	name.MAS
NPL datafile	name/D.DATA	name.D.TEXT	name.DAT	name.DAT
NPL Index file	name/I.fld	name.I.fld	name.Inn	name.Inn
NPL Exec file	name/E.TEXT	name.E.TEXT	name.EXC	name.EXC
Number of characters:				
in "name"	8	8	6	8
in suffix	4	4	3	3

Volume Names

Some operating systems use names for the disk drive devices, and some systems name the disks themselves. UCSD and Apple systems provide for both kinds of volume names (volid).

Apple II Pascal and the UCSD p-System

Disk drives are named:

$$\#5:, \quad \#4:, \quad \#11:, \quad \#12:, \quad \#9:, \quad \#10:$$

and they are searched in the order shown. A diskette or a hard disk volume may have any name, provided it begins with a letter, ends with a colon, and has eight or fewer characters (excluding the colon). Full filenames look like this:

```
volid:name/M.TEXT
YR82:CLIENTS/M.TEXT
YR82:CLIENTS/D.DATA
YR82:CLIENT/I.LNAM
```

The index filename suffix is the first four characters of the alias for LASTNAME.

476

Apple III Pascal

Disk drives are named:

```
.D1, .D2, .D3, .D4, .PROFILE (Apple hard disk),
.C1, .C2, .C3, .C4 (Corvus hard disk)
```

Any name may be given to a volume, provided it begins with a slash character, has eight or fewer nonblank characters, and is separated from the filename by a slash, as in:

```
/volid/name.M.TEXT
```

e.g.
```
/YR81/CLIENTS.D.DATA
/YR81/CLIENTS.I.LNAM
```

Under the Apple III SOS operating system the volid may be a *pathname* consisting of a directory name and subdirectory names, each separated by slashes, as in:

```
/CORP/NORTHERN/SALES/CLIENTS.D.DATA
```

CP/M Operating System

Disk drives are named:

```
A:, B:, C:, D:, E:, F:, G:, H:
```

Names may not be assigned to disk volumes. Names may have up to eight characters and must begin with a letter. Full filenames look like this:

```
E:CLIENTS.MAS
E:CLIENTS.DAT
E:CLIENTS.EXC
E:CLIENTS.I03
```

The index file suffix I03 refers to the third field in the CLIENT master file.

IBM/PC DOS Operating System

IBM/PC DOS Disk drives are named:

```
A:, B:
```

Names may not be assigned to disk volumes. Names may have up to eight characters and must begin with a letter. Full filenames look like this:

```
B:CLIENT.MAS
B:CLIENT.DAT
B:CLIENT.EXC
B:CLIENT.IO3
```

The index file suffix IO3 refers to the third field in the CLIENT master file.

RT11 Operating System for the PDP-11

Disk drives are named:

```
SY0:, SY1:, SY2:, SY3:
```

Names may not be assigned to disk volumes. Names may have up to six characters and must begin with a letter. Full filenames look like this:

```
SY1:CLIENT.MAS
SY1:CLIENT.DAT
SY1:CLIENT.EXC
SY1:CLIENT.IO3
```

KEYBOARD DIFFERENCES

The NPL manuals use a descriptive name for several of the special key functions. The actual keys to be pressed vary from keyboard to keyboard. Typical cases are listed:

Function name	Apple II & UCSD p-System*	Apple III	CP/M Televideo Terminal	PDP-11 VT52/VT100 Terminal	IBM/PC DOS
Back-Space key	Left-Arrow	Left-Arrow	BS	BS or DEL	BS
Tab key	Right-Arrow	Right-Arrow	TAB	TAB	TAB
Exit key	ESC	ESC	Control-X	Control-X	Control-X
Interrupt key	ESC		Control-X		
Override key	Control-O	Control-O	Control-F	Control-F	Control-F
Stop key	Control-S	Control-7	Control-S	Control-S	Control-Num Lock
Start key	Control-S	Control-7	Control-S	Control-Q	any key

* varies with terminal

DATA FORMAT DIFFERENCES

Some versions of NPL, particularly those for the 8-bit microcomputers, do not have the D, L, and S data format options. There are two reasons:

- Long integer (L format) and Strings (S format) are unique to the Apple and UCSD Pascal operating systems

• Double precision or Dollar format (D format) provides routines to perform arithmetic on 40-bit integers. This additional code may not fit into certain small computers.

If you have datafiles with fields having L and S formats on, say, the Apple III system and wish to move them to an Apple II version of NPL, the files can be converted to compatible files if you:

• **DEFINE** new variables in F or A format for each L or S formatted field.

• Issue a **PRINT** request for the new variables plus all the fields excluding the L and S format items.

• **HOLD** the result as a new datafile and master file.

To move such a file of alphanumeric characters to the PDP-11 where D format is available, simply **PRINT** and **HOLD** all fields to produce a file with alphanumeric file formats for all fields. Do not use **HOLD BINARY**.

End-Of-Record Fields

Datafile formats are determined by operating system designs, and the character(s) used to mark the end of a record in a file vary among operating systems. For example:

	EOR Characters	Standard File Format
UCSD p-System & Apple Pascal	Return	A1
CP/M	Return	A1
RT11	Return & Line-feed	A2
IBM/PC DOS	Return & Line-feed	A2

Some datafiles may have no End-of-Record characters. Such files are commonly written by Pascal and Fortran programs. Files created in NPL with the **HOLD BINARY** phrase have no End-of-Record field.

The size of the EOR field, or its absence, does not affect the use of a particular file on computers different from the computer that created the file. It is critical, however, that the master file match the datafile. If the master file is **CRE-ATE**d on the second computer, it may be necessary to change or delete the EOR field to conform with the datafile.

BIBLIOGRAPHY

Goetz, Martin: "Engineering 4th Generation System Software, In Depth," *Computerworld*, June 1982.

IBM: *SQL/Data System Application Programming* (SH24-5018-0), White Plains, NY, 1981.

——: *SQL/Data System Concepts and Facilities* (GH24-5013-0), White Plains, NY, 1981.

——:*SQL/Data System Terminal Users Guide* (SH24-5016), White Plains, NY, 1981.

Infodata Systems Inc.: *INQUIRE User Language Tutorial*, Pittsford, NY, 1980.

Information Builders Inc.: *Focus Users Manual*, New York, NY, 1979.

Keen, Peter G.W., and Michael S. Scott Morton: *Decision Support Systems: An Organizational Perspective*, Addison-Wesley Publishing Company, Inc., Reading, MA, 1978.

McCracken, D.D.: "The Changing Face Of Applications Programming," *Datamation*, 1978.

——: *A Guide to NOMAD Applications Development*, National CSS Inc., Wilton, CT, 1980.

——: "Software Systems in the 80's: An Overview," *Computerworld*, September 1980.

Management Decision Systems Inc.: *Express Reference Manual*, Tymcon-370, 2 vol., Tymshare Inc., Cupertino, CA, Jan., 1980.

Martin, James: *Application Development Without Programmers*, Prentice-Hall, Inc., Englewood Cliffs, NJ, 1982.

Mathematica: *Ramis II*, Mathematica Products Group, Princeton, NJ, 1978.

MRI Systems Corporation: *System 2000 General Information Manual*, Austin, TX, 1972.

National CSS, Inc.: *NOMAD2 Reference Manual* (2 vol.), Wilton, CT, 1981.

Relational Database Systems Inc.: *Marathon Relational Database Systems*, Sunnyvale, CA, 1981.

Sandberg G.: "A Primer On Relational Data Base Concepts," *IBM Systems Journal*, vol. 20, no. 60, 1981, pp. 23-39.

Sperry Univac: *MAPPER 1100 User Reference Guide* (UP9193,-5), New York, 1980.

Zloof, M. M., "Query-by-Example: A Data Base Language," *IBM Systems Journal*, no. 4, 1977.

INDEX

SYSTEM SYMBOLS

$	131
&	142, 153
&variable	153, 156, 366
( )	367
*	367
+	367
−	367
/	367
/D	391
/E	391
/I	391
/M	391
<n	367

A

A FORMAT,	66, 127, 132, 133, 187
ABS,	70, 76, 315
ACROSS,	315
ACTUAL,	315
ALIAS,	124, 126, 134–136, 145, 224, 316, 416–418
ALL,	290, 291, 293, 294, 316
Alphanumeric,	127
AMPER VARIABLES,	142, 152, 155, 156, 158
AND,	13–15, 25–27, *43, 52,* 85, 185, *186,* 316, 388
ANY,	293, 294, 316
APPEND,	165, 167–168, 170, 177, 182, 203, 257–258, 316, 422, 429, 432
Appending new records,	165–167
Apple Pascal,	376–377
Apple Pascal Editor,	429
Apple II Pascal,	476
Application programs,	219, 243
Array,	276, *277, 280,* 284, 316, 277–281
Array variable,	275–276
AS,	25–27, 81, 85, 89, 98–101, 111, 117, 202, 304, 308, 317
ASQ,	34, 38, 317
Attribute,	318
AVE,	33, 49, 70, 118, 252, 292, 306, 318
Averaging,	33
AVG,	34, 37, 40, 41, 44, 112, 118, 318

B

Back-Space Key,	164–165, 162, 318

BINARY,	111, 112, 128, 130, 133, 135, 136, 318, 468
BINARY file formats,	133
BINARY format,	136
BINARY integer,	111
Blank fields,	135
BOTTOM,	164, 169, 319
Brackets,	131
BY,	11, 13, 14, 18–22, 25, 28–30, 33, 36, 38, 39, 49, 52, 63, 66–67, 85, 104, 110, 113, 125, 149, 194, 197–201, 203, 209, 251, 273, 287, 289, 292–294, 299
BY Field,	393, 395, 397
BY Phrase,	394–398
BY Phrase Modifiers,	81, 85–92
Bytes,	378

C

C>,	18, 27, 167, 380, 387, 403
Calculating,	63
Calculations,	33
Capture,	373
Center,	319
Changing of Master file,	194–196
Choosing formats,	187–192
CLEAR,	12, 144, 320
CLEAR DEFINE,	197
CLEAR SELECT,	197
CLIP,	64, 78, 201, 320
CNT,	33, 34, 37, 40, 44, 45, 49, 118, 320
Column heading,	29, 98–103, 125
COLUMNTOTAL,	33, 48, 71, 128, 320
Command Mode,	10
Commas,	85, 131
Comment statements,	156
COMPUTE,	11, 66–71, 76–77, 79, 97, 103, 109–110, 114–115, 134, 153, 194, 197, 231, 294, 308
COMPUTE Phrase,	98, 66–69
CONSOLE:,	12, 13, 30, 31, 321, 389, 391, 424
CONTAINS,	51, 57–60, 73, 321
CONTROL-A,	386–387
CONTROL-C,	432–433
CONTROL-O,	430
CONTROL-S,	391
CONTROL-Z,	387–388
Conversion,	132, 322
Coordinated request,	294–297, 301–305, 308
Copying,	167
Copying files,	185–186
COPYFILE,	11, 171, 185, 322
Correcting entry error,	407
COUNT,	11, 33, 44–45, 68, 109, 124, 273, 304, 323, 397
Counting,	21, 33

CP/M Operating system,	477
CREATE,	8, 11, 121–123, 134, 136, 323, 417, 426, 479
Creating DATA-FORMS,	415
Creating index,	148
Crunching,	119

D

D FORMAT,	130–133, 187, 189, 197, 479
Data,	53
Database,	xii, 220, 221
Database function,	257
Database names,	219, 221–224
Data entry,	403, 406
Data field,	416
Data items,	373, 378, 416
DATA-FORM,	6–11, 161–162, 179, 182, 183, 173, 174, 373, 403, 406
DATA-FORM programs,	179–182
Data records,	373
DATA>TEXT,	323
DATAFILE,	14, 35, 109, 373
DBMS,	220, 221
DEFINE,	8, 11, 64–67, 69–70, 76–77, 79–80, 88, 97, 101, 103, 132, 134, 138, 144, 147, 226, 231, 236, 250, 253, 260, 263, 295, 324, 380, 479
Defining,	63–66
DELETE,	167–170, 203, 257–258, *259,* 260, 325, 433
DELETEFILE	11, 325
Deleting,	167–168
Descriptors,	124
Direct Action,	11
DIRECTORY; DIR,	11, 119, 202, 325, 223, 380, 381
Disk address,	145
Disk Space,	118, 171, 202–203
DISK:,	11, 31, 185, 186, 197, 325
Diskette,	378
Division,	68
Dollar format,	479
Dollars & Cents,	131
Double precision,	479
Dummy field,	186

E

ECHO*,	157–159
ECHO ALL,	157
ECHO Commands,	9, 157, 159, 326
ECHO OFF,	12, 157, 159
ECHO ON,	12, 157, 159, 162, 182, 435
Edit,	326
Edit checks,	177
Edit criteria,	175

Edit Mode,	8
ELSE,	246, 248
END,	13–14, 27–29, 53, 64, 144, 250, 263, 326, 387, 388
ENDFOR,	246, 248
End-of-record,	124, 134–135, 479
Engineering format,	130, 190
EQ,	51, 52, 73, 145, 232, 235, 247, 260, 292, 326
Error correction,	18
Error Messages,	183
ESCAPE; ESC,	12, 18, 28, 165, 326, 379, 381, 387, 405–408, 413, 420, 435
EXCEEDS,	51, 73, 327
EXCHANGE,	327, 433
EXEC File; Program,	156, 158–159, 161, 173, 207, 327
EXEC Level,	8, 11
EXEC; EX,	151–152, 197, 413, 434–435
Exit Key,	156, 163–167, 170, 162, 182, 327
Expanding the record,	186–187
Expressions,	64, 66, 72, 246
External Sorting,	30, 196–199
Extending a file,	186
Extract file,	109

F

F FORMAT,	66, 129, 131–132, 187, 189
FETCH,	308, 328
FIELD,	125–126, 188, 276, 328
FIELD Editing,	175, 176
FIELD Markers,	92–97, 103, 178, 182
FIELDNAME,	124–126, 134–136, 224, 328, 416–419
Fieldtype,	328
FIL,	175, 183
FILE,	237, 278, 295, 304, 308, 329, 378
FILE_FMT,	328
FILE FORMAT,	112, 124, 126–130, 132–137, 416–417, 419
File View,	146, 149
FILE?,	114, 137–138, 329
File maintenance,	262–263
Filename,	124, 223, 329, 471, 475
FILER,	389
Filer Mode,	8
FILES?,	329
Finish Command,	9
FINISH; FIN,	11, 183, 329, 429
Floating Point,	133
Floating point variable,	129
FOCUS,	xiii, 443, 444
FOLD,	81, 85, 87–88, 101, 329
Footing,	329
FOR,	245–248
FOR...ELSE...ENDFOR,	255, 230

FORM,	*173,* 174, 178, 179, 182, 183, 193, 258, 330, 427, 429, 431–432
Format,	130
Format Codes,	127–134
Format conversion,	132
Formatted data entry,	427
Formatting the screen,	178–179
Fourth generation,	xiv
Fractional digits,	130
FROM,	260
FST,	33, 34, 37, 41, 208, 331
Functions,	76–77

G

GE,	51, 54, 73, 331
GETFILE; GET,	8, 11, 13, 14, 16, 18, 20, 25, 29, 52, 64–65, 81, 141–143, 145, 147, 331
GRAPH,	332
Greater,	54
Group test,	292–294, 305–306
GT,	51, 54, 73, 145, 332, 384

H

HEADING,	14, 81–82, 84–85, 92–93, 103, 178, 203, 333, 389, 427
HI,	144, 149, *187,* 333
Hierarchy,	229, 290, 295
Hierarchical,	267, 269
HIGHEST,	13, 30, 333
HOLD,	11, 109–115, 117–118, 128, 130, 133, 135–136, 149, 168, 185–188, 191, 194, 197–198, 202–203, 274
HOLD AS,	111, 116, 185, *186*
HOLD BINARY,	133, 136, 479
HOLD Master file,	135

I

I FORMAT,	66, 128, 132, 187
IBM Computer,	441
IBM/PC DOS Operating System,	477
Identifier,	125–126
IF,	11, 14, 29, 49, 51–63, 66–67, 72–73, 80, 97, 103, 110, 185, 188, 192, 197, 203, 232, 235, 237, 259–260, 291–294, 299–301, 305, 308, 335
IF Phrase,	51, 55, 238–240, 242, 384, 387, 392, 395
IF...THEN...ELSE,	60, 64, 70, 72–76, 78–79, *209,* 211, 246, 263, 335
IN,	145, 188, 336
INDEX,	12, 141, 145, 147, 168–170, 177, 182, 192, 200–203, 231, 240, 241, 297, 336
Index file,	141
Indexing,	141, 145–147

IN-GROUPS-OF,	337
Input,	203
INQUIRE,	xiii, 443, 460
INSERT,	167–170, 203, 257–258, 260, 263, 337, 433
I)NSERT,	337
Inserting,	167–168
Integer,	128, 337
Interactive Error Correction,	387
INTO,	111, 338
IS,	14, 49, 51–55, 73, 145, 148, 338
IS-LESS-THAN,	51, 73, 339
IS-MORE-THAN,	51, 73, 339
IS-NOT,	51–53, 55, 73, 338
IS-NOT...TO...NOR,	51, 54
IS...TO...OR,	51, 54–55

K

Key,	339
Keyboard differences,	478
Keyfields,	148, 149, 240, 339,
Keylength,	197–198, 201, 203
KEYFLD,	145
Keyword,	339

L

L FORMAT,	132, 479
Languages,	xii, 3
LAST,	64, 78–80, 101, 251–253, 255, 340
LE,	51, 54, 73, 340
Left-arrow,	380, 390, 403–404, 407, 413, 418–420, 422, 430–433
Length,	92
Less,	54
Letter Reports,	103–107
Limits,	161, 341, 194
Line-feed,	134
Listing,	13
Literals,	341
LO,	144, *187,* 341
Locating Records,	163, 164
LOG,	263, 341
Long Integer format,	132
Lookup table,	229–231
LST,	33, 34, 38, 41, 43, 78, 208, 342
LT,	51, 54, 73, 145, 342
LTR,	175, 176, 183

M

M>,	163–165, 167–170
Masks,	59–60, 342
MASTER,	343
Master File,	14, 34, 109, 121–139, 343, 221, 277–279, 297, 415–417, 465, 468

Match,	343
Matching,	228–237, 240–241, 263, 290, 292, 295
Matching IF Phrase,	232, 239
MAX,	33, 34, 37, 38, 41, 49, 70, 112, 118, 294, 306, 343
MEMORY?; MEM,	12, 344
Memory space,	197
Microcomputer characteristics,	475
MIN,	33, 34, 37, 38, 41, 49, 112, 118, 294, 344
Modes,	379
Modifiers,	344
MODIFY,	11, 173, 174, 344, 406, 421, 422, 429, 434, 436
Multipath files,	272–274
Multiple values,	53–55
Multiplication,	68
Multisegment records,	265
Multiverb request,	305

N

Names,	344, 225–226
NBR,	175, 176, 183
NE,	51–53, 73, 168, 345
NEWRECS,	169, 345
New variable names,	63
NOC,	177, 183
NOMAD,	xiii, 443
NOMAD2,	450
NOMATCH,	346
Nonprocedural,	xiii, xiv, 3, 219–221, 243, 441
NOPRINT,	43, 69–70, 81, 85, 90, 104, 308, 346, 413
NOR,	53–55, 346
NOSORT,	13, 25, 113, 116, 198, 201, 203, 346
NOTOTAL,	33, 49, 70–71, 85, 90, 346
NPL,	161, 183
NPSORT.DATA,	196, 200, 202
Numbering,	13
Numeric codes,	187–188, 191

O

OMITS,	51, 53, 57–59, 73, 347
Operating System,	7–9, 11
Operator messages,	157–159
OR,	14, 53–55, 58–60, 147–148, 347
OVER,	13, 15, 25–27, 88–89, 99–101, 348, 411, 413
Override Key,	156, 166, 162, 348
Owner,	348

P

PAGE,	14, 81, 85, 91–93, 348, 398
PAGE#,	81, 92–93, 97–98, 348

Page length,	91
Page size,	92
Page number,	92
PARENT,	268–269, 274, 349
PAUSE,	92, 349
PCT.fld,	293, 349
Portability,	475
Practicing data entry,	421
Precision,	130
Prefix,	34–47, 118, 349
Prefixed field,	70–72
PRINT,	11, 13–16, 18, 20–21, 25–26, 28–29, 33, 36, 52, 68, 109–110, 197, 248, 263, 273, 479
PRINTER:,	8, 11, 13, 30, 31, 92, 197, 350, 388, 391, 394, 424
Printing Format,	112, 124, 126–137, 350, 416–419
PRINTING_ FMT,	351
Procedural,	4, 220, 243
Procedural commands,	246–248
PROFILE,	278–280, 293, 351
PROFILE variable,	225, 252–253, 280, 293
Program file,	151
Program variable,	294
Programming Language,	xii
PROMPT,	*173*, 174, 175, 177–179, 182, 183, 258, 351, 427, 429
Protected field,	176–177

Q

Query,	xii, 7, 373
QUIT,	13, 18, 27, 28, 156, 352, 387, 406
Quote,	82, 353
Quote character,	76

R

R>,	14, 27, 380, 387, 403
RAMIS,	xiii, 443, 447
RAM Memory,	30
Range,	54
Rapid Access,	147–148
Rapid searching,	168–170
Real Numbers,	129, 189
Real values,	111
REC#,	81, 97–98. 170, 240, 353
RECODE,	229, 230–231, 241, 353
Record,	378
Record format,	373
Record length,	124
Record segment,	265–266
RECTYPE,	244, 267–268, 353
Relating records,	226–230
Relational Operator,	51, 52, 246, 385
Relations,	241–242

REMOUT:,	11, 30, 353
REPEAT:,	255
REPEAT:...UNTIL,	245, 246, *247*, 251, 255, 354
Repeating field,	265
REPLACE,	11, 65, 354
Report,	7
Report Mode,	8, 28
Report writing,	377
REQ,	175, 176, 183
Request,	8
RESET,	354
RESET#,	13, 21, 22, 354
Return,	14, 18, 27, 82, 134, 158, 163–169, 182, 355, 379, 380, 387, 403–404, 406–408, 419
Revising field values,	164–165
Right-Arrow,	406–407, 409, 413, 420, 430, 432–433
Root segment,	267
ROW#,	13, 16, 21, 22, 92, 97–98, 112, 277, 355
ROWPCT,	355
ROWTOTAL,	355
RT11,	478
Rules,	355–357
RUN,	173, 174, 182, 357
Runtime Variables,	151–156

S

S FORMAT,	133, 479
Saving changes,	171
Scientific format,	190
Schema,	221
Screening,	51, 66, 72–73, 144, 291–292
Screen pictures,	162–163
SEGMENT,	265–269, 273–274, 357
SELECT,	8, 11, 62, 141, 143–145, 148–149, 168–170, 182, 185, 187, 197, 200, 203, 257, 259–260
Selecting,	141–145, 148–149
Sequence,	243
SET,	248, 250–253, 255, 358
SET WIDTH,	81, 92
SET?,	92, 359
SET statements,	253
SET Variables,	250–252, 255
SKIP,	81, 85–88, 100, 359, 397–398, 411
Skip fields,	135, 189, 193
Sort keys,	30, 393
Sort keylength,	197
Sort key table,	195
Sort Sequences,	29
Sorted view,	200
Sorting,	13, 18, 19–21, 30, 201, 203
Sorting large files,	194–196
Space character,	25, 27, 78, 82
SQL,	xii, 443, 454

SQRT,	359
String format,	133
SUBS,	360
Subfile,	141, 143, 148, 149, 169
SUBSCRIPT,	278–280, 282, 284, 360
Subscript relations,	280–285
Substring comparisons,	58–61
SUBTOTAL,	33, 49–50, 85, 71, 360, 398
SUM,	11, 33–34, 36, 39, 43–45, 49, 54, 67–68, 109–110, 208, 273, 289, 293, 304, 306
Summing,	33
System Guide,	7
System Variables,	97, 98

T

Tab,	84, 164, 166–168, 162
Tab key,	361
Terms,	361
Testing,	182–183
TEXT>DATA,	362
THRU,	144–145, 149, *187,* 362
Time and Space,	193, 194
TO,	54, 55, 145, 282, 362
TOP,	163–164, 167–169, 363
TOT.fld,	293, 363
Transactions,	204–205, 208, 261–262
Transfer,	363
Tutorial,	373
TYPEFILE; TYPE,	11, 30, 31, 185, 186, 189, 191, 363, 380, 423
Types of data,	127
Types of variables,	252–253

U

UCSD p-System,	476
UNDERLINE,	363
Unique key,	199
UNTIL,	248, 255
UP,	164, 169, 364
Updating,	170, 257, 260, 261, 263, 364, 203–208
USAGE,	364
Using the printer,	423

V

VAL,	175, 176, 183
Validate,	*173,* 174, 175, 177–179, 183, 258, 364
VALIDATION,	177–178
Variable,	225, 251–253
Verb Object,	15, 21, 26, 66, 67, 70, 92, 104, 118
Verb Phrase,	15, 67, 103, 106, 395
View,	149
VOLID,	365
Volume,	365
Volume name,	390, 476

W

Whole numbers,	131
Width,	92
WRITE,	11, 33, 34, 36–44, 49, 50, 68, 103–104, 109–110, 273, 288–289, 304, 308, 366